LIBRARY OF
AND
MONEY BANKING
HISTORY

A SHORT HISTORY OF

PAPER MONEY & BANKING

Also Published In

Reprints of Economic Classics

By WILLIAM M. GOUGE

THE FISCAL HISTORY OF TEXAS [1852]

A

SHORT HISTORY

OF

PAPER MONEY AND BANKING

IN THE UNITED STATES

TO WHICH IS PREFIXED

AN INQUIRY

INTO THE

PRINCIPLES OF THE SYSTEM

BY

WILLIAM M. GOUGE

[1833]

With An Introductory Essay

" William M. Gouge and the Formation of
Orthodox American Monetary Policy "

By JOSEPH DORFMAN

Reprints of Economic Classics
AUGUSTUS M. KELLEY PUBLISHERS
New York 1968

First Edition 1833

(Philadelphia: *Printed by* T. W. Ustick; *and for Sale
by* Grigg & Elliott, *No. 8 N. Fourth St.*, Uriah Hunt,
No. 19 N. Third St., Hogan & Thompson, *No. 139½
Market St.*, 1833)

Reprinted 1968 by

AUGUSTUS M. KELLEY · PUBLISHERS

New York   New York   10010

PRINTED IN THE UNITED STATES OF AMERICA
by SENTRY PRESS, NEW YORK, N. Y. 10019

William M. Gouge and the Formation of Orthodox American Monetary Policy

Few areas in American history have undergone such intensive study in recent years as the Jacksonian era. A major subject of controversy in that period is monetary and banking policy. It began with President Jackson's successful veto of the bill for rechartering the embryonic central bank, the Second Bank of the United States, in 1832. The subsequent struggle on both the federal and state levels rocked the nation intermittently for a decade. The ablest writer on the orthodox Jacksonian hard-money side was William M. Gouge (1796-1863); the bible of the movement was his *A Short History of Paper Money and Banking in the United States, . . . to which is Prefixed an Inquiry into the Principles of the System* (1833).[1]

It seems to have been the first American economics treatise to win an international reputation. An abridged version was published in the influential Brussels journal, *La Revue Universelle*; in England the second part, the history part, was brought out by the leading political journalist, the radical William Cobbett. The foremost popularizer of the dominant British classical school, J. R. McCulloch, commended the treatise for its detailed history of American banking. The praise which it received at home as well as abroad was in good part due to

---

[1] The edition which is reprinted below is the first edition. Subsequent editions contained only minor changes. The last appeared in 1841-1842 as supplements to his bi-weekly *The Journal of Banking*.

Gouge's careful research. For this he spent over two years at the library of the American Philosophical Society, Philadelphia, a rough counterpart of the famed British Museum. Gouge supplemented this by correspondence with knowledgeable persons in various states. Such was the level of the work that it is still a primary source for information on the history and organization of American banking, especially for the first third of the nineteenth century, a period when the veil of secrecy surrounding banking was even tighter than in other fields.

Gouge was an agile writer, shy in personal contact and adverse to speech making, but possessed of a persuasive pen, steeped at times in wit and satire. He "was one of the most thorough students of our early banking [including the security and money markets] and also one of its keenest and most influential critics."[2]

To furnish perspective on his monetary and banking views, it seems desirable to provide a short biographical sketch and a statement of his general economic philosophy. The son of an apothecary, he was born and raised in Philadelphia. Though he was to spend most of his mature life in Washington, he always preferred large cities, especially New York.[3]

---

[2] Harry E. Miller, *Banking Theories in the United States Before 1860* (Cambridge, Mass.: Harvard University Press, 1927) p. 86.

[3] While inspector of customs in New York in 1843, Gouge was reluctant to be transferred to Washington on the ground that New York "affords a greater variety of objects with which to divert the mind." (Gouge to J. C. Spencer, October 25, 1843, National Archives, Treasury.)

His career consisted largely of his activities as a financial journalist and as an employee of the United States Treasury; he pursued these occupations simultaneously for a good part of his life. He began as a journalist and first achieved prominence in Philadelphia while serving as co-publisher and editor (with Stephenson Smith) of the *Philadelphia Gazette and City Advertiser* from 1823 to 1831. He devoted the newspaper chiefly to monetary and banking reforms, advocating primarily what became a part of the Jacksonian creed, the prohibition of small bank notes, as a first step in the elimination of all bank notes. At the same time he helped prepare a so-called "workingmen's" memorial to the Pennsylvania legislature which sought to prohibit the chartering or rechartering of banks with the corporate power of limited liability.[4] But this was one of those periods when there was relatively little public interest in currency and banking questions. Gouge's newspaper constantly lost subscribers and he was forced to give up what "had promised to be one of the most lucrative newspaper establishments in the country."[5]

Ten years later, he again attempted the role of

---

[4] For a discussion of this memorial, see Joseph Dorfman, "The Jacksonian Wage Earner Thesis," 1949, reprinted in *The Economic Mind in American Civilization* (1946; reprinted by Augustus M. Kelley • Publishers, 1966) II, appendix.

[5] Gouge to F. P. Blair, August 17, 1831, Blair Papers, Princeton University Library. He explained that the *Gazette* had not attacked that "terrific institution," the Second Bank of the United States, because he would soon have been without adequate funds just to print the paper.

editor and publisher; he started the bi-weekly *The Journal of Banking,* but the result was the same. After a year he was forced by the loss of subscriptions to suspend publication, complaining of the public's antipathy to economic abstractions, especially "the science of currency." He pointed to the fate of *The Journal of Banking* as further evidence that "no journal of political economy or statistics, in either Europe or America . . . has ever repaid expenses."[6]

Gouge's journalist activities were not limited to his own ventures; from the 1830's down to the Civil War he was a valued contributor to and adviser of such influential financial and economic journals as *Hunt's Merchants' Magazine* and *The Bankers' Magazine and Statistical Register,* and such leading Democratic party organs as the Washington *Globe* and *The United States Magazine and Democratic Review.*

From about 1834 to March 1862, Gouge was with the Department of the Treasury except for relatively short periods when the Democrats did not occupy the presidency. Even when the Whigs and their successors were in power, he managed to retain his post for a part of the time.[7] He began, as he put it, as a "mere accountant and copyist," but was

---

[6] "Notice," *The Journal of Banking,* June 22, 1842, p. 404.

[7] Gouge was dismissed in April 1841 when the Whigs came to power, but he came back in 1843. In April 1851, after the Whigs had won the presidency, Gouge was again forced out and finally on March 3, 1862, after the Republicans had been in office for a year, he was dismissed. At the time his salary was $1,600 a year.

soon charged with the duties of what may be called "the statistical and politico-economical clerk" of the bureau that served as the immediate staff of the Secretary of the Treasury.[8] In this capacity he should be credited with services of value not only to government but also to the growth of economic science and especially monetary and banking policy. As he described it, his was the task of collecting and arranging the materials that went into the detailed statement of the condition of the banks throughout the Union which the Secretary of the Treasury laid before Congress each year.[9] He used his skills as accountant and statistician to improve the collection and systematization of monetary and banking data that Treasury, Congress and the business world used in making decisions.[10]

Perhaps more important for our purposes was his involvement in policy making. He served as an economic adviser to secretaries of the treasury in Democratic administrations and such outstanding Jacksonian leaders in the monetary controversies as Senator Thomas Hart Benton of Missouri and Benjamin F. Butler, Attorney General in Jackson's second administration. Occasionally Gouge worked directly with President Martin Van Buren.

---

[8] Gouge to President Van Buren, July 17, 1840, Van Buren Papers, Library of Congress; Gouge to James G. Guthrie, March 10, 1853, National Archives, Treasury.

[9] Even when out of government service, he continued to collect data in part with the help of correspondents such as his fellow collector of statistics and future Democratic party candidate for the presidency, Samuel J. Tilden.

[10] This function is now largely performed by the Comptroller of the Currency.

His general economic philosophy was in the Jefferson-Jackson *laissez faire* tradition. This view he showed more formally in his adherence to Adam Smith and "the axioms of political economy" of the British classical school typified by David Ricardo and its continental counterpart led by Jean-Baptiste Say.[11] Gouge, like the classical economists, held that the theory of value was basic in any economic discussion. The laws of supply and demand were all-powerful in the determination of value. For natural value, cost of production was the determining condition of supply, and back of demand was the adaptation of the goods to the wants and desires of the people. "The market value . . . is in the compound ratio of their utility and of their scarcity."[12] Thus the prices of goods and all factors of production would be "much better regulated by free competition than . . . by governmental enactments."[13]

---

[11] His favorite was always Adam Smith. He complained that *The Wealth of Nations* was seldom reprinted in the United States whereas English translations of Say's treatise were reprinted many times; "but this is chiefly owing to its having been adopted as a textbook in the colleges, and to a study of it being requisite to enable young men to take their degrees." ("Political Economy," *The Journal of Banking,* February 2, 1842, p. 242).

[12] Below, Part I, pp. 10, 11.

Gouge commented on what came to be called marginal utility analysis: "Value is, according to some approved writers, in its ultimate analysis, 'a judgement of the mind.' It would carry us too far into the regions of metaphysics to show how they make this out." ("The Standard of Value," *The Journal of Banking,* March 16, 1842, p. 290).

[13] "Remarks," *The Journal of Banking,* December 22, 1841, p. 196.

Business corporations, especially banks, possessed of the privilege of limited liability and other perquisites, were "incompatible with the equality of rights and unfavorable to the progress of national wealth." In the absence of "the Argus eyes of private interest . . . their affairs are much more carelessly and . . . expensively conducted than those of individuals."[14]

He questioned the desirability of laws fixing a maximum rate of interest; here he differed from his master, Adam Smith, and followed instead Jeremy Bentham's *Defence of Usury* (1787).[15] "Loanable capital in the form of money, varies in value . . . [Consequently] it is as absurd to attempt to fix the rent or interest of money . . . as it would be to fix the rent of houses or lands that are bought with money." Furthermore, if banks were free to raise the interest on loanable capital, as its value in the market increased, this action would "put the whole community on their guard, and many a fever of wild speculation would be checked" at the very start.[16] Similarly governments might issue bonds at a heavy discount but they must redeem them at their nominal price lest the affected states lose their credit.

---

[14] Below, Part I, p. 41.

[15] Gouge commented humorously that the tract "was free from those peculiarities of phraseology which render other of Bentham's works sealed books to the great mass of readers." ("Bentham on Usury," *The Journal of Banking*, April 18, 1841, p. 52).

[16] "Banking as It Ought to Be," *The United States Magazine and Democratic Review*, April 1843, p. 427.

The claims of the honest capitalist, Gouge insisted, were just as sacred as those of the honest laborer. His theory of wages was the traditional wages-fund doctrine: "Every increase of capital increasing the fund out of which wages would be paid, would increase the reward of the laborer." Gouge chastised the lazy and improvident for neglecting to accumulate a capital and thus making themselves independent of "others for means of both subsistence and employment."[17]

On the other hand, on matters such as the safety of steamboat passengers, he was a strong supporter of the policy of regulation which President Jackson had promoted. Thus in reporting in 1854 to the Secretary of the Treasury on the workings of the steamboat inspection law, he said that so many disasters occurred from steam navigation unregulated by law that passengers had to look to the government for protection.

On matters of central concern to him, money and banking, Gouge argued that the precious metals — gold and silver — were chosen to be money, because their particular qualities "fitted them to be standards and measures of value, and to serve, when in the shape of coin, the purposes of a circulating medium." They were the most convenient instruments of valuation, especially since they varied less than all other goods "from changes in the relation of supply and demand."[18] At the same time, he pointed out that bank deposits must be viewed

---

[17] Below, Part I, pp. 91, 132.
[18] Below, Part I, p. 10.

as part of the circulating media, that they might be created by the process of bank loans, and that they had exactly the same effects on prices as bank notes.[19]

Gouge deprecated any deviation from a metallic currency. He contended in the treatise that the present mixed system of currency, of specie and bank notes redeemable on demand in specie, was the primary source of economic evils, especially inflation and subsequent severe depression. Anything that excites the spirit of speculation encourages a tendency to increase the amount of bank issues. With the increase of paper money, prices rise, though in uneven fashion, until eventually the prices of some goods substantially exceed their prices abroad. The resulting adverse balance of trade brings a halt in the rise of prices. Since the foreign sellers will not accept the paper money, importers demand specie from banks. The bankers in turn start calling in loans and refuse extensions and their debtors in turn press their own debtors in what seems an endless chain. The contraction causes a rapid, sharp fall

---

[19] "He who has deposited money in the bank, and he to whom it has been loaned, appear as competitors in the same market. . . . It is the same sum of money. . . . But there are two credits for this money in the bank, and the credit is equivalent to cash, both to him who has deposited the money and him to whom it has been lent." (Below, Part I, p. 23.)

In 1859 Gouge argued that "dullness of business complained of at the beginning of the present year in some parts of the country" was due to the fact that "many chose to let deposits lie inactive rather than employ them in enterprises in regard to which they could come to no satisfactory conclusion." ("The Banks of the United States," *The Bankers' Magazine and Statistical Register*, July 1859, p. 5.)

of prices and goods cannot be sold except at a heavy loss. Multitudes become bankrupt but as prices decline, imports fall and gold eventually returns. The confidence of the banks is revived and they begin to issue paper money again, and the circle of expansion and contraction is on. The effect of the restriction of the money supply under a bank-note currency was much worse than under a specie standard because of the multiple contraction that results in the ''pressure'' on the community. Gouge estimated it as fourfold. Not least of the effects of the contraction is the substantial unemployment. Here he brought into play what is called the income approach: ''as one man is thrown out of employment, his effective demand for the product of his neighbor's labor is diminished. . . . If twenty clerks are deprived of employment, the shoemaker may find it necessary to dismiss one of his assistants . . . and so of all other trades.''[20] In more modern terminology: ''as contraction of the currency, by diminishing purchasing power, spoils the market, one employer after another must release his workers. The discharge of a considerable number of employees, depriving them of their incomes, prevents their purchasing as freely as usual, thus tending to diminish production in other lines and further to increase unemployment. A progressive deterioration of the market is introduced, and with it goes like slackening of production.''[21]

[20] Below, Part I, p. 27.
[21] Miller, *Banking Theories in the United States Before 1860*, pp. 203-204.

Gouge insisted that this must not be interpreted as giving approval to the heretical doctrine that general overproduction was the cause of the crisis: "If the real wants of the community, and not their ability to pay, be considered, it will not perhaps be found that any one useful trade or profession has too many members. . . . But, in one sense, all businesses may be said to be 'overdone' since all businesses are by this system rendered unprofitable to those who are engaged in them." Gouge concluded that any good done by corporate banks is overbalanced by "their continual alterations of the measures of value, by the uncertainty they give to trade, and by the advantages they confer on some men over others."[22]

He maintained that the various restrictions on banks that were proposed would not be effective. Take for example, what was then becoming the orthodox view of the proper kind of bank loans; namely, that, if banks would not discount "accommodation notes" but only short term business paper, real commercial bills, they would not overissue.[23]

---

[22] Below, Part I, pp. 27, 49.

[23] A good statement of the theory, later called the "real-bills" doctrine, is as follows: "Restriction of bank earning assets to real bills of exchange will automatically limit, in the most desirable manner, the *quantity* of bank liabilities; it will cause them to *vary* in quantity in accordance with the 'needs of business' and it will mean that the bank's assets will be of such a nature that they can be turned into cash on short notice and thus place the bank in a position to meet unlooked for calls for cash." [Lloyd W. Mints, *A History of Banking Theory in Great Britain and the United States* (Chicago: University of Chicago Press, 1945) p. 29.]

But the discounting of such bills, said Gouge, might cause inflation because ''the same lot of goods might be sold to a dozen persons, and each might give a note, and each of these twelve notes might be discounted at bank.'' Furthermore, the most stringent legislation could not restrict banks to commercial bills, ''if this paper did not afford full employment to all their 'capital' and all their 'credit.' '' He expresses sympathy with the proposal to limit bank dividends on the ground that it ''would remove many inducements to over-banking,'' but felt that such a measure would not be adequate.[24]

He ruled out rechartering the Bank of the United States as a regulator of the state banks not only on constitutional grounds but also on the ground that as an incorporated paper money bank it would produce as in the past the same evils as the state banks. As a profit making institution, the central bank could hardly be expected to act to restrain the inflationary tendency of state banks, but would itself expand and contract as they did.

As an ideal remedy Gouge proposed prohibition of all incorporated paper money banks; that is, to eliminate their privileges of limited liability and note issue. In their place he would have banks subject to unlimited liability, lending only their own capital plus savings deposits (time deposits) and maintaining a hundred per cent specie reserve

---

[24] Below, Part I, pp. 50, 51, 52.

against demand deposits. In this sense, banking, like all other businesses, should be free.[25]

Gouge expected that private banks would rise up to receive deposits, discount promissory notes and deal in exchange. ''The bankers would be men of great wealth, for it is in lending money that men of large fortune can employ their capitals with most profit and convenience.''[26] Their competition would result in more favorable terms to borrowers. They should and would allow interest on savings deposits. At the same time, these banks should impose a small charge in proportion to the amount of service they rendered customers ''in the collecting of bills, the receipt of [demand] deposits, or the payment of drafts. In this way, they who derive advantage from the banks would pay their neces-

---

[25] Historians of American banking theory have generally held that Gouge in the late 1830's began to look favorably on banks of issue if they followed the real bills doctrine. This view was based on certain ambiguous statements in his ''Commercial Banking,'' (*Hunt's Merchants' Magazine*, April 1843). Interestingly, the same article caused a fellow journalist and opponent of banks of issue to express regret that Gouge sanctioned such banks. Gouge in a private letter to a friend said that he had been misunderstood. ''I intended it as an introduction to other articles in which it was my desire to show that banks of issue cannot be so managed as not to produce evil. In *The [United States Magazine and] Democratic Review* for April, I have published an article entitled 'Banking As It Ought to Be,' in which I have given a compendious view of the whole subject.'' (Gouge to Henry Lee, May 1, 1843, Lee Papers, Massachusetts Historical Society). In the latter article, Gouge bluntly states ''we are for having the money of the country exclusively metallic.'' The article has been overlooked by scholars, doubtless because it was anonymous.

[26] Below, Part I, p. 49.

sary expenses. Now, these expenses are paid by a tax levied in an indirect way, on the whole community.''[27]

Gouge granted that the sudden ending of the old banking system, especially the prohibition of all bank notes, ''would be ruinous'' to the economy. The answer was to begin with small notes and proceed gradually to those of the highest denomination.[28] This suggestion became a basic monetary policy for President Jackson and his followers, and it enjoyed some success for a time as regards denominations under $5.

---

[27] ''Banking As It Ought to Be,'' *The United States Magazine and Democratic Review*, April 1843, p. 426.

[28] Below, Part I, p. 138. Gouge originally proposed that the minimum denomination be $5; by 1837, he held that the minimum should be ''$50 or perhaps $100.'' (Gouge to Nathan Bunker, November 15, 1837, Princeton University Library).

As late as 1897, Gouge's view in a modified form was maintained by the eminent Harvard economist Frank W. Taussig. He argued that a way of achieving the circulation of gold was to prohibit bank notes of denominations of $20 and smaller. (Answer to questionnaire in ''United States Monetary Commission, Currency Reform,'' 1897, Typescript, p. 707. Columbia University Libraries).

Gouge's underlying logic was: ''[since] an efficient demand ensures a supply . . . abundant issues of paper cause ''specie to flow out of a country''; and elimination of the paper causes an inflow of specie. ''[A]n efficient demand for gold and silver . . . of all demands . . . is the one which is the most readily met. Light of carriage and small in bulk, when compared with their value, the precious metals defy all political regulations which are intended to prevent their obeying the laws of effective demand.'' *An Inquiry into the Expediency of Dispensing with Bank Agency and Bank Paper in the Fiscal Concerns of the United States* (Philadelphia: Stavely, 1837) p. 43. Hereafter referred to as *An Inquiry.*

Another of Gouge's proposals which had much greater success and one with which his name is most closely identified was the Independent Treasury, or Sub-Treasury System. After President Jackson's veto of the bill for rechartering the Second Bank of the United States there arose the question of the future handling of the fiscal concerns of the federal government; that is, the holding, receiving and disbursing of federal funds. There was a discussion over whether this should be largely performed by selected state banks or exclusively by the government. Gouge had argued in *A Short History* for the latter; government fiscal operations would be handled through the treasury with the help of sub-treasuries; and only specie would be used. He had explained that:

If the state banks were made the depositories of the public funds, and if their notes were made receivable in payment of duties, the evils of the [paper money] system would be increased. If the Government should, after the expiration of the present charter of the United States Bank [in 1836], resolutely refuse to receive anything but gold and silver in payment of debts, and also refuse to employ any bank as an agent in its fiscal operations, the evils of the system would be greatly diminished.[29]

As the foremost work on the history of American banking theory summarized his basic doctrine:

Gouge ... desired a "constitutional treasury system", as he called it, for the reason that it would abolish all connection between the banks

---

[29] Below, Part II, p. 218.

and the government. If the government deposited its balances in the banks, the latter would then have larger reserves upon the basis of which they might expand; if the government allowed itself the privilege of borrowing from the banks, such a practice would surely lead to inflation; and even if the government merely accepted bank notes in payment of taxes, the result would be inflationary. Under the sub treasury system, however, there was a continual flow of gold between the banks and the treasury, and this fact served as a constant check on the banks, "not as does the foreign demand at uncertain intervals of months and years, but daily, nay, hourly." The only rational objection, he thought, was that even so, the check was not strong enough.

[Most important of all] . . . a larger quantity of specie would be in circulation, thus bringing the money supply a step nearer that of a hard money system. . . . It was his contention that, if the government received and paid out only coin, additional specie would be imported, and thus the supply of specie in circulation would be increased and the volume of bank obligations decreased. The increase of specie, he claimed, would have the further advantage of producing an increased supply of reserve money available to the banks upon the contraction of their loans. He pointed to the advantage of the "constitutional treasury system" in furnishing an improved means of interregional transfer of funds. Finally, he contended that in the case of a large payment of gold by the government there would be no disturbance to business, whereas, if the banks were acting as the fiscal agents of the government, such a payment would result first in inflation and later in contraction, with all its unfortunate consequences.[30]

Gouge showed imagination when he described the government as ''the greatest capitalist and the greatest dealer in the country'' because of the immense volume of transactions, especially those growing out of land sales and customs duties, the main sources of its income; and proceeded to say ''Let such a capitalist and such a dealer decline receiving and paying bank paper,'' and the issues of the banks would be substantially reduced.[31]

President Jackson at first went contrary to Gouge's views by ordering Secretary of the Treasury Roger B. Taney in October 1833 to begin the process of removing the deposits from the Bank of the United States to selected state institutions. But Jackson and some of his cabinet had grave doubts as to whether this should be the permanent policy. So much so that, when Gouge entered the Treasury, Levi Woodbury, the new secretary, had him prepare ''A Memoir on the Expediency of Establishing Sub-Treasury Offices.'' [32] In the ''Memoir'', dated April 1835, he outlined not only the argument ''in the abstract'' but also the details of its practical operation and cost.

No action was then taken on the proposal, according to Gouge, because men supporting the idea of a

---

[30] Mints, *A History of Banking Theory in Great Britain and the United States,* pp. 174-175.

[31] *An Inquiry,* p. 15.

[32] The ''Memoir'' is in the Woodbury Papers, Library of Congress.

league of state banks to perform the role of fiscal agent had the ear of the administration and especially Woodbury. But when a money panic began in May 1837 and banks suspended specie payments, Gouge, immediately and without informing the administration, published an elaborated version of the "Memoir" under the title, *An Inquiry into the Expediency of Dispensing with Bank Agency and Bank Paper in the Fiscal Concerns of the United States.* He archly explained to Secretary Woodbury that "I did not mention to you, or to any other member of the cabinet, my intention of making this publication, because I thought that from my peculiar position, it might be regarded by some as a *feeler* put forth by the administration, and I wished no person but myself to be compromitted by it, in case it should not prove acceptable to the public."[33]

President Van Buren made the Independent Treasury system the major issue for the special session of Congress in September 1837. After a three year fight and a temporary split in the party, it became law in 1840. Gouge, who during the battle was saluted by the supporters of the measure as a master mind and by opponents as the evil genius, began installing the system. The law was repealed after Van Buren was defeated for re-election at the end of 1840, but in 1846 it began a long career as the major regulator of the monetary and banking system of the country until the establishment of the Federal Reserve System in 1914.

Gouge not only established the system but he also

---

[33] Gouge to Woodbury, June 29, 1837, Woodbury Papers.

was on the alert to close loopholes. Thus in 1854 he proposed, and Secretary of the Treasury James G. Guthrie adopted, a scheme for reducing transfers of specie to a minimum without making the drafts a currency. These could be obtained at any sub-treasury on deposit of the specie at the issuing office, but they had to be drawn on a specified sub-treasury in order "to prevent their passing from hand to hand as currency. For with the restrictions as to the place of redemption, if they circulated at all, they would remain in the neighborhood of the sub-treasury at which they were payable."[34]

The sub-treasury system won such general approval that ex-president Martin Van Buren could state in the late 1850's that it was the only clear case of a public measure or act "entirely acceptable to all sides."[35] It gained this strong support from its practical success in maintaining the credit of the government, especially during the panic of 1857. As President Buchanan noted in his annual message of December 7, 1857, "Thanks to the Independent Treasury, the Government has not suspended [specie] payments, as it was compelled to do by the failure of the banks in 1837." By this measure as well as by his writings, Gouge played a large role in solidifying if not in rendering more rigid the tradition of hard money that continued to dominate American mone-

---

[34] David Kinley, *The Independent Treasury of the United States and Its Relation to the Banks of the Country* (Washington: Government Printing Office, 1910) p. 67.

[35] *Inquiry into the Origin and Course of Political Parties in the United States* (New York: Hurd and Houghton, 1867) p. 261.

tary and banking policy down to World War I, despite the modifications that were made in the original legislation.[36]

American historians have until very recently widely held that Gouge was the militant champion of the downtrodden western farmer or of the exploited wage earner of the urban east, or of both. Interestingly, he refuted that view in the 1840's in *The Journal of Banking*. After noting a number of leading business men who supported hard money, he exclaimed that "the friends of sound currency and sound credit have . . . borne too long in silence the reproach of being 'a miserable set of loco-focos, disorganizers, radicals, levellers, destructives, agrarians, infidels, and atheists'." The substantial number of "large (solid) capitalists" and professional men on the subscription list should dispose of the diatribe that "dissatisfaction with the present banking system is confined to those whose own hard fortune has made life bitter to them."[37]

He also noted that his essay "The True Principles of Commercial Banking" (*The United States Maga-*

---

[36] Under the National Bank Act of 1863, the treasury could use the banks chartered by the federal government as depositories for its revenues, except customs duties, and by an act of 1907 the exception was dropped. Even after the establishment of the Federal Reserve System in 1914, it was not until 1916 that the secretary of the treasury began to transfer funds from the sub-treasuries to the Federal Reserve district banks. The last sub-treasury was closed in 1921 under the Act of May 19, 1920.

[37] "Obituary," *The Journal of Banking*, March 16, 1842, p. 310; "Subscribers' Names," *The Journal of Banking*, June 22, 1842, p. 404.

zine and Democratic Review, May 1838) "was much commended by many commercial men, and others, who, from their position and previous studies, were well qualified to judge of its merits and defects. Among others . . . a Director of the Bank of England was so pleased with it, that he sent to this country for copies of all the writings of [its] author."[38]

Gouge conceived of himself as an "intellectual," belonging to the growing class of "disinterested political economists."[39] To achieve necessary banking reform, he realized that more was required than the arguments of a "disinterested political economist." "It is partly by assistance . . . coming from men who would as willingly, if their political ambitions could thereby be gratified, . . . aid the banks as oppose them, that I hope for reform. . . . [I]t is remarked by a theological writer that the wicked are frequently the instruments of doing more good than the righteous, inasmuch as worldly ambition in the minds of the first is generally a much stronger passion than disinterested benevolence in the minds of the latter, and, therefore, when the worldly ambitious happen to seize hold on a *right* measure, they push it with far more energy than would be done by those actuated solely by desires to promote the public good."

He felt that the church had been and could be a powerful force for reform, but the ministers were

[38] "The True Principles of Commercial Banking," *The Journal of Banking*, August 4, 1841, p. 36.

[39] The phrases are from Gouge to President Van Buren, July 17, 1840, Van Buren Papers, and Gouge to Henry Lee, May 1, 1840, Lee Papers.

so split on bank reform that not too much dependence should be placed on the church on this question. Suppose people's minds will not "yield to the disinterested effort of political economists, to the more selfish efforts of ambitious politicians, or even the heavy artillery of the church. What then? We must do what we can to check the evils we cannot cure. To preserve the *balance* between evil and good in the world, is all that, according to some writers, can be done. If moral effort ceases, evil will quickly predominate."[40]

The obituary of Gouge which appeared in that conservative journal, *The Bankers' Magazine,* summed up the dominant opinion on the man and his book: He was "exceedingly well informed on all questions of finance" which he discussed with considerable skill and his book was "a very able and clear exposition of the principles of banking and of the mistakes made by our American banking institutions."[41]

[40] Gouge to Henry Lee, November 7, 1840, Lee Papers.

[41] Editorial, "William M. Gouge," *The Bankers' Magazine and Statistical Register,* September 1863, p. 242.

JOSEPH DORFMAN

Columbia University
October 1967

To

Asa C. Dunham Esq.

From

Wm. M. Gouge

A

SHORT HISTORY

OF

PAPER MONEY AND BANKING

IN THE

UNITED STATES,

INCLUDING AN ACCOUNT OF

PROVINCIAL AND CONTINENTAL PAPER MONEY.

TO WHICH IS PREFIXED

AN INQUIRY

INTO THE

PRINCIPLES OF THE SYSTEM,

WITH

CONSIDERATIONS OF ITS EFFECTS

ON

MORALS AND HAPPINESS.

THE WHOLE INTENDED AS

A PLAIN EXPOSITION OF THE WAY IN WHICH PAPER MONEY
AND MONEY CORPORATIONS, AFFECT THE INTE-
RESTS OF DIFFERENT PORTIONS
OF THE COMMUNITY.

BY WILLIAM M. GOUGE.

Philadelphia:

PRINTED BY T. W. USTICK,

AND FOR SALE, BY GRIGG & ELLIOTT, NO. 8 NORTH FOURTH STREET, URIAH HUNT,
NO. 19 NORTH THIRD ST., HOGAN & THOMPSON, NO. 139½ MARKET ST.

....

1833.

CONTENTS.

PART II.

A Short History of Paper Money and Banking in the United States.

PREFACE.

A brief exposition of the principles of Banking, was all that the writer originally intended to give. In the first draft of the work, the historical sketch was part of a chapter. It has been extended to its present length, from a belief that a tolerably full account of incidents in the History of American Banking would be acceptable to the reader.

If additional illustrations of the nature of the system were wanted, they might be derived from its history in Great Britain. These, our limits will not permit us to introduce. We have, however, room for a sketch of the changes of opinion that have taken place in that country, in regard to paper money.

Mr. Joplin, in his History of the Currency Question, after collating different passages in the treatise on "The Wealth of Nations," gives the following as a summary of the views of Adam Smith.

"1. That he would prefer the circulation between consumers or what may be termed the *consumptive* circulation, to be metallic : but that he thought it a greater advantage for the circulation between dealer and dealer, to be paper ; admitting at the same time,

"2. That if Bankers were subjected to the obligation of an immediate and unconditional payment of their notes in coin on demand, as soon as presented, their trade might, with safety to the public, be rendered in all other respects perfectly free.

"3. That the amount of notes which the country required was an amount equal to the sum of metallic money which would circulate if there were no paper.

"4. That this amount could not be exceeded without producing an immediate demand for gold to be sent abroad previous to its passing into general circulation : by which, of course, no derangement of prices, from excess of issues, could at any time be produced : the evils of over-issues being confined to the Banks upon which the demand for gold would arise.

" 5. That besides this, if the Banks confined their loans to real bills of exchange and real transactions, they would not be liable to any excess of issues whatever."

" With these views of the working of our paper system, nothing," says Mr. Joplin, " could be more reasonable than his (Smith's) conclusions as to its value. It was evidently one from which much good might be derived, and no harm."

What Adam Smith had immediately in view, was the Scotch system of Banking, which is carried on by *unincorporated* companies, each of the members of which is responsible, in his whole personal and real estate, for the whole amount of debts due by the company : and the English country system, which is carried on by private co-partnerships, the members of which enjoy no special privileges or exemptions. His views afford little or no support to the American Banking System. To a small note circulation he was a decided enemy. His judgment was, that country Banks should issue no notes of a less denomination than five pounds sterling, or twenty-four dollars Federal money : and that city Banks should issue no notes of a less denomination than ten pounds sterling, or forty-eight dollars Federal money. The whole tenor of his book is in decided opposition to the practice of conferring peculiar privileges or exemptions, on any men, or any bodies of men, and is, consequently, in decided opposition to a fundamental principle of the American Banking System.

The principles of Smith were generally received till the year 1797. The Bank of England then suspended specie payments, and permission was given to it and to the country bankers, to issue notes of as low a denomination as one pound. The country Banks were required to make payment in notes of the Bank of England : while the Bank of England itself was placed under no restraint whatever but the discretion of its directors.

This state of things necessarily drew the attention of political economists to the subject; and, as Bank of England paper did not, for some years, undergo any sensible depreciation, guineas began to be regarded as an unnecessary incumbrance. So strong a hold did this notion take in the minds of men, that when Bank notes passed in the market at a considerable discount, many writers affirmed that paper had not fallen, but that gold had risen in value.

Mr. Boyd, Lord King, and other Economists, showed the incorrectness of this opinion, and Mr. Ricardo placed its erroneousness in a strong point of view, in a pamphlet published in the latter part of the year 1809, entitled, " The high price of Bullion, a proof of the depreciation of Bank notes." This work, Mr. Joplin avers " was the immediate cause, and formed the ground-work of the Report of the Bullion Committee."

" The principles of this Committee, supported by a host of writers, became now," says the historian, " the received opinions upon the subject, and they were as follows :

" They entirely agreed with Smith in the general principle, that if Banks were obliged to pay their notes in specie on demand, the trade might, in all other respects, be left perfectly free. They agreed with him, that the sum of paper in circulation ought not to exceed the sum of metallic money that would be in circulation if there were no paper · and they further agreed with him, that, if this amount of paper was not exceeded, no great demand for gold for exportation would ever arise: and that, if it were exceeded, a demand would arise for exportation, adequate to the excess. But in every other respect they differed from him, and laid down principles equally new and important.

" In the first place, they repudiated the principle that Banks could not issue to excess if they confined themselves to advancing money on real bills of exchange. This principle they proved totally incorrect.

" In the next, they denied that an excess of issues would be discovered by the merchant *previously* to the money's entering into consumptive circulation, and be returned upon the Banks for gold: though they admitted that an excess of issues would produce a demand upon the Banks for gold for exportation. But this, they proved, would take place *after* the paper had been introduced into circulation, and had depreciated the value both of itself and of the gold

in which it was payable; that gold, by this operation, becoming less valuable in England than in other countries,
would be exported to other countries; that the excess of
paper would be returned upon the Banks in demand for it,
to be sent abroad until the excess was withdrawn; and
that the value of both paper and gold would *then* rise to
its previous level, and the exportation of gold cease. This
doctrine negatived the idea of Smith, that an excess of issues did not find its way into consumptive circulation. It
was contended, on the contrary, that prices must be raised
above their proper level, before 'the exportation of gold
could be brought about.

" Thus, two important principles of Smith's which would
be very much calculated to affect his views as to the value
of a paper currency, were set aside : first, that the Banks
had an easy rule by which to guard against excess;
and next, that if they did issue to excess, no derangement
of prices would be produced by it; that the injury would
be felt by themselves, and not by the public.

" To this derangement of prices, however, which according to their views must precede an importation of
gold, the Committee did not appear to attach much importance.

" In the third place, they contended, that the issues of the
Bank of England regulated those of the country Banks. This
theory was new, though appearing to be suggested and
borne out by experience."

When Mr. Joplin says that the principles of the Bullion Committee became the received opinions, we are to
understand thereby that they became the opinions of a
large part of the British nation. The Anti-Bullionists were
so closely wedded to their favorite theory, that neither facts
nor reasonings could separate them from it. Such was
their influence, and such was the force of circumstances,
that, though it had been determined that specie payments
should be resumed one year after the close of the war, the
Government delayed, for four or five years, to take the necessary measures for effecting this object.

In May 1821, the Bank of England regularly resumed
the payment of gold on demand.

In the twenty-four years in which inconvertible paper
was the circulating medium, many hundred millions had

been added to the national debt, and the amount of private debts had been swelled immensely. The paying in specie of the interest of a national debt contracted in paper, and the discharging of private contracts in a currency of enhanced value, necessarily produced much embarrassment. No sooner, however, had the difficulties attendant on the resumption of specie payments been surmounted, than the Bank of England began to extend its issues. In 1824, it reduced the rate of discount from 5 to 4 per cent., and as the country Banks at the same time increased their circulation, such an *appearance* of prosperity was produced, as was unexampled in the annals of the kingdom.

This lasted till September 1825. Then, difficulties began, and in December there was a convulsion which threatened all interests with destruction.

" Such a panic," says Mr. Joplin, " occurring in a period of profound peace, after a good harvest, and traceable to no other cause but defects in our system of Banking and Currency, rendered it, of course, incumbent on the ministers to bring forward measures to remedy, if possible, the evils which had been produced, and also to prevent the recurrence of such diasters in future."

One of the principal measures they recommended was, the abolition of one and two pound notes; and, on this occasion, they, according to the British author just quoted, " adopted a mode of speaking of our currency different to any that had hitherto been adopted. When the withdrawal of the small notes was enacted in 1819, all the arguments were in favor of paper payable in gold. The Bullion Committee, whose views had been implicitly adopted, observed, that they fully agreed with Dr. Adam Smith, and all the most able writers and statesmen of this country, in considering a paper circulation constantly convertible into specie as one of the greatest practical improvements which can be made in the political and domestic economy of any State, and that such convertibility was a complete check against over issue.

" Nor had this doctrine ever been impugned by those who differed from the Bullion Committee in other respects. They, on the contrary, always contended, that paying in cash would not merely prevent over-issues, but would prevent enough being issued. It was too great a check upon

issues.   But in explaining the principles thus laid down in
the letter to the Bank, the Ministers, now, for the first time,
gave up this doctrine."

Mr. Charles Grant stated, that "the great problem with
respect to currency, is to discover that check whereby the
evil we wish to avoid may be arrested before it takes place.
The principle should be preventive rather than corrective.
His honorable friend opposite (Mr. Smith) seemed to think,
that the convertibility of paper into gold would operate as
a sufficient check to arrest its progress ; and in this opinion
he was certainly supported by high authorities, amongst
whom were some of the wisest men that composed the Bullion Committee.   They all agreed upon the necessity of
the convertibility of paper into gold, in order to establish
a sound currency.   The science of currency (for it deserved
the name of a science) was every day acquiring additional
light ; in fact, it was now in a state of experiment.   It appeared to him that those who supported the Bullion Report
were led to rely too exclusively on this check, not merely
to correct the evil when it does take place, but to operate
as a preventive, by which to guard against the extension of
it beyond a certain point.   There was no doubt of the
check ; but it may be so tardy in its progress as to produce
the evil itself : because, it is a check that operates not by
necessity, but by the discretion and judgment of those by
whom the paper is circulated.

"It was clear from what had occurred, that the check
provided by the convertibility of notes into gold, operated
so tardily, as to be inadequate to avert the evil, and it ought
to be the leading principle in every sound currency, to provide the means of arresting the evil before it arrives at its
height."

Lord Liverpool took a similar view of the subject, and
the Chancellor of the Exchequer, for the first time, impugned the doctrine of the regulating power of the Bank
of England.   He observed, "that by an investigation into
the different issues of different years, it would be found,
that the issues of the Bank of England had no relative connection with the issues of the country Banks, it happening
in several instances, that, when the Bank of England issues had increased, the country note issues had diminished,
and *vice versa.*"

This was also maintained by Lord Liverpool, who joined with the Chancellor of the Exchequer and with Mr.Huskisson, in descanting on the merits of a metallic medium. The latter observed, that, " It was the natural course, that, in such a fluctuating state of our currency, all classes of society must, in their turn, be afflicted by it, and, therefore, the sooner we get rid of that fluctuation, and returned to a sound, and healthy, and permanent, circulating medium, the better for the community at large. If they wished to prove the value of a steady and unchangeable currency, they had it in the history of France ; that country had been twice invaded by a foreign army, her capital had been twice taken possession of, and she was obliged to pay large sums to foreign countries; but they had a steady metallic currency, and however such visitations might have affected the great—however the extensive contractor might have been injured or ruined, the body of the population remained unoppressed. The storm might have crushed the forest tree, but it passed over without injuring the humble reed. This was to be attributed to the permanent footing upon which the currency of that country had been established."

In conformity with these views, an act was passed to prohibit, after the —— day of —— 1829, the issue of all notes of a less denomination than five pounds sterling, In 1828, a vigorous effort was made to repeal the law, but it was steadfastly and successfully resisted.

In a debate on the subject on the 3d of July, 1828, the Duke of Wellington said, " The measure of 1826 was not founded on any theory, but on experience which the few last years had confirmed. That experience had proved the fallacy of a theory which stated that a paper currency was perfectly safe as long as it was convertible into gold and silver. Experience during the three last years had proved this theory not to be true. It had likewise proved another theory not true—the theory that one pound notes and sovereigns could circulate together."

In the same debate Lord King remarked, that " those persons who considered paper money as an excellent thing to be established in a country, he was disposed to view as heretics. He had no hesitation in saying that the superstition attached to paper money was idolatrous in the highest degree. He looked upon it as the most dangerous heresy of all heresies."

The opinions of such men as Mr. Huskisson, Mr. Grant, Lord King, Lord Liverpool, and the Duke of Wellington, are, on such a subject as this, entitled to the respectful attention of every candid American. In their country, paper money Banking has been known longer than in ours. Every thing that can be said in favor of convertible paper, has been said in the various publications that have issued from the British press. These statesmen were familiar with all the arguments usually adduced in support of the system. They had ample opportunities of observing its practical effects.

If, however, we are disposed to disregard the result of their experience, let us examine the system for ourselves.

If paper money Banking requires only new restrictions to prevent its producing evil, the nature and number of those restrictions cannot be known, till we know all the evils it has produced.

If, as some seem to think, the system is to be perpetual, the effect it has on society, is a rational subject of inquiry. Such an inquiry, if faithfully made, will prevent us from ascribing to other causes such evils as have their origin in Banking, and thereby prevent us from increasing those evils by applying improper remedies.

AN INQUIRY

INTO THE PRINCIPLES

OF THE

AMERICAN BANKING SYSTEM.

CHAPTER I.

Importance of the Subject.

In an address to the stockholders of the United States Bank, at their meeting in 1828, Mr. N. Biddle, the President of that institution, stated, that, of five hundred and forty-four Banks in the United States, one hundred and forty-four had been openly declared bankrupt, and about fifty more had suspended business.

Mr. Gallatin, in his "Considerations on the Currency and Banking System," published in 1831, gives a list of 329 State Banks then in operation, having nominal capitals of the amount of $108,301,898, which, added to the capital of the United States Bank, made the whole nominal capital of these institutions, upwards of one hundred and forty-three millions of dollars.

These Banks issue notes which serve as substitutes for coin.

They grant credits on their books, and transfer the amount of credit from one merchant to another.

They receive money on deposit.

They buy and sell bills of exchange.

They discount mercantile notes.

They buy and sell public stocks.

All these are important functions, and if only one of them be ill performed, the community must suffer inconvenience.

The Banks are scattered through nearly all the States and Territories which compose our Union ; but they may all be embraced in one view, inasmuch as they all substitute paper for specie, and credit for cash, and are all endowed with privileges which individuals do not possess.

By their various operations, immediate and remote, they must affect, for good or for evil, every individual in the country.   Banking is not a local, temporary, or occasional cause.   It is general and permanent.   Like the atmosphere, it presses every where.   Its effects are felt alike in the palace and the hovel.

To the customs of trade which Banking introduces, all are obliged to conform.   A man may, indeed, neither borrow money from the Banks, nor deposit money in their vaults : but if he buys or sells it is with the medium which they furnish, and in all his contracts he must have reference to the standard of value which they establish.   There is no legal disability to carrying on commerce in the old-fashioned safe way : but the customs of Banking have introduced a practical disability.   It is no longer possible for the merchant to buy and sell for ready money only, or for real money.   He must give and take credit, and give and take paper money, or give up business.

Bank paper is not a legal tender in the discharge of private debts : but it has become, in point of fact, the only actual tender, and the sudden refusal of creditors to receive it would put it out of the power of debtors to comply with their engagements.

Credit, the great rival of cash, is completely controlled by the Banks, and distributed by them as suits their discretion.

These institutions may contribute little to the *production* of wealth ; but they furnish the means to many for the *acquisition* of wealth ; they appear to be the chief regulating cause of the present *distribution* of wealth, and as such are entitled to particular attention.

" In copying England " says Mr. Jefferson " we do not seem to consider that like premises induce like consequences.   The *Bank mania* is one of the most threatening of these imitations : it is raising up a monied aristocracy in our country which has already set the Government at defiance, and although forced to yield a little on the first essay of their strength, their principles are unyielded and unyielding. They have taken deep root in the hearts of that class from which our legislators are drawn, and the sop to Cerberus, from fable has become history. Their principles take hold of the good, their pelf of the bad, and thus, those whom the Constitution has placed as guards to its portals, are sophisticated or suborned from their duties. That paper money has some advantages must be admitted : but its abuses are also inveterate ; and that it, by breaking up the measure of value, makes a lottery of all private property, cannot be denied. Shall we ever be able to put a constitutional veto upon it ?"

"In most disquisitions upon the noxious tendency of Banks," says another writer* " much stress has been laid upon the injuries they have a power to inflict, by excessive loans and consequent bankruptcy, and by creating and circulating a permanent excess of currency. Could these two evils be avoided, many believe that Banks would be innoxious. I regret to differ. I am not of those who imagine that Banks incorporated with a liberal capital, will ever endanger their solvency by extending their loans ; nor of those who believe that Banks controlled by specie payment, can circulate a *permanent* excess of paper. And yet, I think I can perceive a portentous power that they exercise over commercial enterprize. I am of opinion that they can circulate a *temporary* excess of paper, which, from time to time, finds a corrective, in a run upon the Banks for specie ; that this temporary excess is succeeded by a temporary deficiency, one extreme invariably tending to another ; that the consequences of this alternate excess and deficiency are, in the former case to impart an undue excitement, and in the latter an undue depression to commercial enterprize ; that the effect of the former is to create an unnatural facility in procuring money, and to enhance unnaturally the price of commodities ; while that of the latter is to produce an artificial scarcity, and to cheapen prices artificially ; that the victims of these vibrations are the great body of merchants, whose capital and average deposits cannot always command discounts ; that the gainers are a few intelligent and shrewd capitalists, the

* Letter to Mr. Gallatin, by Publicola, New York, 1815.

magnitude of whose deposits commands enormous discounts at all times, and who, being behind the curtain,
know when to buy and when to sell. I am of opinion that
these vibrations inflict evils which close not with mercantile speculation; that they tend to unhinge and disorder
the regular routine of commerce, and introduce at one moment a spirit of wild and daring speculation, and at another,
a prostration of confidence, and stagnation of business :
that these feelings are transferred from the counting-house
to the fire-side ; that the visionary profits of one day stimu-
late extravagance, and the positive losses of another en-
gender spleen, irritation, restlessness, a spirit of gambling
and domestic inquietude.

" I appeal to the commercial history of our country, during the last seven years, and to the aching hearts of many
of my fellow-citizens, for the truth of these reflections.

" I wish not to be misunderstood. Let no one suppose
me so weak as to attribute every unfortunate speculation,
and every fluctuation in prices, to an undue management
or organization of our Banking Institutions. That would
be a folly, from the imputation of which I trust the preceding remarks will rescue me. There are commercial
fluctuations, and they are wholesome. They invigorate
enterprize, and their benefits are directly felt by all. There
are Banking fluctuations, and they are highly deleterious.
They intoxicate enterprize, only to enfeeble it ; and the
benefits are restricted to a few.

" This evil of Banking fluctuation, ends not with the
mercantile community. It extends to every thing that
commercial enterprize reaches. It injures the farmer and
the mechanic, in the precise ratio of the vacillations of
public feeling.

" The injuries which it has inflicted have been as universal as the insinuation of bank paper ; and the peculiar
manner of its operation renders it doubly distressing. It
does not affect the wealthy man, because he can always
control discounts; but it falls with single and dreadful severity upon the industrious poor man, whose capital is not
sufficient to command permanent accommodations; upon the
inexperienced, who purchase knowledge by a sacrifice of
property, and upon the merchant whose skill and sagacity
are superior to his wealth. *   *   *   *   *   *

Against a power so tremendous, what barrier has been erected? Against a power which, at different periods, has baffled the legislative wisdom of our revolutionary sages, of the Governments of Europe, and of Great Britain; what check have we imposed? THE INTEREST ACCOUNT OF EACH BANK. As well might Canute have controlled the waves of the ocean with a breath."

"Of all aristocracies," said a Committee of the New York Legislature, in 1818, "none more completely enslave a people than that of money; and in the opinion of your committee, no system was ever better devised so perfectly to enslave a community, as that of the present mode of conducting Banking establishments. Like the Syren of the fable, they entice to destroy. They hold the purse strings of society; and by monopolizing the whole of the circulating medium of the country, they form a precarious standard, by which all property in the country, houses, lands, debts and credits, personal and real estate of all descriptions, are valued; thus rendering the whole community dependent on them; proscribing every man who dares to expose their unlawful practices: if he happens to be out of their reach, so as to require no favors from them, his friends are made the victims. So no one dares complain.

" The committee, on taking a general view of our State, and comparing those parts where Banks have been for some time established, with those that have had none, are astonished at the alarming disparity. They see, in the one case, the desolations they have made in societies that were before prosperous and happy; the ruin they have brought on an immense number of the most wealthy farmers, and they and their families suddenly hurled from wealth and independence into the abyss of ruin and despair.

"If the facts stated in the foregoing be true, and your committee have no doubt they are, together with others equally reprehensible and to be dreaded, such as that their influence too frequently, nay, often already begins to assume a species of dictation altogether alarming, and unless some judicious remedy is provided by legislative wisdom, we shall soon witness attempts to control all selections to offices in our counties, nay the elections to the very Legislature. Senators and members of Assembly will be indebted to the Banks for their seats in this Capitol, and thus the wise end of our civil institutions will be prostrated in the dust of corporations of their own raising."

Not a few of those who have a personal interest in the continuance of the system, acknowledge and deplore the evils it produces. Indeed we have found no men more sensible of those evils, than some of the officers of Banks. They retain their offices on the same principle that they would, if they lived in England, retain offices under a Government they could not approve. To the established system of a country, whether political or commercial, men may deem it expedient, perhaps believe it necessary, to conform ; but this need not prevent their discovering the necessity for reformation.

One of these gentlemen, Mr. John White, the Cashier of the United States Branch Bank at Baltimore, makes the following candid and correct statement, in a letter to the late Secretary of the Treasury, under date of February 15th, 1830:

" Looking back to the peace, a short period, fresh in the memory of every man, the wretched state of the currency for the two succeeding years, cannot be overlooked ; the disasters of 1819, which seriously affected the circumstances, property, and industry of every district in the United States, will long be recollected. A sudden and pressing scarcity of money prevailed in the Spring of 1822 ; numerous and very extensive failures took place at New York, Savannah, Charleston, and New Orleans, in 1825 ; there was a great convulsion among Banks and other monied institutions in the State of New York in 1826 ; the scarcity of money among traders in that State, and eastward, in the Winter of 1827 and 1828, was distressing and alarming ; failures of Banks in Rhode Island and North Carolina, and amongst the manufacturers of New England and this State, characterize the last year ; and intelligence is just received of the refusal of some of the principal Banks of Georgia to redeem their notes with specie—a lamentable and rapid succession of evil and untoward events, prejudicial to the progress of productive industry, and causing a baleful extension of embarrassment, insolvency, litigation, and dishonesty, alike subversive of social happiness and morals. Every intelligent mind must express regret and astonishment, at the recurrence of these disasters in tranquil times, and bountiful seasons, amongst an enlightened, industrious, and enterprizing people, comparatively free from taxation, unrestrained in our pursuits, possessing abundance of fertile lands, and valuable minerals, with capital and capacity to improve, and an ardent disposition to avail ourselves of these great bounties.

" Calamities of an injurious and demoralizing nature, occurring with singular frequency, amidst a profusion of the elements of wealth, are well calculated to inspire and enforce the conviction that there is something *radically* erroneous in our monetary system, were it not that the judgment hesitates to yield assent, when grave, enlightened, and patriotic Senators, have deliberately announced to the public, in a recent report, that our system of money is in the main excellent, and that in most of its great principles, no innovation can be made with advantage."

The " grave, enlightened, and patriotic Senators," to whom Mr. White alludes, are those who, with Mr. Smith, of Maryland, at their head, made a report, in the year 1830, in which they represented certain kinds of Bank paper as being as good as gold, and even better. If their opinion is correct, it ought to be confirmed. If it is not correct, its erroneousness ought to be exposed; for error in such a subject as this, may be productive of incalculable mischief.

CHAPTER II.

Of Real Money.

Paper money is the foundation of the American Banking System. But, as, without a knowledge of what is genuine, it is impossible to have a clear conception of what is spurious, it will be necessary to give a statement of the qualities and functions of real money.

Money is not, as was asserted by a late Secretary of the Treasury, (Mr. I.) "merely the representative of property." Money of gold and silver *is* property—is *wealth*. A hundred dollars in silver can no more be considered as the representative of a hundred dollars' worth of flour, than a hundred dollars' worth of flour can be considered as the representative of a hundred dollars' worth of iron. Each is the *equivalent* of the other ; but each is *real* wealth— not a mere symbol or representative.

But money is not, as is supposed by some others, superior in its nature to all other kinds of wealth. The precious metals do not differ *essentially* from other items of wealth. This is distinctly seen when they are in the form of bullion. Converting them into coin, does not change their nature. It only adapts them to a particular use—fits them for passing from hand to hand, without the trouble of weighing and assaying each piece at each transfer. An increase of the stock of gold and silver in our country, is very desirable ; but it is for precisely the same reasons that an increase of other kinds of wealth is desirable.

Some fancy that it is the authority of Government that gives money its value. But the true value of money, as measured by the amount of goods for which it will honestly exchange, cannot be affected by edicts of Princes or acts of Parliament. Monarchs and Ministers may alter the weight of coins, or lessen their purity ; but they cannot make a coin containing an half of an ounce of pure silver, worth as much as a coin containing an ounce. The stamp of the State is a mere certificate of the weight and fineness of the piece.

Others suppose that the precious metals owe their value entirely to their *scarcity*. But if gold and silver were not useful in the arts, they would have no value in commerce. Their utility is so great, that even if they were not the material of money, they would exchange for great quantities of corn and other commodites. If they were as plentiful as copper and tin, they would be more valuable than these base metals; because they are applicable to more various uses. The market value of the precious metals is, as that of all other things, *in the compound ratio of their utility and of their scarcity.* It does not depend on their scarcity alone.

Money is, simply, that valuable by reference to which the value of other things is estimated, and by the instrumentality of which the interchange of other things is effected. There is nothing mystical in its nature; nor is it likely that its character would ever have been misunderstood in the United

States, if the avoirdupois ounce of silver had been made the unit of reference, and if coins had been struck of the weight of an ounce, and of aliquot parts of the ounce. Men would then have had as clear conceptions of the nature of the transactions into which money enters, as they now have of those in which iron is exchanged for wheat. They would then have seen that there is no essential difference in these transactions—that trade by barter, is exchanging wheat for one metal, and that trade with money, is only exchanging wheat for another metal. It has been by taking for the unit of reference a fractional part of the Troy ounce, which is a weight with which the people are not familiar, and by giving to this unit the arbitrary name of "a dollar," that the subject has been rendered obscure to many minds.

As whatever is extended may be made the standard of length, in like manner, whatever is valuable may be made the standard of value. Instead of saying, this tract of land, or this bale of cloth, is worth so many ounces, or so many pieces of silver, men might say, it is worth so many horses or cows, or so many pounds of lead or of iron. The *principle* of valuation would be identical with that which is adhered to in countries where only solid money is used. But he who had a small article to sell, would find it difficult to calculate its exact value in the *fractional* parts of a horse or a cow, and pounds of lead or of iron would be a very inconvenient circulating medium.

Corn, cattle, iron, leather, cacoa, tobacco, and other commodities, have all, in point of fact, been used as money, in different ages and different countries; but they have long ceased to be so used, by commercial nations, for reasons similar to those which have induced men to choose for their standard of length, some object less liable to variation than the foot of a Chancellor, or the fore arm of a King.

The high estimation in which the precious metals have been held, in nearly all ages and all regions, is evidence that they must possess something more than merely ideal value. It is not from the mere vagaries of fancy, that they are equally prized by the Laplander and the Siamese. It was not from compliance with any preconceived theories of philosophers or statesmen, that they were, for many thousand years, in all commercial countries, the exclusive cir-

culating medium. Men chose gold and silver for the material for money, for reasons similar to those which induced
them to choose wool, flax, silk, and cotton, for materials for
clothing, and stone, brick, and timber, for materials for
building. They found the precious metals had those *specific* qualities, which fitted them to be standards and measures of value, and to serve, when in the shape of coin, the
purposes of a circulating medium. To this use they are
admirably adapted :

1. Because they are divisible into extremely minute
portions, and capable of re-union without any sensible loss
of weight or value ; so that the quantity may be easily
apportioned to the value of the articles of purchase.*

2. They have a sameness of quality all over the world.
The difference between iron from different parts of our
own country and of Europe, is well known to all dealers
in that article. The copper of Siberia is superior to that
of Germany, while that of Sweden is better than that of
Siberia, and that of Sweden is surpassed by that of Japan.
But, one grain of pure gold is exactly similar to another,
whether it comes from the mines of Europe or of America,
or from the sands of Africa. Time, weather, and damp,
have no power to alter the quality : the relative weight of
any specific portion, therefore, determines its relative quantity and value to every other portion ; two grains of gold
are worth exactly twice as much as one.

3. Gold and silver, especially with the mixture of alloy
that they admit of, are hard enough to resist very considerable friction, and are therefore fitted for rapid circulation.

4. Their rarity and consequent dearness are not so great,
that the quantity of gold or of silver, equivalent to the
generality of goods, is too minute for ordinary perception :
nor, on the other hand, are they so abundant and cheap,
as to make a large value amount to a great weight.

5. They are capable of receiving a stamp or impression,
certifying the weight of the piece, and the degree of its
purity.

6. They are liable to less variation than any other article, from changes in the relations of supply and demand,
including the cost of production among the conditions of
supply.

*See Say, Book, Chap. xxi, Section 2.

By the discovery of America, the supply from the mines was increased tenfold, but as there was at the same time an increase of demand, owing to the increase of other kinds of wealth, the rise of prices from 1520 to 1620, was only fourfold. An opinion prevailed about fifty years ago, that the value of silver had been gradually declining from the year 1620, but Adam Smith, who inquired carefully into the facts, came to the conclusion that the opinion was unfounded, and Jean Baptist Say, the celebrated French economist, is of the belief that there has been hardly any variation in the value of silver in the last two centuries.

During the eight years preceding 1819, the supply from the mines is supposed to have fallen short one-half, owing to the troubles in South America. Such a diminution in the supply of any other article, would have made a great alteration in its value; but the annual product of the mines is so small in proportion to the whole quantity of the precious metals in the market of the world, that it requires very nice calculations to show that their value has been affected by this falling short of the supply.

According to the estimate of Mr. Gallatin, the stock of the precious metals on hand is between four and five thousand millions. From 1803 to 1809, when the mines are believed to have been most productive, the annual supply was fifty millions. In the last twenty years, it is said to have been but twenty-seven millions. But when the annual supply was most abundant, it was only in the proportion of one and a quarter per cent. to the stock on hand, and when it was lowest it had fallen only to three-fifths of one per cent. The ordinary supply of gold and silver does not exceed one hundredth part of the stock on hand, while the annual supply of agricultural products always exceeds, and that of manufactures often equals, the stock on hand.

The demand for the precious metals may be measured by the whole amount of other commodities in the market of the world, and the whole amount of labor. In this, but little variation can take place from year to year, or even in a series of years. There may be a glut of corn, cloth, cotton, or other merchandise. More of these articles may be produced than can be consumed, at a particular time or place : but there is never a glut of gold or of silver. The demand for these metals is universal and incessant. We do, indeed, say that "money is scarce, or money is plenty," but what we mean thereby is, that *loanable capital* is scarce or abundant. With the great body of men, money, and the material of which it is composed, are always scarce : and must continue scarce, as long as they want those things which money can procure.

From the durability of silver, and its other physical properties, from the steadiness and universality of the demand for it, and from the small proportion the annual supply bears to the stock on hand, it appears to unite all the qualities that can *reasonably* be desired in a commercial standard of value.

If it is not, as has been asserted by some, " an absolutely perfect and altogether permanent standard of value," it, in this respect, resembles our standard measure of length. Even a platina rod is affected by changes of temperature. All things here below are in a state of mutat on. The very figure of our earth is changing ; and an arc of the meridian will not, in the cycles of futurity, be of precisely the same length that it was when measured by the French Academicians.

It is true, our standard of value is liable to be affected by more causes than our standard of length. But we can calculate the force of these causes, and construct tables showing the effective power of money in exchanges in different ages. Such tables have been published by Sir George Shackford, in the Philosophical Transactions, by the Rev. Arthur Young, in one of his treatises, and by Admiral Rainer, as an accompaniment of his valuable charts of fluctuations in the price of corn. The difficulty of showing the effective power of money in remote periods, is not owing to any inherent defect in the material of which it is composed : but owing to the chroniclers of ancient times not having recorded a sufficient number of facts for the satisfaction of modern inquirers.

In solving problems in Political Economy, it is necessary sometimes to use labor as a measure of value, sometimes corn, and sometimes other commodities. So, to measure heights, we sometimes use the foot rule, sometimes the barometer, and sometimes the theodolite. But as, whatever instruments they may use, men find it convenient to express their mensuration of height in feet and inches their fractional parts and multiples, so, whatever measure of value writers may adopt, they seldom find it convenient to proceed far in their calculation, without reducing their expressions of value into the common money of account.

In no way can a clear conception of the wealth of a man in a distant time or place, be so easily acquired, as by a comparison of his income in money with the money price of labor and commodities at the same time and place.

Those who object to silver as an imperfect standard of value, appear to have fixed their minds on our common measures of length, and finding in them some qualities which silver does not possess, have hastily concluded that, as a standard of value, it is more imperfect than it really is. But, as value and length are *essentially* different, we must expect to find the standard and measures of the one essentially different from those of the other. The causes of variation must also be different; and the extent of variation must be different. The analogy between the standards and measures of different things, cannot be greater than the analogy between the things themselves. Value and length agree only in this—that each admits of increase and decrease by homogeneous degrees, whence it is that each is mensurable by like quantities.

If the reader will not suffer his mind to dwell exclusively on measures of length, but extend his thoughts to measures of duration, of heat, and of atmospheric pressure, he will probably be convinced that the common measures of value are not more defective than the common measures of time, temperature, and gravity.

To talk of *absolute* value is as absurd as to talk of absolute distance. As the distance of the earth from the sun increases as it passes from its perihelion to its aphelion, the distance from the sun to the earth must increase also.

As the value of other things falls, that of gold and silver rises. If the mercury in the thermometer did not rise as the heat increases, we should not be able, by that instrument, to measure degrees of temperature. If the mercury in the barometer did not fall, as we ascend mountains, we should not be able, by that instrument, to measure heights.

For an *absolute* standard of value, we should have to find something, the cost of production of which should be the same at all times, and in all places, and the demand and supply of which should never vary in the smallest degree. It is impossible even to fancy such a thing. It would be as reasonable to wish for a pendulum which should beat seconds in all latitudes, and in all elevations.

The effective power of money is much greater in some countries, and some ages, than in others. But we do not complain of our common measures of weight as imperfect, because ponderous bodies weigh more when on a level with the sea, than when on the tops of the highest mountains.

To object to the precious metals, on account of their being affected by the costs of production, and by the relations of supply and demand, is to object to them on account of the very things that fit them for standards and measures of value. If the causes of their value were not similar to the causes of the value of other items of wealth, and if they were not liable to be affected by the same causes of variation, they could not serve as a material for money. There must be some homogeneousness in the measure and the thing to be measured.

An ounce of pure silver is a quantity which never changes. We may make this our standard of value—our unit of reference in estimating other things. It is our own fault, if we afterwards vary this standard.

In many minds the notions of *value* and *utility* appear to be confounded. But the two things are distinct, though frequently conjoined. A fine lady and a merchant of the society of Friends have very different views of the utility of diamonds; but if the merchant has diamonds for sale, the creed of his church does not induce him to value them at less than the fine lady is able and willing to give. The value of commodities is in proportion to their adaptation to the wants and wishes of mankind, rational or irrational, and to the facility or the difficulty with which those wants and wishes can be gratified.

With others, *value* and *wealth* appear to be synonymous terms. But the various items that constitute wealth are positive in their nature. They are all those things that conduce to the gratification of human wants and desires, and which may be estimated by reference to a given standard—all those things which may be bought and sold, or estimated at a price. The word *value* is used to denote certain relations among these items. It always implies comparison of two or more objects. In its strict sense, it denotes the effective power of things in exchanges; but it is, without impropriety, sometimes used to designate that property in things which makes them effective in exchanges, and sometimes to signify the judgment the mind forms of different things, on a consideration of their effective power in exchanges. All these meanings of the word are closely connected, and grow out of one another.

Various views may be taken of value; but in whatever light it may be regarded, we shall find gold and silver money the most convenient instruments of valuation, though certainly not the *only* ones it is expedient to employ. The political economist, to determine the natural value of things, may compute their cost of production in days' labor and capital; but he will find it very difficult to estimate accurately these elements of production, except by the instrumentality of money. If he cannot bring his calculations into the common money of account, his labor will be of very little use to the practical man, for the effective power of things in exchanges is always estimated in this way, and it is the relation the natural value bears to the market value, that induces the enterprizing to incur the toil and expense of production.

In countries in which paper money is unknown, the common standards and measures of value appear to approach as near theoretic perfection, as the common standards of weight, length, or capacity. The standard of reference has no variation, except such as necessarily arises from the nature of value. The measures are composed of the same material as the standard.

The calculations necessary to show the effective power of money in different countries, and different ages, may not unaptly be compared to those which show the length of pendulums to beat seconds in different latitudes; or to those which show the loss of weight ponderous bodies sustain on being carried to different elevations above the surface of the sea.

In all such countries, the people suffer no more practical inconvenience from the want of any theoretic perfection philosophers may discover, or may fancy they discover, in the common measures of value, than from similar imperfections in the common measures of time and weight.

Where metallic money is exclusively used, the value of land, of labor, and of all commodities, great and small, can be determined with great accuracy. If, in such countries, the trade between different men is not always an interchange of equivalents, the fault is not in the instrument of valuation, but in those who use it.

If the labor of a man, for a day, or for a year, produces more than is necessary for his immediate support, he can, by exchanging the surplus product for gold or silver, secure the means of supplying his wants in future days or years. Time will not corrupt his treasure or lessen its value. If he should not require it all for his personal wants, he may, at the end of fifty years, endow his children with a portion.

The use of money renders it unnecessary for families to keep on hand a large stock of provisions and other necessaries, and thus saves them from the risk of loss from provisions spoiling, and from various accidents. Having money, they may procure whatever else they want, in just such proportions, and at just such times, as they want.

If business or duty calls a man to a distant country, he finds in money the means of procuring comforts similar to those be enjoys at home. The instrument by which he procures all these advantages, is light of carriage, and is unaffected by any climate into which he may travel.

As the value of silver has undergone hardly any variation in the last two centuries, and probably will not undergo any great variation for a hundred years to come, a man may, in solid money countries, enter into a contract to pay a sum of money, ten, twenty, or thirty years hence, and rest assured that more wealth will not be exacted from him than he intends to give. In such countries, contracts can be complied with in equity.

As the standard of value in most countries is the same, the coins differing only in weight, purity, stamp, and denomination, the value of different articles in different countries at the same time, can be ascertained with sufficient accuracy for each country to determine what articles it is expedient to export and what to import.

Without money, the division of labor could never be carried to any great extent, and the wealth of society would be small. Money, by promoting commerce, advances civilization.

All these advantages are procured at a small cost, for the product of the labor of a commercial nation, for a few weeks, will procure it enough of metallic medium for all the purposes of domestic trade, and this medium will not require renewal for centuries.

If the sovereign power refrains from unnecessary alteration in the coinage, commerce is, in countries where metallic money is exclusively used, liable to derangement only from great natural or political causes. If the supply of gold and silver from the mines is greatly increased, it does not produce a great rise of local price, for the metals diffuse themselves over the whole commercial world. If any country gets a large portion of these metals, manufactures absorb a part, and the increase of money is only in proportion to the increase of trade. If the supply from the mines is diminished, manufactures absorb less.

To the state of trade in different countries, the supply of gold and silver money naturally adapts itself; and also to the state of trade in each county and town, and to the condition of each individual. If any country, any county, any town, or any individual wants money, it is for the same reason that that country, that county, that town, or that individual, wants corn, cloth, coaches, or other commodities.

If the laws regulating trade introduce a new state of things, the supply of gold and silver soon conforms to the new relations of supply and demand.

No prohibitions can prevent money's departing from those countries where its amount is beyond what their trade and industry require. No country can be deprived of its just proportion of the precious metals, except by the use of paper, or by such causes as ruin the commerce and industry of a nation. No obstacle, except spurious money, can prevent the precious metals from flowing into countries where wealth is increasing.

No instance is on record of a nation's having arrived at great wealth without the use of gold and silver money. Nor is there, on the other hand, any instance of a nation's endeavoring to supplant this *natural* money, by the use of paper money, without involving itself in distress and embarrassment.

CHAPTER III.

Of Barter, Leger Entries, Bills of Exchange and Promissory Notes.

It is not necessary for carrying on business *honestly*, to introduce gold or silver money into every transaction. After we have measured a scantling by a foot rule, we may use that scantling to measure another, and that again to measure a third. We can, after having measured several scantlings in this way, make a tolerably correct estimate of the length of others by the eye. In like manner, after the value of given quantities of corn, cloth, and other commodities, has been ascertained by exchanging them for gold or silver, the value of other parcels of the same commodities may be determined without the intervention of money. In commercial countries in which there is no paper money, little trade is carried on by direct barter, not because it is difficult to make a correct barter estimate, but because purchases and sales can be better regulated in regard to time and quantity by other modes of business.

Hence the practice of leger entries, or running accounts. The amount of transactions between two traders may be very great, and yet, if, in all their dealings, they have strict reference to the specie price of goods, the commerce may throughout be an interchange of equivalent, though not an ounce of gold or of silver may have passed from one merchant to the other.

By promissory notes, the use of real money is *deferred*, and in some cases *superseded*. If A gives a promissory note to B, and B gives it to C, in exchange for goods, and C passes it to D, the use of money is in two cases superseded, and in one deferred.

Bills of exchange have, in some respects, a similar effect. A merchant at Paris sending goods to Alsace, and wishing money for them, would be forced to wait till the goods could be sold, and the money brought from Alsace, if he could not procure a bill of exchange. In like manner, a manufacturer at Alsace, sending goods to the capital, would be forced to wait for payment till the money could be brought from Paris. Here would be two sums of money passing in opposite directions. Supposing the whole trade of France carried on in this way, the amount of money continually on the road would be equal to the whole amount of goods in passage. The amount of money to be annually transferred from one country to another would be equal to the whole amount of trade between different countries, except when the business of importing and exporting was carried on by the same merchant. By the use of bills of exchange, the merchant receives the money for which the manufacturer's goods were sold at Paris, and the manufacturer receives the money for which the merchant's goods were sold at Alsace. In this way, it becomes necessary to transfer from one part of a country to another, or from one country to another, such sums only as are equivalent to the balances of trade.

Bills of exchange, where the practice is to pass them from hand to hand, may serve as a local commercial medium, though not a very convenient one, since it is necessary for the nice adjustment of transactions, to calculate the difference of the interest on each transfer.

Each of these three kinds of mediums has its *specific* uses; and each is, as an *auxiliary* of gold and silver money, productive of great benefit. A clear view of their operations is necessary, for the distinction between the representatives of private credit, and of bank credit, is as important as the distinction between genuine money and spurious.

Leger entries, promissory notes, and bills of exchange, agree with money in being a medium by which valuables are circulated. They differ from it in being evidences of debt owing by one man to another—which money is not.

In a far more important particular do they differ from money. They are *mere* commercial medium. They are neither *standards* nor *measures* of value. The amounts expressed in them are the estimations made of goods, by reference to the article which law or custom has made the standard of value. They may be conveniently distinguished as *commercial* medium, restricting the term *circulating* medium to money.

An increase of these three kinds of commercial medium may have the same effect on prices as an increase of money. Where the spirit of speculation is excited, men, after having exhausted their cash means, strain their credit. Cash and credit are then competitors in the market, and raise prices on one another. In the year 1825, a year of great speculation, the amount of bills of exchange, negotiated in England, was, according to the returns to Parliament, 600 millions sterling. Supposing one-eighth of these in circulation at the same time, this branch of the commercial medium of England amounted in that year to 75,000,000 pounds.

But the rise of prices produced by these occasional multiplications of the representatives of private credit, is always temporary. At the end of a given period the balance of the running account is demanded, and payment of the promissory notes, and of the bills of exchange, is required in money. If they are paid, their effect on prices ceases. The result is the same, if they are dishonored. In 1826, the amount of bills of exchange negotiated in England, was 400 millions. Supposing one-eighth part in circulation at one time, this branch of the commercial medium of England amounted, in this year, to 50 millions, and was one-third less than in the year preceding.

In countries where the money is of a sound character, and the state of credit sound also, leger entries, bills of exchange, and promissory notes, serve rather to keep prices on a level, than to cause them to fluctuate. In some seasons of the year, as when crops are brought to market, or cargoes arrive from foreign ports, there is naturally more trade than in other seasons. By the use of private credit payments are divided among the different months more equally than would otherwise be practicable.

Thus, in whatever way trade is carried on, whether by barter, running accounts, promissory notes, or bills of exchange, or money, one principle of valuation is adhered to in countries having a sound money system. The cash sales regulate the credit sales, and the cash prices regulate the credit prices.

If the money of a country is paper, whether issued by the government, or by a corporation, the expressions of value in the running accounts, promissory notes, and bills of exchange, are according to the new standards and measures of value.

Into the nature of these we shall inquire in other chapters.

CHAPTER IV.

Of Banks of Discount.

Let us suppose that all the Banks in the country were destroyed, and that our circulating medium consisted exclusively of gold and silver coin.   In such a state of affairs, every merchant would keep about his person, or in his house, his whole stock of money.

Let us next suppose an *Office of Deposit*, established in any one of our large towns.   For the sake of security against fire and robbers, the wealthy would here deposit whatever money they did not require for immediate uses.   All the money employed in the wholesale trade would thus become the deposit of the Bank.   It might be drawn out a few times, but as every large dealer would keep an account at the Bank, the absurdity would soon become evident, of drawing out the money by one man, that it might be deposited in the same place by his neighbor.   The amount would, therefore, be transferred from the credit of one merchant to that of another, and the Bank would become an *Office of Transfer* as well as of *Deposit*.   The only money that would circulate, would be that employed in retail trade. All wholesale transactions would be adjusted by checks on the Bank, and transfers on its books.

The Bank having issued no paper, the only demand on it would be for specie to send abroad.   This demand would be limited, for every merchant would make it a rule to retain enough money in Bank for his domestic trade.   It would be only as the trade of the town fluctuated, that the amount of money in the vaults of the Bank would fluctuate.   We may suppose that it rose as high, sometimes, as six millions, and sunk as low, sometimes, as four millions. In a little time, the Bank would discover the lowest amount to which its permanent deposits would be liable to be reduced : and it might lend nearly the whole of this amount without much risk of discovery.   The money might, indeed, be sent abroad by him to whom it was lent, but he by whom it had been deposited would still have a credit at the Bank, and as all the wholesale transactions of the town would be carried on by checks on the Bank, his credit on the books of that institution would serve him the same purposes as money.   Retaining the sum of 500,000 dollars to meet contingencies, the Bank might safely grant discounts to the amount of 3,500,000, and thus realize a profit of more than 200,000 dollars per annum, without lending a cent of its own capital, and without issuing any paper.

It is worthy of note, that the Bank of Amsterdam acted on this principle.   Millions of money, which the merchants had deposited in its vaults, and for the safe-keeping of which, and the transferring of which from one account to another, they paid a premium, were lent by the Bank to the India Company, and to the Provinces of Holland and West Friesland.   The fact was long kept secret; but was disco-vered when the French entered Amsterdam in 1794.

What was regarded as a shameful breach of confidence in the Bank of Amsterdam, is, with our American Banks, an avowed principle of action.   They all lend the money deposited with them for safe keeping, and it is in this way that the Banks in the large cities make great part of their profits.   All the money required for wholesale transactions is their permanent deposit.   It may go out one day, but it returns the next; and it may be transferred from one Bank to another, but it is never long out of some of the Banks; and for the same sum of money there are frequently two creditors—one in favor of him by whom the money has been deposited, and another in favor of him to whom it has been lent.

These Bank credits have a very different effect from the leger entries of private traders.   Whoever sells on trust, puts on his goods an additional price, equivalent to the in-terest for the time to which payment is deferred.   Sellers may persuade purchasers to the contrary, and, in some cases, capital may be so plentiful that the amount of interest on a small sum, for a short period, may be scarcely appre-ciable.   In other cases, the increase of price is greater than the amount of interest; as with fashionable tailors and shoemakers, who are forced to charge *insurance* on each item, and make the honest pay for themselves and the dishonest also.   Their business would not otherwise yield the common profits of stock and the common wages of labor.

But Bank credits are in all cases equal to cash. The Bank check goes as far as Bank notes, for Bank notes can be obtained for it on demand.

Increase of Bank credits has the same effect on prices as increase of Bank notes. He who has deposited money in the Bank, and he to whom it has been loaned, appear as competitors in the market, and raise prices by bidding against one another. It is the same sum of money with which they are contending, and the seller of goods can get it from one only. But there are two credits for this money in the Bank, and the credit is equivalent to cash, both to him who has deposited the money, and him to whom it has been lent.

Our American Banks of Discount must be distinguished from *Loan Offices*, or institutions which lend no more than the amount of their own capital. As some express it, the business of the American Banks is " to lend credit."

These Banks must also be distinguished from the Bank of Amsterdam, as it once was, and the Bank of Hamburg, as it now is. Into those cities there was a great influx of foreign coin, of various denominations, and much of it clipped or worn. To save the trouble of ascertaining the exact value of each parcel, by sorting it on every transaction, it was deposited in Bank, and credit granted to each merchant for the amount he deposited, according to mint valuation, a small sum being deducted for warehouse rent, and a small fee charged on each transfer. These Banks were mere offices of deposit and transfer—not of discount. They were very different from our American Banks.

CHAPTER V.

Of Banks of Circulation.

Our American Banks are not contented with the profits derived from lending the money of depositors to other people.

As soon as the first instalment of the capital is paid in, the Bank commences issuing notes. To those who come to borrow, it lends paper or coin. The paper being exchanged for coin, serves, at least at the place where it is issued, the same purposes as coin.

Every man desires money, because he can therewith procure whatever else he desires. If paper can procure for him the object of his desire as readily as gold and silver, paper is as desirable to him as gold and silver. The Bank, therefore, finds borrowers for all the coin it has to lend, and all the paper it deems it safe to issue. This addition of notes to the amount of metallic money previously in circulation, raises first the price of some articles and then of others. The borrower from the Bank having more money, either paper or coin, at command, can offer an additional price for the object of his desire, or perhaps procure some desirable object that was before unattainable. He from whom the borrower has bought, having made a speedier sale, or perhaps received a higher price than would otherwise have been possible—he also has it in his power to obtain some object of desire that was not before within his reach. A third, a fourth, a fifth, a sixth, each in his turn, derives a like advantage from this increase of circulating medium. The rise of prices is confined for a time to store goods, but it at length reaches real estate, and finally the wages of labor. Industry is stimulated, and enterprize encouraged. Speculation is excited, private credit is strained, and the representatives of private credit are multiplied. Every body is active, and all branches of business appear to be prosperous.

Nothing could be prettier than this, if prices could be kept *continually* rising. But it is, unfortunately, only while the amount of Bank issues is actually increasing, or for a short time after they have attained their maximum, that society derives this benefit from paper money. So far it has the same effect as an increase of *real* money—as an increase of real wealth. But in due time it affects all articles in nearly equal proportions : and men then discover that for an object of desire for which they had formerly to give one dollar, they have now to give one dollar twenty-five cents, or one dollar fifty : and that it is not more easy to get the one dollar and fifty cents to make the purchase with, than it was formerly to get one dollar. The *value* of land, labor, and commodities, as compared with one another, is the same as it was before. It is only the *money price* that is enhanced. The effect this has on public prosperity, is much the same as that which would be produced by changing accounts from pounds, shillings, and pence, to federal money. The sum total of dollars would exceed that of pounds, but the articles of the value of which they would be the exponents, would be unaltered in number and in quality.

It would be well if the issues of the Banks had no other effect than that of *apparently* increasing the wealth of the community, by raising the money valuation of all kinds of property. But these institutions do not continue their issues long, before they raise the price of some commodities above the price they bear in foreign countries, added to the costs of importation. In foreign countries the paper of the Banks will not pass current. The holders of it, therefore, present it for payment. The Banks finding their paper returned, fear they will be drained of coin, and call upon their debtors to repay what has been advanced to them. In two ways, then, is the quantity of circulating medium diminished: first, by the specie's being exported : secondly, by the paper's being withdrawn from circulation. Prices fall as rapidly as they had before risen. The traders find that the goods in their stores cannot be disposed of, unless at a loss. The different members of society had entered into obligations proportionate to the amount of circulating medium in the days of Banking prosperity. The quantity of circulating medium is diminished, and they have not the means of discharging their obligations. The merchandise, the farms, the houses, for which they contracted debts, may be still in their possession ; but the product of the farms will not bring, perhaps, half as much as will pay the interest of the original purchase money ; the houses will not rent for as much as will pay the interest on the mortgages ; and the store goods must, if sold at all, be sold below prime cost. Bills of exchange are dishonored, and promisory notes protested. One man is unable to pay his debts. His creditor depended on him for the means of paying a third person to whom he is himself indebted. The circle extends through society. Multitudes become bankrupt, and a few successful speculators get possession of the earnings and savings of many of their frugal and industrious neighbors.

By the reduction of the amount of Bank medium, the prices of things are lowered, the importation of some kinds of foreign goods is diminished, and specie is brought back. Then the confidence of the Banks is renewed, and they re-commence their issues of paper. Prices are raised again, and speculation is excited anew. But prices soon undergo another fall, and the temporary and artificial prosperity is followed by real and severe adversity.

"Such is the circle which a mixed currency is always describing."

CHAPTER VI.

General Effects of this System.

The rise of prices that follows an expansion of Bank medium, and the fall that follows a contraction, do not affect all descriptions of labor and commodities, at the same time, in an equal degree. The usual effect of an increase of issues, appears to be to raise still higher those articles which are rising from some natural cause; and the effect of a contraction, to sink still lower those which are falling from some natural cause. As Malthus has observed, the tendency of paper money is in some instances to sink prices to their lowest point, and raise them in others to their highest. The natural value no longer regulates exchanges. We had melancholy proof of this effect of contraction in 1820, when, according to Mr. Niles' calculation, the average price of flour throughout the country was only two dollars and fifty cents a barrel. Of rise of prices produced by expansions of Bank issues, we had striking examples in 1825 and 1831.

Wages appear to be among the last things that are raised by an increase of Bank medium. The working man finds all the articles he uses in his family rising in price, while the money rate of his own wages remains unchanged. In the year 1831, which was a year of great expansion, rents rose enormously in many parts of the town, store goods advanced in price, and such fresh provisions as are sold in the market were higher than they

had been at any time since the resumption of specie payments ; but the money rate of wages was hardly affected.*

If wages are not the first to fall on a contraction of issues, it is because the effects of the contraction fall unequally on different kinds of labor. "Contractions" never
proceed far, without breaking up some productive establishments. Some men are thus deprived of employment :
they enter into competition with the workmen in other establishments, and finally reduce wages in the branches
of business not immediately affected by the contraction
of Bank issues.

Hence the complaint we sometimes hear of " all branches of trade being overdone." A great number of enterprizes, undertaken with a cheering prospect of success when
the Banks "make money plenty," come to an unfortunate
conclusion when the Banks " make money scarce." As
one man is thrown out of employment, his effective demand for the product of his neighbor's labor is diminished,
and he, perhaps, becomes the competitor of his neighbor,
instead of his customer. The merchant is compelled to
offer his services as a clerk. The master mechanic becomes a journeyman. If a clerk is thrown out of employment, the shoemaker has one good customer less. If
twenty clerks are deprived of employment, the shoemaker
may find it necessary to dismiss one of his assistants.
If twenty shoemakers are without employment, the baker
may find his sales of bread materially diminished : and so
of all other trades.

If the real wants of the community, and not their ability to pay, be considered, it will not, perhaps, be found
that any one useful trade or profession has too many mem-

* This is not the first time this remark has been made. In the British Bullion Report, made in 1811, the following passage occurs: "The
wages of common country labor, the rate of which, it is well known.
adapts itself more slowly to the changes which happen in the value of
money, than the price of any other species of labor or commodity."

Hutchison, in his History of Massachusetts, vol. 2, page 401, makes
a remark which shows that the effect of paper money is, in this respect,
the same, whether it is issued by a Government or by a Bank.

" I recollect one advantage from paper money. Upon the depreciation from time to time, the *wages* of seamen, and the rate at which
coasting vessels and others were hired, did not immediately rise in
proportion to the rise of silver, and exchange with London and other
parts of the world."

bers. The number of educated physicians, for example, is not too great for the population. But, not a few physicians remain without employment, while many persons, from inability to pay for medical advice, suffer all the evils of sickness. It cannot be said that we have too many shoemakers, tailors, or cabinet-makers, while multitudes are but indifferently provided with clothing and furniture. But, in one sense, "all businesses" may be said to be "overdone," since all businesses are by this system rendered unprofitable to some who are engaged in them.

On the operations of manufacturers, these contractions and expansions are productive of most pernicious consequences. Expansions of Bank medium are always incitements to them to extend their business. The paper need not be put in circulation by direct loans to the manufacturers. Lending it to such as will buy their commodities has the same effect. Having, by the increase of Bank medium, been enabled to sell his goods at an advanced rate, the manufacturer re-commences operations with new spirit. So facile is production with modern machinery, that a small rise of prices causes a great increase of cotton and woollen goods. The production of the articles for which these fabrics are ultimately to be exchanged, cannot, unfortunately, be increased with equal facility. Unfortunately, also, the Bank medium is soon contracted. There is then a glut of manufactures, and a scarcity of money.

On the operations of the agriculturists, these expansions and contractions operate more slowly, but not less perniciously. Of this we had a striking example in 1825, when the speculations in cotton (speculations which can be distinctly traced to an extension of the paper system in Europe and America,) caused much corn to be uprooted that cotton might be planted in its place. The consequence was, a glut of cotton in the next year, and a scarcity of corn, in some districts of the South.

But, increase of Bank medium has the most obvious effect on real estate, as that varies most slowly in value from natural causes. Whenever the Banks make money plenty, speculation in real estate is excited, because men are very desirous to possess that which will afford them a permanent revenue. As the custom is to pay only part of the price agreed upon, and give mortgages for the remainder, a small increase of Bank issues produces a considerable rise in the price of immoveable property. In Philadelphia and some other large towns, it is the practice with many not to give any money in the purchase of building lots, but to contract to pay a specified sum annually by way of ground rent. Thus, when the currency is plentiful, men enter into obligations, binding themselves and their heirs to pay perpetual annuities; which annuities, when the currency becomes scarce, sweep away half or all their property. .

A four story house on Market street, the erection of which cost $10,000 about the time of the last war, was offered for sale some years afterwards for *five* dollars. Nobody would take it at this price, because the rent the house would bring was not equal to the ground rent. A few furlongs higher up this street, several three story houses were bought for a dollar apiece; and the purchaser did not get for rent of houses and ground together, as much as he had, a few years previous, bargained to receive for the ground alone.

In the less commercial parts of the town, many mechanics took lots on ground rent, and invested their little savings in houses, which they hoped would be the property of themselves and of their children after them. The Bank issues were contracted, and these hard-working men lost the net proceeds of many years of industry and economy.

Now, the owners of the ground meditated no injustice towards these mechanics. When they fixed the rent of the lots, they supposed they were asking no more than they were worth in perpetuity; and the mechanics supposed they were agreeing to pay no more than they were worth. Their value was correctly estimated, but in a debased currency. If the landlords had abated part of their demand, when a fall of prices took place through the enhancement of the currency, they would have acted on principles different from those which usually govern men of business.

For more than a century it had been the practice with men of limited means to lease lots on perpetual ground rent, erect houses thereon, and give mortgages for so much of the cost of building as they could not defray without borrowing. There was little risk in entering into these obligations, as both the ground and the buildings rose in value with increase of capital and population. In each succeeding year a portion of the debt was paid off, and the mechanic had, at the end of no long period, the satisfaction of calling his house his own. The mechanics whose melancholy fate we have recorded, were acting on a method which had been successfully pursued from the first settlement of the country. Their only misfortune was, being ignorant of the principles of currency, and having rulers as ignorant as themselves.

In all parts of the Union, except New England, property passed in the same manner from those who had an equitable to those who had only a legal claim to it. Farms rose in price from fifty to a hundred per cent., and sunk again as rapidly as they had risen. Thousands were reduced to poverty, and scores rose to wealth on the ruin of their neighbors.

It may be said that we are only describing the effects of a suspension and a resumption of specie payments. To this it is sufficient to reply, that occasional suspensions of specie payments are *necessary incidents* of the Banking system. Those who fancy that the Bank of the United States would be able to continue specie payments in time of war, forget the fate of the more powerful Bank of England. Twice in the midst of profound peace, has this very Bank of the United States been on the verge of suspending specie payments; and the Bank of England itself was, in 1825, saved from bankruptcy, only by the intervention of a Sunday, the discovery in the cellar of the Banking-house of 800,000 one pound notes, by putting which in circulation again, the Bank *evaded* its promises to pay, and by an unexpected supply of gold from the continent.

Suspensions and resumptions of specie payments only make the effects of contraction and expansion more obvious. The money of the country is paper money now, as it was in 1815 and 1816. Its "convertibility" fixes limits on its expansion; but frequent contractions are necessary to keep it "convertible," and these expansions and contractions are followed by very pernicious consequences.

As in the case of all public evils, the system bears with the most hardship on the poor. The rate of wages is, as we have seen, the last thing that is affected by an expansion ; and one necessary consequence of a contraction is, to deprive some men of employment. If a rich man cannot sell his merchandise to-day, he can sell it to morrow ; and if he cannot sell it for full price, he can sell it for half-price. But labor is the poor man's only commodity. If he cannot sell it to-day, it is lost to him forever.

The substantial capitalist is a frequent loser, though sometimes a gainer, by these fluctuations. If his capital is small, and his credit in proportion, it is with difficulty he escapes from total ruin in times of contraction.

The reckless speculator, who has no capital of his own, but who operates extensively on the capital of other people, has much cause to be well pleased with this system. If a loss is sustained by a fall of prices, the loss falls on his creditors, for he has nothing to lose. If there is a gain, through a rise of prices, the gain is all his own.

If the speculator is a Bank Director, or a favorite with Bank Directors, happy is his lot. Is there a scarcity of money ? It affects not him. Money is made more scarce with other men, that it may be plenty in his pockets. Whatever may be the condition of others, he is enabled to meet his engagements, and to support his credit. He has the means of purchasing the goods and real estate of distressed debtors at reduced prices, and of holding them till prices rise again. A year seldom passes over without an opportunity of this kind occurring, and such opportunities sometimes occur several times in the course of a single year.

In the facility with which these speculators can obtain loans in troublous times, they have another source of profit. In some seasons, they make more gain by discounting notes out of doors, at 2, 3, and 4 per cent. a month, than the Banks of a city acquire by their regular operations. A " go-between" usually manages these transactions, and the speculator, though generally suspected, cannot be proved to be a usurer : but instances have been known of Directors following unsuccessful applicants for " renewals of accommodation" out of the Banking-house, and then discounting their notes for an extortionate premium. In times of " expansion," men are invited to receive " accommodations" from the Banks ; and in time of " contraction" these " accommodations" are made the instruments by which they are fleeced of their property.

Much is said against lotteries, and they are certainly great evils. But a lottery, if there is no fraud on the part of the Managers, is perfect fairness when contrasted with some of our commercial operations. Some must gain, and some must lose, in every lottery: but if it is fairly conducted, the chances of loss and gain are equal to all adventurers. In the present great game of Banking, in which the fortunes of the whole community are the stakes, the very nature of the game gives great advantages to the Managers.

It is no reply to this to say, that many Bank Directors are too high-minded to make an improper use of their opportunities for making money. Bank Directors are like other men—some of them good, some of them bad. The great majority of them are worthy of all respect as private citizens: but even they must, if they are candid, admit that the *system* gives great advantages to some members of the community over others; and it is of *the system* that we are treating.

Nor is this view of the subject altered by the fact that all the favorites of Banks do not become men of great wealth. They have great advantages in the great game of society, but there is a bye-game among themselves, and one speculator wins from his fellow speculator what the latter had gained from the people at large.

Besides this, they are affected, in common with other men, by the various Banking processes which make business in general so uncertain as frequently to baffle all calculation. These affect all classes of society. These place us all astride of the see-saw of fortune. Now we go up, and now we go down. The fate of the frequenters of the Palais Royal is hardly more uncertain.

These vicissitudes of fortune are most striking in the cases of men of a bold turn of mind, who commence life without capital, and who, not satisfied with the gain acquired by a few years of successful speculation, continue their operations till fortune turns against them. But the regular merchant, the plodding mechanic, and the painstaking farmer, are not exempted from similar vicissitudes. It is said, that, in one of the most commercial streets of Philadelphia, there were, a few years ago, but three or four mercantile houses of twenty years standing, which had not broken once or oftener, been compelled to ask for an extension of credit, or been in some way seriously embarrassed. When we consider that the same causes are now in operation, how many of our present commercial houses may we hope will remain unembarrassed for twenty years to come ? No doubt many men will, in that period, retire from business, with handsome estates : but of such as shall continue operations for twenty years, how many will escape the vicissitudes which the present system of things entails on the community ?

We have become so accustomed to this system of breaking, that we begin to consider it a part of the system of nature. But it was not so always. Previous to the revolutionary war, there were but three bankruptcies among the large dealers in Philadelphia.* A bankruptcy in the olden time, spread as much gloom over a family as a death; and if the bankruptcy was the result of misfortune, the family had the sympathy of all their neighbors.

There is reason to believe, that in some periods of six months, more bankruptcies have been recorded in Philadelphia and New York, than in Hamburg and Bremen in twice that number of years : and that there are more insolvencies in the United States in one year, than happen in Holland in a whole century.

No natural causes exist to make trade more uncertain in the United States than in France, Germany, and Holland. The commerce of those countries is, in fact, exposed to shocks, from which ours is exempt, from the operations of hostile armies in and near their territories, and from every change that happens in the political world immediately affecting their mercantile operations. But the expansions of Bank medium lead our merchants to overtrading, and the contractions force them to make sacrifices of their property : and as these expansions and contractions are as incessant, though not as regular, as the ebbing and flowing of the sea, many kinds of business are with us rendered more uncertain by this one cause, than they are in some other countries by all natural and political causes put together.

---

* They were those of Scott and M'Michael, Peter Baynton & Co., and of one other firm, the name of which is not recollected by our informant.

CHAPTER VI.

Effects on Credit.

In a rising country, sound credit is of equal importance
with sound currency. Through its operation, the advantages of capital are more equally diffused than would otherwise be possible. The man who has more capital than he
wishes to employ in his own business, and the aged and
infirm who possess wealth, lend it to the young and active.
By these means, much capital is made productive, which
must otherwise have remained unproductive; and many
persons find employment who must otherwise have been
idle. The wealth of the nation is increased, and lenders
and borrowers are mutually benefitted. The former receive their just share of profits, in the shape of interest;
and the latter keep another share as a recompense for the
trouble of management.

To have a system of sound credit, nothing more is necessary than to have a sound money system, and to enforce
the faithful performance of honest contracts.

In the countries forming the present United States, credit
has never been perfectly sound. In an early period of our
colonial history, arbitrary alterations were made in the legal
valuation of the current coin. Then came the paper
money of the Provincial Governments, and the Continental money of the Revolutionary Congress, together with
tender laws, supported by penal enactments. Men of
property were careful in making loans, as they knew not
but that, between the time of lending and receiving back,
such alterations might be made in the currency, that they
would be paid in money of much less value than that which
they lent.

Notwithstanding this, as business was much less uncertain than it is now, men whose moral character was such
as to afford a guarantee that they would not take advantage
of unjust laws to injure their creditors, found little difficulty in borrowing. But moral character is no longer
security for the re-payment of loans; for, the sudden vicissitudes of fortune, which are produced by the Banking system, make very great changes in the moral feelings of men.

Many a one who has, while his affairs are prosperous, every disposition to fulfil his engagements, becomes very careless about them, when he finds his affairs declining.

As industry and economy no longer insure success in business, nothing short of real estate is regarded as adequate security for the re-payment of a loan. This security many men, in whose hands capital would be very productive, are unable to give. And thus, while the rich are prevented from lending their funds in the manner which would be most advantageous to themselves, not a few industrious and enterprizing persons are prevented from exerting their faculties in the way which would be most beneficial both for themselves and for the community. Some, from the impossibility of obtaining capital to work with, are like mechanics without tools—useless both to themselves and to the nation.

This practice of lending on bond, to which Banking has nearly put an end, was, perhaps, more advantageous to the country, than any other kind of lending. Men who have real estate, could find means for employing their faculties to advantage, even if they were not able to borrow on mortgage. They might till their farms, if their real estate consisted of farms ; or if it consisted of houses, they might, by renting their houses, obtain capital enough to engage in some active business. But men having no capital of their own, and unable to borrow, must, unless employment is afforded them by others, remain in absolute idleness.

It is now, indeed, possible for such men to borrow from the Banks, if their indorsers please the Directors. But the loans of the Banks are for 60 or 90 days, while months, and even years, are required for bringing the enterprizes of the farmer and the mechanic to successful completion. Short loans are useless to them. The Banks may, indeed, renew the accommodation, but this depends on contingencies; and the curtailments in time of pressure are so ruinous, that a man acts very unwisely who borrows large sums from the Banks, or who borrows them for a long period.

When Dr. Franklin arrived in this city, more than a century ago, he was a poor and friendless journeyman printer. The amount of loanable capital held by the Philadelphians was small. Yet, he had been here but a short time, before his neighbors, without solicitation on his part, offered to lend him money to establish him in business. A thrifty young mechanic who should now attempt to borrow 500 or 1000 dollars, for a term of two or three years, on his personal security, would be regarded with astonishment. Yet this young mechanic has a capital in his faculties which would entitle him to a loan of more than 500 dollars, if the state of credit were sound. If his labor yields him six dollars a week, and his expenses of living are four, he will have a surplus of 104 dollars at the end of the year. This would pay the interest on upwards of 1700 dollars. His chance of living, if he is twenty-one years old, is, according to the doctrine of life-insurances, at least thirty years. After making every allowance for contingencies, a loan of 500 dollars to such a young man, might be considered quite a prudent act, and such a loan might enable him to double his weekly revenue. But the uncertainty of business, and the instability of moral character which is produced by uncertainty of business, are such, that capitalists deem the chances of re-payment not sufficient to justify lending to young mechanics: and the embryo Doctor Franklins who are among them, are left to contend with adversity, without assistance from their richer neighbors.

As there is no borrowing at present on personal security, except from the Banks, many persons suppose that if there were no Banks, there would be no borrowing at all. But Banks do not increase the amount of loanable capital in the country. The loanable capital of each year, is the wealth which its owners do not choose to employ in their own business. All Banking can do, is, to take this loanable capital out of the hands of its owners, and place it under the control of irresponsible corporations.

If those who have honestly paid their cent. per cent. for Bank stock, could get their money back, and lend it on bond, it would be more secure than it is at present. Much of that money has been lent by the Banks to wild speculators. It would be in safer hands, if lent to industrious farmers and mechanics, and plain dealing merchants and storekeepers. We mean, of course, if we had a sound money system, and a sound credit system built thereon, and that sound moral character which proceeds from a sound money and sound credit system. At present, it is not prudent to lend on any security short of real estate. Such is the precariousness of business, that men who do not like to incur debts which they may be unable to pay, are scrupulous about borrowing on bond, unless their personal estates are so large as to cover all risk.

CHAPTER VII.

The same subject, continued.

It is a very pernicious kind of credit which Banking substitutes for the kind of credit which would exist, if we could escape the evils of government paper money, and of unnecessary alterations in our coinage.

The lender and the borrower do not, under the present system, meet each other face to face. The capital is placed in the hands of irresponsible Boards of Directors, who, in managing it, have regard to little but their own personal interest and that of their favorites. Great facilities are thereby afforded to many men for borrowing, to whom no man ought to lend. They are led by Bank loans to engage in business for which they are not fitted by either nature or education. The enterprizes fail, and the wealth of the community is diminished in proportion as the amount of capital thus employed is great or small.

Instances have occurred of men obtaining credit for an immense amount, who were not entitled to credit for one cent. They were neither skilful, industrious, nor economical. They had no capital in their faculties; and none in the form of real or personal estate; or, if they had, it was previously loaded with debts of equal amount to its whole value. On an investigation of the affairs of a petty Bank in Buck's county, it was found that the President was indebted to it, either individually, or as a co-partner with other men, in the sum of $112,000, which was three times the amount of the active capital of the Bank. In the case of a Bank in Connecticut, the loans of which were 1,900,000, no less a sum than 1,500,000 was lent to two commercial firms, consisting of two persons each. In another instance, four gentlemen of Baltimore, who had previously borrowed $1,957,700 from a certain Bank in the regular way, borrowed an additional sum of $1,500,000 from the same Bank, without even asking the consent of the proper officers. From a statement recently published, it appears that, on the 9th of April, 1832, the whole amount of notes and bills discounted at the principal Bank in Philadelphia, was $7,939,679 52; of which sum, more than two-thirds wvs loaned to ninety persons. More than $3,000,000 were in the hands of seventeen individuals, and nearly one-seventeenth part in the hands of one person. Deducting from the total the bills of exchange, the discounts of the Bank on that day, amounted to $5,964,085 26; and nearly five millions and a half of this amount were distributed as follows:

In loans of not less than $20,000,	each to 72 persons,	$2,404,278
do. 50,000,	do. 19 do.	1,274,882
do. 100,000,	do. 3 do.	341,729
do. 200,000,	do. 4 do.	995,456
do. 400,000,	do. 1 do.	417,766
		$5,434,100

Leaving only $529,974 26, to be divided among the rest of the community.

A small amount borrowed from a Bank, gives a man great credit with the community. By paying down a few thousand dollars and giving mortgages for the remainder of the purchase money, he may get real estate in possession of the value of fifty thousand dollars. He is then regarded as a rich man by the multitude, who know of his houses and lands, but know nothing of the mortgages. They are willing to let him have any kind and any amount of goods on credit. The second year he may be insolvent; but his credit remains unimpaired, and he satisfies those from whom he bought goods in the first year, by the proceeds of goods purchased on credit in the second year. Every year the amount of debt he owes beyond what he is able to pay, goes on increasing; but ten or twelve years may elapse before his insolvency becomes apparent. In the mean time he is living in splendor on the property of other men.

This facility of credit leads many into extravagant modes

of living. What they have obtained by the sweat of their brow, men know the value of, and are careful of. But what they obtain in a less laborious way, they expend more freely. The easiness with which they can run into debt, is to multitudes a great misfortune.

It is well if extravagant living is the only fault this facility of credit brings with it. When men accustomed to splendor, have the property of others in possession, and can secure an independent fortune by so simple an act as a false oath in an insolvent's court, the temptation may prove too strong to be resisted. When they break, the ruin that follows spreads far and wide : for a system of guaranteeing has grown out of our present mode of doing business, through which every man's success in life is made to depend quite as much on the good conduct of those with whom he is connected, as on his own frugality and industry. The Banks are secured by special assignments in which the endorsers of notes are made "preferred creditors," but all others with whom the bankrupt has had commercial dealings, are injured. As every merchant depends in part on what is owing to him by others to pay his own creditors, bankruptcies seldom occur singly. One dishonest, or one simply unfortunate man, may break twenty.

When credit has caused such a distribution of wealth as renders that capital productive which would otherwise be unproductive, and gives employment to those persons who would otherwise be idle, or less profitably employed, it effectuates all the good that it is in its nature capable of accomplishing. Left to itself, it would regulate itself—would reach this limit, and seldom pass beyond it. Pushed beyond this extent, it becomes pernicious ; and it is pushed far beyond this extent, by our present system. There is now little buying or selling, except on credit. Even the trade of consumption is on credit. A pass book goes to the grocer's ; and the tailor and the shoemaker think themselves happy if their bills are paid at the end of the year.

The retail storekeeper (if he does not commence business without any capital of his own,) lends his capital to his customers by selling to them on credit. This forces him to borrow another capital from the wholesale merchant : for, buying goods on credit, is the same as borrowing capital—it is borrowing in the shape of goods instead of money, and giving a note instead of a bond, and an additional price instead of interest. The wholesale merchant, having lent his capital to the retailer, is forced to borrow another capital from the Bank. The Bank, in its turn, borrows the capital of its depositors, and of those who receive its notes. In this way, the whole community becomes indebted—the private families to the storekeepers, the storekeepers to the merchants, the merchants to the Banks, and the Banks to the community at large.

Nothing is gained by this forced extension of the credit system. It does, indeed, increase the gambling trade of speculation : and that kind of trade in which sheriffs, constables, and assignees, are the active agents. It also increases, in particular years, the trade of consumption : but then it draws from the productive capital of the country, and diminishes the trade of consumption in the following years. The amount of *bona fide* trade for a series of years depends on the amount of goods produced and to be exchanged. The aggregate of this trade would be much increased through the habits of industry and economy which a cash and sound credit system would introduce.

On a cash system, men with small capitals could do as much business as they do at present. They would then turn their capital more frequently. By each act of trade, they would get back their own capital. Now, when they turn their capital once, they turn it out of their own hands, and it remains out of their hands for a year or eighteen months. In the interim they must employ themselves in turning other people's capital, or give up business.

If an account should be rendered of the amount lost by bad debts in the course of a year, some notion might be formed of *one* of the evils of super-extended credit : for, nine bad debts in ten may fairly be laid to the account of this system. The aggregate must be enormous, as from 600 to 800 persons annually take the benefit of the insolvent laws in Philadelphia alone, and numerous compromises are made of which the the courts take no cognizance.

CHAPTER IX.

Of Banks as Corporations.

Against corporations of every kind, the objection may be brought, that whatever power is given to them, is so much taken from either the Government or the people.

As the object of charters is to give to members of companies powers which they would not possess in their individual capacity, the very existence of monied corporations is incompatible with equality of rights.

Corporations are unfavorable to the progress of national wealth. As the Argus eyes of private interest do not watch over their concerns, their affairs are much more carelessly and much more expensively conducted than those of individuals. What would be the condition of the merchant who should trust every thing to his clerks, or of the farmer who should trust every thing to his laborers? Corporations are obliged to trust every thing to stipendiaries, who are oftentimes less trustworthy than the clerks of the merchant or the laborers of the farmer.

Such are the inherent defects of corporations, that they never can succeed, except when the laws or circumstances give them a monopoly, or advantages partaking of the nature of a monopoly. Sometimes they are protected by direct inhibitions to individuals to engage in the same business. Sometimes they are protected by an exemption from liabilities to which individuals are subjected. Sometimes the extent of their capital or of their credit, gives them a control of the market. They cannot, even then, work as cheap as the individual trader, but they can afford to throw away enough money in the contest, to *ruin* the individual trader, and then they have the market to themselves.

If a poor man suffers aggression from a rich man, the disproportion of power is such, that it may be difficult for him to obtain redress; but if a man is aggrieved by a corporation, he may have all its stockholders, all its clerks, and all its proteges for parties against him. Corporations are so powerful, as frequently to bid defiance to Government.

If a man is unjust, or an extortioner, society is, sooner

or later, relieved from the burden, by his death. But corporations never die.

What is worst of all, (if worse than what has already been stated be possible,) is that want of moral feeling and responsibility which characterizes corporations. A celebrated English writer expressed the truth, with some roughness, but with great force, when he declared that "corporations have neither bodies to be kicked, nor souls to be damned."

All these objections apply to our American Banks.

They are protected, in most of the States, by direct inhibitions on individuals engaging in the same business.

They are exempted from liabilities to which individuals are subjected. If a poor man cannot pay his debts, his bed is, in some of the States, taken from under him. If that will not satisfy his creditors, his body is imprisoned. The shareholders in a Bank are entitled to all the gain they can make by Banking operations; but if the undertaking chances to be unsuccessful, the loss falls on those who have trusted them. They are responsible only for the amount of stock they may have subscribed.

For the old standard of value, they substitute the new standard of Bank credit. Would Government be willing to trust to corporations the fixing of our standards and measures of length, weight, and capacity? Or are our standards and measures of value of less importance than our standards and measures of other things?

They coin money out of paper. What has always been considered one of the most important prerogatives of Government, has been surrendered to the Banks.

In addition to their own funds, they have the whole of the spare cash of the community to work upon.

The credit of every business man depends on their nod. They have it in their power to ruin any merchant to whom they may become inimical.

We have laws against usury: but if it was the intention of the Legislature to encourage usurious dealings, what more efficient means could be devised than that of establishing incorporated paper money Banks?

Government extends the credit of these institutions, by receiving their paper as an equivalent for specie, and exerts its whole power to protect and cherish them. Whoever infringes any of the chartered privileges of the Banks, is visited with the severest penalties.

Supposing Banking to be a thing good in itself, why should Bankers be exempted from liabilities to which farmers, manufacturers, and merchants are subjected ? It will not surely be contended that Banking is more conducive than agriculture, manufactures, and commerce, to the progress of national wealth.

Supposing the subscribers to Banks to be substantial capitalists, why should artificial power be conferred on them by granting them a charter ? Does not wealth of itself confer sufficient advantages on the rich man ? Why should the competition among capitalists be diminished, by forming them into companies, and uniting their wealth in one mass.

Supposing the subscribers to Banks to be speculators without capital—what is there so praiseworthy in their design of growing rich without labor, that Government should exert all its powers to favor the undertaking?

Why should corporations have greater privileges than simple co-partnerships?

On what principle is it, that, in a professedly republican Government, immunities are conferred on individuals in a collective capacity, that are refused to individuals in their separate capacity ?

To test this question fairly, let us suppose that a proposition were made to confer on fourteen individuals in Philadelphia, and three or four hundred individuals in other parts of the country, the exclusive privileges which three or four hundred incorporated Banks now possess. How many citizens would be found who would not regard such a proposition with horror. Yet privileges conferred on corporations are more pernicious, because there is less moral feeling in the management of their concerns. As directors of a company men will sanction actions of which they would scorn to be guilty in their private capacity. A crime which would press heavily on the conscience of one man, becomes quite endurable when divided among many.

We take much pride to ourselves for having abolished entails, and justly, in so far as the principle is concerned : but it seems to be lost sight of by many that entails can prove effective only when the land is of limited extent, as in Great Britain ; or where the mass of the population are serfs, as in Russia. In those districts of our country where negro slavery prevails, entails, aided by laws of primogeniture, would have kept estates in a few hands : but in the Middle and Northern States, a hundred ways would have been contrived for breaking the succession. If direct attempts had proved unsuccessful, the land would have been let on leases of 99 or 999 years, which would have been nearly the same in effect as disposing of them in fee simple. The abundance of land prevents its being monopolized. Supposing the whole extent of country, from the Atlantic to the Pacific, and north of the 39th degree of latitude, parcelled out among a few great Feudatories ; those Feudatories, in order to derive a revenue from their domains, would be forced to lease them in a manner which would give the tenants the whole usufruct of the terrene ; for, the quit rent would be only an annual payment, instead of a payment of the whole in advance.

But the floating capital of the country is limited in amount. This, from the condition of things, may be monopolized. A small portion of the community have already, through the agency of Banking operations, got possession of a great part of this floating capital, and are now in a fair way of getting possession of much of the remainder. Fixed and floating capital must be united to produce income, but he who has certain possession of one of these elements of revenue, will not long remain without the other.

The difference between England and the United States, is simply this : in the former country, exclusive privileges are conferred on individuals who are called *Lords ;* in the latter, exclusive privileges are conferred on corporations which are called *Banks.* The effect on the people of both countries is the same. In both the many live and labor for the benefit of the few.

CHAPTER X.

Of the Popular Arguments in favor of Banking.

The objections to the American Banks are tripartite. They are, first, such as arise from their substituting paper money for metallic. Secondly, such as arise from their introducing an unsound system of credit. And, thirdly, such as arise from their nature as corporations. If the reader will take a view of all the different operations of the Banks, connecting them together in his mind as they are connected in fact, he will require no refutation of the popular arguments in favor of the system. Nevertheless, it may not be amiss, for the satisfaction of some, to consider these arguments in the form in which they are commonly presented.

" *Banks make money plenty.*"

Nay, they make *real* money scarce. As Bank notes are circulated, gold and silver are driven away. It is contrary to the laws of nature that two bodies should fill the same space at the same time : and no fact is better established than that, where there are two kinds of currency authorized by law or sanctioned by custom, that which has the least value, will displace the other. If Banks at any time make money more plentiful than it would be if only gold and silver circulated, they diminish its value in increasing its quantity. The valuation, or relative estimation of things is thereby enhanced, but not an atom is added to the wealth of the community.

" *Banks diminish the rate of interest.*"

So far is this from being true, that the Banks tend to increase the rate of interest, by collecting capital into large masses, and diminishing the competition among money lenders. They, also, by their various operations, immediate and remote, give rise to a multitude of usurious transactions.

" *Banks do much good by lending money to individuals.*"

But much less good than would be done, by the owners of this money lending it themselves. Banks, as was observed in a previous chapter, do not increase the loanable capital of the country, but only take it out of the hands of its proprietors, and place it under the control of irresponsible Bank Directors.

"*If there were no Bank paper, specie must of necessity be frequently transported to and from distant parts of the country, at great expense and great risk.*"

The trade between different parts of the country does not consist of an interchange of Bank notes or of specie, but of the products of the soil and the industry of the inhabitants. By private bills of exchange, the sums due to one trader could be transferred to another; and it would be necessary only occasionally to discharge balances in specie. This is, in fact, the present custom of trade, Bank notes being to only a limited extent, substitutes for bills of exchange.

"*Banks diminish the rate of exchange between different parts of the country.*"

Then they do great evil. The rate of exchange is the natural balance wheel of trade between different parts of the country. Banks cannot interfere with this, without doing harm. When they lessen the rate of exchange, they remove a natural check on overtrading.

"*Banks give greater security than individuals in buying and selling exchange.*"

If so, it is because the other operations of Banking have rendered all kinds of business uncertain. In countries where paper money is unknown, no more risk attends dealings in exchange than other kinds of dealings.

"*Such are the customs of trade in the United States, that Banking seems necessary.*"

But the customs herein referred to have their origin in Banking, and, as they are pernicious, ought to be abolished.

"*All commercial countries have some systems of Banking.*"

And none have a worse system than the United States. In all commercial countries, there are men who receive money on deposit, lend money, and deal in exchanges; but the system of Banking on *paper* money, is of modern origin. The cities of Greece, and Rome, and Egypt, and ancient Asia, attained to wealth far greater than we can boast of, without the aid of chartered Banks. In all countries in which paper money Banking, or paper money of any kind, has been introduced, it has done much evil. Austria, Russia, Sweden, France, Denmark, Portugal, Brazil, and Buenos Ayres, all bear witness to this truth, as well as England and the United States. To these countries we may add China, in which paper money was tried before the commencement of our era, and, on experience of its ill effects, abandoned.

" *The various evils that are mentioned as flowing from Banking, proceed, in fact, from abuses of it. Banking on proper principles is productive of great benefits.*"

We willingly admit that Banking on *proper* principles would be productive of great benefits : but we deny that Banking with paper money, or by corporations possessing peculiar privileges, is Banking on proper principles.

" *Paper is more convenient than specie in large payments.*"

Deduct from the total of large payments, all those that are made on account of accommodations at Bank, and all those made on account of the wild speculations introduced by Banking, and it will be found that so few large payments would remain to be made, that we should be able to get through them all without difficulty. To count out a sum in ten or twenty dollar gold pieces, would be as easy as to count it out in ten or twenty dollar Bank notes. Before the establishment of a Bank in Montreal, guineas were done up in rouleaus, and such was the confidence the merchants had in one another, that the paper envelopes of the guineas were seldom broken. We mention this merely to show that the effecting of large payments with metallic money, would not be a work of so much difficulty as some imagine. In cases where great despatch was required, the silver or gold money might be weighed, as was done by the Bank of England in 1825, when the demands for gold was so urgent, that the tellers had not time to count the sovereigns they paid out.

If we wish to effect large payments with the least possible inconvenience, we must establish a *single* Office of Deposit and Transfer in each large town. This would save the time which is now lost in running from Bank to Bank.

" *Paper saves the wear and tear of coin.*"

The saving is too insignificant to be taken into a national account, in a subject of so much importance as the soundness of the currency. Mr. Gallatin says that " the annual amount wanted to repair the loss occasioned by friction in gold and silver coin, cannot exceed, taking the highest computation, seventy thousand dollars a year in a coinage of forty millions, and is probably much less." This estimate has been formed by Mr. G., "from various opinions deduced from actual experiments."

Dr. Moore, the Director of the United States Mint, in a report made to the President in 1826, computes the loss on gold coins at two per cent. in fifty years, and on silver coins at only one per cent.

Agreeably to the report made to the Senate by the Committee of which Mr. Sanford was chairman, half-dollars and half-eagles will circulate for one hundred years, and dollars and eagles for two hundred years, without being so much worn or defaced as not to serve the purposes of a circulating medium.

"*Banks affoi d the public a safe place for depositing their funds.*"

Not always. One hundred and sixty of these safe depositories, have broken in the last twenty years, and one hundred and sixty more may break in the twenty years next to come.

Again : all those who deposited money in the Banks in the early part of 1814, received back their deposits in money of inferior value. What has happened once, may happen again.

The probability is, that ten times as much has heen lost by depositing money in Banks, as would have been lost if people had kept their money in their own houses.

"*Every man ought to be allowed to use his own credit.*"

Exactly so : and, therefore, we ought not to have incorporated Banks, which give credit to some, by taking it from others. These institutions owe their credit to acts of Assembly. If their charters were taken from them, not even their own stockholders would trust them. Every man ought to be allowed to use his own credit ; but he ought to get that credit fairly, and use it properly.

"*If there were no Banks, it would be easy to borrow money on bond or mortgage, for long periods, but it would not be possible to obtain discount of merchants' business paper, which has but a few months to run.*"

Not so : If the corporate Banks of Philadelphia were abolished, many private Banks would spring up in their place. The owners of these private Banks would be men in whom the public could place confidence, for they would be responsible in the whole amount of their estates. They would be men of great wealth, for it is in lending money that men of large fortunes can employ their capitals with most profit and convenience. The competition among them would be such, that business notes would be discounted on more favorable terms than at present. They would allow interest on such sums as their customers might leave in their hands. For their own convenience, they would establish a public Office of Transfer and Deposit, and pay the greater part of the expenses of this institution.

The system of private Banking in England, has done much evil, (though much less evil than the system of corporate Banking in the United States,) because the private Banks of England have traded partly on paper money issued by themselves, and partly on that issued by the Bank of England.

In Scotland, where the regulating power is in the unincorporated Banks, the system does less evil than in England, although paper money is used in both countries.

Private Banking in Switzerland, Holland, France, Hamburg, and Bremen, does much good and no evil. Such a system will we have in the United States, when paper money shall be abolished. In every town in the United States, in which there is trade enough to require it, private Bankers will spring up, who will receive money on deposit, and pay interest for the use of it: Lend money on interest: Buy and sell bills of exchange: Attend to the collection of debts, and in various ways facilitate business. Operating on sufficient capital, these private Bankers will not ruin their customers by violent " contractions." Neither will they incite them to engage in improper enterprizes, by sudden and great "expansions."

Our corporate Banks do no good to compensate for the evils they occasion, by their continual alterations of the measures of value, by the uncertainty they give to trade, and by the advantages they confer on some men over others. With private Banks, and public Offices of Transfer and Deposit, we should have all that is good in the present system, without the evil.

CHAPTER XI.

Of Restrictions on Banking Corporations.

The evils which are produced by paper money Banking, are so great as necessarily to force themselves on the attention of those who are most deeply interested in the continuance of the system. To remedy these evils, they propose various restrictions on Banking corporations, or new modes of conducting their business.

A common opinion is, that, *if* the Banks would not discount accommodation notes, and *if* they would confine themselves to business paper of short dates, their operations would not be injurious to the community.* But, a little reflection may convince us, that, by discounting business paper might be set afloat, as much Bank paper might be set afloat, as by discounting accommodation notes. The same lot of goods might be sold to a dozen persons, and each might give a note, and each of these twelve notes might be discounted at Bank. The limit on Bank issues would be the same as at present—that is, the demand for specie for foreign trade. The anxiety of the Banks to extend their issues would be in no way diminished. The inducement, then, would be to buy and sell goods that notes might be discounted at Bank. Now, it is to have notes discounted at Bank, that goods may be bought and sold. The spirit of speculation being excited by any cause, notes would flow in for discount, and the Banks would, as at present, discount as many as they might deem prudent.

The severest legislative enactments could not confine the Banks to discounting business paper of short dates, if this paper did not afford full employment to all their "capi-

---

* This opinion was sufficiently refuted by the Bullion Committee, so long ago as 1811; and the correctness of their conclusion is confirmed by those who have had the best opportunities for observing the operations of the Banking system. "I consider the opinion entertained by some," says Sir F. B., "that the Bank ought to regulate its issues by the public demand, as dangerous in the extreme; because I know by experience, that the demand for speculation can only be limited by want of means." The general practice in England is to discount only business paper, but this does not prevent the recurrence of evils similar to those we suffer in the United States.

tal" and all their " credit." They would soon find sufficient reasons for " renewing" the business notes of some
of their customers, and those notes, thus renewed, would
become accommodation notes.

Except in the cases of applications from Directors, and
their favorites, the Banks now prefer business notes, because
these place their issues more immediately under their control. More than a certain amount they cannot lend on
accommodation paper, for they must keep so much capital
under command as is necessary to support their credit.
Their deposits would otherwise be withdrawn, and the circulation of their notes would cease. It does not appear
that these accommodation notes have any specially mischievous effect on prices. They are permanent in amount,
or nearly so. The fluctuation of prices appears to be occasioned by that part of Bank " capital" and of Bank
" credit," which is always varying in amount.

Limiting the amount of issues to double the amount of
capital, and the amount of loans to thrice the amount of
capital, is a favorite provision with legislators. But, Mr.
Gallatin says, " amongst more than three hundred Banks,
either now existing, or which have failed, and of which we
have returns, we have not found a single one, the loans of
which amounted, so long as specie payments were in force,
to three times, or the issues to twice, the amount of capital.
It is clear, that provisions applicable to such improbable
contingences, are purely nominal."

Compelling the Banks to give an annual statement of
their affairs, is also a favorite measure. But it is not easy
to compel them to give a *faithful* statement. The accounts
of the Banks that break look nearly as well on paper as
the accounts of the Banks that continue payments. They
who are acquainted with the secrets of Bank management,
say, little reliance is to be placed on these accounts.

Preventing the Banks from issuing notes of a less denomination than five dollars, is a measure which is effective
so far as it goes. But it still leaves the Banks the power
to substitute paper for specie, and to carry on credit dealings to an extent which is very pernicious. In England,
where the issue of notes of a less denomination than one
pound sterling, or about four dollars and eighty cents, has,
for many years, been prohibited, the contractions and ex-

pansions of the Bank have done so much evil, that it has been found necessary to prohibit the emission of any notes of a less denomination than five pounds sterling, or about twenty-four dollars Federal currency. The Bank of France issues no notes of a less denomination than 500 francs, equal to about ninety-four dollars of our money, yet the Bank of France is at times forced to make such sudden and great curtailments, as inflict much evil on many of those who are within the sphere of its influence. The manufacturers in Alsace had doleful experience of this power of the Bank in France, in 1825. The merchants of Paris, and throughout the kingdom, felt it in 1819. In 1822, also, the contractions which the Bank of France found it necessary to make, produced much commercial embarrassment in many parts of that country.

In the charter of the Bank of France, there is a provision that all profits above six per cent. shall be converted into a reserved stock, on which reserved stock the Bank may make dividends not exceeding five per cent. Such a provision in the American Bank charters, would remove many inducements to over-banking, and would make speculations in their stock less frequent.

In proportion as the personal responsibility of those concerned in Banking is increased, and in proportion as the denomination of the notes they are permitted to issue, is raised in amount, the system becomes less pernicious. But no legislative enactments can afford an adequate remedy for the evils which flow from incorporated paper money Banks. The system is, to use the language of the lawyers, *malum per se*—or a thing which is evil in its nature. The very principle of its foundation is wrong. No immunities should, in a Republican Government, be granted to any, save those which are common to all. To impart to corporations a moral sense of right and wrong, is impossible. They may be made nominally responsible, but to impose on them an *effective* responsibility is impracticable. To a certain extent they obey the laws, and respect public opinion, but it is only so far as, and so long as, is necessary for making their business profitable. The interest account of the Banks is, in point of fact, the only effective check we have on the abuse of those powers which our legislative bodies have conferred on them by charter.

Such privileges as the Banks possess, ought neither to be sold nor to be given away, by a republican legislature, to any men or any body of men.   A control over the whole of the cash and the credit of the community, is a power as despotic in its nature as any possessed by the nobility of Germany.

The regulation of the currency is one of the most important prerogatives of sovereignty.   This prerogative is now, in point of fact, surrendered to the Banks.   They drive away what may be called the *natural* money of the country, and substitute for it something which differs from this natural money in both the *nature* of its value, and the *causes* of its value.   A quantity of this money may be put afloat, but, whatever may be the discretion of Directors of Banks, and whatever may be the legal restrictions on corporations, it must fluctuate in quantity, and be affected in value, by all the causes, natural and political, by which credit is affected.   It is flexible, vacillating, agitated by every wind that blows.   If any man can invent a method by which the hardness and other properties of platina can be imparted to lead, that man may hope to discover the means by which Bank credit may be made as stable as gold and silver medium.

To prove that the task is hopeless, we shall give an analysis of the standard and measures of value introduced by Banking.

CHAPTER XII.

Of the Essential qualities of Bank Notes.

Bank notes are considered by some as "representatives of specie."   But, for every silver dollar they have in their vaults, some of the Banks have two paper dollars in circulation, some three, some five, some eight, and some thirteen.   Bank notes cannot represent that which the Banks have not, and which is not in the country.   If Bank notes can, in any sense, be considered representatives of specie, the paper dollar of the same Bank sometimes represents fifty cents, and sometimes forty cents : and the paper dollars of different Banks represent at the same time, thirty-three and a third cents, twelve and a half cents, ten cents, and seven cents of the silver dollar.   Yet they are all current, and all have the same effective power as silver in exchanges.

Various other erroneous views are entertained of the nature of Bank notes, the consideration of which would be tedious.   Examining them one by one, would be merely showing what Bank notes *are not*.   Instead of doing this, it will, it is presumed, be sufficient to show what Bank notes really *are*.

Bank notes are *simple evidences of debt* due by the Banks.   This is their true character.

As mere *evidences* of debt, they differ not from the promissory notes of merchants.   They are also, in common with bills of exchange and business notes, a commercial medium ; but in some respects, there is an essential difference between Bank notes and the notes of merchants.*

For *their* promissory notes, the merchants *pay* interest. For the promissory notes of the Banks, the Banks *receive* interest.

The promises to pay of the merchants are fulfilled, when the notes arrive at maturity.   Bank notes are never paid.†
Payment of them in the aggregate is never demanded,

---

* " A bill of exchange drawn by an individual or individuals who do not issue notes having the character of currency, appears to us to be clearly distinguished from a Bank note, though it is a substitute, and lessens the amount of currency which would otherwise be required. A payment made in Bank notes is a discharge of the debt, the creditor having no further recourse against the person from whom he has received it, unless the Bank had previously failed.   The bill of exchange does not discharge the debt, the person who receives it having recourse against the drawer and every preceding endorser, in case the drawer should fail or refuse to pay.   But the essential distinction is, that bills of exchange are only promises to pay in currency : and that the failures of the drawers, drawees, and endorsers, does not in the smallest degree, affect the value of the currency itself, or impair that permanent standard of value by which the performance of all contracts is regulated."
                                                                            Gallatin.

† " The essential difference between Banking and other commercial business is that merchants rely for the fulfilment of their engagements on their resources, and not on the forbearance of their creditors, whilst the Banks always rely, not only on their resources, but also on the probability that their creditors will not require payment of their demands."
                                                                            Gallatin.

because what could be got in payment, would, for most purposes of domestic trade, serve no better purpose than Bank notes themselves.

Bank notes are thus a kind of *paper money*. In the countries where they are used, bills of exchange, the promissory notes of merchants, and balances of running accounts, are paid in Bank notes, as they are paid in other countries with metallic money.

The sales for prompt payment in Bank notes regulate sales for deferred payment in Bank notes, as, in solid money countries, cash transactions regulate credit transactions.

Like real money, Bank notes are instruments of valuation. The quantities they express are the exponents of the effective power in exchanges of land, labor, and commodities.

An increase or decrease of Bank notes in the United States, has the same effect on prices, that an increase of solid money has on prices in Spain or Switzerland.

Increase the amount of Bank notes, and, *other things being the same*, prices will rise.

Diminish the amount of Bank notes, and, *other things being the same*, prices will fall.

In our first chapter, the several qualities of gold and silver were enumerated, *all* which qualities an article must possess in the *same* degree, to serve as well as the precious metals the purposes of money. In proportion as the qualities of articles recede from those of gold and silver, they are unfitted for these uses. By a comparison of the different qualities of Bank notes and coin, the reader may acquire a clear conception of the difference between *real* money and *fictitious*.

In susceptibility of receiving an impression, and in comprising a great value (i. e. market value) in a small space, Bank notes agree with coin. But in every thing else they disagree. Of utility in the arts, the very attribute that gives gold and silver their value in commerce, Bank notes are utterly destitute. They are also destitute of the important qualities of unchangeableness of value, and of uniformity of value.

We, however, because we have never changed our *money of account*, fancy that we have never changed our standard of value. We call a Bank dollar by the *same name* as a silver dollar, and then fancy there is no essential difference between them.

In our mensuration of other things which admit of increase or decrease by homogeneous degrees, we use instruments possessing the same physical properties as the thing to be measured. The judgment the mind forms of weight or length, is regulated by a *material* standard. The judgment the mind forms of value, is regulated by an *ideal* standard ; for Bank credit is something altogether intangible.

In solid money countries, in all sales of goods for cash, the products of labor are exchanged for the products of labor. The product of the miner's labor, is made the instrument for circulating the products of the farmer's and of the manufacturer's labor. The transactions are removed but one step from simple barter, and do not differ from it in its essential principle. The exchanges on both sides are of articles possessing *inherent* value—articles in the production of which *labor* has been bestowed, and articles which possess the physical qualities which adapt them to the satisfaction of human wants and desires. We receive commodities from one another, and give in return some uncertain representatives of credit, and fancy that trade is conducted with us on the same principles as it is in those countries where paper money is unknown. We pass from hand to hand certain promises to pay, and call that making payment.

The relations in the supply and demand of the precious metals are so slow in changing, that hardly any perceptible variation in the value of silver has, according to some able authors, taken place in the last two centuries. But the supply of Bank notes may vary several per cent. in different periods of the same year, and twenty or thirty per cent. in three or four years. Thence come great rises and falls of price : but we have only an imperfect apprehension of the cause, for our intangible standard of value never changes its name, how great soever may be the extent in which it is contracted or expanded.

It is folly to say that the *money* of the country is not *paper money*. In Virginia, Pennsylvania, and Maryland, payments of a less amount than five dollars are made in real money : but in the other States, dollar notes circulate, so that payments in specie are made for only fractional parts of the dollar. In North Carolina, South Carolina, and some other parts of the Union, notes for 25 cents, 12½ cents, and even 6¼ cents, are current. There even small silver change is a rarity.*

Of large payments, nine hundred and ninety-nine in a thousand are made with paper. Of small payments, ninety-nine in a hundred. The currency of the country is, we repeat it, essentially a paper currency. The sprinkling of silver has only the effect of keeping up the reputation of the paper. This paper varies in amount, from day to day, from month to month, and from year to year. Every thing that affects the spirit of enterprize, affect scom mercial credit, and through that, Bank credit.

The importance of adjusting measures of value with the greatest exactness, is enforced by all who have written on the subject. An order has recently been issued to re-coin the whole of the silver money of France, amounting to not less than eighty millions of dollars, on account of its having been discovered that the mode of assay by cupellation, indicates but 1000 grains of pure silver in a mass containing 1004 grains. The difference between the legal and the practical standard, is less than a half of one per cent.; yet this difference has been deemed important enough to make necessary a re-coinage of the whole of the silver money of the country. Our own statesmen bear a silent testimony to the truth of this doctrine, by their attempts to

---

* It is observed by Mr. White, Cashier of the United States Branch Bank at Baltimore, in a letter to the Secretary of the Treasury, under date of Feb. 30th, 1830 : " Congress fixed the relative value of gold at 15 for 1 of silver; and under the natural presumption that gold and silver coin would compose a portion of the general circulating medium, it has also been enacted, that a tender of either of those metals should be the only legal mode of discharging obligations. *In practice, however, and in fact, our currency consists altogether of paper.* In this State, (Maryland,) and in Pennsylvania, Virginia, and perhaps some others, the fractional parts of a dollar circulate in sufficient quantity to purchase with coin, marketing, or other low priced necessaries; but in the Carolinas, Georgia, and all that great district eastward of Pennsylvania, composing the States most distinguished for commerce and manufactures, and for wealth, there is no transfer of the value of the established unit that is not effected by paper. This Bank paper is sustained by public confidence on a specie basis, *considered* sufficient to liquidate balances accruing among the several States, and to supply the demands for foreign commerce."

determine the ratio of gold and silver, carrying out their calculations in some tables to the five hundredth thousandth part of a grain.

Such is the care that Governments (our own among others) take in fixing metallic standards and measures of value. If by any accident a dollar coined at our mint should contain but 369 grains of pure silver instead of 371¼, it would not be put in circulation. The nicest chemical and mechanical operations are resorted to that the different pieces may have an exact uniformity. But, having done this, our next care is to drive metallic measures of value from the country, and substitute those of the most uncertain nature possible.

CHAPTER XIII.

Of the " Convertibility" of Bank Medium.

Many who are inimical to paper money in every other form, are friendly to the use of Bank paper, because it is, they say, equal to specie, inasmuch as specie can be obtained for it at the will of the holder.

But what does this " convertibility" amount to ? Though we have between three and four hundred Banks, we have not yet one at every man's door; and, if we had, every man would, in the course of business, be compelled to receive the paper of distant Banks. A man may prefer silver, and yet not choose to walk even half a mile, to have his note changed.

Those whose money dealings are most extensive, like not to offend the Banks by too frequent calls on them for specie. It might lead to a curtailment of their accommodation. They have as deep an interest as the stockholders and the directors in keeping the notes in circulation.*

* In a debate in Parliament in July 1828, Lord King said, that " as for payment in gold, he knew there was an *esprit de corps* among the Bankers, and people who wished to get accommodations from them would find it no easy thing to obtain gold. The Banker would inquire if the individual was in the habit of asking for gold, and if so, accommodations would be withheld. Paying in gold was not, therefore, that check to over-issues which some people imagined."

In addition to this, it must be remembered, that Bank paper is "convertible" into only one of those species which should, according to law and constitution, be the money of the United States. An incorrect valuation of gold at the Mint, and paper money together, have driven this precious metal from the country. Bank paper is "convertible" into silver only, which is inconvenient for large payments, and for transportation to distant places in large amounts.

From this combination of causes, not more than one-twentieth of the paper is actually "convertible" at any one time, and herein consists the safety of the Banks. An attempt to convert but one half of the Bank medium, into specie, would, though several months were allowed for the operation, break all the Banks in the country.

Now, can such a "convertibility" make Bank notes "equal" to specie? We mean equal to specie as money, in its *three* functions of a circulating medium, and of a standard and measure of value. We know the two articles are equal in the market, but the question is, if they ought to be so.

"Convertibility," so far from being an assurance of the soundness of Bank notes *as money*, is not even an assurance, for three days together, of their soundness as bills of credit. This is verified in the case of Banks whose paper is in one week at par, and in the next at a discount of fifty per cent.

When the contingencies on which convertibility depend, are taken into consideration, the risk appears so great as of itself to outweigh all the arguments usually adduced in favor of Bank medium.

The practice of the Banks is to make provision for those demands only which it is *probable* will be made upon them, which provision is seldom for more than one-fifth of the amount of their actual engagements to pay on demand. It is very easy for the Directors to make a mistake in their estimate of probabilities. Events which they could not foresee may occur, and circumstances they cannot control. It is not always easy to say where the line of safety should be drawn; and the Directors are at all times tempted to transcend it, from the desire of making large dividends, and raising the price of their stock in the market. Sudden changes in the political and commercial world, may render

the best conducted Banks unable to comply with their engagements, though they may have in store double the
amount of specie, which would, in other times, be necessary to support their credit.

On a certain day in 1819, there were but $80,000 be-
tween us and universal bankruptcy. This was the whole
amount of specie in the United States Bank at Philadelphia; and if that had been exhausted, a shock would have
been given to Bank credit, which would have caused a
general suspension of specie payments. In 1825, the condition of both England and the United States was hardly
less critical. The failure of two or three of our principal
Banks would cause a run upon all the others. They could
then comply with but a part of their engagements, and
their inability to satisfy the claims of the holders of their
notes and of depositors, would render the fulfilment of
other money contracts impossible. The credit which
Bank notes enjoy, has been called "suspicion lulled to
sleep." Events may awaken that suspicion.

Attempts are sometimes made to show the perfect security of the Banks, by contrasting the amount due by them
for notes in circulation and for deposites, with the amount
falling due to them every sixty or ninety days on account
of mercantile paper discounted by them. But such calculations, even when they rest on indisputable data, prove
only the ultimate solvency of a Bank. The amount due
by the Bank, on account of deposites and on account of
notes in circulation, may all be legally demanded in one
day; nay, in one hour. A greater amount may be owing
to the Bank, but it is payable at different times, and the
extremes of the term are sixty or ninety days apart. The
individuals who owe this money to the Bank may be rich
men: but their ability to pay, within the time agreed upon,
depends on the credit of Bank paper being maintained.
Let the depositors suddenly withdraw but one-half the
amount of specie ordinarily retained by the Banks, and
the credit of Bank notes necessarily falls. A portion of
the debts due to the Banks may be paid in this depreciated
paper; but the Banks will not have the means of satisfy-
ing all their creditors. There being little specie in the
country, the collection of debts due by individuals to indi-

viduals, would be suspended, (if Bank paper should suddenly lose its credit.)   *   *   *   *   *   *

The danger of such an event may not be very imminent; but it is sufficient to show that the stability of Bank medium depends on contingencies which, as they cannot always be foreseen, cannot always be guarded against. What was called "a panic" in England, in 1825, broke up a number of private Bankers who were perfectly solvent, and was near proving destructive to the whole system. If a suspension of specie payments should again occur in this country, we should be left for a time without a sufficient medium of exchanges. Too many men are now aware of the nature of "inconvertible" Bank paper for it to have general circulation. It would soon run the course of the Continental money, and of the French assignats.

So long as Bank paper is "convertible," more than a certain amount cannot be kept in circulation for a long time without undergoing a sensible depreciation. Hence "convertibility" fixes a limit which Bank issues cannot pass. By carefully watching one another, by attending to the course of foreign exchanges, and by guarding against a drain of specie, the Banks may, in ordinary times, maintain the "convertibility" of their paper; but the history of Banking, both in England and the United States, since the resumption of specie payments, shows that this "convertibility" cannot give to Bank medium that stability which is essential to a sound money system.

In the means by which "convertibility" is maintained, we have an abundant source of evils. It is by one Bank pressing on another, and thereby forcing the debtor Bank to press on its customers. When there is a foreign demand for specie, the "convertibility" of Bank medium is maintained by a general pressure on the community.

Lord Liverpool, in a debate in the British House of Peers, in Feb. 1826, placed the doctrine of convertibility in its true light. " The doctrine," he said, " maintained by some noble lords, that nothing was better than a paper circulation convertible into gold, is true to this extent— that if convertible into coin, the evil would cure itself, whilst one not convertible would lead to nothing but ruin. But how is the cure to be operated ? By the downfall of thousands and hundreds of thousands, and the convulsion of all kinds of property. It is true that the evil carries its own cure, but with such terrible consequences that the cure is worse than the evil."

CHAPTER XIV.

Of the " Elasticity" of Bank Medium.

" The value of Bank medium," says a writer on this subject, " consists in its elasticity—in its power of alternate expansion and contraction to suit the wants of the community. In truth, the merit of a Bank is nearly in proportion to the flexibility of its means."

Most unfortunately for this argument, when the demand for money is greatest, the Banks are compelled to contract their issues. When the natural demand is least, they are able to expand most. These " alternate contractions and expansions" do not, therefore, " suit the wants of the community."

It is not a regard to " the wants of the community" that regulates these " alternate expansions and contractions." It is a simple regard to their own profits that induces the Banks to expand their issues. In contractions, the Banks have regard only to their own safety.

Every thing is not, indeed, left to the arbitrary discretion of the Directors. The natural and political causes that affect trade, affect also their operations.

If wars, or other political operations, cause a flow of specie to a particular point, the Banks are immediately compelled to reduce their issues of paper. As a demand on the Banks for a million of specie usually causes them to reduce their accommodations to the amount of four millions, the pressure on the community is four times as great as it would be if the foreign demand operated singly.

A rise in the price of our staples in foreign markets enables the Banks immediately to expand their issues. The spirit of speculation is then excited, and the Banks supply it with aliment. Hence, immediately after news of a rise in the price of flour and cotton, in foreign markets, these articles rise so high at home that they cannot be exported

and sold at a profit abroad. The original holders gain
something by selling their stock to the speculators. The
price is raised on the domestic consumer ; but very little
is added to the wealth of the nation, for the rise of price
at home causes little to be exported.

To enumerate all the causes that affect expansions and
contractions of Bank issues, would be to enumerate all the
causes, immediate or remote, that affect trade, or affect the
confidence man has in man. Any thing that excites the
spirit of enterprize, has a tendency to increase the amount
of Bank issues. Whatever damps the spirit of enterprize
or of speculation, has a tendency to reduce the amount of
Bank issues. As the wild spirit of speculation has in most
cases its origin, and in all its aliment, in Banking transactions, these various causes operate in a circle. The
Banks, by expanding their issues, give aliment to the wild
spirit of speculation when it begins ; and by their contractions, they aggravate the evils of the natural reaction.

One of the principal inducements for preferring the
precious metals as the material for money, is their *want* of
this very " elasticity" or " flexibility" which the writer
above quoted, declares is the principal excellence of Bank
medium. The mere desire of one man to have money,
and of another to gratify that desire that he may make a
profit by it himself, will not increase the supply of the precious metals. The spirit of wild speculation, therefore, in
solid money countries, wants that aliment which is so readily afforded to it in our own. The production of gold and
silver requires an expenditure of labor equal to that which
must be expended in the production of those articles which
gold and silver can procure. The supply is regulated by
natural causes which are as powerful as those which regulate the demand.

When an addition is made to the stock of gold and silver in a solid money country, it does not immediately
affect prices. It usually comes in the shape of bullion or
foreign coin. The importer considers whether a profit may
not be acquired by shipping it to some foreign country. If
he decides on retaining it, part of it is probably wrought
up into plate or jewellery. If he sends it to the mint, some
time must elapse before it can be converted into coin. After it is converted into coin, he may not choose to put it

immediately into circulation. He may make it part of his reserved stock, and wait for months, perhaps, for an opportunity for making advantageous purchases. If he can make no advantageous purchases at home, he sends the money abroad. Thus while there are powerful causes in operation throughout the commercial world, which make the demand and supply of silver and gold to vary in only an imperceptible degree, from year to year, there are particular causes operating, which make the supply in all solid money countries, just equal to the effective demand, and thereby truly " to suit the wants of the community."

In such countries, when the spirit of enterprize is awakened by fair prospects of a profitable trade, no sudden plentifulness of money follows to convert the spirit of enterprize into a spirit of wild speculation.

If the enterprizes prove unsuccessful, the evil is not aggravated by an artificial scarcity of money.

If wars, or other political operations, create a demand for specie, the pressure is only equal to the foreign demand —not fourfold, as with us.

If there is a rise abroad in the prices of the staples of exports of a solid money country, no sudden increase of currency raises prices so high as to make the exportation a losing business.

Such are the advantages of an " *inflexible*" and " *non-elastic*" money.

CHAPTER XV.

Is Paper Money Cheaper than Specie?

The events of the last thirty years, have created a suspicion in most men's minds, that there is something not exactly right in our Banking system. Indeed, the very head of the system, the President of the United States Bank, seems at times half a sceptic as to its utility. He acknowledges that it is attended with great danger ; but then he says, " the substitution of credit for coin, enables the nation to make its exchanges with less coin, and of course saves the expense of that coin."

Mr. Gallatin, who is now President of the National Bank at New York, goes still farther. " The substitution of a paper currency for the precious metals, does not," he says, " appear to be attended with *any* other substantial advantage than cheapness."

Bank notes, it must be confessed, come *very cheap* to those who *issue* them. But to those who *receive* them, Bank notes come as dear as gold and silver. The farmer must give as much of the product of his labor for a paper dollar, as for a silver dollar.

It is alleged by some, that " Bank notes increase the aggregate capital of the community, since they cause silver, which produces nothing, to be exchanged abroad for commodities useful in the arts, or for household consumption."

But it is not true that silver money produces nothing. It is as productive as any other labor saving machine. Its uses in commerce, are as great as those of the steam engine in manufactures.

Neither is it true, that the aggregate capital of the country is increased, when silver coin is displaced by Bank notes. A mere exchange is made of one kind of capital for another. The precious metals are exported, and laces, wines, silks, satins, and ostrich feathers, are received in return. A nation that carries its consumption of foreign luxuries so far, as to leave itself without a suitable medium for domestic exchanges, may be compared to a mechanic who barters the tools of his trade for the enjoyments of the ale house. *Money is the tool of all trades.*

But on the supposition most favorable to the friends of the Banking system, what sum is gained by the nation by the substitution of paper for specie ?

According to the calculation of Mr. Gallatin, the currency of the country consisted, on the 1st of January, 1830, of about ten millions of dollars in specie, in the hands of the people, of 54 millions of Bank notes, and 55 millions of Bank credits; making a total of 109 millions of Bank medium, for the support of which the Banks keep 22 millions of specie dead in their vaults.

Now, supposing Bank medium to fall into disuse, these 22 millions of specie would be set free, and 87 millions more would be required to bring up our currency to its present amount. What is this, when compared with the whole capital of the country, which is estimated by Mr. Lee of Boston, at ten thousand millions of dollars, and by two other able economists, at twelve thousand millions. What is it, even when compared with the aggregate of incomes, which, according to Mr. Niles and Mr. E. Everett, is one thousand millions a year ?

It should be recollected, that, on the supposition of something being gained by the nation, by the use of paper money, the saving is once for all, and the annual gain is no more than the interest on the amount of medium.   Now, the interest on 87 millions, at six per cent., divided among the individuals who constitute our nation, is about 40 cents a piece !

Is it wise, for so trifling a gain, to derange all our monied operations ?

But if the inquiry be pushed further, it will be found that nothing is gained by the nation, (we do not say that nothing is gained by certain persons,) even on the supposition most favorable to the Banks.

For a specie medium, but one mint would be necessary. To maintain a paper medium, we have from 300 to 400 paper mints. The expenses of these mints press heavily on the people. The expenses of the Bank of the United States and its offices, are about 500,000 dollars a year.

According to Adam Smith, three million people, in the countries now forming the United States, were governed, and well governed, before the Revolution, at an expense not exceeding 350,000 dollars a year.

The labors of the American people for a few weeks would purchase them a sufficiency of metallic medium, which would not require renewal for a hundred years.   To support our paper medium, we are frequently obliged to purchase specie abroad, at a disadvantage.   As there is no profit on paper money, except by keeping down the amount of specie in the vaults of the Banks, the precious metals are frequently exported and sold at a loss.

The cheapness or dearness of an instrument, is to be estimated by the annual expense to which it puts us, in addition to its original cost, and by the manner in which it serves the uses intended.   Bank medium is a machine which requires continual watching, which is always getting out of order, which requires frequent and expensive repairs, and which, after all, performs its work badly.

Men have passed from one extreme to the other. A hundred years ago, the chief feature in the commercial policy of nations, was the amassing of gold and silver, as a kind of wealth *par excellence.* Now, he is the wisest statesman, who is most successful in driving the precious metals from a country.

In their attempts " to economize specie," as they call their absurd and nefarious policy, they seem to be forgetful of economy in every thing else. Correct measures of value, it must be confessed, cost something. So, likewise, do correct measures of weight and of capacity. A metallic medium cannot be obtained without paying for it; but whatever it may cost, it is well worth its cost. Our roads and our canals, which are, like money, instruments for facilitating exchanges, cost immense sums. So, also, do our ships, and our manufacturing machinery.

Among labor saving machines, gold and silver coin are entitled to the first place. In no way can a nation invest a portion of its capital more profitably, than in a sound circulating medium. It will return its original cost a hundred fold. Without such a medium, it is impossible for contracts to be complied with in equity, or for productive industry to exert all its energies.

CHAPTER XVI.

Of the Tax paid by the People to the Banks.

The thirty-one chartered Banks of Pennsylvania had, in November 1829, according to the statement of Mr. Gallatin, a nominal capital of $12,032,000. One million three hundred and ten thousand dollars of this amount was invested in real estate, and 4,620,000 in stocks of various descriptions, leaving the Banks 6,102,000 to employ in discounting notes.* From the $5,930,000, invested in

* Some corrections might be made in Mr. Gallatin's estimates, but we take them as we find them, they being accurate enough for the illustration of principles, which is our only object in introducing them.

stocks and real estate, it is to be presumed they derive as much advantage as private persons derive from similar investments. With the remaining 6,102,000, they discount notes to the amount of 17,526,000. On this amount they draw interest at 6 4-10 per cent., for the usage of the Banks is to charge 64 days' interest on loans for 63 days.

The revenue which private capitalists would derive from lending $6,102,000 at the legal rate of six per cent., would be $366,120 per annum. The revenue which the Banks derive from the management of this amount, is 1,121,664 dollars.

If the Banks do not, by the use of a nominal capital of $6,102,000, draw interest from the people on the sum of 17,526,000 dollars, their returns to the Legislature are deceptive. If they actually draw interest on this amount, they draw from the people $755,544 per annum more than would be drawn by private persons lending bona fide capital of the same amount as the nominal capital of the Banks.*

Supposing the sums paid in each year, since the passage of the Bank act of 1814, to equal that paid in 1829, the total amount paid by the people in sixteen years, over and above six per cent. on the loanable capital of the Banks, is $12,088,704. A direct tax of half the amount for the support of government, would have produced a rebellion.

The Bank of the United States had, on the 1st of November, 1829, a nominal capital of $34,996,270. Of this amount, $11,717,071 were invested in public stocks, and $3,876,404 in real estate, leaving it $19,402,795 of nominal capital for its proper business of accommodating bor-

Algebraic signs would, if they were generally understood, serve the purposes of illustration as well as the most correct estimates.

* It may, perhaps, be argued, that the "surplus funds" of the Banks ought to be added to their loanable capital. But, as Mr. Gallatin has said, "it will easily be perceived, that what is called the surplus, and sometimes the reserved or contingent fund, is nothing more than that which balances the account, or the difference between the debits and credits of the Banks." The surplus funds of the Banks of Pennsylvania were, in November, 1829, according to Mr. G.'s statement, $1,142,000. If it be thought proper to add this amount to the loanable capital, the estimate of the tax paid by the people of Pennsylvania for the support of their local Banks should be reduced from 755,544 to 687,024 dollars per annum. It is of little moment which mode of estimation is adopted. Either proves that the tax amounts to hundreds of thousands of dollars in each year.

rowers and dealers in bills of exchange. On this amount of bona fide capital lent at six per cent., private persons would draw a revenue of $1,164,167. But the Bank, with this amount of nominal capital, discounts notes and bills of exchange, to the amount of 40,017,445 dollars, from which it derives an annual revenue of $2,561,114, or $1,396,947 more per annum than would be received by private capitalists. In this estimate, we do not include what is paid to the Bank on the rate of exchange, though this must amount to hundreds of thousands of dollars.

Of the tax paid by the people for the support of the local Banks in other States than Pennsylvania, it is not so easy to form an estimate. Mr. Gallatin gives a statement of 297 institutions having nominal capitals of the amount of 97,381,935 dollars, but he does not state what portion of their capital is invested in stocks and real estate. The loans made by certain local Banks, out of Pennsylvania, having capitals of the amount of 81,363,224 dollars, he states to be 108,341,268; but he gives no statement of the loans made on 20,412,711 dollars of nominal Bank capital. Supposing the loans on this amount to be in the same proportion, the total amount loaned by the local Banks out of Pennsylvania, is 135,522,331 dollars, and the annual Bank interest on it 8,673,427 dollars.

Supposing these Banks to have the same proportion of their capital invested in stock and real estate, as the Banks of Pennsylvania, they have 49,387,015 dollars left for the business of discounting. From such an amount of *bona fide* capital lent at six per cent., private persons would draw an interest of $2,963,220. But the amount the Banks draw is, 8,673,427 dollars, or 5,710,207 more than would be drawn by private capitalists.

The sums, then, extracted from the people, over and above six per cent. on so much of the Bank capital as is employed in discounting, or the tax paid by the people for the support of the Banks, would appear to be—

For the support of the Banks of Pennsylvania, $ 755,544
    do.   local Banks of other States,   5,710,207
    do.   United States Bank,   1,396,947

                                         $7,862,698

We cannot pretend to be very exact in our estimate.

The local Banks in the other States, may have a greater proportion of their capital invested in stocks and real estate, than the Banks of Pennsylvania, or they may have a less proportion. The total amount of their loans may be greater or may be less than has been calculated from the data furnished by Mr. Gallatin. It is enough to know that the extra interest is *millions* per annum.

The principle on which this tax is levied, cannot be misunderstood. With a loanable capital of 100,000 dollars, a Bank can, by the help of its deposits and circulation, make loans to the amount of 200,000 or 300,000. Hence, for every hundred thousand of their own capital employed in discounting, the Banks draw twice or thrice as much interest as is drawn from the same amount in the hands of private capitalists. The gain of the Banks from their practice of taking the discount in advance, and charging 64 days interest on notes which have but 63 days to run, is also considerable.

CHAPTER XVII.

Of the Formation of Bank Capitals.

When the uninitiated hear of Banks having capitals of 500,000 or of 1,000,000 dollars, they suppose that these institutions had at their commencement, or some time after, real money to this amount. It is a very natural supposition; but not a true one. The Banks create their own capitals in the same manner that they create the money they lend to the people.

The usual method of proceeding is as follows:

An act is passed by the Legislature to authorize the establishment of a Bank, and certain persons, called Commissioners, are appointed to receive subscriptions. It is provided in the act that the amount subscribed shall be paid in instalments of five or ten dollars in specie, or the notes of specie-paying Banks, and that after one or two instalments shall have been paid in, the Bank shall commence operations.

The first instalment, which we shall suppose to be five

dollars on a share, enables the Bank to purchase desks and a counter, and to pay for engraving and printing its notes. It has then the necessary apparatus for commencing operations, and has, perhaps, a specie fund in reserve of three or four dollars for each share of stock, to meet contingencies.

It then begins to discount notes and circulate paper. The spare cash of those who have dealings with it, are deposited in its vaults. This fund enables it to extend its operations. As the Bank notes will serve the purposes of trade in the neighborhood, the specie is sent to distant places to procure commodities. This leaves open a new channel for the circulation of paper : and the Bank increases the amount of its issues. Then comes the time for paying the second, third, or fourth instalment. The Bank makes a call on the stockholders. Some of them hypothecate their stock, that is, pledge it to the Bank, and with the means obtained from the Bank itself pay in their proportion. Others have obtained the means by discounts of accommodation notes, without any hypothecation of stock. Some few pay in real money : but they generally pay in the notes of the Bank itself, or of similar institutions.

It is by this kind of hocus-pocus that Bank capitals are formed. After the first instalment is paid, the Bank by its own operations, facilitates the paying of the others.

The Bank of Pennsylvania and that of the United States have more pretensions than most others to solidity of capital. It was provided in their charters, that a portion of their instalments should be paid in Government stock. This is not a convenient form for loanable capital, which, it might be supposed, is what Banks should possess. But the peculiar profits of Banks are derived from credit and circulation, and they want no more real capital of any kind than is necessary to support their credit.

It is difficult to say in what the capitals of the other Banks ever consisted, unless it be in what it consists at present—in the promissory notes of individuals. Now, the Banks did not obtain these promissory notes by lending real money of their own, for they had it not to lend. They obtained these promissory notes of the stockholders, by giving in exchange for them the promissory notes of the Bank. Thus Bank capitals are formed by exchanging one kind of promises to pay for another kind of promises to pay.

This mode of forming Bank capitals, with the stock notes of the subscribers, is not peculiar to Banks of the second and third order. The Banks of the most approved standing have formed their capitals in the same way.

The nominal capital of the old Bank of the United States, was ten millions of dollars. One-fifth part of this, or two millions of dollars, was subscribed by the National Government ; but the National Government having no money to pay its subscription, professed to borrow from the Bank. And the Bank having no money to lend, passed a *credit* of two millions in its books to the Government on which it paid six per cent. The Government, in its turn, received the dividends on 5,000 shares of stock of 400 dollars each at par value.

The residue of the capital, or eight millions, was subscribed by individuals, and was to be paid, three-fourths in six per cent. stock, and one-fourth in specie, in four six-monthly instalments of five hundred thousand dollars each. " No more," says Dr. Erick Bollman, " or little more than the first instalment, can ever be considered as having been received by the Bank actually in hard money."*

The capital of the present Bank of the United States was fixed by its charter at thirty-five millions, of which Government subscribed seven ; but Government having, as in the former instance, no money, the Bank granted it a credit to this amount.

The remaining twenty-eight millions of stock were subscribed for by individuals. On each share of the stock, they were, agreeably to the terms of charter, to pay five dollars in gold or silver coin at the time of subscribing ; at the expiration of six months the further sum of ten dollars : and at the expiration of twelve months, the further sum of ten dollars. At each of those three periods, twenty-five dollars more were to be paid, on each share, either in United States stock, or in gold and silver coin, at the option of the sub scribers.

No more or very little more, than the first instalment of five dollars on each share, was paid in gold or silver coin.

* Paragraphs on Banks, Philadelphia, 1811. Dr. Bollman was a zealous advocate for the renewal of the charter of the Bank.

The Directors, indeed, proceeded on the principle that no more was necessary. "It is clear," says one of them, " that having commenced business, and put its paper in circulation, it (the Bank) could not enforce the specie part of the second and third instalments of the capital, in new *acquisitions* of specie. * * * * The Directors acted wisely in discounting the notes of the stockholders, payable in specie, sixty days after date, for the payment of the second instalment."*

It is contended by the founders of these institutions, that this mode of forming Bank stock, is perfectly correct. If it is, stock may be created to almost any amount. The Bank risks nothing, and does not increase its circulation; for the notes which it pays out at one counter in discounting stock notes, are paid in at another counter in subscriptions. The subscribers pay a certain sum to the Bank as borrowers : but they receive back the same amount as stockholders. The whole business, is nothing but a paper transaction between the Bank and its stockholders.

Many of the present owners of stock have paid their hundred dollars' worth of property, or perhaps given an advance of twenty per cent. for the shares they hold : but what they paid, never went to form the capitals of the Banks. They paid it to the original subscribers or to those who bought script from the original subscribers.

CHAPTER XVIII.

Of Speculations in Bank Stock, and of other Stock-Jobbing.

It is well worthy of remark, that, though the Banks derive as much profit as private capitalists, from so much of their capital as is invested in real estate and public securities, however they may have got that capital, and however they may have formed it : and though they derive from 12 to 18 per cent. from so much of their capital as is employed in discounting, they do not, on an average, divide more

* " A Friendly Monitor," Philadelphia, published December 15, 1819, and re-published September 17, 1822.

than six per cent. When the proposal was made to form a " safety fund," by a tax on the Banks, the proprietors of stock in the city Banks of New York objected to it as a great hardship, alleging that they had not, for a series of years, received more than $5\frac{1}{2}$ per cent. per annum. The heavy expenses of these institutions in the payment of Presidents, Cashiers, and Clerks, and the heavy losses that are necessarily sustained when corporate interest superintends the business of lending, are the reasons that the stockholders get much less than the people pay. Such being the fact, the anxiety to establish new Banks might create surprise, if we did not know that the object of the projectors of such institutions is not *to lend* money, but *to make* money. People who have money, can lend it without the intervention of Boards of Directors. They can lend it more securely, and watch over it more easily. But a new Bank will afford to some favored gentleman a snug birth as President for life, and to another an equally snug birth as Cashier. Poor cousins can be very conveniently provided for by giving them clerkships. To some, the new Bank will afford facilities for borrowing ; to others, it will afford facilities for lending—at two or three per cent. a month. To those who are to be Directors, it will impart additional consequence in society, and give great advantages over their neighbors in business. Others hope to make fortunes by speculations in the script. To further all these objects, nothing is necessary but a charter from the Legislature, and the means of paying the first instalment. By the convenient contrivance of stock notes, the stock of the Bank can be completed. The circulation and deposits will prove a certain source of revenue.

When a charter is granted, the speculators evince great anxiety to possess the stock, and thereby create an idea that it is something very valuable. In New York, their practice is to subscribe a much greater amount than the nominal capital, and then clamor for a *pro rata* division. In the case of the Broome County Bank, the capital of which was fixed at 100,000 dollars, the subscriptions amounted to eight millions. In Pennsylvania, where subscriptions are not received beyond the amount of nominal capital, draymen and other able-bodied persons are hired by the speculators to get the script for them. They struggle at the windows with so much violence, as to give and receive severe personal injury. The most disgraceful riots that occur in Philadelphia, are those which are produced by the opening of the books of subscription for a new Bank.

These doings have their effect on simple-minded people; and, from the prospect of large profits, they prefer Bank stock to land and houses. The founders of the Bank kindly spare them some of the script at an advance of five or ten per cent., retaining only enough to keep the control of the institution in their own hands.

Even those who are not simple-minded, do not hesitate to buy the script at an advance, for they hope to sell it at an additional advance. They know that the price of Bank stock in the market is regulated principally by the rate of dividends, and that few make inquiry into the solidity of these institutions, or have, indeed, the means of ascertaining whether, on the winding up of affairs, they can pay fifty cents in a dollar.

From the peculiar nature of their operations, Banks may sustain their credit, and continue to make high dividends, even when nearly all their capital is gone. In one instance, in Philadelphia, a sum equal to the whole capital of a Bank, was actually taken from it by some of its clerks and their coadjutors out of doors, without the Directors knowing any thing about it. The Bank continued its operations as before, supported by its deposits and its circulation. Its stock sold as high in the market as ever. When the defalcation was discovered, the credit of the Bank received a shock. But the Directors called in one or two additional instalments, and the Bank recovered its credit. Its stock is now much above par.

On common gambling principles, speculations in Bank stock are, perhaps, as eligible as speculations in any thing else. But it may be made a question, if executors, guardians, and trustees, act with sound judgment, when they, merely for the sake of facility of management, invest the property entrusted to their care in stocks of this description. The ability of a Bank to pay any thing to the purchasers of its shares, depends on the ability of the original subscribers to pay their stock notes and accommodation notes, and on the ability of borrowers to pay their promissory notes. This ability depends on various contingencies, all which ought to be duly considered by those who contemplate making permanent investments of the funds in their hands.

In making *temporary* investments, there is less risk. " The house is crazy," says the weary traveller to himself, " and must fall ; but not to-night. I may therefore venture to sleep in it." When it has no profits, the Bank may make dividends on its capital, and the fact be concealed from all but the Directors. If its stock should fall in the market, it may be raised again by a few pretended sales, effected through the instrumentality of brokers.

Sometimes the funds of a Bank are employed in purchasing its stock, and then, if the price offered be sufficiently high, those who have the management contrive to sell their own shares. In 1826, four thousand eight hundred and eighty-three shares of the Franklin Bank of New York, were bought up with the funds of the Bank, at an advance of 62,850 dollars. When an investigation was made of the affairs of the Bank, in 1828, it was found there was not enough left to pay the remaining stockholders 50 cents in a dollar.

When a Bank gets into difficulties, it sometimes sustains itself for a period, and affords its agents a considerable chance of profit, by allowing them to have its notes at a discount, on condition of their putting them in circulation in distant places. On an investigation of the affairs of the State Bank at Trenton, in 1825, it was proved that one of its agents had sold bills of the Bank to the amount of 18,500 dollars, at an average discount of $37\frac{1}{2}$ per cent. The very day before the Bank stopped payment, its notes were quoted in the Philadelphia Price Current, at only $1\frac{1}{2}$ per cent. discount.

Every now and then the speculators find it convenient to break a Bank. This enables them to purchase up the notes at a discount, and therewith pay what they owe to the Bank. " There are instances," says Mr. Gallatin, " in which the stockholders, by paying for their shares in their own notes, and afterwards redeeming their notes with the stock in their name, suffered no loss ; and this fell exclusively on the holders of Bank notes and depositors."

In the New York American, for June 1825, the follow-

ing account is given of a mode of operation which was
adopted by the knowing ones of that city.

" The mode of proceeding is simple and not expensive,
and acquires strength by its own action. We will illustrate
it by a case. It is desired to get possession of Insurance
Company A, for example. The stock bears a premium in
the market, say of five per cent. Enough money is raised
among the contributors to pay the premium; and the residue is borrowed from other individuals or companies, on a
pledge of the stock A, at par. The original advance of the
combination is thus small, and they are thence enabled to
be operating in the stock of many Companies at once, till,
having acquired a control in the several concerns, they
turn out all the old administrators, put in their own men,
and then go to work again with renewed energy, and means
increased by the whole amount of the capitals they have
thus acquired the control of. By artful management, assi-
duous puffing, magnificent predictions, and supplies of
stock skilfully curtailed as the demand increases—any one
of the stocks thus owned, may be blown up to an absurd
rate—and *spared* as a favor to the public, until the Managers have sold all out, and realized their profits, leaving
the new purchasers to come in and assist at the bursting
of the bubble."

The Editor of another New York paper, the Inquirer,
said in June, 1826, that certain men had, " by their bonds,
rags, and hypothecation of stock, managed to control a
nominal capital of nearly *four millions of dollars* in different
institutions, and I do not believe" said he, " the whole
confederacy is worth 100,000 dollars."

The same editor afterwards gave a list of *thirty-four*
Banking, Insurance, and other companies, all which, he
asserted, were under the control of a certain gang of stock-
jobbers.

If a Legislature will only grant charters enough, the
speculators will have no difficulty in providing a full
" assortment" of stocks—Banking, Insurance, and of every
other description that may be wanted to suit all the varieties of taste to be found in men and women who have money to part with. If they have one Bank under control,
they can use that as a means of putting half a dozen other
Corporations into active business. So, the Northern Bank

of Pennsylvania was set a going by means of a *certificate* for thirty-five thousand dollars *said* to be deposited in one of the New York Banks: and so, the Sutton Bank of Massachusetts was put in operation by means of 50,000 dollars in specie, borrowed for one day from the City Bank of Boston.

Several of the kind of doings described in this chapter, are regarded with horror by Banks which have reputations to sustain. But, in a view of the *whole* system, it is necessary to take them into consideration. The aggregate of loss sustained by simple-minded people, through such doings, is enormous.

Another way of making money through the medium of incorporated paper-money Banks, is by dealing in Government stocks. Voltaire gives us some insight into this, in one of his letters from Ferney, in Switzerland.

" Here I am," he says, " living in a way suited to my habits, and caring but little for to-morrow; for I have a friend, a Director in the Bank of France, who writes to me whenever money is to be made in the public funds. Sometimes he writes to me desiring me to sell, because the Bank is going to withdraw its notes : at other times, he bids me to buy, for we are going to issue a quantity of notes ; and so, through the kindness of my friend, I always make money, though living two hundred miles from Paris."

CHAPTER XIX.

Of the Ways and Means by which Bank Charters are obtained and renewed.

When a bill was under consideration in the year 1828, to renew the charter of the New York State Bank, General Root, then speaker of the Senate of that Commonwealth, made a speech, from which the following is an extract:

" This Bank was chartered in 1803. Who were the original applicants, and what were the representations made to the country members, it is not necessary to state : at all events, it was to be a State Bank, and a democratic one.

I was urged to be a subscriber to the Bank; it was said the shares were to be scattered over the State, and the members of the Legislature were to have shares. It was one of the most open, palpable, barefaced acts of bribery that can be imagined. I was induced to subscribe ; but I lost all the shares but a few : they said they had lost the subscription paper, or some such thing. So I told them I would not take any. Afterwards a gentleman who came from Albany to Delaware (*i. e.* Delaware county, N. Y.) brought me a script for eight shares. I told them I would not have any; so they kept them to themselves, I suppose."

In the year 1816, Mr. Hopkinson, of Philadelphia, had the boldness to declare in Congress, that " he considered the litter of Banks lately created in Pennsylvania, as the offspring of private legislation and legislative fraud."

A few years since, a senator from Philadelphia County, was heard to lament that a number of shares had been reserved for him in a certain Corporation, the bill for establishing which, he had assisted in passing through the Legislature. The speculation turning out unfortunate, he had lost, instead of gaining, by his services as a stock-jobbing lawgiver.

There was great struggling for the script of the Spring Garden Bank. But we know a member of the Legislature who merely intimated his wish to have a certain number of shares in that Institution, and his wish was gratified.

A distinguished statesman has lately intimated " that there is no law against the Banks subsidizing the public press." With equal truth, it may be said, that there is no law to prevent members of the Legislature from partaking of the advantages of the Corporations they themselves establish. Still it is proper that such facts should be known.

Another great inducement with members of the Legislature to vote for new Banks, is that they may have the means of rewarding the township and ward politicians, the " delegates" and " conferees," to whom they are indebted for their nominations. In selecting " Commissioners," they have the means of paying a debt of gratitude to some men, and of laying others under personal obligations which they hope will not be forgotten.

To get a majority to vote for a new Bank, is, in some instances, no difficult undertaking. In Pennsylvania, there is a mode of running bills through both houses, known technically as "log-rolling." The figure of speech is borrowed from the practice of the original settlers, who, after cutting down the trees on their tracts of land, used to assemble together to roll the logs into heaps. What could not be done by one man, the united strength of many made easy. In like manner, the members of the Legislature who are interested in local, personal, or corporation bills, unite their strength, and roll them all through both houses. In this way, it may chance that fifty or a hundred bills are passed in the course of a session, each of which, if suffered to rest on its own merit, would have been rejected.

Many members of the Legislature are averse to this practice; but some of them are reluctantly brought into it, by the refusal of the "log-rolling" members to vote for good public bills, unless their own private bills are passed at the same time.

The same system is known in the other States, by other names; and it will readily be believed, that where it prevails, special privileges will be conferred on companies under any and every pretext. Such is the effect it has on American Legislation, that a stranger, on inspecting the list of acts annually passed, might suppose our State Governments had been established for the special benefit of stock-jobbers and speculators. In 1826, the Governor of Massachusetts declared that, within the preceding five years, charters had been granted to corporations within that Commonwealth, with authority to hold thirty millions of property. This was exclusive of charters to Banking, Insurance, Canal and Rail Road Companies. The Governor of Delaware stated, in his official message in 1825, that there were then *eighty* corporations in that small State.

No doubt many legislators think that, in voting for new Banks, they are promoting the welfare of their constituents. But the prevalence of false views of the money corporation system, in legislative bodies, is to be attributed mainly to the exertions of those members who have a personal or political interest in establishing and supporting such institutions.

If a Bank only preserves a tolerable credit, the *renewal* of its charter follows as a matter of course. At least, we have met with no instance on record, of refusal to renew the charter of a State Bank which had not committed some open act of bankruptcy. How far a Bank may be entitled to the credit it enjoys, is seldom inquired into. Too many interests are then concerned. Those who have bought stock at second hand, know not, if the Bank were compelled to wind up, if its assets would cover its debts. Some of the borrowers from the Bank feel alarmed, for, if called on to pay what they owe, their insolvency may be made apparent, and the means of living in splendor be taken away from them. A clerkship of 600 dollars per annum, makes a man a firm friend of the Banking system : and he who has had an accommodation note discounted, of the amount of only 500 dollars, feels unpleasant if you hint at the possibility of a charter's not being renewed. Such is the weakness of human nature, that if a man owns only a hundred dollars' worth of stock, it makes him less an enemy to money corporations than he otherwise might be.

Whenever the Legislature creates a Bank, it, at the same time, creates an interest sufficient to sustain that Bank, under all circumstances but those of open bankruptcy. And, as if to give these various interests as much power as possible, it has been contrived in Pennsylvania, that the charters of nearly all the Banks shall expire at the same time.

The extent of Bank influence is not easily appreciated. It is seldom we see a "Bank ticket," or a "money corporation ticket," on the election ground : but when questions are agitated which affect this interest, the Banks have agents at work, whose operations are the more effective because they are unseen. The result usually is, placing the names of friends of paper money on all the tickets.

Over the periodical press, the Banks have great power. Few journalists can venture to expose the money corporation system, in such plain terms as every body would understand, without risking the means of support for themselves and families. Newspaper editors have as much independence of principle as other men ; but they are far from being independent in circumstances. The neglect of subscribers to pay up arrears, has brought many of them in debt to the Banks. Others who are not in debt, are supported principally by the patronage of the Banking interest.[*]

* In a speech in Congress in 1816, Mr. Calhoun, referring to the state of the currency, said, " the evil he desired to remedy, was a deep

In England it is possible to assail both the ecclesiastical and the hereditary aristocracy, through the medium of the periodical press. Under all the evils the people of that country suffer, they have the consolation of enjoying freedom of discussion : but, notwithstanding our boasted liberty in the United States, free and full expositions of the principal cause of our social evils would not be tolerated.*

In some respects, the Banks have more power than the Government itself. They hold the purse-strings of the nation. They can buy off enemies, and they have the means, in various ways, of rewarding friends. *Their* fund for the circulation of pamphlets is not easily exhausted. They require no formal treaties to induce them to act in

one; almost incurable; because connected with public opinion, over which Banks have a great control: They have, in a great measure, a control over the press ; for the proof of which he referred to the fact, that the present wretched state of the circulating medium, had scarcely been denounced by a single paper in the United States."

* "Previous to commencing this pamphlet," says Mr. Carey, in a publication made in 1816, " and during its progress in my hands, prudence and discretion have been constantly exerting themselves to repress my zeal, and to deter me from the undertaking. They have incessantly spread before my eyes the risk of offending those powerful bodies, the Directors of the Banks, who have so many opportunities of making their indignation be felt, and some of whom may not be above the mean and malignant desire of availing themselves of those opportunities.

"To the soundness of these suggestions, I must freely assent. It is plain and practicable. And were I to consult my own personal advantage or comfort, I should bow down in humble submission to their authority. I am well aware of the risk I run. I know if there be at any of the Boards any portion of malice or resentment, (and were there ever twelve men assembled togther without a portion of malice and resentmen ?) it will be roused into action to persecute the man who has dared to arraign their institutions at the bar of the public, and to accuse them of gross errors, which have produced a fertile crop of misfortunes and distress to our citizens.

"Another consequence equally clear, is present to my view. One Bank Director, actuated by malice and resentment, would do me more injury in a day, than one hundred of those whose cause I undertake to defend, would do me good in seven years. The malice of the one would be strong, lasting, insatiable, and as vigilant as Argus, with his hundred eyes, to gratify his spleen. The friendship, or the gratitude, of the others would be cold, torpid and lifeless."

Mr. Carey then was, and perhaps still is, a supporter of the Banking system. The object of his letters was simply to investigate the *policy* of a curtailment of accommodations made by the Banks.

concert. They are ready organized for all occasions. The direct power their charters give them, and the additional power they acquire by their diversified operations, make them all but resistless.

In the United States, there always have been, and there are now, a great number of men opposed to the money corporation and paper money system; but their opposition has produced little effect. In the Bank controversy, there is, on the one side, the strong feeling of private interest supported by party discipline; and, on the other side, the comparatively weak feeling of patriotism, without any aid from party organization. The friends of the Banking system act in concert; its opponents act singly, if they act at all. Against any kind of action, there are various discouragements. If a proposition is made to establish a new Bank, it seems hardly worth while to oppose it, for one Bank more or less can have no great effect. The question immediately occurs on such occasions, why should not these men, as well as others, be permitted to share the profits of Banking? Every new Bank does, indeed, increase the difficulty of reform; but the prospect of reform seems so remote as to be with many thought hardly worthy of attention.

Other difficulties arise from the system's having received the sanction of the Federal Government, as well as that of the State Governments. If any one of the States was disposed to establish a system of sound currency and sound credit, it would find the work impracticable so long as a paper money Bank incorporated by the United States Government continues in existence. If a proposition is made to suffer the charter of the United States Bank to expire, we are startled with the horrors of a multitude of State Banks, issuing paper without limits, and failing to redeem their notes with specie.

It ought to excite no surprise that, under such circumstances, the paper money system has, notwithstanding the great evils it has produced, been prolonged to the present time, and that it is daily strengthening and extending itself. To get rid of it suddenly is impossible. To remove it would require a regular plan of operations, the carrying of which into effect would employ a series of years. Such a plan of operations could be carried into effect by a party which would be willing to sacrifice all merely personal predilections and antipathies for the grand object of breaking down the money corporation and paper money system, and restoring to the great body of the American people their *natural* right of acquiring property by industry and economy.

CHAPTER XX.

Summary View of the Advantages which the System gives to some men over others.

If two individuals should trade with one another, on the same principle that the Banks trade with the community, it would soon be seen on which side the advantage lay. If A should pay interest on all the notes he gave, and finally pay the notes themselves with his own wealth, and if B should receive interest on all the notes he issued, and finally pay the notes themselves with A's wealth, A's loss and B's gain would be in proportion to the amount of transactions between them.

This is the exact principle of American Banking operations; but, owing to the multitude of persons concerned, the nature of the transaction is not discovered by the public. Regard the whole Banking interest as one body corporate, and the whole of the rest of the community as one body politic, and it will be seen that the body politic pays interest to the body corporate for the whole amount of notes received, while the body corporate finally satisfies the demands of the body politic by transferring the body politic's own property to its credit.

In private credit, there is a reciprocity of burdens and of benefits. Substantial wealth is given when goods are sold, and substantial wealth is received when payment is made, and an equivalent is allowed for the time during which payment is deferred. If A took a note from B, endorsed by the richest man in the country, he would require interest for the time for which payment was postponed. But the Banking system reverses this natural order. The interest which is due to the productive classes that receive the Bank notes, is paid to the Banks that issue them.

If the superior credit the Banks enjoy, grew out of the natural order of things, it would not be a subject of complaint. But the Banks owe their credit to their charters—to special acts of legislation in their favor, and to their notes being made receivable in payment of dues to Government. The kind of credit which is created for them by law, being equipollent with cash in the market, enables them to transfer an equal amount of substantial wealth from the productive classes to themselves, giving the productive classes only representatives of credit, or evidences of debt, in return for the substantial wealth which they part with.

To test the Banking principle fairly, let us bring down our minds from a country to a county, and, to give definiteness to our ideas, let us, in all instances, make round numbers the basis of our calculation.

Suppose a county to contain a thousand families of ten persons each, and each family to be worth 5,000 dollars. The wealth of the community is, then, 5,000,000 dollars. One-tenth of this wealth, or 500 dollars for each family, we will suppose to be in silver money. The rest is in land, houses, and various commodities. The state of credit in this county is as sound as the state of the currency. The distribution of wealth is left to natural laws. The *production* and *acquisition* of riches are never separated. Every man enjoys what he produces, and what he saves ; and no man enjoys what is produced or what is saved by another. We will suppose the income of this community to be 1,000,000, dollars, or 1,000 dollars a year for each family, and that 700,000 dollars of this aggregate income is derived from industry, and the rest from capital, profits being at the rate of six per cent.

In this county are ten men of a speculative turn of mind, who grow tired of working and saving, and wish to grow rich in some more easy way. They apply to the Legislature for a charter for a Bank, with a nominal capital of 100,000 dollars, divided into a thousand shares of 100 dollars each : and their prayer is granted. It is provided in the charter that, as soon as five dollars shall be paid on each share, the Bank shall commence operations. The payment of the other instalments is, according to the custom of Pennsylvania, left to the discretion of the Directors.

The business of Banking is new in this county, and as none clearly understand its operation but the ten speculators, they subscribe for the whole of the stock, or for one hundred shares each. Each of them pays down 500 dollars, making the whole capital paid in, 5,000 dollars.

The Bank then commences business, and issues notes to the amount of 25,000 dollars. By the contrivance of " convertibility," and by another contrivance by which they are made receivable in payment of dues to Government, the notes become current. The notes are borrowed by the speculators. Each speculator has then 2,500 dollars at command, instead of 500. It is true, he pays interest to the Bank as a borrower : but he receives the same interest back as a stockholder. It is evident that the equality of wealth is destroyed. The possession of a monied capital so much greater than that of his neighbors, will give him advantages in trade equal to double the amount of interest. But, estimating his advantages as equal to only six per cent., his annual income is increased from 1000 dollars to 1120, his 500 dollars formerly yielding him but 30 dollars a year, and now, by their conversion into Bank-stock, yielding him 150 dollars; for, each metallic dollar is, by this contrivance, made to produce to him as much as five did formerly.

But this is only the first operation of the Bank. Some of the families in the county deposit their silver in the vaults of the Bank, for safe-keeping. Other families, finding that Bank notes serve all the purposes of domestic trade, export their silver. This creates a new demand for Bank notes as a circulating medium. In time, the Bank finds that its permanent deposits of silver are not liable to be reduced beyond a certain amount : and to increase its profits, it lends a great part of the silver to those who export it.

It may require some years to bring the machine into complete operation. The " prejudices " of some men against paper, and in favor of metallic money, are not easily subdued. But even those with whom the " prejudices " remain, are brought at length, through the force of example, through necessity, or through some other cause, to make deposits in Bank, and to pay and receive Bank paper. Bank medium then becomes the money of the

county : and as soon as this is accomplished, the regular
receipts of the Bank may be estimated as follows :

On 100,000 of Bank notes lent, at 6 40,   - $6,400
On 100,000 of active Bank credit lent,   -   6,400
On 100,000 of silver deposited by some, and
   lent by the Bank to others who export it, -   6,400
                                                   ─────────
                                                    $19,200

On this supposition, 200,000 of metallic money will be
left in the county, half of which may be in the vaults of
the Bank, and the other half circulate as the medium of
retail trade.

In our haste we passed over the payment of the second,
third, and subsequent instalments of the stock. It was
not of much moment. The payments were merely nominal. The speculators could easily have paid all the instalments, after the first, by the profits derived from the operations of the Bank itself. But where would have been the
use of this ? The money, if paid in, would have been lent
and exported. It would have added something to the
income of the Bank. But each speculator can make
as much by keeping it in his own hands. The original
sum of 5,000 dollars, and so much of the silver of depositors as is retained, are sufficient to support the credit of
the Bank. Each of the speculators, therefore, throws in
a note for 500 dollars, when the second instalment becomes
due. The Bank discounts it : pays out its own paper at
one counter, and receives it back at another, or, perhaps,
only makes a new credit entry in its books. It is true, that the
speculators are made debtors to the Bank for a certain
amount as borrowers : but they are credited with an equal
amount as stockholders : and in this way the whole of the
remaining instalments may be arranged. By this contrivance
the sum of 95,000 dollars will be added to the debts due
to the Bank, but nothing to its circulation or responsibilities.

The time has now come, in which the speculators may
sell a part or the whole of the stock. They may with safety
dispose of seven hundred and fifty shares, to widows, orphans, and literary and charitable institutions, for these
will never interfere with Bank management.

We will deduct 9,200 dollars from the gross income of

the Bank, for expenses, losses, and reservations for a contingent fund. It will then be able to divide ten per cent. on its nominal capital : and at the rate at which permanent annuities are calculated, stock yielding ten per cent. will be estimated as worth in the market 150 dollars a share. Each of our speculators sells seventy-five shares of his stock at this rate, or for 11,255 dollars, and invests the proceeds in land, houses, or merchandise. The risk of payment to the Bank of the notes discounted, he transfers to the purchaser of the stock.

Thus we see that our ten speculators have, by the "*judicious*" use of 5,000 dollars of metalic money, got transferred to them 112,550 dollars' worth of real and personal estate. Retaining two hundred and fifty shares of stock, they keep the control of the institution in their own hands.

Now, we pretend not to say that the accounts of any one of our American Banks would, if faithfully exhibited, accord in every particular with this supposed case. Their profits do not appear to be usually as great : but extreme cases serve best to illustrate *principles;* and these are the *fundamental* principles of the American Banking System. A small amount of metalic money is paid in : the other instalments are arranged by the discounting of stock notes. The Bank extends its operations by discounts on deposits, and by substituting a paper for a metalic medium : and, at a suitable time, the founders of the Bank sell a portion of the stock, and invest the proceeds in lands, houses, and merchandise.

The Bank of Chester had, on the 3d of November, 1829, a capital of 90,000 dollars, notes in circulation to the amount of 209,064 dollars, and deposits to the amount of 166,374 dollars. The specie in its vaults amounted to 61,462 dollars, and the investments on which it was drawing interest amounted apparently to 451,663 dollars. The circulation and deposits of the Bank of Chester, were altogether 375,438. Those of the Bank in the case supposed, for the sake of illustrating the principle, were only 300, 000 dollars. The investments of the Bank of Chester, yielding interest, amounted to 451,663. Those of the supposed Bank, to only 395,000, including the stock notes of the ten founders of the Bank.

It may be, that the whole 90,000 of the capital of the

Bank of Chester was paid in, without any resort to discounting of stock notes, or any similar contrivances. But if it was, there was nothing in the principles of the system to prevent the stock of the Bank of Chester from being filled up in the way which is usual in establishing new Banks in America. The Bank of Chester County having gone into operation in the year in which specie payments were suspended, the filling up of its stock must have been an easy process, whatever method was adopted.

As it is public credit that supports the Banks, and not the Banks that support public credit—as the deposits of the Banks are the property of the community generally, and as the profits derived from circulation come from the community generally, they ought to go to the community generally, and be used (if used at all) to lighten the burdens of taxation. "If," says Ricardo, "a charter were about to expire, the public might question the policy of permitting a company to enjoy all the advantages which attend the supplying of a great country with paper money. Paper money may be considered as affording a *seignorage* equal to its *whole* exchangeable value—but seignorage in all countries belongs to the State."

If, after the manner of the Scotch Banks, the American Banks paid four per cent. interest on deposits, and granted discounts at the rate of five per cent. there would be something like equity in this department of their operations, for one per cent. would not be more than a fair commission. But they allow no interest on deposits, except in Boston, and perhaps in Baltimore, though it is, in point of fact, through the means of the deposits, that they support the credit of the notes they have in circulation.

But the reader will have a very imperfect idea of the advantages the present Banking system gives to some men, if he extends his view no further than the profits derived from trading on deposits, from substituting a credit medium of commerce for a metallic medium, from the formation of Bank stock *secundum artem*, and the subsequent exchange of that Bank stock for lands, houses and merchandise.

In addition to this, he must take into consideration—

What some have gained and others have lost, by the various kinds of stock-jobbing and usury, to which Banking has given rise:

What some have gained and others lost, by that fluctuation of prices which is produced by "contractions" and "expansions" of Bank medium, and which has made most kinds of business more uncertain than a lottery:

What some have gained and others lost, through that super-extended system of commercial credit, which has its origin and support in Banking:

What some have gained and others lost, by the breaking of upwards of one hundred and sixty Banks between the years 1811 and 1830:

What some have gained and others lost, through the circulation of counterfeit notes:

What some have gained and others lost, by receiving genuine notes at one rate, and passing them at another:

Let him add all these accounts together, and he will have a pretty correct idea of what some have gained and others have lost by the *direct* operations of the system.

CHAPTER XXI.

Of the Remote Consequences of the System.

Our view of the extent to which paper-money Banking affects our social condition, will be very imperfect, if we confine it to the *direct* operations of the system. These are, as it were, but the first links of a long extended chain. Each effect becomes in its turn a cause; and the remote consequences are of more importance than the immediate. To prove this, a few plain truths will suffice.

If two men start in life at the same time, and the one gets, at the commencement, but a small advantage over the other, and retains the advantage for twenty or thirty years, their fortunes will, at the end of that period, be very unequal.

If a man at the age of twenty-one years, is deprived of one hundred dollars which he had honestly earned, and honestly saved, the injury done to this man must be estimated by the advantage he would have derived from the use of his little property during the rest of his life. The want of it may prevent his turning his faculties to the best account. The loss may dispirit his future exertion.

If a man is, at any period of his life, deprived of a property, large or small, accumulated for him by the honest industry and economy of his ancestors, the wrong done to him is of the same character as that which he sustains when he is unjustly deprived of property which was the fruits of his own industry. It is the dictate of nature that parents shall leave their wealth to their children, and the law of the land, in this case, only confirms the dictate of nature.

It is not easy to set bounds to the effects of a single act of injustice. If you deprive a man of his property, you may thereby deprive him of the means of properly educating his children, and thus affect the moral and intellectual character of his descendants for several generations.

Such being the consequences of single acts, we may learn from them to estimate the effects of those political and commercial institutions which operate unequally. They lay the foundation of an *artificial* in equality of wealth : and, whenever this is done, the wealth of the few goes on increasing in the ratio of compound interest, while the reflux operations of the very causes to which they owe their wealth, keep the rest of the community in poverty.

Where the distribution of wealth *is* left to natural and just laws, and the natural connection of cause and effect is not violated, the tendency of " money to beget money," or rather of wealth to produce wealth, is not an evil. A man has as strong a natural right to the profits which are yielded by the capital which was formed by his labor, as he has to the immediate product of his labor. To deny this, would be to deny him a right to the whole product of his labor. The claims of the honest capitalist and of the honest laborer, are equally sacred, and rest, in fact, on the same foundation. Nor is it the law of nature that the idle and improvident shall suffer temporary inconvenience only. By neglecting to form a capital for themselves, they render their future labor less productive than it otherwise might be : and finally make themselves dependent on others for the means of both subsistence and employment.

But, unequal political and commercial institutions *invert* the operation of the natural and just causes of wealth and poverty—take much of the capital of a country from those whose industry produced it, and whose economy saved it, and give it to those who neither work nor save. The natural reward of industry then goes to the idle, and the natural punishment of idleness falls on the industrious.

Inasmuch as personal, political, commercial, and accidental causes, operate sometimes in conjunction, and sometimes in opposition, it is diffiult to say, in individual cases, in how great degree wealth or poverty is owing to one cause or to another. Harsh judgments of rich and poor, taking them individually, are to be avoided. But it is notorious, that, as regards different *classes* in different countries, wealth and poverty are the consequences of the positive institutions of those countries. Peculiar political priviliges are commonly the ground of the distinction : but peculiar commercial privileges have the same effect : and when the foundation of the artificial inequality of fortune is once laid, (it matters not whether it be by feudal institutions or money corporations,) all the subsequent operations of society tend to increase the difference in the condition of different classes of the community.

One consequence of unequal institutions is increasing the demand for luxuries, and diminishing the effective demand for necessaries and comforts. Many being qualified to be producers of necessaries, and few to be producers of luxuries, the reward of the many is reduced, and that of the few raised to an enormous height. The inventor of some new means of gratification for the rich, is sure to receive his recompense, though thousands of able-bodied men may be starving around him.

This may be illustrated by a case drawn from England, where the favorite opera-singer receives her thousands per annum, while the able-bodied agricultural laborer is forced to draw on the parish rates for subsistence.

Something similar to it may be found in our own country, where the second rate singers, dancers, and players of Europe, accumulate fortunes in a few years, while multitudes of humble but useful women in all our large cities, struggle hard for the means of a bare subsistence.

Now, there is no cause of complaint in people's lavishing their thousands on favorite singers and dancers, if those thousands have been honestly earned and fairly got. But if they owe their thousands to political or commercial institutions operating specially to their advantage, those political and commercial institutions are not of the kind most conducive to social happiness.

Through all the operations of business, the effects of an

unequal distribution of wealth may be distinctly traced
The rich have the means of rewarding most liberally the
professional characters whom they employ, and the trades-
men with whom they deal. An aristocracy in one department of society, introduces an aristocracy into all.

These effects are, it is true, most obvious in countries
where the causes of an artificial inequality of wealth are of a
permanent character, and connected with political organization : but they can be discovered in our own country. The
inequality of reward our lawyers and physicians receive, is
caused but in part by inequality of talent. It is owing in
part to the inequality of the means of those who employ
them : and to the disposition the many have to prefer the
lawyer or the physician who is patronized by the rich and
fashionable. They feel that their own education disquali-
fies them for forming a proper estimate of professional
talent, and take the judgment of those they suppose must,
from their superior wealth, have better means of information.

It is, however, among the hard-working members of
society, that the ultimate effects of such causes are most
observable.

The condition of a multitude of poor women in our large
cities, has lately attracted the attention of the benevolent.
It appears from the statements that have been published,
that they can, by working ten or twelve hours every day,
earn no more than from seventy-five cents to a dollar
a week. Half of this sum goes for house rent and fuel,
leaving them from thirty-seven and a half cents to fifty
cents a week for food and clothing for themselves and children. Some thousands are said to be in this situation in
Philadelphia alone.

Various proposals have been made to better their condition : some futile, others absolutely pernicious. The laws
of supply and demand are too powerful to yield to ser-
mons and essays. The low rate of the wages of these poor
women, is the effect of general causes—causes which affect,
in one way or another, every branch of business. In the
great game we have been playing, much of the wealth of
the country has passed into a few hands. Many men dying, have left nothing to their widows and children ; and
others who still live, cannot support their families, except

by the additional industry of their wives. The work of a seamstress can be done by a woman in her own house, in the intervals she can spare from attention to her children. In this way, the number of seamstresses has been increased.

On the other hand, many families who would gladly employ these poor women, are compelled by their own straitened circumstances, to do this kind of work themselves. In this way the demand for seamstresses is diminished.

Private benevolence may improve the condition of individuals of this class : but the class itself can be benefitted by such causes only as will diminish the number of seamstresses or increase the demand for their labor. The cause that will improve the condition of one of the industrious classes of society, will improve the condition of all. When an end shall be put to unfair speculation, then, and not till then, will honest industry have its just reward.

CHAPTER XXII.

Effects on Moral Character.

The practices of trade seem, in most countries, to fix the standard of commercial honesty. In the Hanse towns and Holland, while they were rising to wealth, this standard was very high. Soldiers were not more careful to preserve their honor without stain, than merchants were to maintain their credit without blemish.

The practices of trade in the United States, have debased the standard of commercial honesty. Without clearly distinguishing the causes that have made commerce a game of hap-hazard, men have come to perceive clearly the nature of the effect. They see wealth passing continually out of the hands of those whose labor produced it, or whose economy saved it, into the hands of those who neither work nor save. They do not clearly perceive *how* the transfer takes place : but they are certain of the fact. In the general scramble they think themselves entitled to some portion of the spoil, and if they cannot obtain it by fair means, they take it by foul.

Hence we find men, without scruple, incurring debts which they have no prospect of paying.

Hence we find them, when on the very verge of bankruptcy, embarrassing their friends by prevailing on them to indorse notes and sign custom-house bonds.

Instances not unfrequently occur of men who have failed once or twice, afterwards accumulating great wealth. How few of these honorably discharge their old debts by paying twenty shillings in the pound !

How many evade the just demands of their creditors, by privately transferring their property.

It is impossible, in the present condition of society, to pass laws which will punish dishonest insolvents, and not oppress the honest and unfortunate.

Neither can public opinion distinguish between them, The dishonest share the sympathy which should be given exclusively to their unfortunate neighbors : and the honest are forced to bear a part of the indignation which should fall entirely on the fraudulent.

The standard of commercial honesty can never be raised very high, while trade is conducted on present principles. " It is hard," says Dr. Franklin, " for an empty bag to stand upright." The straits to which many men are reduced, cause them to be guilty of actions which they would regard with as much horror as their neighbors, if they were as prosperous as their neighbors.

We may be very severe in our censure of such men, but what else ought we to expect, when the laws and circumstances give to some men so great advantages in the great game in which the fortunes of the whole community are at issue—what else ought we to expect, but that those to whom the law gives no such advantage, should exert to the utmost such faculties as remain to them in the struggle for riches, and not be very particular whether the means they use are such as the law sanctions or the law condemns.

Let those who are in possession of property which has been acquired according to the strict letter of the law, be thankful that they have not been led into such temptations as those on whom the positive institutions of society have had an unfavorable influence.

But, Banking has a more extensive effect on the moral character of the community, through that distribution of

wealth which is the result of its various direct and remote
operations. Moralists in all ages, have inveighed against luxury. To it they attribute the corruption of morals, and the
downfall of nations. The word luxury is equivocal. What is
regarded as a luxury in one stage of society, is, in another,
considered as a comfort, and in a still more advanced stage
as a necessary. The desire of enjoyment is the great stimulus to social improvement. If men were content with bare
necessaries, no people would, in the arts and sciences, and
in whatever else renders life desirable, be in advance of
the lowest caste of the Hindoos, or the unhappy peasantry
of the most unhappy country of Europe.

But, whatever moralists have said against luxury, is true
when applied to that *artificial* inequality of fortune which
is produced by *positive* institutions of an unjust character.
Its necessary effect is to corrupt one part of the community, and debase the other.

The bare prospect of inheriting great wealth, damps the
energies of a young man. It is well if this is the only evil
it produces. "An idle man's brain," says John Bunyan,
" is the devil's workshop." Few men can have much leisure, and not be injured by it. To get rid of the *ennui* of
existence, young men of wealth resort to the gambling table, the race ground, and other haunts of dissipation. They
cannot have these low means of gratification, without de-
basing those less favored by fortune.

The children of the poor suffer as much in one way, as
the children of the rich suffer in another. The whole energies of the father and mother are exhausted in providing
bread for themselves and their family. They cannot attend properly to the formation of the moral character of
their offspring—the most important branch of education.
They can ill spare the means to pay for suitable intellectual instruction. Their necessities compel them to put
their children to employments unsuited to their age and
strength. The foundation is thus laid of diseases which
shorten and imbitter life.

Instances occur of men, by the force of their innate
powers, overcoming the advantages of excess or defect of
wealth ; but it is true, as a general maxim, that, in early
.life, and in every period of life, too much or too little
wealth, is injurious to the character of the individual, and,

when it extends through a community, it is injurious to the character of that community.

In the general intercourse of society, this artificial inequality of wealth produces baneful effects. In the United States, the pride of wealth has more force than in any other country, because there is here no other pride to divide the human heart. Some of our good republicans do, indeed, boast of a descent from the European nobility; but when they produce their coats of arms, and their genealogical trees, they are laughed at. The question is propounded, if their noble ancestors left them any *money*. Genius confers on its possessor a very doubtful advantage. Virtue, with us, as in the days of the Roman poet, is viler than sea weed, unless it has a splendid retinue. Talent is estimated only as a means of increasing riches. Wealth alone can give permanent distinction, for he who is at the top of the political ladder to-day, may be at the bottom to-morrow.

One mischief this state of things produces, is, that men are brought to consider wealth as the *only* means of happiness. Hence they sacrifice honor, conscience, health, friends—every thing, to obtain it.

The other effects of artificial inequality of wealth, have been treated of at large, by moralists, from Solomon and Socrates downwards. To their works, and to the modern treatises on crime and pauperism, we refer the reader. The last mentioned treatises are, for the most part, only illustrations of the ultimate effects of positive institutions, which operate unequally on different members of the community.

CHAPTER XXIII.

Effects on Happiness.

The inferences the intelligent reader must have drawn from what has already been stated, preclude the necessity of much detail in this part of our inquiry.

Wealth is, if independently considered, but one among fifty of the causes of happiness: and poverty, viewed in the same light, is but one among fifty of the causes of misery. The poorest young man, having health of body and peace of mind, and enjoying the play of the social sympathies, in the affections of wife, children and friends, is happier than the richest old man, bowed down with sickness, oppressed with anxiety for the future, or by remorse for the past, having nobody to love, and beloved by nobody.

But though we may, by mental abstraction, consider wealth independently, or poverty independently, neither the one or the other is absolutely independent in its operation. There is no cause in either the physical or the moral world, but which works in conjunction with other causes. Health of body and peace of mind, with the just play of the social affections, may give happiness, independently of wealth: but in extreme poverty, it is difficult to preserve either health of body or peace of mind, and the play of the social affections becomes then a source of misery.

Some little wealth, at least enough for daily subsistence, is necessary for the enjoyment of life and the pursuit of happiness: and hence it is, that the right to property is as important as the right to life and the right to liberty. " You take my life when you do take the means by which I live."

The majority of men are of such temperament, that something more than the means of subsistence for the bare twenty-four hours, is necessary for their happiness. They must also have a prospect of enjoying the like means of subsistence in future days. But this is a prospect which, with the reflecting part of the poor, is frequently overcast with clouds and gloom. Few journeymen mechanics are able to make adequate provision for sickness and old age. The wages of a laborer will support him and his family while he enjoys health and while employment is steady: but in case of long continued sickness he must look for relief from the hand of public or of private charity. If he casts his eyes on his wife and children, his dying hours are imbittered with thoughts of the misery which may be their portion. Corroding care is the inmate of the poor man's breast. It is so heart-withering, that it may be made a question, if the condition of some slaves in the Southern States is much worse than that of many citizens of the other States. The want of liberty is a great drawback on happiness: but the slave is free from care. He knows that when he grows old, or becomes infirm, his master is bound to provide for his wants.

There would be less objection to that artificial inequality of wealth which is the result of unjust positive institutions, if it increased the happiness of one class of society in the same proportion that it diminishes the happiness of another class. But, increase of wealth beyond what is necessary to gratify the rational desires of a man, does not increase his happiness. If it gives birth to irrational desires, the gratification of them must produce misery. Even when inordinate wealth does not give birth to irrational desires, it is attended with an increase of care, and this is a foe to happiness.

With some men, the love of wealth seems to be a blind passion. The magpie, in hiding silver spoons in its nest, appears to act with as much reflection as they do, in piling money-bag on money-bag. They have no object in view beyond accumulation. But, with most men, the desire of great wealth appears subordinate to the love of great power and distinction. This is the end, that the means. They love fine houses, splendid equipages, and large possessions, less for any physical gratification they impart, than for the distinction they confer, and the power they bestow. It is with some, as much an object of ambition to be ranked with the richest men, as it is with others to be ranked with the greatest warriors, poets, or philosophers.

The love of that kind of distinction which mere wealth confers, is not a feeling to be highly commended : but it is hardly to be reprobated, when it is constitutional, and when it is under the government of proper moral principle. In this case, it is a simple stimulus to vigorous industry and watchful economy. With some men, the love of ease is the ruling passion, with others the love of pleasure, and with others the love of science. If the love of riches was not, with many men, stronger than any of the other loves we have mentioned, there might not be enough wealth accumulated to serve the general purposes of society. They may claim the liberty of gratifying their particular passion in a reasonable way : but it is a passion which derives less gratification from the actual possession of a large store, than from the constant increase of a small one. The man whose wealth increases gradually from 100 dollars to 1000, thence to 5000, thence to 10,000, and thence to 50,000, has more satisfaction in the process than he who suddenly becomes possessed of 100,000 dollars.   As to the distinction which mere wealth confers, it would be obtained in a state of society in which the distribution of wealth was left to natural laws, as certainly as in a state in which positive institutions operate to the advantage of the few, and to the disadvantage of the many.   If the riches of men were made to depend entirely on their industry, economy, enterprize, and prudence, the possession of 100,000 dollars would confer as much distinction as the possession of 500,000 dollars confers at present. Those worth " a plum," would then rank among the " first men " on 'change : those who are worth " five plums " can rank no higher now.

But the system has not a merely *negative* effect on the happiness of the rich.   Such is the uncertainty of fortune in the United States, that even the most wealthy are not exempt from painful solicitude for the future. Who can be sure that he will be able to navigate his own bark in safety to the end of the voyage, when he sees the shore strewed with wrecks?   If a man leaves an estate to his children, he knows not how long they will keep possession of it.   If he extends his views to his grand children, the probability will appear strong that some of them will be reduced to abject poverty.

Such is the present custom of trade, that a man who has a considerable capital of his own, not unfrequently gives credit to four or five times the amount of that capital.   He is a rich man, but even if the debts due to him are perfectly secure, the perplexity which is created by a long train of credit operations, the failure of but one of which may prove his ruin, must leave him little ground for solid satisfaction : and the necessity he is under in times of embarrassment, of courting the good-will of Bank Directors, goes far towards destroying his personal independence.   " The servile dependence on Banks, in which many of our citizens pass their lives," was observed by Mr. Carey as long ago as the year 1811.

There is one other evil resulting from the super-extended system of credit which has its origin in Banking, and with a few observations on this, we shall close our remarks

on this head of the subject. We allude to the *misery* suffered by an honest man, who is involved in debts. We
have known cases in which none of the common rules of
prudence had been transgressed in incurring the debts, in
which the creditors were perfectly convinced of the
honesty of the debtor, and neither pressed for payment,
nor reflected on his disability to comply with his engagements : in which the debtor was sensible that his failure
would not subject his creditors to any serious inconvenience; and yet a gloom would overspread the mind of the
debtor, and remain there for years.

CHAPTER XXIV.

*Of the Evils that would be produced by a sudden dissolu-
tion of the System.*

If every Bank note in the country were consumed by
fire to-morrow, the wealth of the nation would be diminished just as much as it would be by the destruction of so
much waste paper.

So, if all the title-deeds of estates were destroyed, the
loss of positive wealth would be equivalent to the loss of so
many skins of parchment. But very great injustice would
be done to individuals by the destruction of these skins of
parchment ; and not less, probably, by the sudden destruction of Bank notes.

It is an easy thing to establish a Banking system : but
it is not very easy to get rid of it after it has been some
years in operation. The *sudden* abolition of it, would produce an entire destruction of private credit, a universal
pressure for the payment of debts, and a general disability
to comply with engagements. Business of nearly every
kind would be suspended, and the laboring part of the
community would be deprived of employment.

If all the Bank notes in the country should be destroyed
to-morrow, the twenty-two millions of specie which are
said to be in the vaults of the Banks, would be put in circulation, which, added to the ten millions of specie sup-

posed to be at present in circulation, would make a total
of thirty-two millions. Supposing Bank credits to be destroyed at the same moment, the circulating medium would
suddenly be reduced from one hundred and nineteen millions (which is, according to Mr. Gallatin, the present
aggregate of specie, notes, and Bank credits) to thirty-two
millions. If an end were not put to all transactions except
by means of barter, the fall of prices would be at least
seventy-five per cent.

If but *half* of the Bank notes and Bank credits should
be suddenly abolished, the fall of prices would be in
greater proportion than the reduction of medium, from the
immense quantities of land and of merchandise which
would be thrown into the market.

If the Bank medium should be suddenly reduced only
one-fourth, the fall of prices would be at least twenty-five per
cent., and universal embarrassment would be the consequence.

Many of those who have acquired capital by the different operations of Banking, would not, perhaps, desire any
thing better than the sudden destruction of the system.
Most estates which are now mortgaged for only one-third
or fourth of their worth, at the present rate of valuation,
would fall into the hands of speculators. The condition of
the whole country would be like that of Kentucky when
she adopted her " relief laws." The people would clamor
for the issue of paper money by the State Governments,
and a worse system than the present might be adopted, if a
worse be possible.

Public opinion in the United States, when it once takes
root, runs so rapidly to maturity, that this caution is not
unnecessary. Some who are now living may see the time
when the popular feeling against the Banking system will
be stronger than the feeling ever was in its favor.

CHAPTER XXV.

Of the Proper Mode of Proceeding.

As paper drives specie out of circulation, so, the with-drawal of paper brings specie Bank again. Wherever there is a vacuum it flows in, unless political regulations counteract its tendency to find its own level.

If we *gradually* withdraw Bank notes from circulation, no evil will ensue, for specie will immediately supply their place.

The proper mode of proceeding would be, to begin with the smallest notes, and proceed gradually to those of the highest denomination.

Mr. White, of New York, in his report to Congress, made in February, 1831, estimates the amount of notes in circulation of a less denomination than five dollars, at not more than seven millions. This does not exceed the amount of gold and silver we sometimes import in one year. But, through the use made of paper, the gold and silver imported in one year are exported in the next. Let small notes fall into disuse, and an equal amount of specie will be retained in the country.

The amount of five dollar notes in circulation is esti-mated by Mr. White at ten millions. Two years after the act to prohibit the issuing of small notes, it would be per-fectly safe to prohibit the issuing of notes of a less deno-mination than ten dollars.

In two years more, the prohibition might be extended to notes of a less denomination than twenty dollars. Our currency would then be on a par with that of Great Britain.

In two years more the issue of notes of a less denomina-tion than fifty dollars might be forbidden ; and in two years after that, the issue of notes of a less denomination than 100 dollars.

In this way, in the short period of ten years, and without producing any commercial convulsion, specie might be made to take the place of paper.

We speak from experience. The principles of the mea-sure have been tried in Virginia, Maryland, and Pennsyl-vania. In the way in which these States have got rid of small notes, the other States may get rid of them.   In the way in which small notes have been driven from circulation, notes of every denomination may be made to give place to specie.

In some parts of Pennsylvania, violent opposition was made to the act to prohibit the circulation of small notes, from an opinion that it would "make money scarce." The grand juries of the counties of Beaver and Erie went so far as to present it as a nuisance. But the Legislature remained firm in its purpose, and many of the former opponents of the law are now among its warmest supporters.   The effect of the measure was just such as its friends predicted. An immense quantity of trash disappeared from circulation, and its place was supplied with silver.

The principles of the measure have also been tried in England, where, in 1829, the issue of notes of a less denomination than five pounds sterling was prohibited. The proceeding there was from notes of one pound, or four dollars eighty cents, to notes of five pounds, or twenty-four dollars—a greater jump than would be advisable in America.

Some of our most distinguished statesmen appear to be of opinion that, if it were possible to substitute a metallic for a paper medium, it would greatly promote the interests of the country.   Nothing hinders, but *want of inclination.* If either of the great political parties into which our nation is divided, would take a decided stand in favor of sound currency and sound credit, the cause of sound currency and sound credit would be triumphant.   The industrious classes of the nation would array themselves with that party, as soon as they could be made to understand the question, and the speculators and their satellites would be vanquished in the contest.

If our national debt was of great amount, and if our taxes were heavy, some difficulties might be experienced in passing from a paper to a metallic medium.   But our national debt is now merely nominal, and the taxes payable to the United States may, if necessary, be reduced, without diminishing the efficiency of Government.   A country and a people possessed of so much elasticity, could bear greater changes than any here proposed.

Of the perfect feasibility of the measure, we may be

convinced in another way. Our exports of domestic produce amount annually to between fifty and sixty millions
of dollars. If we should buy from five to ten millions a
year of gold and silver, for ten years, we should still have
between forty and fifty millions to expend in the purchase
of European manufactures, and East and West India products. If, by the withdrawal of paper, a demand for specie
to the amount of twenty millions annually should be created, it could readily be supplied. England, in four years,
on the resumption of specie payments, imported twenty
millions sterling in gold alone. Our demand could be
supplied by both gold and silver.

Supposing the withdrawal of the Bank notes should
cause a diminution of Bank discounts of equal amount,
the effect, if we proceeded gradually, would be almost imperceptible. If two years were allowed for the withdrawal
of small notes, the diminution of Bank discounts would, in
this period, and on this supposition, be at the rate of
3,500,000 dollars a year. In the single city of Philadelphia, there have been, in periods of less than a year, reductions of Bank discounts to as great an amount as is here
proposed for the whole country.

According to the estimate of Mr. Gallatin, the whole
amount of Bank notes in actual circulation, in 1830, was
about 61,000,000. Surely it will not be said, that our
whole nation cannot pay off an amount of Bank debt, equal
to the amount of Bank notes in circulation, in the period
of ten years.

But, supposing we should, in the course of ten years,
choose to pay off an amount of Bank debt, equal to the
whole amount of Bank medium, or of both Bank notes and
Bank credits, amounting together to 109,000,000, would it
be a work of insuperable difficulty ? In the last seven
years, the Government has paid off the public debt at the
rate of eight or ten millions a year : can we not, all of us
together, pay off between eleven and twelve millions a year
of Bank debt ?

In a pamphlet entitled " Remarks on the Annual Treasury Report," published in 1828, and said to be written by
two practical economists, distinguished for their talents
and information, the whole capital of the country is estimated at 12,000,000,000 dollars, and its productive industry

at 600,000,000 annually. Mr. Lee of Boston, seems to suppose the national capital is not more than 10,000,000,000, but he increases the national income to 700, or 800 millions. In the Harrisburgh address, drawn up by Mr. Niles, in 1828, our productive industry is estimated at 1,066,-000,000. Mr. E. Everett, in his speech of 1830, rates our national income at 1,000,000,000 dollars.

Take the lowest of these estimates; suppose our national capital to be only 10,000,000,000, and our productive industry only 600,000,000 a year, can we not pay off a Bank debt of 109,000,000 in ten years?

In every year, the increase of loanable capital in the country, must exceed the amount of Bank debt it would be necessary to pay. Private credit would take the place of Bank credit. If there should be a greater demand for capital on loan than could be supplied out of the savings of our own people, capital would flow in abundantly from Europe.

If the notes should be withdrawn gradually, in the manner here proposed, there is not a solvent Bank, nor a solvent individual, in the country, that could not sustain the operation. Such are the energies and the resources of the American people, that it would seem practicable to accomplish the work in half the time we have mentioned. The sooner it is accomplished, the sooner will we be delivered from the evils of our present condition. If, however, ten years be thought too short a time for the work of reform, let it be extended through twenty years or through thirty years. The longest of these is but a short period in the life time of a nation.

CHAPTER XXVI.

Of a New Coinage of Gold.

The money unit of the United States is the dollar, consisting of 416 grains of standard silver, or $371\frac{1}{4}$ grains of pure silver and $34\frac{3}{4}$ grains of alloy. All our contracts are to pay and receive dollars; all our accounts are kept in dollars. The dollar is thus our money of both account and contract, and its legal value is fixed by our having a coin of the same name, containing the quantity of pure silver and alloy which has just been mentioned.

Gold is, in the spirit of our laws, a subsidiary currency, its value being computed in silver dollars. At the United States Mint it is rated as fifteen to one—that is to say, one ounce of gold is considered as worth fifteen ounces of silver; or, what is the same thing, as many grains of pure gold as are equal to the number of grains of pure silver contained in a dollar, are coined into an eagle and a half eagle, and estimated at the mint as worth fifteen dollars.

The market rate of gold to silver, as determined by sales of gold bullion and silver bullion, in a series of years past, is about 15.8 to 1. Consequently, if the mint rate corresponded with the market rate, the quantity of pure gold contained in an eagle and a half eagle, ought to be estimated at the mint at about fifteen dollars and eighty cents.

The undervaluation of gold at the mint, is not the reason that it has disappeared from circulation. Eagles have disappeared for the same reason that dollars have disappeared. Whenever Bank notes are used, no more specie is retained in a country than is necessary for transactions of a smaller amount than the least denomination of paper, and is necessary for meeting the few stray notes that may be presented to the Banks for payment. It has been found impossible in England to make sovereigns and one pound notes circulate currently; and we all know that small notes in the United States have not only driven away gold coins, but also such silver coins as are of a higher denomination than a half dollar.

If Bank notes had never been introduced, eagles, half-eagles, and quarter-eagles would have continued in circulation, notwithstanding the undervaluation of gold at the mint. The eagle would not have been current at the rate of ten dollars; but at the rate of ten dollars and fifty cents, ten dollars and seventy-five cents—or whatever else it would have been worth. The calculation of the fraction would have been productive of some inconvenience; but the utility of gold coins, in large transactions, would have made them current at a rate probably a little above that which they have borne in the bullion market.

A new gold coinage is desirable ; but the proposition to coin eagles of a less weight than the eagles of former times, is not entirely free from objection. As all our contracts are to pay dollars, and as there is no gold at present in circulation, an issue of a new coin, called an eagle, which should be of the exact value of ten dollars, would cause no practical injustice. But the issue of a new coin of different weight from the old, and yet bearing the same name, might give countenance to the idea that money is something which owes its value to the authority of Government, and lead, perhaps, at some future time, to an alteration in the dollar—an alteration in our true standard of value.

The Eagle is the proper name of a coin which contains $247\frac{1}{2}$ grains of pure gold, or 270 grains of standard gold, of twenty-two carats fineness. A coin which would contain but 234.84 grains of pure gold, or 256.20 grains of standard gold, ought to be called by another name, and, to prevent all possibility of mistake, should have a different device. When the English ceased to coin pieces containing 118 58-89 grains of pure gold, and began to coin pieces containing 113 grains of pure gold, they did not call the new pieces by the same name as the old. But if the proposition which was laid before Congress, a year or two since, should be adopted, there will be a greater difference in the weight and value of our new half-eagles and our old half-eagles, than there is in those of English sovereigns and English guineas.

To attempt to fix by law what is not fixed by nature, is preposterous. Gold and silver vary in value when compared with one another, in the same manner as copper and iron vary. The variations in the relative value of the precious metals are, it is true, very small; but in different epochs of our history, 232, 234, 238, 247, 250, and 252 grains of pure gold may be worth ten silver dollars. If we should, through all such changes, pertinaciously insist on coining eagles, adapting the quantity of gold in them to the varying state of the bullion market, we should have a dozen different coins, each of a different weight, and yet all bearing the same name.

As there is little use for a gold coin so small as the quarter-eagle, and as we have imitated the Spaniards in our silver coinage, perhaps it would be judicious to imitate them in our gold coinage also, and issue American doubloons, half-doubloons, and quarter-doubloons, of the respective values of sixteen dollars, eight dollars, and four dollars. But, if pieces containing five and ten dollars' worth of gold be preferred, call the ten dollar piece, " the Republican," " the President," or by any name that may please the fancy, except that of " the Eagle." This is a name affixed, by long usage, to a piece containing neither more nor less than 270 grains of standard gold, and calling a piece containing a fewer number of grains by the same name, will certainly lead to confusion of ideas, and perhaps, at some future period, to practical injustice.

Whatever kind of new coins may be preferred, it will be proper to stamp on them the number of grains of pure gold and alloy that they may contain. Each new gold piece will then be a primer of political economy, and help in dissipating the erroneous ideas entertained respecting money.

It will be quite unnecessary to declare by law, that the new gold coins shall be a tender in payment of private debts. People who receive Bank notes at their *nominal* value, will not refuse gold at its *real* value.

To ascertain the quantity of gold it would be proper to put in the new pieces, nothing more is necessary than to strike an average of the price gold bullion has borne as compared with silver bullion, in the principal markets of the world, during the last ten years. The mint regulations of different countries, are of no further account than as they affect the value of gold and silver in the bullion market.

If, from some error in the data made the basis of the calculation, the gold in the new coins should happen to be rated a decimal fraction too low, so small an undervaluation will not cause the coins to be exported. Their utility as a circulating medium will keep them in circulation, the issue of five and ten dollar notes being prohibited.

If the gold should happen to be rated a decimal fraction to high, it will not, as some seem to fear, drive silver out of circulation. The necessity for silver coins in small payments will cause them to be retained in the country.

Should there be a greater error than a decimal fraction either too much or too little, in the valuation of gold, the new coin would continue to circulate, but at a small discount or a small premium, thus correcting the error of the mint valuation.

If one metal be made the standard and the legal tender, neither gold nor silver can be driven from circulation, except by paper, and paper cannot obtain currency except through the sanction or the connivance of government.

Gold is undervalued at the French mint, as well as at our own : but, according to Mr. Gallatin, " it is only during short and extraordinary periods, that the fluctuations have been so great, as that the gold coins did either fall to the par of silver coins, or rise to the premium of one per cent. During by far the greater period of forty-five years, the premium has fluctuated from one-fifth to one-half per cent.: so that the variations in the relative price of the two metals have, with the few exceptions above mentioned, been less than one-third per cent." From the result of experience in France, there is every reason to believe, with Mr. Gallatin, that " the fluctuation in the relative market price of gold and silver, issued under proper mint regulations, would be so small a quantity that it might be neglected."

To establish a system of sound currency and sound credit, it is not absolutely necessary to have a new gold coinage. Only let Bank notes be withdrawn, and eagles, half-eagles, and quarter-eagles, will come into circulation, and pass at their real value. But as four and eight, or five and ten dollar pieces, would be more convenient than pieces of the worth of five dollars and the indeterminate parts of a dollar, or ten dollars and the indeterminate parts of a dollar, a new gold coinage is desirable. It would be attended with injustice to no individual. No seignorage being charged at our mint, whatever quantity of gold bullion a man sent there, he would receive back the same amount in gold coin : and this coin he would pass in the market for whatever it might be worth.

CHAPTER XXVI.

Of the Fiscal Concerns of the Union.

In a report to the Senate, by the Committee of Finance, made March 29th, 1830, it is said—

" The Government receives its revenue from—

> 343 Custom Houses,
> 42 Land Offices,
> 8400 Post Offices,
> 134 Receivers of Internal Revenue.
> 37 Marshals,
> 33 Clerks of Courts.

" These, with other receiving officers which need not be specified, compose an aggregate of more than 9000 persons, dispersed through the whole of the Union, who collect the public revenue. From these persons the Government has, for the ten years preceding the 1st of January, 1830, received $230,068,855 17. This sum has been collected in every section of this widely extended country. It has been disbursed at other points, many thousand miles distant from the places where it was collected ; and yet it has been so collected and distributed, without the loss, as far as the Committee can learn, of a single dollar."

The most difficult point in the business of finance, is to get *possession* of money. If this point is attained, the safe-keeping of the money, the transferring of it from one part of the country to another, and the paying it away, are easy undertakings.

If " not a dollar has been lost," it has not been because the present system contains any extraordinary guards against malversation. The collectors at our custom-houses have the whole amount of money received by them under their entire control, till it is, at stated times, transferred to the credit of the Treasury Department. Under a different system, all the public officers at each particular point might be made checks on one another.

With a sub-treasury office in each State, the safe-keeping and disbursing of the public funds could be effected without any difficulty ; and the expense of each sub-treasury office need not exceed ten thousand dollars per annum.

If it were necessary occasionally to carry silver from one part of the country to another, the Government could do it as easily and cheaply as individuals. The whole amount it would be necessary to transport, would not probably exceed four or five millions a year, nor the cost go beyond one per cent. As the principal part of the United States' revenue is collected in those sections of the country which have usually the rate of exchange in their favor, what the Government would gain by the sale of bills of exchange in the West and South, on Boston, New York, Philadelphia, and Baltimore, would probably exceed what it would be forced to pay for the transportation of specie.

There is no novelty in this. It is the system of all policed nations except our own. In England, the Bank is merely auxiliary to the Exchequer and the Treasury. The revenue collected at Liverpool, is, or was a few years since, remitted to London through the agency of a private Banker.

To incorporate a Bank with a capital of ten millions or of thirty-five millions, to endow that corporation with privileges which individuals do not possess, and to make its paper receivable in payment of dues to Government, is a measure so wide from the proposed end, that it cannot be considered " as necessary and proper," or, if the phrase be preferred, " as natural and appropriate." It is difficult to believe that it would have been even so much as *thought of*, if the measure had not in itself been calculated to promote certain *private interests*. The natural and appropriate way of keeping the public funds, is in the Treasury and in sub-treasury offices. The natural and appropriate way of transferring them from point to point, is by bills of exchange, and the occasional transportation of specie.

Neither is the establishment of a United States paper-money incorporated Bank, the " necessary and proper," or " natural and appropriate" way of correcting the evils occasioned by the State Banks. A National Bank, resting on the same principles as the State Banks, must produce similar evils. It must " contract" and " expand" as well as they.

If Congress should, from excessive caution, or some less

commendable motive, delay the passage of the necessary laws for prohibiting the issue of Bank notes, the "necessary and proper" or "natural and appropriate" way of regulating the State Banks, would be by declaring that nothing but gold and silver should be received in payment of dues to the Government. The State Banks would then be obliged to provide a sufficient fund of specie to meet the demands of the merchants having payments to make to Government. This would force them to diminish the amount of notes in circulation. The Government receiving and paying nothing but gold and silver, the people generally would begin to distinguish between paper and specie—between cash and credit. Simple as the measure is, it would double the amount of metallic money in the country, and prevent, in a great degree, fluctuations of currency, and oscillations of credit, by taking away one of the chief causes of the instability of Bank medium.

The establishing of a paper-money incorporated Bank, is not the "necessary and proper" or "natural and appropriate" way of enabling Government to borrow when borrowing is advisable. A Bank may, when instituted, lend to Government its whole capital, or so much, at least, as is not required for supporting its credit and circulation : but it is not often that it can, after it has been sometime in operation, make any great loan to Government, without either curtailing mercantile accommodations, or issuing an excess of paper. Nearly all the *great* " expansions" and " contractions" that have occurred in both England and the United States, can be traced to attempts to convert Banks into fiscal machines. If the operations of Government could be *completely* separated from those of the Banks, the system would be shorn of half its evils. If Government would neither deposit the public funds in the Banks, nor borrow money from the Banks ; and if it would in no case either receive Bank notes or pay away Bank notes, the Banks would become mere commercial institutions, and their credit and their power be brought nearer to a level with those of private merchants.

The " necessary and proper" or " natural and appropriate" way of placing the financial concerns of the country on such a basis as will enable us to provide for all exigencies, is to make gold and silver coins the exclusive money of the country. We shall then be prepared for either peace or war.

To depend on the Banks in time of war, after the experience of both England and the United States, would be the height of infatuation. The impression produced on the minds of men by the suspension of specie payments, is so fresh, that, on a new declaration of war, it is probable great part of the deposits would be withdrawn. If the Banks should escape this evil, the landing of a hostile force of but a few thousand men on any part of the coast, would create " a run" which would compel most of them to suspend payment. If Government should, to forward its financial schemes, sanction or connive at a suspension of specie payments, it would be instrumental in producing such evils as we have suffered in past years.

A war imposes on Government the necessity of expending the greater portion of its revenues in a section of country distant from that in which it collects it. The payment of the war taxes of a single year, would deprive great part of the Union of its specie. The sources of foreign supply would be cut off, and much of the specie which flowed from the interior to the frontiers, would be exported. It would not return in sufficient quantities, or sufficiently early to meet the wants of either the people or the Government.

A vigorous war of but two years continuance, in which our foreign commerce would be interrupted, must produce one of two results. It must either compel the Banks to suspend specie payments, and thus produce evils which no pen can adequately describe ; or else force them to curtail mercantile accommodations, and thus spread ruin through the community. To sustain the credit of Bank medium, it would be necessary to reduce it to one-third or one-fourth of its present amount : and as it would be impossible in a state of war, immediately to obtain a sufficient supply of gold and silver coin, the Government and the people would suffer all the evils of an insufficient circulating medium.

We have profited in some respects by the experience of the last war. We have built ships, constructed fortifications, and collected military stores. But " money is the sinews of war." And it must be real money. Paper money will not then answer. It is not necessary that the real money should be in the coffers of Government. It is enough that it is in the pockets of the people.

Let Bank notes be withdrawn, and such an accumulation of gold and silver coin will be made by individuals, that in no possible exigency will there be a real scarcity of money. This is evident from the condition of certain countries in which paper money is unknown. In Flanders, for example, every farmer has a little purse of gold or silver—small in proportion to his property, but making the aggregate throughout the country very considerable. Nothing is lost by this practice. It is impossible to keep the whole wealth of a country in constant circulation. If a man's whole stock consists of but two suits of clothes, he cannot wear them both at the same time. It is of little moment, as regards individuals, whether their reserved stock be in money or in those things which money can procure. In a national point of view nothing is lost by this custom. It ensures the punctual performance of contracts. No man has to call twice on a farmer in Flanders, for the payment of a debt. Whatever may be the vicissitudes of war or of commerce, there is never in that country a scarcity of the tool of all trades.

We have that amount of metallic money in the United States which is barely sufficient, in the most favorable state of things, for daily exchanges, and which would not answer even in the most favorable state of things, if we had not various modes of barter, and different credit contrivances. As much time is lost every year, in " dunning for debts," as would, if properly employed, purchase some millions of metallic medium. Let the natural order of things be restored, and a sufficiency of metallic money will be collected, to enable the country to bear transitions from peace to war, and to answer all the demands of commerce, both ordinary and extraordinary. As it is the custom of all prudent families in rural districts, to have on hand a greater quantity of flour and other necessaries, than is required for the use of the twenty-four hours, so it will become the custom for each prudent family to have a little money in reserve. Out of this stock, the war taxes will be paid, and before the original stock is completely exhausted, a portion of it will come back to them in the regular course of trade.

Few people are more able than those of the United States to contribute what is necessary for the defence of their country. Few people—if we had a proper money system, would be more willing. Ask the farmer, if, in a war undertaken in a just and righteous cause, he would not be willing to contribute a certain number of bushels of wheat, to vindicate the honor of the nation or secure its safety. Ask the shoemaker, if he would not be willing to contribute a certain number of pairs of shoes. Ask the day laborer, if he would not be willing, in such a contingency, to labor a certain number of days on the fortifications. Now, what a nation actually consumes in the course of a war, is labor and the products of labor : but the taxes cannot be conveniently collected in kind, and to collect them in money is impossible, for the people have it not to give.

Let those obstacles be removed which prevent our acquiring such a stock of metallic money as is adapted to varying exigencies, and in times of hostilities, neither productive industry nor commercial credit will be affected more than is necessary by the incidents of war. In this condition of things, the Government could easily raise considerable sums by taxation. If it chose to borrow, the negotiation of its loans would not, as in the last war, derange the whole train of mercantile operations. Simply by collecting taxes enough to pay the annual interest, it could borrow to any desirable extent. If the loanable capital of our own country were not sufficient to meet its wants, it would have the market of the world from which to supply the deficiency.

But, let the present system continue, and, in a state of war, the Government must get into financial embarrassments, in attempting to extricate itself from which it will, as in the last war, involve thousands in ruin.

CHAPTER XXVIII.

Of Banking on Proper Principles.

There is nothing novel in the modern system of Banking, except its being carried on by corporations and by the instrumentality of paper money.

Private Bankers were known to the Greeks, the Romans and the Jews. At Rome, especially, they appear to have been very numerous, and to have done an extensive business. The shops round the Great Forum were chiefly occupied by them, and we may learn from Cicero and other ancient authors, that the Romans commonly paid money by their intervention. A Roman would sometimes give an order, or, as we should say, draw a check on his Banker : but the usual way of managing pecuniary transactions, was by writing their names in the Banker's books.*

Previous to the establishment of the Bank of England, the goldsmiths of London performed most of the functions of Bankers. To those who deposited money with them, they sometimes allowed six per cent. interest, but the usual rate did not exceed four per cent.

In Virginia, as is stated by a writer in the Richmond Enquirer, the merchants formerly acted as Bankers to the planters. Governor Wolcot, in his Message to the Legislature of Connecticut, in May 1826, says that "private Banks existed in this country before and a short time subsequent to the Revolutionary War."

As a country advances in wealth and population, the business of dealing in money naturally becomes a distinct profession. It is a business which requires no laws for its special encouragement : no charters to cause it to be conducted to the public advantage. The trade in money is as simple in its nature as the trade in flour or the trade in tobacco, and ought to be conducted on the same principles.

Restore the natural order of things, by abolishing money corporations, and, in those parts of the country where there is little population, little wealth, and little commerce, there will be little Banking : while in those parts of the

* " In foro, et de mensæ scriptura, magis quam ex arca domoque, vel cista pecunia numerabatur."—*Terrence.*

country where commerce is extensively carried on, Bankers will rise up in proportion to the wants of the community.

In most villages, all the call there is for Bankers could be answered by the Postmasters. Offices of deposit, of transfer, and of loan, are not necessary in villages. The only call there for a dealer in money, is to collect debts due to persons at a distance, and transmit the money to to whom it is due. The publishers of periodicals now collect great part of what is owing to them on account of subscriptions through the medium of the Postmasters. Many of the debts due to merchants might be convenient-ly collected in the same way, if Government were careful to appoint none but solvent and trust-worthy persons to be Postmasters: and if it should make a rule to remove them on proof being given of their having neglected to pay over money which they had collected.

But it would not be necessary for Government to go even this far, for us to have a good Banking system. The Postmaster, in most small towns, would stand the best chance of becoming collector of debts for persons at a dis-tance, and the commissions he would receive would, in many cases, exceed the amount paid to him as a public officer: but if he was found untrustworthy, or incapable, the business would be transferred to the storekeeper, or some other respectable inhabitant of the village.

In the larger towns, and even in the small towns which are centres of wealthy districts, the business of dealing in ex-changes, and of acting as an agent between lenders and borrowers, would become a distinct profession.

In each city the number of Bankers would be in pro-portion to the amount of business to be done, and their capital in proportion to the trade of the city. A merchant of Philadelphia who wished a note discounted, would, in-stead of having his choice among a dozen corporations, have his choice among perhaps twice that number of pri-vate Bankers. Instead of being obliged to approach the supercilious Director of some overgrown monied institu-tion, he would deal with a private trader, to whom it would be of as much importance to lend as it would be to himself to borrow. The extent of business these private Bankers would do, would depend, in a degree, on the disposition they showed to accommodate their customers. The competition amongst them would be so lively, that, after the manner of the Bankers of Europe, they would allow a credit on deposits. Being responsible in the whole amount of their private fortunes, they would seldom extend their loans so far as to cherish the wild spirit of speculation. Their whole fortunes would be in the business, and their whole faculties exerted for its proper management, and it is in this way only that *any* business can be well conducted.

If there should be a necessity for placing any restrictions on these private Bankers, it would be simply that of restraining them from issuing notes, bills, or checks, which would circulate in the same way as the present Bank notes. Some intelligent men who have turned their attention to the subject, think that even this would not be necessary. They are of opinion that the competition among private Bankers would be so brisk, that they would effectually check one another.

In opposition to this it may be urged, that much has been lost by the breaking of private Bankers in England ; though it must be admitted, this is not a case exactly in point, since the private Bankers of England are influenced in their operations, though not regulated, by the great corporate institution of that kingdom.

In Scotland, where the private Banks have the predominance, little has been lost by the breaking of these institutions. But, the evils produced by the occasional breaking of a Bank, are far from being the greatest evils of the system. No instance has occurred of a Bank breaking in Philadelphia, and yet who can adequately describe all that the people of this city have endured from Banking. We have satisfactory evidence that the Scotch Banks, by their " expansions" and " contractions," produce evils, the same in kind, though not in degree, as are felt in Philadelphia.

But in neither England nor Scotland, can we, perhaps, be said to have a fair example of private Banking, as the Government receives Bank notes in payment of taxes. When the Government receives one kind of paper, the people lose their clear perception of the difference between cash and credit, and where room is made in this way for the circulation of paper, the most worthless kind sometimes obtains circulation as easily as the best. " Numberless instances," says the Edinburg Review, " have occurred in the history of British Banking, within the last few years, in which the notes of individuals without any real capital, and who were from the beginning in a state of insolvency, have continued to circulate for a long period in company with the notes of the best established houses, and to enjoy an equal degree of credit."

The private Bankers on the continent of Europe do not circulate any paper, but it is not in our power to say, whether this is, in all instances, owing to obstacles thrown in their way by Government, or to the indisposition of the people to receive paper where it is not taken in payment of taxes.

If notes issued by private Bankers should circulate as the notes of the present corporations, they would become money. As a credit money, they would necessarily fluctuate in quantity. It is not desirable that, in addition to changes in the state of credit, proceeding from great natural or political causes, we should have changes in the currency, to add to the uncertainty of trade.*

If these notes produced no other evil, they would prevent us from accumulating that stock of metallic money, which is required for the varying exigencies of peace and war. After this had been for a time in circulation, the receiving of them would be, as in the case of the present Bank notes, a matter of necessity rather than of choice.

The evil would, indeed, in time, correct itself; but if we can prevent it, why suffer it at all ?†

* " Hitherto," says Tooke, " the Legislature has restricted individuals, under the severest penalties, from establishing private mints, and uttering metallic money of intrinsic and discreditable value ; yet, with a degree of inconsistency which strikes us as most extraordinary the more attentively we consider it, our law-makers have permitted individuals to establish private Banks of circulation—and to utter paper money, possessed of only a conventional value, which *a breath of panic may at any time destroy.* On the same principle that the Government protects the public against the probable insecurity which might arise from individuals being permitted to utter metallic currency, it should guard against the more probable, nay *certain insecurity* which is created when individuals utter a paper currency. In every civilized country, supplying and regulating the circulating medium is a function of the sovereign prerogative.

† What is here advanced is not at variance with the principles of Adam Smith, as will be seen by the following extract from his writings:
" To restrain private people, it may be said, from receiving in pay-

We can certainly carry the credit system far enough, by the agency of leger entries, notes of hand, bills of exchange, and bonds and mortgages. We do not require the additional aid of credit money, to run us deeper in debt.

Why should a private Banker, having a capital of his own of five hundred thousand or a million dollars, and deriving therefrom an income of thirty thousand or of sixty thousand per annum, desire to double his income, by the circulation of paper money? He would make a legitimate use of his credit, in receiving money on deposit, at five per cent., and lending it again at six per cent. More than this he ought not to desire.*

If the capital of a private Banker is small, he will derive as much profit from his credit as he is justly entitled to, in his commission on bills of exchange, and in the difference between the rate he will pay for money taken by him on deposit, and that at which he will lend this money to others. The issue of notes by Bankers, for the convenient discharge of their own business, will not be necessary. The private Bankers of London and Lancashire issue no notes. At the clearing-house in London, in which their accounts

ment the promissory notes of a Banker for any sum, whether great or small, when they themselves are willing to receive them; or, to restrain a Banker from issuing such notes, when all his neighbors are willing to accept them, is a manifest violation of that natural liberty which it is the proper business of law not to infringe but to support. Such regulations may, no doubt, be considered as in some respect a violation of natural liberty. But those exertions of the natural liberty of a few individuals, which might endanger the security of the whole society, are, and ought to be, restrained by the laws of all governments: of the most free, as well as of the most despotical. The obligation of building party walls, in order to prevent the communication of fire, is a violation of natural liberty, exactly of the same kind with the regulations of the banking trade which are here proposed."

The proposal Adam Smith here supports, is that of prohibiting private Bankers from issuing notes of a less denomination than five pounds sterling, nearly *twenty-five dollars* Federal money. On the principles on which he proposes to prohibit the issue of notes of some denominations, the issue of notes of all denominations may be prohibited.

* " There is no more reason why a man, or body of men, should be permitted to demand of the public, interest for their reputation of being rich, than there would be in permitting a man to demand interest for the reputation of being wise, learned, or brave. If a man is actually rich, it is enough for him to receive interest for his money, and rent for his land, without receiving interest for his credit also."—*Raymond.*

are daily settled by an exchange of checks, transactions to the amount of four or five millions sterling are adjusted with the help of about two hundred thousand pounds in money.

If arrangements of this kind were not found to answer the desired end, a public Office of Transfer and Deposit might be established in each city, on the model of the Bank of Hamburg, with the exception of buying and selling bullion and dealing in exchange, which ought to be left to private Bankers. The establishing of such an Office would be attended with a little expense, but if it would not be worth paying for, it would not be worth having. If the Bankers objected to paying all the expense, the Government might, as such an office would be a safe and convenient depository of the public funds, share the expense with them. There is nothing in the constitution to prevent the establishment of public Banks, which shall be mere Offices of Deposit and Transfer. And as such Banks would be a great public benefit, the defraying of their necessary expenses out of the public revenue would not be objectionable.

In this way, we should secure all the advantages the present system affords, and avoid all its disadvantages.

We should have places of deposit safer than the present; for the money deposited in a public Bank by one man would not be lent to another.

The business of settling accounts by transfers of credit, would be greatly facilitated. One public Bank would suffice for each city, and the time which is now lost in running from Bank to Bank, would be saved.

The private Banks, paying interest on deposits, would extend throughout the country the advantages of Saving Banks.

Men who wished to borrow, would deal with a private Banker as an equal, instead of dealing, as at present, with an overgrown corporation, as a superior.

The business of dealing in exchange, would be better conducted than at present, for it would be left free to individuals, and they would show the same disposition to oblige and to give satisfaction, that is now evinced by the dry goods merchant, or the importer of groceries.

Instead of having to pay the expense of three or four

hundred public Banks, we should have to pay the expense of only twenty or thirty, for this number of offices of deposit and transfer would suffice for the whole United States. We should escape all the evils that flow from Banks as corporations, from fluctuations of the circulating medium, and from the false system of credit which has its origin in the present banking system.

And what should we lose? The supporters of the present system admit that " the only substantial advantage attending paper money appears to be its cheapness." Taking their own estimates of the amount of Bank notes and Bank credits, the sum thus gained does not amount to more than forty cents a year for each individual in the nation. Is it worth while for so trifling a gain, (admitting it, by way of argument, to be a gain,) to endure all the evils of a bad system, and forego all the advantages of a good?

CHAPTER XXIX.

Probable Consequences of the Continuance of the Present System.

To infer that because a system produces great evil, it must soon give way, would be to argue in opposition to all experience. If mere suffering could produce reformation, there would be little misery in the world.

Too many individuals have an interest in incorporated paper money Banks, to suffer the truth in relation to such institutions to have free progress. Too many prejudices remain in the minds of a multitude who have no such interest, to permit the truth to have its proper effect.

It is, therefore, rational to conclude that the present system may, at least with modifications, continue to be the system of the country—not for ever, as some seem to think, but for a period which cannot be definitely calculated. It is also rational to conclude that the effect it will have on society in time to come, will be similar to the effect it has had in time past. We have, then, in the present state of the country, the means of judging of its future condition.

No system of policy that can be devised, can prevent

the United States from advancing in wealth and population. Our national prosperity has its seat in natural causes
which cannot be effectually counteracted by any human
measures, excepting such as would convert the Government into a despotism like that of Turkey, or reduce the
nation to a state of anarchy resembling that of some countries of South America.

Our wealth and population will increase till they become
equal for each square mile to the wealth and population of
the continent of Europe.

We are now very far from this limit. Under a good
system, we cannot reach it in less than one or two hundred years. Under a bad system, in not less, perhaps, than
three or four hundred.

If we had a political system as bad as that of Great Britain, with its hereditary aristocracy, its laws of entail and
primogeniture, its manufacturing guilds, its incorporated
commercial companies, its large standing army, its expensive navy, its church establishment, its boroughmongering,
its pensions and its sinecures, our advancement would be
seriously retarded. But our wealth and population would,
notwithstanding, continue to increase, till they should bear
the same ratio to the natural resources of the country, that
the wealth and population of Great Britain have to the
natural resources of that island.

The progress of opulence in the United States in the
next forty or fifty years, will probably be very great. Many
of the natural sources of wealth are as yet unappropriated.
In no part of the country has their productiveness been
fully developed. The people have now sufficient capital to
turn their land and labor to more profit than was possible
in any previous period of our country's history.

The daily improvements in productive machinery, and
especially in the application of steam power, the discove-
ries in science, the introduction of new composts and new
courses of crops in agriculture, the extension of roads and
canals, have all a tendency to increase the wealth of the
country, till the aggregate shall be enormous.

But this increase of wealth will be principally for the
benefit of those to whom an increase of riches will bring
no increase of happiness, for they have already wealth
enough or more than enough. Their originally small capi-

tals have, in the course of a few years, been doubled, trebled, and, in some instances, quadrupled. They have now large capitals, which will go on increasing in nearly the same ratio.

As no kind of property is prevented from being the prize of speculation by laws of entail, it is not easy to set bounds to the riches which some of our citizens may acquire. Their incomes may be equal to those of the most wealthy of the European nobility. Think, for a moment, of the immense accession of wealth certain families in the neighborhood of large cities and other improving towns must receive, from the conversion of tracts of many acres into building lots. For ground which cost them but one hundred dollars an acre, they may get ten thousand dollars, twenty thousand dollars, or twenty-five thousand dollars. This will be without any labor or expenditure of capital on their part. The land will be increased in value, by the improvements made around it at the expense of other men.

But this is but one of the ways in which the wealth of the rich will increase. It has heretofore been found that capital invested in lots, even in the neighborhood of the most flourishing towns, doubles itself less rapidly than capital devoted to other purposes of speculation. In whatever way it may be employed the capital of the rich will, in the aggregate, increase in nearly the ratio of compound interest.

The vicissitudes of fortune will be, as they have been in past years, many and great, but they will tend to increase the inequality of social condition, by throwing the wealth of several rich men into the hands of one. It is seldom that the vicissitudes of fortune distribute the wealth of a few among the many.

An increase in the number of Banks must be expected. If the system is to be *perpetual*, an increase in the number of these insititutions would not, in some respects, be an evil; for seven hundred Banks could circulate no more paper than three hundred and fifty. But every new Bank is a new centre of speculation; and one kind of stock-jobbing gives birth to another. We shall have new schemes for growing rich without labor—similar perhaps to the Briitsh bubble companies of 1825—perhaps to the former speculations in Washington City lots—perhaps to the recent speculations in Pennsylvania coal lands. The present rage for rail-road stock shows that part of our population already want something to be crazy about—or rather want something by which to set their neighbors crazy. The old modes of speculation no longer afford full employment for their time and talents.

Nearly all the secondary operations of society will tend to increase the disparity between the rich and poor as different classes of the community, and not a small proportion of the rich will, in due time, become as luxurious and as corrupt, as ostentatious and as supercilious, as the "first circles" in the most dissipated capitals of Europe.

Their early habits of industry and economy cleave to some of the rich men of the present day. Hence they are as useful and, as modest members of society as many who are in moderate circumstances. But when their immense wealth passes, as pass it must in a few years, to their heirs, who know not the value of money, because they never knew the want of it, it will be lavished in every way which corrupt inclination can dictate.

While some will be enormously rich, there will be a considerable number in a state of comfort, as in Great Britain, and very many in a state of disconsolate poverty. Some years must, indeed, elapse, before the number of paupers and criminals, and of persons whose condition borders on pauperism, will bear the same proportion to population in Europe and America. In our immense extent of uncultivated land, the poor have a place to fly to ; but the spirit of speculation will follow them there. We need not wait till the country is fully peopled to experience a measure of these evils. While some parts of the Union will have all the simplicity, the rudeness, and the poverty of new settlements; others will exhibit all the splendor and licentiousness, and misery and debasement of the most populous districts of Europe.

The beginning of this state of things is already observable. According to the estimates of Mr. Niles, the number of paupers in the maratime counties of the United States, was, in 1815, in the proportion of one to every 130 inhabitants ; and, in 1821, in the proportion of two to every 130.

The published accounts do not give the number of *persons* admitted into the almshouses or committed to the prisons of Philadelphia, in the course of the year ; but the number of *commitments* of criminals and vagrants amounts to three or four thousand annually, and the number of *admissions* into the alms-house is equally considerable. As the same person may be *admitted* or *committed* several times, we cannot give the exact number of either paupers or criminals. But at one time last winter, there were upwards of sixteen hundred poor persons in the Spruce Street Alms-house ; and many more were receiving outdoor relief.*

In some years the public expenditures on account of the poor in Philadelphia, exceed the expenditures on the same account in Liverpool.

Some of the members of a Commission appointed about twelve years ago to inquire into the causes and extent of pauperism in Philadelphia, estimated the cost of relieving the poor at between four hundred and five hundred thousand dollars a year. In this estimate was included what is given in private charity, as well as what is given in public : and an allowance was made for rent of almshouses and hospitals, or for interest on the first cost of land and buildings set apart for the use of the poor. At that time the population of the city and suburbs did not much exceed one hundred and twenty thousand.

We may increase the legal provision for the relief of the indigent, and multiply alms-houses and hospitals. But nothing of this kind can supply the want of just laws and of equal institutions.

Efforts may be made in various ways to diffuse the blessings of education, and to promote moral and religious improvement. But these efforts will only alleviate our social evils : They cannot cure them.

In no small degree will the public distress be increased by well-meant but ill-directed attempts to give relief. There is a class of politicians, (and they are unfortunately numerous and powerful,) who have for each particular social evil a legal remedy. They are willing to leave nothing to nature : the law must do every thing.

This is, most unfortunately, the kind of legislation which

* Part of this pauperism and criminality must be attributed to European institutions, as the character of the subjects was formed before they migrated to America. Another part is of domestic origin.

public distress is almost sure to produce. Instead of tracing its cause to some *positive* institution, the removal of which, though it might not immediately relieve distress, would prevent its recurrence, men set themselves to heaping law upon law, and institution upon institution. They in this resemble quacks who apply lotions to the skin to cure diseases of the blood, or of the digestive organs, occasioned by intemperate living.

These projects of relief and efforts at corrective legislation, will be numberless in multitude and diversified in character : but as they will not proceed on the principle of " removing the cause that the effect may cease," they will ultimately increase the evils they are intended to cure.

CHAPTER XXX.

Probable Effects of the Establishment of a System of Sound Currency and Sound Credit.

The laws which govern the moral world are just as certain in their nature as those which govern the physical : but it is not always easy to fortell the effects of a political measure, because it is not easy to foresee the precise combination of causes that will be in operation at any future period. David Hume reasoned with perfect correctness from the permises before him, when he predicted that an increase of the national debt beyond a certain amount would make the British Government bankrupt. But he did not foresee the great increase of wealth, and consequent increase of ability in the people to bear public burdens, which has been caused by the use of steam and of productive machinery ; and the Government has swelled the debt beyond the amount he fixed upon, without becoming bankrupt.

As we have neither a large standing army nor an expensive navy, neither King nor titled nobility to support, neither sinecurists nor pensioners to pay, it would seem rational to believe that, on the destruction of the monied corporation system, honest industry in the United States would be secure of its reward. But it is, perhaps, too soon to assert that the ingenuity of those who wish to grow rich by the labor of others will then be exhausted. The Banking system destroyed, they may invent some other, equally plausible and equally pernicious.

There has been at least an *apparent* improvement in the moral sentiments of men. About three centuries ago, it was customary to insert in the treaties between Christian Kings, a stipulation that the subjects of one King should not plunder the subjects of another, on the high seas, in time of peace—in other words, it was made matter of express covenant that merchants should not be pirates. At a much later period, many Scottish gentlemen thought it quite as honorable and as honest to levy " black mail " on the estates of their neighbors, as to levy rents on their own estates.

Some intelligent writers seem to be of opinion, that the improvement in moral sentiment is rather apparent than real. There is, they assert, so much less personal risk in certain modern modes of acquiring wealth, that men can lay little claim to merit because they do not carry off their neighbors' cattle by force of arms, or rob ships on the high seas. Lord Byron appears to have been of this way of thinking, for he said that " if the funds failed, *he* meant to take to the high-way, as he considered that the only honorable mode of making a living, now left for honest men."

> " For why ?
> The good old rule sufficeth still,
> The simple plan—
> That they shall take who have the power,
> And they shall keep who can."

" Many ingenious men" says an American author, " have amused themselves and others, in forming theories respecting the social compact. Some supposed it to originate in one way, some in another. Some supposed it to have been formed for one purpose, some for another. It is supposed by some to have been formed for defence—others suppose it to have been formed for aggression. It is true, that every thing on this subject is mere speculation; and one man has as much right to form theories as another, but it is very clear, that aggression must precede defence, and that before communities could have been formed for defence, there must have been others formed for aggression. Had there been no such thing as attack, men would never have thought of defence. The primary object, therefore, in forming the *social compact*, must have been plunder; and the first article of that compact no doubt was, " *we will plunder our neighbors.*" The second article probably was, " *we will not plunder each other.*" This article was necessary to enable them to carry the first into effect.

" The first article in the social compact has been faithfully executed, as far as it was practicable. The second article has been and still is evaded, or forcibly violated, by a large portion of every community. How many people do we see in every community, who, instead of supporting themselves by their own industry, contrive to supply themselves with the necessaries and comforts of life, from the industry of others? Some do this by fraud and overreaching. Some by direct violence—some by the exercise of their wits in one way, some in another. Some by the permission, or the express provision, of the law—others in violation of it. What a host would there be, if all the people in the United States even, who live by the labor of others, were collected together.

" The history of mankind, in all ages of the world, shows that they will never labor for subsistence, so long as they can obtain it by plunder—that they will never labor for themselves, so long as they can compel others to labor for them."*

This is a gloomy view of things: and we cannot say that we assent to its correctness in every particular. We trust there has been, in the last three centuries, some *real* improvement in the minds of men. Yet history and experience both show that there is a strong principle of evil which shows itself in different forms in different men, and which changes its appearance in communities with change of circumstances.

As this principle is found in Americans as well as in Europeans and Asiatics, we may rest assured, that, if the money corporation system shall be abolished, attempts will be made, under the plausible pretext of promoting the public good, to have other laws passed, and other institutions established, which will give to some members of the community advantages over the rest. The attempts of this

* Raymond. Elements of Political Economy. Baltimore 1823.

kind will probably be numerous, for even those who apparently pay most regard to the principles of natural justice, think themselves fairly entitled to such advantages as the law gives them, and deem it quite proper to endeavor to advance their private speculations by procuring legislative enactments in their especial favor. If these attempts shall be successfully resisted, we may rationally expect—being delivered from the curse of paper money and of monied corporations—a considerable improvement, in the following particulars.

1. The demand for most articles of commerce and manufactures will become regular, and the supply will conform itself to the demand, the variations being seldom so sudden or so great as to prevent men of good common sense from managing their business successfully. At present, men find it difficult to make the operation of the natural causes that affect supply and demand the basis of an estimate, in engaging in any enterprize, because these causes are confounded with others growing out of the present system of business.

2. Bankruptcies will be as rare as they were before the Revolution, and losses by bad debts will be inconsiderable. More or less uncertainty will always attend foreign commerce. Events which may happen abroad may, from time to time, have an injurious effect on bodies of merchants engaged in a trade with particular countries: but, as is correctly observed by Mr. Gallatin, the effects of commercial revulsions in a country having a metallic currency, are generally confined to dealers, extending but indirectly and feebly to the community, and never affecting the currency, the standard of value, or the contracts between persons not concerned in the failures.

3. The value of that which forms the principal item of wealth in every country, the land and its improvements, is affected slowly by natural causes. It seldom rises or falls, except in particular situations, more than one or two per cent. in the course of a year. Such variations would not be great enough to prevent the majority of men from forming correct estimates of the value of real estate: and as there would be a continuous rise in the value of land, with the increase of wealth and population, sellers would be quite secure in receiving one-fourth of the purchase money

and a mortgage for the remainder, and buyers would run little risk of losing, from a fall in the price of property. The special causes which would affect the value of lands in particular localities, might be estimated with some degree of exactness.

4. The prices of land and commodities being left to the regulation of natural causes, it would, in most instances, be easy to form a judgment of the probable result of different undertakings. The risk, in the great majority of enterprizes, would not be greater than that of the farmer when he ploughs and sows his fields. It would be easy to tell what businesses are adapted to the state of the country, and to different parts of the country. The developement of the natural sources of wealth would proceed in natural order, and men would grow rich, not by impoverishing others, but by the same causes that enrich nations.

5. Credit would be diffused through the community, and each man would get that share to which he would be justly entitled. The thrifty young mechanic, and the industrious farmer, though not possessed of real estate, would be able to borrow on bond, for such periods as might be necessary to bring their little undertakings to a successful issue.

6. Every increase of capital increasing the fund out of which wages would be paid, would increase the reward of the laborer. Through the new distribution of capital which would be produced by a just apportionment of credit, the number of the competitors of the working-man would be diminished, and the number of his employers increased. He would thus reap a double advantage, from the increase of competition on the one side, and its decrease on the other.

7. The present order of things, by rendering the condition of some members of society almost hopeless, takes away from them almost every inducement to industry and economy. They labor only from the stimulus of necessity; and if, in particular seasons, they obtain more than is necessary for immediate subsistence, they expend it in procuring some sensual gratification. But, open to these men a fair prospect of acquiring a little property and of being secure in its possession, and many who are now indolent

will become industrious, and many who are extravagant will become economical. Give them an object worth working and saving for, and but few, even of those who are least gifted with natural prudence, will become a burden to their friends, or to the public.

8. The moral character of a great part of the nation has been stamped so deeply by causes which have been in operation for half a century, or for nearly a century and a half, if we count from the first issue of paper money by Massachusetts, that many years perhaps, will, elapse, before it can be essentially changed. But one of the first effects of abolishing the money-corporation system, will be that of raising the standard of commercial honesty in a perceptible degree, and the standard of political honor will, in a few years, be sensibly elevated.

9. In a state of things in which industry was sure of its reward, few persons would be destitute of the pecuniary means for obtaining instruction. The intellectual powers of the great body of the people would then be fully developed, and this could not fail to promote the correct management of public and private affairs.

10. The causes of evil are as numerous as the varieties of evil. The Banking system must be regarded as the *principal* cause of social evil in the United States; but it is by no means the *only* one. There are other positive institutions in our land which are very pernicious. Remove the Banking system, and the extent in which most other evil institutions operate, will become evident. The application of the proper remedies will then be an easy task.

In the best social system that can be imagined, that is, in one in which there should be no laws or institutions of any kind except such as are absolutely necessary, and in which the few laws and institutions which are really necessary should be perfectly just in principle and equal in operation, there would necessarily be an inequality in the condition of men. It would proceed in part from differences in mental and bodily strength, in skill, in industry, in economy, in prudence, and in enterprize. In part, it would proceed from causes beyond human control. But this would be a *natural* inequality, and it would not be an evil. The sight of one man enjoying the reward of his good conduct, would induce others to imitate his example.

We have evidence in the condition of Switzerland and Holland, of what patient industry can accomplish. One of these countries is mountainous and rugged; the other is a marsh, great portion of which has been reclaimed from the sea. Yet they are, in proportion to the number of square miles they contain, among the richest countries in the world.

In Switzerland there are, or were till lately, many absurd restrictions on the liberty of the people. The national debt of Holland is very great, and the taxes are consequently heavy. Switzerland is an inland country, and has intercourse with distant nations, through the permission of the neighboring kingdoms. It owes its independence to the sufferance of its powerful neighbors. Holland is frequently devastated by hostile armies. It is not free from commercial monopolies. In both Holland and Switzerland there is an inequality of political rights quite incompatible with our American ideas of natural justice. Yet, under all these disadvantages, natural and political, Holland and Switzerland have arrived at a degree of improvement whcih excites the admiration of every candid observer.

Now, if the Union of the States can be preserved, to what may we not rise, under our free political institutions, with the immense extent of our natural resources, with all our advantages for foreign and domestic trade, and exempted as we are by our situation from a participation in the wars of Europe.

It would really appear that, if we could only get rid of a few laws and institutions which give advantages to some men over others, we might arrive at a state of improvement which would surpass that of any country of which mention is made in history. We have more means of happiness within our reach, than any other people. If we turn them not to a good account, the fault will be our own, and we must patiently bear the consequences.

CHAPTER XXXI.

Summary.

To place the subject fairly before the reader, we shall bring together the principal propositions that have been supported in this essay, and leave the decision to his candid judgment.

We have maintained:

1. That real money is that valuable by reference to which the value of other articles is estimated, and by the instrumentality of which they are circulated. It is a *commodity*, done up in a particular form to serve a particular use, and does not differ *essentially* from other items of wealth.

2. That silver, owing to its different physical properties, the universal and incessant demand for it, and the small proportion the annual supply bears to the stock on hand, is as good a practical standard of value as can reasonably be desired. It has no variations except such as *necessarily* arise from the nature of value.

3. That real money diffuses itself through different countries, and through different parts of a country, in proportion to the demands of commerce. No prohibitions can prevent its departing from countries where wealth and trade are declining; and no obstacle, except spurious money, can prevent its flowing into countries where wealth and trade are increasing.

4. That money is the tool of all trades, and is, as such, one of the most useful of productive instruments, and one of the most valuable of labor saving machines.

5. That bills of exchange and promissory notes are a *mere commercial medium*, and are, as *auxiliaries* of gold silver money, very useful: but they differ from metallic money in having no inherent value, and in being evidences of debt. The expressions of value in bills of exchange and promissory notes, are according to the article which law or custom has made the standard; and the failure to pay bills of exchange and promissory notes, does not affect the value of the currency, or the standard by which all contracts are regulated.

6. That Bank notes are *mere evidences of debt* due by

the Banks, and in this respect differ not from the promissory notes of the merchants; but, being received in full of all demands, they become to all intents and purposes the money of the country.

7. That Banks owe their credit to their charters; for, if these were taken away, not even their own stockholders would trust them.

8. That the circulating quality of Bank notes is in part owing to their being receivable in payment of dues to government; in part to the interest which the debtors to Banks and Bank stockholders have in keeping them in circulation; and in part to the difficulty, when the system is firmly established, of obtaining metallic money.

9. That so long as specie payments are maintained, there is a limit on Bank issues; but this is not sufficient to prevent successive " expansions" and " contractions," which produce ruinous fluctuations of prices; while the means by which Bank medium is kept " convertible" inflict great evils on the community.

10. That no restriction which can be imposed on Banks, and no discretion on the part of the Directors, can prevent these fluctuations; for, Bank credit, as a branch of commercial credit, is affected by all the causes, natural and political, that affect trade, or that affect the confidence man has in man.

11. That the " flexibility" or " elasticity" of Bank medium is not an excellence, but a defect, and that " expansions" and " contractions" are not made to suit the wants of the community, but from a simple regard to the profits and safety of the Banks.

12. That the uncertainty of trade produced by these successive " expansions" and " contractions," is but *one* of the evils of the present system. That the Banks cause credit dealings to be carried to an extent that is highly pernicious—that they cause credit to be given to men who are not entitled to it, and deprive others of credit to whom it would be useful.

13. That the granting of exclusive privileges to companies, or the exempting of companies from liablities to which individuals are subject, is repugnant to the fundamental principles of American Government; and that the Banks, inasmuch as they have exclusive privileges and exemp-

tions, and have the entire control of credit and currency, are the most pernicious of money corporations.

14. That a *nominal* responsibility may be imposed on such corporations, but that it is impossible to impose on them an effective responsibility. They respect the laws and public opinion so far only as is necessary to promote their own interest.

15. That on the supposition most favorable to the friends of the Banking system, the whole amount gained by the substitution of Bank medium for gold and silver coin, is equal only to about 40 cents per annum for each individual in the country; but that it will be found that nothing is in reality gained *by the nation*, if due allowance be made for the expense of supporting three or four hundred Banks, and for the fact that Bank-medium is a machine which performs its work badly.

16. That some hundreds of thousands of dollars are annually extracted from the people of Pennsylvania, and some millions from the people of the United States, for the support of the Banks, insomuch as through Banking the natural order of things is reversed, and interest paid to the Banks on evidences of debt due by them, instead of interest being paid to those who part with commodities in exchange for bank notes.

17. That into the formation of the Bank capital of the country very little substantial wealth has ever entered, that capital having been formed principally out of the promissory notes of the original subscribers, or by other means which the operations of the Banks themselves have facilitated. They who have bought the script of the Banks at second hand, may have honestly paid cent. per cent. for it; but what they have paid has gone to those from whom they bought the script, and does not form any part of the capital of the Banks.

18. That if it was the wish of the Legislature to promote usurious dealings, it could not well devise more efficient means than incorporating paper money Banks. That these Banks, moreover, give rise to many kinds of stock-jobbing, by which the simple-minded are injured and the crafty benefitted.

19. That many legislators have, in voting for Banks, supposed that they were promoting the welfare of their consti-

tuents; but the prevalence of false views in legislative bodies in respect to money corporations and paper money, is to be attributed chiefly to the desire certain members have to make money for themselves, or to afford their political partisans and personal friends opportunities for speculation.

20. That the banking interest has a pernicious influence on the periodical press, on public elections, and the general course of legislation. This interest is so powerful, that the establishment of a system of sound currency and sound credit is impracticable, except one or other of the political parties into which the nation is divided, makes such an object its primary principle of action.

21. That through the various advantages which the system of incorporated paper money Banking has given to some men over others, the foundation has been laid of an *artificial* inequality of wealth, which kind of inequality is, when once laid, increased by all the subsequent operations of society.

22. That this artificial inequality of wealth, adds nothing to the substantial happiness of the rich, and detracts much from the happiness of the rest of the community. That its tendency is to corrupt one portion of society, and debase another.

23. That the sudden dissolution of the Banking system, without suitable preparation, would put an end to the collection of debts, destroy private credit, break up many productive establishments, throw most of the property of the industrious into the hands of speculators, and deprive laboring people of employment.

24. That the system can be got rid of, without difficulty, by prohibiting, after a certain day, the issue of small notes, and proceeding gradually to those of the highest denomination.

25. That the feasibility of getting rid of the system, is further proved by the fact, that the whole amount of Bank notes and Bank credits, is, according to Mr. Gallatin's calculation, only about one hundred and nine million dollars. By paying ten or eleven millions a year, the whole can be liquidated in the term of ten years. If, however, twenty or thirty years should be required for the operation, the longest of these is but a short period in the life time of a nation.

26. That it has not been through the undervaluation of gold at the mint, that eagles and half-eagles have disappeared ; but from the free use of Bank notes. Nevertheless, a new coinage of pieces containing four and eight, or five and ten dollars worth of gold is desirable, to save the trouble of calculating fractions. The dollar being the money of contract and account, no possible confusion or injustice can be produced by an adjustment of the gold coinage to the silver standard.

27. That incorporating a paper money Bank is not the " necessary and proper," or " natural and appropriate" way of managing the fiscal concerns of the Union ; but that the " necessary and proper," or " natural and appropriate" way, is by sub-treasury offices.

28. That incorporating a paper money Bank is not " the necessary and proper," or " natural and appropriate" way of correcting the evils occasioned by the State Banks, inasmuch as a National Bank, resting on the same principles as the State Banks, must produce similar evils.

29. That " convertible" paper prevents the accumulation of such a stock of the precious metals as will enable the country to bear transitions from peace to war, and insure the punctual payment of war taxes, and that the " necessary and proper," or " natural and appropriate" way of providing for all public exigencies, is, by making the Government *a solid money Government*, as was intended by the framers of the Constitution.

30. That if Congress should, from excessive caution, or some less commendable motive, decline passing the acts necessary to insure the gradual withdrawal of Bank notes, they may greatly diminish the evils of the system, by declaring that nothing but gold and silver shall be received in payment of duties, and by making the operations of the Government entirely distinct from those of the Banks.

31. That, on the abolition of incorporated paper money Banks, private Bankers will rise up, who will receive money on deposit, and allow interest on the same, discount promissory notes, and buy and sell bills of exchange. Operating on sufficient funds, and being responsible for their engagements in the whole amount of their estates, these private Bankers will not by sudden and great " expansions" and " curtailments" derange the whole train of mer-

cantile operations. In each large city, an office of deposit and transfer, similar to the Bank of Hamburgh, will be established, and we shall thus secure all the good of the present Banking system, and avoid all its evils.

32. That, if the present system of Banking and paper money shall continue, the wealth and population of the country will increase from natural causes, till they shall be equal for each square mile to the wealth and population of Europe. But, with every year, the state of society in the United States will more nearly approximate to the state of society in Great Britain. Crime and pauperism will increase. A few men will be inordinately rich, some comfortable, and a multitude in poverty. This condition of things will naturally lead to the adoption of that policy which proceeds on the principle that a legal remedy is to be found for each social evil, and nothing left for the operations of nature. This kind of legislation will increase the evils it is intended to cure.

33. That there is reason to *hope* that, on the downfall of monied corporations, and the substitution of gold and silver for Bank medium, sound credit will take the place of unsound, and legitimate enterprize the place of wild speculation. That the moral and intellectual character of the people will be sensibly though gradually raised, and the causes laid open of a variety of evils under which society is now suffering. That the sources of legislation will, to a certain extent, be purified, by taking from members of legislative bodies inducements to pass laws for the special benefit of themselves, their personal friends and political partisans. That the operation of the natural and just causes of wealth and poverty, will no longer be inverted, but that each cause will operate in its natural and just order, and produce its natural and just effect—wealth becoming the reward of industry, frugality, skill, prudence, and enterprize, and poverty the punishment of few except the indolent and prodigal.

PART II.

A

SHORT HISTORY

OF

PAPER MONEY AND BANKING

IN THE

UNITED STATES.

A

SHORT HISTORY

OF

PAPER MONEY AND BANKING.

CHAPTER I.

Of the Medium of Trade, before the Introduction of Paper Money.

The first settlers of a country may be greatly in want of capital, but they do not need a great sum of money as a medium of domestic trade. A few exchanges of products for gold and silver coin, will regulate barter transactions with sufficient accuracy for general dealings. A great portion of the stock of money which the original emigrants brought with them, was, therefore, soon exchanged for the comforts and conveniences which Europe could supply, and trade by barter became the custom of the country.

If the Government had not interfered, all would have been well. But, as early as 1618, as is stated by Holmes, in his American Annals, Governor Argall of Virginia, order-ed " that all goods should be sold at an advance of 25 per cent., and tobacco taken in payment at three shillings per pound, and not more or less, on the penalty of three years servitude to the colony."*

* Mr. Burk says, in the appendix to the first volume of the History of Virginia—

"I find in the proclamations of the Virginia Governors and Councils, the rates of some commodities and something like a scale of exchange between specie and tobacco. During the administration of Captain Argall, tobacco was fixed at three shillings the pound. In 1623, Ca-nary, Malaga, Alicant, Tent, Muskadel, and Bastard wines, were rated at six shillings in specie, and nine shillings the gallon payable in tobacco. Sherry, Sack, and Aquavitae, at four shillings, or four shil-lings and six pence tobacco. Wine vinegar at three shillings, or four

In 1641, as we learn from the same authority, the General Court of Msssachusetts " made orders about payment of debts, setting corn at the usual price, and making it payable for all debts which should arise after a time prefixed."   In 1643, the same General Court ordered " that Wampompeag should pass current in the payment of debts to the amount of forty shillings, the white at eight a penny, the black at four a penny, except for county rates."

Wampompeag being an article of traffic with the Indians, had a value in domestic trade, but an attempt to fix its value by law was an absurdity, and making it a legal tender was something worse than absurdity.   The measure was, however, in perfect accordance with the orders given by the General Court in 1633, declaring, "that artificers, such as carpenters and masons, should not receive more than two shillings a day, and proportionably, and that merchants should not advance more than four pence in the shilling above what their goods cost in England."

shillings and six pence tobacco.   Cider and beer vinegar at two shillings, or three shillings in tobacco.   Loaf sugar one shilling and eight pence per pound, or two shillings and six pence in tobacco ; butter and cheese eight pence per pound, or one shilling in tobacco.   Newfoundland fish per cwt. fifteen shillings, or one pound four shillings in tobacco.   Canada fish, two pounds, or three pounds ten shillings in tobacco.   English meal sold at ten shillings the bushel, and Indian corn at eight.   After a careful inspection of the old records, I cannot find any rates of labor specified, although they too are mentioned, as forming a part of the subject of proclamations."

Holmes, in his Annals, supplies one deficiency in Burk's price current, namely, the price of a passage from Europe.

" The enterprizing colonists being generally destitute of families, Sir Edward Sandys, the treasurer, proposed to the Virginia Company to send over a freight of young women to become wives for the planters. The proposal was applauded ; and ninety girls, " young and uncorrupt," were sent over in the ships, that arrived this year, (1620) and, the year following, sixty more, handsome and well recommended to the company for their virtuous education and demeanor.   The price of a wife, at the first, was *one hundred pounds of tobacco :* but, as the number became scarce, the price was increased to *one hundred and fifty pounds,* the value of which, in money, was three shillings per pound. This debt for wives, it was ordered, should have the precedency of all other debts, and be first recoverable."

The Rev. Mr. Weems, a Virginia writer, intimates that it would have done a man's heart good, to see the gallant, young Virginians, hastening to the water side, when a ship arrived from London, each carrying a bundle of the best tobacco under his arm, and each taking back with him a beautiful and virtuous young wife.

In Pennsylvania, as well as in the other colonies, a considerable traffic was carried on by barter : and we recollect having read in the Minutes of Assembly, that, about the year 1700, a proposition was made to make domestic products a legal tender, at their current rates. The proposition was rejected. But Holmes states that, in Maryland, as late as the year 1732, an act was passed " making tobacco a legal tender at one penny a pound, and Indian corn at twenty pence a bushel."

The colonists had hardly become numerous enough to require more than two or three hundred thousand dollars of medium for domestic uses, before specie began to flow in abundantly. Their trade with the West Indies and a clandestine commerce with the Spanish Maine, made silver so plentiful, that, as early as 1652, a mint was established in New England for coining shillings, sixpences and three penny pieces.*

Gabriel Thomas, in his account of Pennsylvania, published about the year 1698, says silver was more plentiful in that province than in England.

Plentiful, however, as it was, there was not enough to satisfy the wishes of every body. Attempts were, therefore, made to keep the precious metals in the country, by raising the official value of the coin. Virginia, in 1645, prohibited dealings by barter, and established the Spanish piece of eight at six shillings, as the standard currency of

* " The law enacted that " Massachusetts" and a tree in the centre, be on the one side : and New England, and the year of our Lord, and the figure XII, VI, III, according to the value of each piece, be on the other side."—Massachusetts Laws. The several coins had N. E. on one side, and the number denoting the number of *pence*, with the year 1652, on the other. The date was never altered, though more coin was stamped annually for thirty years."—Holmes.

In 1662, the Assembly of Maryland besought the proprietary "to take orders for setting up a mint," and a law was passed for that purpose. " The great hindrance to the colony in trade for the want of money" is assigned as the reason for the measure. It was enacted, that the money coined shall be of as good silver as English sterling; that every shilling, and so in proportion for other pieces, shall weigh above nine pence in such silver; and that the proprietary shall accept of it in payment of his rents and other debts. This coin being afterwards circulated, the present law of Maryland was confirmed in 1676. This is the only law for coining money, which occurs in colonial history, previous to the American Revolution, excepting the ordinance of Massachusetts in 1652."—Chalmers, 1. 248.

that colony. The other colonies affixed various denominations to the dollar, and the country exhibited a singular
spectacle. Its money of account was the same nominally
as that of England. Its coin was chiefly Spanish and
Portuguese. But, what was a shilling in Pennsylvania,
was more than a shilling in New York, and less than a
shilling in Virginia.

In the third year of Queen Anne, an attempt was made
to put an end to this confusion, by a Royal Proclamation
and act of Parliament, fixing the plantation pound at two
ounces sixteen pennyweights sixteen grains of silver, of
the fineness of common pieces of eight, at six shillings and
ten pence half-penny per ounce ; but, from various causes,
the act proved effective in Barbadoes only. In South Carolina, the dollar was estimated at 4s. 8d , in Virginia and
New England at 6s., in Pennsylvania, New Jersey, and
Maryland at 7s. 6d., and in New York and North Carolina at 8s.

These are to be understood as the rates at which the
currencies of the different colonies were finally settled.
They were varied from time to time to suit the varying
views of the lawgivers.*   Confusion in dealing was thereby introduced, and some injustice was done to individuals :
but the chief object of these changes, namely, that of keeping a great stock of the precious metals in the country,
was not effected. In proportion as the denominations of
the coin were raised, the merchants raised the price of
their goods. The laws of nature counteracted the laws of
the land. The people exchanged their surplus gold and
silver for such things as they wanted still more than gold
and silver—leaving just as much money in the country as
its domestic trade required, and not one shilling more.

   * Dr. Franklin, in his Historical Account of Pennsylvania, says,
" During this weak practice, silver got up by degrees to eight shillings
and nine pence per ounce, and English crowns were six, seven, and
eight shillings a piece."

CHAPTER II.

Of Provincial Paper Money.

Paper money was first issued by Massachusetts in 1690. The object was not to supply any supposed want of a medium for trade, but to satisfy the demands of some clamorous soldiers. Other issues were subsequently made, partly with the view of defraying the expenses of Government, and partly with the view of making money plenty in every man's pocket. But, as the quantity increased, the value diminished, as will be seen on inspecting the following table.*

	Exch. with London.		1oz. Silver.		Exch. with London.		1oz. Silver.
1702	- 133	-	6s. 10½d.	1728	- 340	-	18s.
1705	- 135	-	7	1730	- 380	-	20
1713	- 150	-	8	1737	- 500	-	26
1716	- 175	.	9 3	1741	- 550	-	28
1717	- 225	-	12	1749	- 1100	-	60
1722	- 270	-	14				

The ill-judged expedition of the Carolinians against St. Augustine, in 1702, entailed a debt of 6000 pounds on that colony, for the discharge of which a bill was passed by the Provincial Assembly for stamping bills of credit, which were to be sunk in three years by a duty laid upon liquors, skins and furs. For five or six years after the emission, the paper passed in the country at the same value and rate as the sterling money of England.†

To defray the expenses of an expedition against the Tuscaroras, and to accommodate domestic trade, the Legislature of South Carolina established a public Bank in 1712, and issued 48,000 pounds in bills of credit, called Bank bills, to be lent out on interest on landed and personal security, and to be sunk gradually at the rate of 4000 pounds a year. Soon after the emission of these Bank bills, the rate of exchange and the price of produce rose, advancing in the first year to 150, and in the second to 200 per cent.‡

* Holmes. Vol. II, p. 179.   † Ib. Vol. II, p. 58.   ‡ Ib. Vol. II, p. 82.

By the year 1731, the rate of exchange rose to 700, at which, says Holmes, " it continued with little variation upwards of forty years."

In the year 1723, " the province of Pennsylvania made its first experiment of a paper currency. It issued, in March, 15,000 pounds, on such terms as appeared likely to be effectual to keep up the credit of the bills. It made no loans, but on land security, or plate deposited in the loan office : obliged the borrowers to pay five per cent. for the sums they took up ; made its bills a tender in all payments, on pain of confiscating the debt, or forfeiting the commodity ; imposed sufficient penalties on all persons, who presumed to make any bargain or sale on cheaper terms in case of being paid in gold or silver; and provided for the gradual reduction of the bills, by enacting that one-eighth of the principal, as well as the whole interest, should be annually paid."*

Governor Pownall, in his work on the Administration of the Colonies, bestows high praise on the paper system of Pennsylvania, " I will venture to say" he declares, " that there never was a wiser or a better measure, never one better calculated to serve the interests of an increasing country that there never was a measure more steadily pursued, or more faithfully executed, for forty years together, than the loan office in Pennsylvania, founded and administered by the Assembly of that province." Dr. Franklin, also, bestowed high commendation on the system. And Adam Smith, apparently guided by Governor Pownall and Dr. Franklin, says " Pennsylvania was always more moderate in its emission of paper money than any of our other colonies. Its paper currency accordingly *is said* never to have sunk below the value of the gold and silver which was current in the colony before the first emission of its paper money."

All things go by comparison. The credit bills of Pennsylvania were so much better than those of the other Governments, that there was a demand for them throughout the country as bills of exchange: but it was not a fact that they never· sunk below the value of the gold and silver which was current in the colony before the first emission

* Holmes. Vol. II, p. 110.

of its paper. The following table taken from an official document to be found in Proud's History of Pennsylvania shows that the paper was never at a less discount than eleven per cent. if gold be taken as the standard, or seven per cent. if silver be the standard.

			Gold.				Silver.
1700 to 1709	-	-	l5 10s. 0d.	-	-	9s. 2d.
1709 to 1720	-	-	5 10 0	-	-	6 10½
1720 to 1723	-	-	5 10 0	-	-	7 5
1723 to 1726	-	-	6 6 6	-	-	8 3
1726 to 1730	-	-	6 3 9	-	-	8 1
1730 to 1738	-	-	6 9 3	-	-	8 9

We have no account of the bullion market in provincial Pennsylvania, subsequent to the year 1738, but this table shows that those who represented to Adam Smith that the paper of the colony suffered no depreciation, were misled by making neither gold nor silver the standard, but by making the paper the standard of itself. As the Pennsylvania pound current never changed its name, they thought it never changed its value.*

The following table shows the rate of exchange of the

* It is curious to observe the similarity of the reasoning of the supporters of this paper money with that of the anti-bullionists of a subsequent period. A merchant of Boston writing to his friend in England in 1740, uses the following language.

"Upon the continuance of a favorable turn in the trading circumstances of the province of New England, the Government might stop at any rate which silver should fall to, and make that rate the fixed silver pound, and make it a lawful tender; and common consent or acceptance of the people would complete the scheme of silver money. And thus the pound sterling is fixed in England at three ounces seventeen penny weights and two grains of silver, of a certain fineness, or silver at five shillings and two pence per ounce.

"But if that kingdom were under our unhappy circumstances, as not having a sufficiency in value in silver and all other exports to discharge the whole demand of their imports : it would then be next to a miracle if silver did not rise to above five shillings and two pence per ounce in the market, in proportion to the balance of debt against them ; and their trading circumstances continue to decline, as ours have ; their silver would be brought to twenty seven shillings per ounce, as ours is, and the current money of Great Britain be at the rate of twenty shillings per ounce, whatever the lawful money might be."

Anderson, vol. iii. p. 498.

Here we have the doctrine clearly stated that when paper is at a discount, it is not paper that has fallen, but silver that has risen ; and the English Anti-Bullionists are thus deprived of all claim to originality in

currencies of the different colonies, for £100 sterling, at
two different periods.*

		1,740		1,748
New England,	-	525	-	1,100
New York, -	-	160	-	190
New Jersey, -	-	160	-	180 and 190
Pennsylvania,	-	170	-	180
Maryland, -	-	200	-	200
North Carolina,	-	1,400	-	1,000
South Carolina,	-	800	-	750
Virginia, -	-		-	120 a 125.

The Government of Virginia appears not to have issued
any paper money previous to the Revolutionary War.

In respect to the paper money of the colonies generally,
we may say, in the language of Adam Smith, " allowing
the colony security to be perfectly good, a hundred pounds
payable fifteen years hence, in a country where interest is
at six per cent., is worth little more than forty pounds ready
money.   To oblige a creditor, therefore, to accept of this
as a full payment for a debt of a hundred pounds actually
paid down in ready money, was an act of such violent injustice as has scarce, perhaps, been attempted by the Government of any other country which pretended to be free.
It bears the evident marks of having originally been, what
the honest and downright Dr. Douglass assures us it was,
a scheme of fraudulent debtors to cheat their creditors.
The Government of Pennsylvania, indeed, pretended, upon
their first emission of paper money, to render their paper
of equal value with gold and silver, by enacting penalties
against all those who made any difference in the price of
their goods when they sold them for colony paper, and
when they sold them for gold and silver : a regulation
equally tyrannical, but much less effectual than that which it
was meant to support. A positive law may render a shilling
a legal tender for a guinea, because it may direct the courts
of justice to discharge the debtor who has made that tender.   But no positive law can oblige a person who sells

error.   All the arguments they used during the suspension of specie
payments were mere plagiarisms from the Boston merchant."

* The items in the first column are from Anderson: those in the
second from Dr. Douglass.

goods, and who is at liberty to sell or not to sell as he pleases, to accept of a shilling as equivalent to a guinea in the price of them."

Dr. Williamson, the historian of North Carolina, says: " Of all the varieties of fraud which have been practised by men who call themselves honest, and wish to preserve a decent appearance, none have been more frequent in legislative bodies than the attempt to pass money for more than its proper value. There are men who conceive that crimes lose their stain, when the offenders are numerous: that in the character of legislators they cannot be rogues: " defendit numerus." There are men who would be ashamed to acquire five shillings by stealing, picking a pocket, or robbing on the high-way ; but they would freely and without blushing assist in passing a law to defraud their creditors of their just demands. There are instances of men being banished from North Carolina for stealing a hog not worth five dollars: while the men who banished them would contend for paying a debt of seven pounds with the value of twenty shillings : the moral sense is depraved by tender laws, or laws that enable the debtor to defraud his creditor, by offering him a fictitious payment. By such laws the mind is alienated from the love of justice, and is prepared for any species of chicane and fraud."

Hutchinson, the historian of Massachusetts, has preserved many curious particulars of the introduction of paper money into this country, and of its operation on society. After relating the unsuccessful expedition of the Massachusetts troops against Quebec in 1690, he says :

" The Government was utterly unprepared for the return of the forces. They seem to have presumed, not only upon success, but upon the enemy's treasure to bear the charge of the expedition. The soldiers were upon the point of mutiny for want of their wages. It was utterly impracticable to raise in a few days such a sum as would be necessary. An act was passed for levying the sum, but the men would not stay until it should be brought into the treasury. The extreme difficulty to which the Government was thus reduced, was the occasion of the first bills of credit ever issued in the colonies, as a substitute in the place of money. The debt was paid by paper notes from two shillings to ten pounds denomination, which

notes were to be received for payment of the tax which
was to be levied, and all other payments in the treasury.
This was a new expedient. They had better credit than
King James' leather money in Ireland, about the same
time. But the notes would not command money, nor
any commodities at money price. Sir William Phipps, it
is said, exchanged a large sum at par in order to give
them credit. The soldiers in general were great sufferers,
and could get no more than twelve or fourteen shillings in
the pound. As the time of payment of the tax approach-
ed, the credit of the notes was raised, and the Government
allowing five per cent. to those who paid their taxes in
notes, they became better than money. This was gain to
the possessor, but it did not restore to the poor soldier
what he had lost by the discount.

" The Government, encouraged by the restoration of
credit to their bills, afterwards issued others for charges of
Government. They obtained good credit at the time of their
being issued. The charges of Government were paid in
this manner from year to year. Whilst the sum was small
silver continued the measure, and bills continued their value.
When the charges of Government increased, after the second
expedition to Canada in 1711, the bills likewise increased,
and in the same or greater proportion, the silver and gold
were sent out of the country. There being a cry of scarcity of
money in 1714, the Government caused £50,000 to be
issued, and in 1716, £100,000, and lent to the inhabitants,
to be paid in at a certain period, and in the mean time to
pass as money. Lands were mortgaged for security. As
soon as the silver and gold were gone and the bills were
the sole instrument of commerce, pounds, shillings, and
pence were altogether ideal, for no possible reason could
be assigned why a bill of twenty shillings should bear a
certain proportion to any one quantity of silver more than
another. Sums in bills were drawing into the treasury
from time to time, by the taxes or payment of the loans :
but then other sums were continually issuing out, and all
the bills were paid and received without any distinction,
either in public or private payments, so that, for near forty
years together, the currency was in much the same state
as if an hundred thousand pounds sterling had been stamped on pieces of leather, or paper of various denominations,

and declared to be the money of the Government, without any other sanction than this, that, when there should be taxes to pay, the treasury would receive this sort of money, and that every creditor should be obliged to receive it from his debtor. Can it be supposed that such a medium could retain its value? In 1702, 6s. 8d. was equal to an ounce of silver. In 1749, 50s. was judged equal to an ounce of silver. I saw a five shilling bill which had been issued in 1690, and was remaining in 1749, and was then equal to eight pence only in the lawful money, and so retained but one-eighth of its original value. Such was the delusion, that not only the bills of the Massachsetts Government passed as money, but they received the bills of the Governments of Connecticut, New Hampshire, and Rhode Island also as a currency. The Massachusetts bills passed also in those Governments.*

By the year 1713, "silver and gold were entirely banished. Of two instruments, one in use in a particular State only, the other with the whole commercial world, it is easy to determine which must leave the particular State and which remain. The currency of silver and gold entirely ceasing, the price of every thing bought or sold was no longer compared therewith, but with paper bills, or rather with mere ideal pounds, shillings, and pence. The rise of exchange with England and all other countries was not attributed to the true cause, the want of a fixed staple medium, but to the general bad state of the trade. Three parties were formed, one very small, which was for drawing in the paper bills and depending upon a silver and gold currency. Mr. Hutchinson, one of the members for Boston, was among the most active of this party. He was an enemy all his life, to a depreciating currency, upon a principle very ancient, but too seldom practised upon, *nil utile quod non honestum*, [nothing which is not honest is useful.]

" Another party was very numerous. These had projected a private Bank, or rather had taken up a project published in London in the year 1684 : but this not being generally known in America, a merchant in Boston was the reputed father of it. There was nothing more in it

* Hutchinsons' History of Massachusetts, vol 1, p. 402-3. London edition, 1765.

that issuing bills of credit, which all the members of the company promised to receive as money, but at no certain value compared with silver and gold : and real estates, to a sufficient value, were to be bound as a security that the company should perform their engagements. They were soliciting the sanction of the general court and an act of Government to incorporate them. This party, generally, consisted of persons in difficult or involved circumstances in trade, or such as were possessed of real estates, but had little or no ready money at command, or men of no substance at all : and we may well enough suppose the party to be very numerous. Some, no doubt, joined them from mistaken principles, and an apprehension that it was a scheme beneficial to the public, and some for party sake and popular applause.

" A third party, though very opposite to the private Bank, yet were no enemies to bills of credit. They were in favor of a loan of bills from the Government to any of the inhabitants who would mortgage their estates as a security for the re-payment of the bills, with interest, in a term of years, the interest to be paid annually, and applied to the support of Government. This was an easy way of paying public charges, which no doubt, they wondered that in so many ages the wisdom of other Governments had never discovered.

" The controversy had a universal spread, and divided towns, parishes, and particular families. At length, after a long struggle, the party for the public Bank prevailed in the General Court for a loan of fifty thousand pounds in bills of credit, which were put in the hands of trustees, and lent for five years only, to any of the inhabitants at five per cent. interest, one-fifth part of the principal to be paid annually. This lessened the number of the party for the private Bank, but it increased the zeal and raised a strong resentment in those that remained."*

Under this system the trade of the province declined, and in the year 1720, there was a general cry for want of money. " The bills of credit, which were the only money, were daily depreciating. The depreciation was grievous to all creditors, but particularly distressing to the clergy

---

* Hutchinson, vol. I. pp. 206, 7, 8 & 9. Boston edition of 1765.

and other salary men, to widows and orphans whose estates consisted of money at interest, perhaps just enough to support them, and being reduced to one-half the former value, they found themselves on a sudden in a state of poverty and want. Executors and administrators, and all who were possessed of the effects of others in trust, had a strong temptation to retain them. The influence a bad currency has upon the morals of the people, is greater than is generally imagined. Numbers of shemes, for private and public emissions of bills, were proposed as remedies, the only effectual one, the utter abolition of the bills, was omitted."*

In 1721, the Governor recommended measures for preventing the depreciation of the currency : and the Assembly gave him for answer, that they " had passed a bill for issuing one hundred thousand pounds more in bills of credit." This alone, as Hutchinson justly observes, had a direct tendency to increase the mischief: but they added that " to prevent their depreciation, they had prohibited the buying, selling and bartering silver, at any higher rates than set by acts of Parliament." This certainly could have no tendency to lessen it. Such an act can no more be executed than an act to stop the ebbing and flow of the sea."†

" In 1733 there was a general complaint throughout the four Governments of New England of the unusual scarcity of money. There was as large a sum current in bills of credit as ever, but the bills having depreciated, they answered the purposes of money so much less in proportion. The Massachusetts and New Hampshire Governments were clogged with royal instructions. It was owing to to them that those Governments had not issued bills to as great an amount as Rhode Island. Connecticut, although under no restraint, yet consisting of more husbandmen and fewer traders than the rest, did not so much feel the want of money. The Massachusetts people were dissatisfied that Rhode Island should send their bills among them and take away their substance and employ it in trade, and many persons wished to see the bills of each Government current within the limits of such Government only. In the midst of this discontent, Rhode Island passed an act for

* Hutchinson, pp. 231, 2.   † Ib. pp. 245, 6.

issuing £100,000 upon loan, for, I think, twenty years, to their own inhabitants, who would immediately have it in their power to add £100,000 to their trading stock, from the horses, sheep, lumber, fish, &c., of the Massachusetts inhabitants. The merchants of Boston, therefore, confederated and mutually promised and engaged not to receive any bills of this new emission, but, to provide a currency, a large number formed themselves into a company, entered into covenants, chose directors, &c., and issued £100,000, redeemable in ten years; in silver at 19s. per oz. the then current rate, or gold in proportion, a tenth part annually. About the same time the Massachusetts treasury, which had been long shut, was opened, and the debts of two or three years were all paid at one time in bills of credit: to this was added the ordinary emission of bills from New Hampshire and Connecticut; and some of the Boston merchants, tempted by an opportunity of selling their English goods, having broke through their engagements and received Rhode Island bills, all the rest soon followed the example. All these emissions made a flood of money, silver rose from 19s. to 27s. the oz. and exchange with all other countries consequently rose also, and every creditor was defrauded of about one-third of his just dues. As soon as silver rose to 27s., the notes issued by the merchants at 19s., were hoarded up and no longer answered the purposes of money. Although the currency was lessened by taking away the notes, yet what remained never increased in value, silver continuing several years about the same rate, until it took another large jump. Thus very great injustice was caused by this wretched paper currency, and no relief of any sort obtained; for, by this sinking in value, though the nominal sum was higher than it had ever been before, yet the currency would produce no more sterling money that it would have done before the late emissions were made.*

Towards the close of the year 1738, a great clamor arose against the Governor for adhering to his instructions about paper money, and an agent was appointed at the expense of the colony, to procure, if possible, a relaxation of the instructions. A petition was presented by him from the House to his Majesty in Council, but it had no effect.

* Hutchinson, p. 380, 1.

" A general dread of drawing in all the paper money without the substitution of any other instrument of trade in the place of it, disposed a great part of the province to favor the Land Bank or manufactory scheme, which was begun or rather revived in this year, 1739, and produced such great and lasting mischiefs, that a particular relation of the rise, progress, and overthrow of it, may be of use to prevent any attempts of the like nature in future ages. By a strange conduct in the General Court they had been issuing bills of credit for eight or ten years annually, for charges of Government, and being willing to ease each present year, they had put off the redemption of the bills as far as they could, but the Governor being restrained by his instructions from going beyond the year 1740, that year was unreasonably loaded with thirty or forty thousand pounds sterling taxes, which, according to the general opinions of the people, it was impossible to levy. Royal instructions were no bar to the proceedings of private persons. The project of a Bank in the year 1714 was revived. The projector of that Bank now put himself at the head of seven or eight hundred persons, some few of rank and good estate, but generally of low condition among the plebians, and of small estate, and many of them perhaps insolvent. This notable company were to give credit to £150,000, lawful money, to be issued in bills, each person being to mortgage a real estate in proportion to the sum he subscribed and took out, or to give bond with two sureties, but personal security was not to be taken for more than £100 from any one person. Ten directors and a treasurer were to be chosen by the company. Every subscriber or partner was to pay three per cent. interest for the sum taken out, and five per cent. of the principal, and he that did not pay bills might pay the produce and manufactures of the province at such rates as the directors from time to time should set, and they should commonly pass in lawful money. The pretence was, that by thus furnishing a medium and instrument of trade, not only the inhabitants in general would be better able to procure the province bills of credit, but trade, foreign and inland, would revive and flourish. The fate of the project was thought to depend on the opinion the General Court should form of it. It was necessary therefore to have a House of Representatives

well disposed. Besides the eight hundred persons, subscribers, the needy part of the province, in general, favored the scheme. One of their votes will go as far in popular elections as one of the most opulent. The former are
most numerous, and it appeared that by far the majority of
representatives for 1740 were subscribers to or favorers of
the scheme, and they have ever since been distinguished
by the name of the Land Bank House.

" Men of estates and the principal merchants in the province abhorred the project and refused to receive the bills,
but great numbers of shopkeepers who had lived for a long
time before upon the fraud of a depreciating currency, and
many small traders, gave credit to the bills. The directors,
it was said, by a vote of the company became traders, and
issued just what bills they thought proper without any fund
or security for their ever being redeemed. They purchased every sort of commodity, ever so much a drug, for
the sake of pushing off their bills, and by one means or
other a large sum, say perhaps fifty or sixty thousand
pounds, was abroad. To lessen the temptation to receive
the bills, a company of merchants agreed to issue their
notes or bills redeemable by silver and gold at distant periods, much like the scheme in 1733, and attended with no
better effect. The Governor exerted himself to blast this
fraudulent undertaking, the Land Bank. Not only such civil
and military officers as were directors or partners, but all
who received and paid any of the bills, were displaced. The
Governor negatived the person chosen Speaker of the House
being a director of the Bank, and afterwards negatived 13
of the new elected counsellors who were directors or partners in, or reputed favorers of, the scheme. But all was
insufficient to suppress it. Perhaps the major part, in number, of the inhabitants of the province openly or secretly
were well-wishers to it. One of the directors afterwards
acknowledged to me that although he entered into the
company with a view to the public interest, yet when he
found what power and influence they had in all public
concerns, he was convinced it was more than belonged to
them, more than they could make a good use of, and therefore unwarrantable. Many of the most sensible, discreet
persons in the province saw a general confusion at hand.
Application was therefore made to Parliament for an act to

suppress the company, which, notwithstanding the opposition of the agent, was very easily obtained, and thereon it was declared that the act of the 6th of King George the First, chapter eighteenth, [the Bubble Act] did, does, and shall extend to the colonies and plantations in America. Had not the Parliament interposed, the province would have been in the utmost confusion, and the authority of Government entirely in the Land Bank Company."*

Every scheme for fixing the value of the provincial bills of credit having failed, " a new project was, in 1741, reported by a committee of the House and accepted, and afterwards concurred in by the council and consented to by the Governor. This was a scheme to establish an ideal measure, in all trade and dealings, let the instrument be what it would. The act which passed the Court declared that all contracts should be understood payable in silver at 6s. 8d. the ounce, or gold in proportion. Bills of a new form were issued, 20s. of which expressed in the face of the bill three ounces of silver, and they were to be received accordingly in all public and private payments, with this saving, that, if they should depreciate in their value, an addition should be made to all debts as much as the depreciation from the time of contract to the time of payment. How to ascertain the depreciation from time to time was the great difficulty in framing the act. To leave it to a common jury would never do. There were some doubts whether a House of Representatives would be wholly unbiassed. At length it was agreed that the eldest counsellor in each county should meet once a year to ascertain the depreciation.

" This at best must have been a very partial cure. It did not prevent the loss from the depreciation of the bills in those persons' hands through which they were continually passing. All debts which were contracted and paid between the periods when the value of the bills was fixed annually, could not be affected by such fixing, and unless in debts of long standing which the debtor would not pay without an action at law, demand was not ordinarily made for depreciation, and what rendered it of little effect in all other cases, the counsellors appointed to estimate the de-

* Hutchinson, pp. 392, 3, 4, 5 and 6.

preciation never had firmness enough in any instance to
make the full allowance, but when silver and exchange had
risen 20 per cent. or more, an addition was made of four or
five only. The popular cry was against it, and one year
when Nathaniel Hubbard, Esq. the eldest counsellor for the
county of Bristol, a gentleman of amiable character, and
who filled the several posts he sustained with applause, endeavored to approach nearer to a just allowance than had
been made in former years, he felt the resentment of the
House, who left him out of the council the next election.
In short, the act neither prevented the depreciation of the
bills nor afforded relief in case of it, and was of no other
service than to serve as a warning, when an act passed for
establishing the currency a few years after, *to leave nothing
to be done by any person or bodies of men, or even future
legislatures*, to give the act its designed effect, but in the
act itself to make full provision for its execution in every
part."*

" By the expedition to Lewisburgh, the preparations for
the reduction of Canada, and the several supplies of men
for Nova Scotia, the province had," by the year 1747, " issued an immense sum in bills of credit, between two and
three millions, according to their denomination in the currency. The greater part of this sum had been issued
when between five and six hundred pounds was equal to
one hundred pounds sterling, and perhaps the real consideration the Government received from the inhabitants who
gave credit to them, was near four hundred thousand pounds
sterling : but by thus multiplying the bills they had so
much depreciated that, at the end of the war, eleven or
twelve hundred pounds was not equal to more than a hundred pounds sterling, and the whole debt of the province
did not much exceed two hundred thousand pounds sterling. Thus the people had paid two hundred thousand
pounds sterling in two or three years, besides a large sum
raised by taxes each year, as much as it was supposed the
people were able to pay; but to pay by the depreciation
of the bills, although infinitely unequal, yet, as they
were shifting hands every day, it was almost insensible, a
possessor of a large sum for a few days not perceiving the

* Hutchinson, pp. 402, 3, 4.

difference in their value between the time when he received them and the time when he parted with them. The apprehension of their depreciation tended to increase it, and occasioned a quick circulation; and for some time, even for English goods, which ordinarily sell for the longest credit, no body pretended to ask credit. They were constantly, however, dying in somebody's hands, though nobody kept them long by them. Business was brisk, men in trade increased their figures, but were sinking the real value of their stock, and, what is worse, by endeavors to shift the loss attending such a pernicious currency from one to another, fraudulent dispositions and habits are acquired, and the morals of the people depreciate with the currency.

" The Government was soliciting for the reimbursement of the charges in taking and securing Cape Breton, and by the address, assiduity, and fidelity of William Bollan, Esq.; who was one of the agents of the province for that purpose, there was a hopeful prospect that the full sum, about £180,000 sterling, would be obtained.

" Mr. Hutchinson, who was then Speaker of the House of Representatives, imagined this to be a most favorable opportunity for abolishing the bills of credit, the source of so much iniquity, and for establishing a stable currency of gold and silver for the future. About two millions two hundred thousand pounds would be outstanding in bills in the year 1749. One hundred and eighty thousand pounds sterling at eleven for one—which was the lowest rate of exchange with London for a year or two before, and perhaps the difference was really twelve to one—would redeem nineteen hundred and eighty thousand pounds, which would leave but two hundred and twenty thousand pounds outstanding: it was therefore proposed that the sum granted by Parliament should be shipped to the province in Spanish milled dollars and applied for the redemption of the bills as far as would serve for that purpose, and that the remainder of the bills should be drawn in by a tax on the year 1749. This would finish the bills. For the future, silver of sterling alloy at 6s. 8d. the ounce, if payment should be made in bullion, or otherwise milled dollars at 6s. each, should be the lawful money of the province, and no person should receive or pay within the province,

bills of credit of any of the other Governments of New
England. This proposal being made to the Governor, he
approved of it, as founded in justice and tending to promote
the real interest of the province, but he knew the attach-
ment of the people to paper money, and supposed it impracticable. The Speaker, however, laid the proposal before
the House, when it was received with a smile, and generally thought to be a Utopian project ; and, rather out of
deference to the Speaker than from an apprehension of any
effect, the House appointed a committee to consider of it.
The committee treated it in the same manner, but reported that the Speaker should be desired to bring in a bill for
the consideration of the House. When this came to be
known abroad, exceptions were taken and a clamor was
raised from every quarter. The major part of the people
in number, were no sufferers by a depreciating currency ;
the number of debtors is always more than the number of
creditors, and although debts on specialities had allowance
made in judgments of courts for depreciation of the bills,
yet on simple contracts, of which there were ten to one
speciality, no allowance was made. Those who were for
a fixed currency were divided. Some supposed the bills
might be reduced to so small a quantity as to be fixed and
stable, and, therefore, were for redeeming as many by bills
of exchange as should be thought superfluous; others were
for putting an end to the bills, but in a gradual way, otherwise it was said a *fatal shock* would be given to trade.
This last was the objection of many men of good sense.
Douglass, who had wrote well upon the paper currency and
been the oracle of the anti-paper party, was among them,
and, as his manner was with all who differed from him,
discovered as much rancor against the author and promo-
ter of this new project as he had done against the fraudulent contrivers of paper money emissions."*

After many weeks spent in debating and settling the several parts of the bill, it was rejected : but, afterwards, on
motion, reconsidered, passed by the House and Council,
and approved by the Governor.

" The provision made by this act for the exchange of the
bills and for establishing a silver currency, was altogether

* Hutchinson, pp. 435, 6, 7.

conditional, and depended upon a grant of Parliament for reimbursement of the charge of the Cape Breton expedition.
This being at a distance and not absolutely certain, the act
had no sudden effect upon the minds of the people, but when
the news of the grant arrived, the discontent appeared more
visible, and upon the arrival of the money there were some
beginnings of tumults, and the authors and promoters of
the measure were threatened. The Government passed an
act with a severe penalty against riots, and appeared determined to carry the other act for exchanging the bills into
execution. The apprehensions of a *shock* to trade proved
groundless : the bills being dispersed through every part
of the province, the silver took place instead of them, a
good currency was insensibly substituted in the room of a
bad one, and every branch of business was carried on to
greater advantage than before. The other Governments,
especially Connecticut and Rhode Island, who refused,
upon being invited, to conform their currency to the Massachusetts, felt a *shock* in their trade from which they have
not yet recovered. The latter had been the importers for
Massachusetts, of West India goods for many years, which
ceased at once."*

From this account of the operation of the provincial paper money of Massachusetts, the reader may judge of its
operation in the other colonies ; and thereby learn to estimate properly that provision of the United States' Constitution, which forbids any State " to emit bills of credit, pass
any law violating the obligation of contracts, or make any
thing but gold and silver a legal tender in the payment of
debts."

The successful issue of the experiment in Massachusetts
did not induce the other Governments to take the necessary
measures for substituting a metallic for a paper medium.
But, as the British merchants trading to the colonies were
sufferers by the monetary system of the day, an act of
Parliament was passed in 1763, " to prevent paper bills of
credit, hereafter to be issued in any of his Majesty's colonies or plantations in America, from being declared to be a
legal tender in payment of money, and to prevent the legal
tender of such bills as are now subsisting from being pro-

* Hutchinson, p. 440.

longed beyond the periods for calling in and sinking the same."

The preamble to the act declared, with great truth, that, by means of paper bills of credit, " debts have been discharged with a much less value than was contracted for, to the great discouragement and prejudice of trade and commerce of his Majesty's subjects, by occasioning confusion in dealings and lessening credit in the said colonies or plantations." The body of the act made void all acts of Assembly thereafter passed to establish or keep up such tender; and inflicted a fine of 1000 pounds (with immediate dismissal and future incapacity to fill any public office or place of trust,) on any Governor who should give his assent to such act of legal tender.

This measure caused much murmuring, for the speculating classes of society, who are always the most noisy, liked not to be deprived of so many opportunities of profit as a vacillating currency afforded them. They appeared to have had influence enough to prevent the act from being effective in some of the colonies; for we find that ten years after, another act with the same title was passed by the British Parliament.

The two acts together seem to have reduced the paper bills of credit to a very small amount; for Pelatiah Webster, a respectable merchant of Philadelphia, estimates the whole circulating cash of the thirteen States, just before the war, at twelve million dollars, or perhaps, not more than ten million hard dollars in value. "Not more than half, or at most three-fifths of the circulating cash in this State (Pennsylvania,) was paper; and I am well convinced that that proportion was not exceeded in the other States where paper money was circulated."

This provincial paper may be regarded as a species of Government script which by an act of tyranny was made a legal tender. It fluctuated in value, according to the changes in the credit of the Government by which it was issued, and the amount thrown into the market. Being more liable to great depreciation, it was inferior to Bank paper as money: but its character was better understood by the people. They knew the authority of the Government, and the resources of the Government. When they were injured, they knew by whom they were injured, if not to what extent.

In one respect the provincial paper money system had an effect directly opposite to that of the present Banking system. Through the present Banking system, dealings on credit are carried to an extent beyond that in which they are useful, and in which they become highly pernicious. Through the old paper money system, confidence was destroyed, and credit prevented from spreading to its natural extent.

The profits gained by the Governments by the issues of paper money, enabled them to diminish the regular taxes; but this gain was insignificant, and the evils produced by the system were incalculably great. All that honest men lost by highwaymen, house-breakers, foot-pads, and horse-thieves, was trifling in amount when compared with that which they lost through the instrumentality of the paper money of the different colonies.

CHAPTER III.

Of Continental Money.

According to an estimate by the Register of the Treasury, in 1790, the issues of continental money were as follows, viz :

				Old Emission.		New Emission.	
				Dolls.	*90ths.*	*Dolls.*	*90ths.*
In	1776	-	-	20,064,464	66		
	1777	-	-	26,426,333	1		
	1778	-	-	66,965,269	34		
	1779	-	-	149,703,856	77		
	1780	-	-	82,908,320	47	- 891,236	80
	1781	-	-	11,408,095	00	- 1,179,249	00
				$357,476,541	45	$2,070,485	80*

The first emission was dated May 10 1775, but the notes were not actually in circulation till the August following.†

* See the American Almanac for 1830.

† Most of the facts in this chapter have been derived from a series of essays by Pelatiah Webster, a merchant of Philadelphia, and an uncle of Noah Webster, the grammarian. They were published at different intervals, from 1776 to 1780, in pamphlet form, and collected into a volume, with notes, in 1790.

Till the issues exceeded nine millions, the bills, according to the concurrent testimony of Mr. Jefferson and Mr. Paine, passed at their nominal value. The depreciation afterwards was very great. The rate of exchange for hard money at Philadelphia, from January 1777 to May 1781, was as follows, according to a table take from the merchants' books and published by Mr. Pelatiah Webster.

1777.	January,	-	$1\frac{1}{4}$	1779.	April,	$12\frac{1}{2}$, 14, 16, 22
	February,	-	$1\frac{1}{2}$		May,	-	-	22, 24
	March,	-	-	2		June,	-	22, 20, 18
	April,	-	-	$2\frac{1}{2}$		July,	-	18, 19, 20
	May,	-	-	$2\frac{1}{2}$		August,	-	-	20
	June,	-	-	$2\frac{1}{2}$		September,	-	20, 28
	July,	-	-	3		October,	-	-	30
	August,	-	-	3		November,	-	32, 45
	September,	-	3		December,	-	45, 38
	October,	-	-	3	1780.	January,	-	-	40, 45
	November,	-	3		February,	-	45, 55
	December,	-	4		March,	-	-	60, 65
1778.	January,	-	4		April,	-	-	60
	February,	-	5		May,	-	-	60
	March,	-	-	5		June,	-	-	60
	April,	-	-	6		July,	-	-	60, 65
	May,	-	-	5		August,	-	-	65, 75
	June,	-	-	4		September	-	75
	July,	-	-	4		October,	-	-	75, 80
	August,	-	-	5		November,	-	80, 100
	September,	-	5		December,	-	100
	October,	-	-	5	1781.	January,	-	-	100
	November,	-	6		February,		100, 120
	December,	-	6		March,	-	120, 135
1779.	January	7, 8, 9		April,	-	135, 200
	February,	10		May,	-	200, 500
	March,	10, 11			

On the 31st of May, 1781, the continental bills ceased to circulate as money, but they were afterwards bought on speculation at various prices, from 400 for 1, up to 1000 fot 1.

The value of continental paper was not the same in different parts of the country. The exchange was, for example, December 25th 1779, at 35 for 1 in New England, New York, the Carolinas, and Georgia, and at 40 for 1 in Pennsylvania, New Jersey, Delaware, Maryland and Virginia.

An account taken from the books of merchants in Virginia shows that the depreciation there regularly followed that in Philadelphia, though, towards the close, it sometimes lagged a month or more behind. Thus, when exchange was at Philadelphia at 100 for 1, in January, 1781, it was in Virginia at 75 for 1 : and in April, when exchange in Philadelphia was at 135 for 1, it was in Virginia at 100 for 1.

As late as May, 1781, speculations were entered into at Philadelphia, to purchase continental money at 225 for 1, and sell it at Boston at 75 for 1.

It is worthy of remark " that the depreciation of continental money never stopped the circulation of it. As long as it retained any value at all, it passed quick enough: and would purchase hard money or any thing else, as readily as ever, when the exchange was 200 for 1, and when every hope, or even idea, of its being ultimately redeemed at nominal value had entirely vanished."[*]

The facility of raising ways and means, in the early part of the war, by issues of paper, led to much extravagance in the commissary department, and prevented the establishment of a sound system of finance. It is said that when a proposition was before Congress to establish a regular revenue system, one member exclaimed, "Do you think, gentlemen, that I will consent to load my constituents with taxes, when we can send to our printer, and get a waggon load of money, one quire of which will pay for the whole !"[†]

Our ancestors were lavish of their blood, in defence of their rights. If it was through a wish to save their treasure, that they resorted to paper money, they did not succeed in their object. As a mode of raising revenue, it might be compared to a tax, the expenses of collecting which were many times as great as the sum brought into the treasury. The benefit the Government derived from it, was in no way commensurate with the burden it imposed on the people. Most of the loss fell on the Whigs as it was in their hands the paper depreciated. The Tories, who had from the beginning no confidence in it, made it a rule to part with it as soon as possible.

This continental money was, in its true character, a sim-

* P. W.   † Ib.

ple evidence of debt due by the Government: and may, as
such, in the first stage of its operation, be compared to the
forced loans which the potentates of Europe have at times
extracted from their subjects. As a *forced currency*, it
may be compared to the base coin which the same potentates have issued in other seasons of difficulty. The resort
to it can be justified (if it can be justified at all,) only on
the plea of state necessity—a plea so easily made that it
ought never to be admitted without close examination.

It is difficult to believe that a people so devoted to liberty
as were the Americans of that day, would have been back-
ward in their contributions for the necessary expenses of
war, if they had not been taught by some of their leading
men that taxation was quite unnecessary, and that paper
money would supply every financial want. " What a shame
it is" said a patriotic old lady, " that Congress should let
the poor soldiers suffer, when they have power to make
just as much money as they choose."

The best, if not the only excuse, for the policy which
was adopted is, perhaps, to be found in the opinion then
prevalent, that money was something which derived its value from the authority of Government. In no other way
can we apologize for the acts which imposed severe penalties on those who refused to exchange their merchandise
for paper, and which in some instances even outlawed the
supposed offender.

When the continental money was first issued, an expression of doubt as to its value, involved suspicion of disaf-
fection to the cause of the country. As the issues increased,
the prices of goods necessarily rose; but this was attributed
to combinations of the merchants to raise the price of their
merchandise, and to sink the value of continental money.
They were called Tories, speculators, and many other hard
names; and their stores were forcibly broken open, and
their goods sold at limited prices by committees of the
neighbors.*

" The fatal error" says Mr. Webster, " that the credit
and currency of continental money could be kept up and
supported by acts of compulsion, entered so deep into the
minds of Congress, and all departments of administration

* P. W. Note to Essay of July, 1779.

through the States, that no considerations of justice, religion, or policy, or even experience of its utter inefficiency, could eradicate it : it seemed to be a kind of obstinate delirium, totally deaf to every argument drawn from justice and right, from its natural tendency and mischief, from common justice, and even from common sense.

"Congress began, as early as Jan. 11th, 1776, to hold-up and recommend this *maxim of maniaism*, when continen tal money was but five months old. Congress then resolved that 'whoever should refuse to receive in payment continental bills, should be declared and treated as an enemy of his country, and be precluded from intercourse with its inhabitants,' i. e. should be *outlawed:* which is the severest penalty (except of life and limb,) known to our laws.

"This ruinous principle was continued in practice for five successive years, and appeared in all shapes and forms, i. e. in *tender acts*, in *limitation of prices*, in *awful and threatening declarations*, in *penal laws*, with dreadful and ruinous punishments, and in every other way that could be devised, and all executed with a relentless severity by the highest authorities then in being, viz. by Congress, by Assemblies and Conventions of the States, and by *committees of inspection* (whose powers in those days were nearly sovereign,) and even by military force : and though men of all descriptions stood trembling before this monster of force, without daring to lift a hand against it during all this period, yet its unrestrained energy always proved ineffectual to its purposes, but in every case increased the evils it was designed to remedy, and destroyed the benefits it was intended to promote : at best its utmost effect was like that of water sprinkled on a blacksmith's forge, which, indeed, deadens the flame for a moment, but never fails to increase the heat and flame of the internal fire. Many *thousand families* of full and easy fortune, were ruined by these fatal measures, and *lie in ruins* to this day (1790) without the least benefit to the country, or to the great and noble cause in which we were then engaged."

After this account of the nature of the system, the reader will readily believe Mr. Webster, when he says, in an essay published in March, 1780, " Frauds, cheats, and gross dishonesty are introduced, and a thousand idle ways of living are attempted in the room of honest industry, economy and diligence which have heretofore enriched and blessed this country."

In various parts of his essays, he adverts to the sufferings of the people from the necessary incidents of the war. The price of foreign commodities was increased many per cent. There was " an extreme scarcity and want of some necessary articles ; for example, much meat was spoiled and lost for want of salt to preserve it : and many trades and manufactures were either wholly stopped or greatly diminished for want of materials. Another hardship very sensibly felt was the force which was used with all descriptions of men in seizing their goods, wagons, stock, grain, cattle, timber, and every thing else which was wanted for the public service. To these may be added the captures, the ravages, and depredations, the burnings and plunders of the enemy, which were very terrible and expensive. They had possession, first or last, in the course of the war, of eleven of the capitals of the thirteen States, pervaded the country in every part, and left dreadful tracks of their marches behind : burning, in cool blood, a great number not only of houses, barns, mills, &c., but also of most capital towns and villages." Yet these evils were not as great in the judgment of Mr. Webster, (and he was an eye witness and a participator of these sufferings,) as those which were caused by continental money and the consequent irregularities of the financial system. " We have suffered more from this cause" he says, " than from *every other* cause of calamity : it has killed more men, pervaded and corrupted the choicest interests of our country more, and done more injustice than even the arms and artifices of our enemies."*

" While we rejoice in the riches and strength of our country, we have reason to lament with tears of the deepest regret, the *most pernicious shifts of property* which the irregularities of our finances introduced, and the many thousands of fortunes which were ruined by it; the generous, patriotic spirits suffered the injury: the idle and avaricious derived benefit from said confusion."†

Certain compulsory measures of the Executive Council of Pennsylvania, designed to support the credit of conti-

* P. W. Essay of Jan. 8th 1780.   † Note to Essay of Feb. 20th 1780.

nental money and of the State bills, gave the fatal blow to the system, in May 1781. Mr. Webster gives a minute account of the proceedings; but we deem it unnecessary to transcribe them, for, as he justly observes, " they will appear to a stranger as intricate and as hard to understand as the prices of stocks in Change Alley." We doubt not, however, " that they were perfectly understood by people of all ranks at that time, inasmuch as every variation of the exchange altered the value of all their cash on hand."

" Thus," he exclaims, after having narrated the proceedings of the Executive Council, and their important effects, " thus fell, ended, and died, the continental currency, aged six years. Bubbles of another sort, such as the Mississipi scheme in France, and the South Sea in England, lasted but a few months, and then burst into nothing : but this held out much longer, and seemed to retain a vigorous constitution to its last : for its circulation was never more brisk than when its exchange was 500 to one ; and yet it expired without a groan or struggle; and I believe of all things which ever suffered dissolution since life was first given to the creation, this mighty monster died the least lamented.

" If it saved the State, it has also polluted the equity of our laws; turned them into engines of oppression and wrong : corrupted the justice of our public administration : destroyed the fortunes of thousands of those who had the most confidence in it, enervated the trade, husbandry and manufactures of our country, and gone far to destroy the morality of our people."

Many who are yet living can attest the truth of this statement.

CHAPTER IV.

Of the Bank of North America.

It is a common opinion that the Bank of North America rendered essential service during our revolutionary struggle —that, without it, the achievement of independence would have been difficult, if not impossible. Assertions to this effect have been made with so much confidence that we once believed them to be well-founded; but on examination we find—

First. That the capture of Cornwallis, which is described by historians as the closing scene of the Revolutionary War, took place on the 9th of October, 1781, and that the Bank did not go into operation till January 7th, 1782.

Secondly. That the whole amount of expenditures of the U. S. Government in the year 1782, was only three million six hundred thousand dollars, and in 1783 only three million two hundred thousand dollars. Large loans were negotiated in Europe in these years; " and such a conviction of the necessities of public supplies generally took place through the States, that considerable sums were obtained by a tax on polls and real estates."*

Thirdly. The whole amount subscribed by individuals to the Bank did not, as appears from the concurrent testimony of Mr. Robert Morris and Mr. Gouverneur Morris, exceed 70,000 dollars.

Fourthly. From statements made by Mr. Robert Morris, in public debate in the Legislature of Pennsylvania, in the year 1786, it appears that the advances made by the Bank to the Government, above the amount of silver money actually paid in by the Government, never did exceed 165,000 dollars, and for a part of the time did not amount to 50,000 dollars.†

The reader, on duly considering these facts, will probably be convinced that the services rendered by the Bank of North America, during our revolutionary struggle, have been grossly exaggerated.

From the beginning of the year 1780, till the close of the war, hard money was very plenty. This " was occa-

---

* P. W.

† From the statements of Mr. Robert Morris, the accounts of the Government with the Bank were as follows:

			Cr.	Dr.				
April 2d,	-	1782	- 252,918	300,000	-	-	-	47,082
July	-	1782	- 252,918	400,000	-	-	-	147,082
October	-	1782	- 253,394	400,000	-	-	-	146,606
January	-	1783	- 53,394	100,000	-	-	-	46,606
April	-	1783	- 53,394	100,000	-	-	-	46,606
July	-	1783	-	129,800	-	-	-	129,800
October	.	1783	-	164,781	-	-	-	164,781

January 1st. 1784, the debt was discharged.

The last column shows the amount in which the Government was in debt to the Bank, at the different periods mentioned.

sioned by large sums, by various means, coming from the
English army at New York, and spreading through the
States ; also by large sums remitted by France to their army
and navy here; also by large importations of hard money
from the Havanna and other places abroad ; so that hard
money was never more plenty nor more easily collected
than at that time." In a note to an essay of later date,
Mr. Webster says, " the States were really overrun with
abundance of cash : the French and English armies, our
foreign loans, Havanna trade &c., had filled the country
with money."

" It has been asked," says Lord Sheffield, " what has
become of the money which we have sent during the war
to America? Some is come back—a considerable part is
the circulating cash within our lines. Many British subjects in New York have very large sums in their possession. The Dutch and Germans, whose number is not inconsiderable, have hoarded up—and it is believed considerable sums are concealed.

" France sent (not included in the debt) above 600,000
pounds sterling in specie to America, being obliged to send
cash."*

The operations of the war caused such a drain of specie
from Europe, that the Bank of England was brought into
jeopardy, and the *Caisse d' Escompte* at Paris actually
suspended payment in 1783 : and such a flux of specie into
the United States, that, as Mr. Webster observes, " hard
money was never more plenty or more easily collected."

Such being the state of the money market, it is difficult
to believe that the Government might not, if the Bank had
not been established, have obtained a loan of 50,000 to
165,000 dollars from some other source. It does not appear that the Bank ever made advances to the Government,
except on the best security. For at least 80,000 dollars of
the amount, the State of Pennsylvania was guarantee. For
the residue of the amount, the Government might have
pledged the proceeds of the taxes, or bills on Europe : and
on the same security, it is probable, individuals would have
made the advances, especially as money was so abundant,
and the news of peace confidently expected.

* Observations on the Commerce of the American States. June 21st
1783.

The truth is, that the project of establishing a Bank in Philadelphia had been conceived by Mr. Robert Morris, before the commencement of the war, as appears from his own declaration :* and he had entered into negociations in Europe with a view to effect this object. But a project for a Bank about the year 1763, had been vigorously opposed on the ground that it would give a few men a monopoly of trade : and it is probable that Mr. Robert Morris's project would have encountered severe opposition, if it had not been brought forward as a *fiscal* measure, and at a time when neither the Legislature nor the people could give it that consideration it deserved.

He submitted his plan to Congress in May, 1780, and on the 26th of the same month it was approved by that body. " Yet," he says, " until the month of September or October following, there were not more subscriptions in the whole, than amounted to about 70,000 dollars. During the time, one of his most Christian Majesty's frigates arrived at Boston, and brought a remittance in specie of about 470,000 dollars. The sum was brought to Philadelphia and deposited in the vaults of the Bank. I determined from the moment of its arrival, to subscribe on behalf of the United States, for those shares in the Bank which remained vacant: but such was the amount of the public expenditures, that notwithstanding the utmost care and caution to keep this money, nearly one-half of the sum was exhausted before the institution could be organized. In November, 1781, the president and directors of the Bank were elected: they obtained a charter of incorporation from Congress—and opened the Bank for transacting business in January, 1782. I subscribed the sum then remaining in the treasury, being about 254,000 dollars, into the Bank stock, per account of the United States, which became thereby the principal stockholder."†

As is remarked by Mr. Gouverneur Morris, the sum subscribed by Government may be said to have been paid in

* See Carey's "Debates and Proceedings of the General Assembly of Pennsylvania, on the memorials praying a repeal or suspension of the law annulling the charter of the Bank." Phil. 1786.

*† It may be made a question, whether the *whole* of the original capital of the Bank was not advanced by Government. Thomas Paine says, in one of his tracts, it is well known " that the Bank originated in another Bank called the Bank of Pennsylvania, which was formed in

with one hand, and borrowed with the other, leaving the Bank but 70,000 dollars at most for its proper operations. On this amount it undertook to make advances to the Government and to individuals; but as the experience of the evils of continental money was fresh in the minds of the people, some difficulty was encountered in giving currency to the notes of the Bank. To remove this "prejudice" the gentlemen who were interested in the institution, were, as we have learned from undoubted private authority, in the practice of requesting people from the country and laboring men about town, to go to the Bank and get silver in exchange for notes. When they went on this errand of neighborly kindness, as *they* thought it, they found a display of silver on the counter, and men employed in raising boxes containing silver, or supposed to contain silver, from the cellar into the Banking room, or lowering them from the Banking room into the cellar. By contrivances like these, the Bank obtained the reputation of possessing immense wealth; but its hollowness was several times nearly made apparent, especially on one occasion, when one of the co-partners withdrew a deposit of some five or six thousand dollars, when the whole specie stock of the Bank did not probably exceed twenty thousand.

By these means, and by the assistance of the United States Government, the notes of the Bank became current;

the spring of 1780. On the 17th of June, it was resolved to open a security subscription to the amount of 300,000 pounds Pennsylvania currency, in real money, the subscribers to *execute bonds* for the amount of their subscription, and to form a Bank for supplying the army." He afterwards speaks of some of *these subscriptions* being transferred to the Bank of North America.

From the journals of Congress, it appears that the Board of Treasury was directed to deposite in this Pennsylvania Bond-Bank, "bills of exchange, in favor of the directors thereof, on the Ministers of the United States in Europe, or any of them, and in such sums as shall be thought convenient, but not to exceed in the whole £150,000 sterling."

Were the 70,000 dollars which were subscribed by individuals to the Bank of North America, paid in bonds or in money? Was a part of the 470,000 dollars received by the French frigate, used in redeeming some of these bonds: and was it in this way subscriptions were transferred from the old Bond Bank to the Bank of North America: or were the 70,000 dollars paid in by individuals without any trafficking with Government? These questions are, perhaps, rather curious than useful: but our knowledge of the contrivances for forming Bank stock in our own day, makes us desire to see an explanation of the 70,000 dollars subscription by individuals.

and so profitable was the business that the early dividends were at the rate of from 12 to 16 per cent. per annum. This naturally created a desire in others to share in so very lucrative a trade. A project was therefrom formed for establishing a second Bank, to be called the Bank of Pennsylvania. This, they who were interested in the Bank of North America strenuously opposed, fearing the effect of a rival institution in Philadelphia. To prevent its being established, they opened their books for additional subscriptions; but not without murmuring loudly at the hardship of receiving new partners.*

In the year 1784, the Bank did a very extensive businsss; and by the beginning of 1785, the effects of its operations began to be very apparent. They are such as

* The following is an extract from a pamphlet, published in 1785, entitled an "Address to the General Assembly of Pennsylvania, on the abolition of the Bank Charter."

"After the peace, when the advantages of the Bank had been felt, and the property of the stock had become secure, an opposition was raised by some of the same persons who are now the opposers, but on grounds somewhat different. For then, instead of considering the Bank as pernicious, it was considered to be so highly beneficial that they must needs have two. They did indeed complain of the old Bank. But for what? Not because the capital was so large as to threaten general ruin: but because the directors would not open a subscription to make it larger. And what was the modest request of that day? Why, truly, such an extension of the capital as might enable those who had waited for events in perfect ease and safety, to enjoy the same advantages with those who had borne the burden, and run the risk of the contest. It was, indeed, a hard case that many worthy gentlemen who would not have given a shilling to save the State, should be obliged to pay either $500 for a share in Bank which had cost but four, or to lend their money on bond and mortgage to the farmers of Pennsylvania. A very hard case; And so loudly did they complain of it, that at last many sensible members of Assembly were prevailed on to believe it would be a good thing to have two Banks. Two shops to go to, for that was the fashionable phrase. And they were the more easily led into this opinion, because it was laid down by some in high stations, for whose sentiments they had acquired a habitual respect.

"The consequence of the noise made at the time, must be well remembered. The Assembly were plagued with long arguments on both sides which might have been spared, and then, all at once, the thing was hushed up and accommodated. Because, such of the promoters of the new Bank as had money, found out their new friends had none. Because they all found out the scheme did not promise so much either of security or profit, as was imagined. And because they had not too much confidence in each other, being (like Nebuchadnezar's image) composed of discordant materials. They agreed, therefore, to abandon their project, on certain conditions acceded to by the old Bank, one of which was to extend the subscription, and this it is which has convert-

Banking has always produced—a temporary plentifulness of money, followed by great scarcity, usury, ruin to the many, riches to the few. These effects were ably set forth in petitions to the Assembly, from the inhabitants of Philadelphia, and those of the counties of Chester and Bucks, presented on the 21st and 23d of March, praying for a repeal of the charter of the Bank. Those petitions were referred to a committee, who, in a report of the 25th of the same month, fully sustained the allegations of the petitioners, and recommended a repeal of the charter. This recommendation was carried into effect, at the *ensuing* session, on the 13th of September, 1785.

Thus we find that the first Bank established in this country produced so much evil, that its charter was taken from it in less than four years after it had commenced operations.

The Bank, however, claiming the right of prosecuting its business under the act of Congress, continued its operations, though on a more moderate scale. In 1786, an attempt was made by its friends to obtain a renewal of the charter from the State of Pennsylvania, but it was successfully opposed by Wm. Findlay of Westmoreland, Mr. Smilie of the same county, and other leading democrats. It is difficult, however, for the people long to withstand the efforts of a powerful monied interest; and it being pleaded, with some show of reason, that the forms of the Constitution had not been properly regarded in taking away the charter, and many persons fearing a return of the old paper money system, the Bank was re-incorporated on the 17th of March, 1787, with limited powers, and for fourteen years. By successive acts of the Legislature, it has been continued in existence to the present day.*

ed all the surplus money of the State into Bank stock. For otherwise, let the price of a share have risen ever so high, nay, had it gone to 4000 instead of 400 dollars, not one penny would have been added to the Bank capital. But in proportion as stock rose, the dividends would have been less valuable.

"It is notorious that if the Directors had not been under compulsion, they would not have extended the subscriptions beyond the first 400,000 dollars. It is notorious that any addition to the number of shares lessens the value of each."

* For further particulars respecting the early history of the Bank of North America, see Appendix.

CHAPTER V.

Of the Old Bank of the United States.

" Let the Americans," said Wm. Pitt, " adopt their funding system, and go into their Banking institutions, and
their boasted independence will be a mere phantom."

No small number of Americans were of a similar opinion : but it was contended by others, that if the revolutionary debt was not funded, injustice would be done to
the public creditors. Out of this funding system sprung
the old Bank of the United States, for three-fourths of its
capital consisted of public stocks. The Bank, its friends
averred, was necessary to support the public credit, and
aid the fiscal operations of the Federal Government. Its
opponents contended that it was anti-republican in its tendency, and that the Constitution gave Congress no power to establish such an institution.

The period immediately succeeding the Revolutionary
War, was, in a peculiar sense, an age of speculation.
Trafficking in soldier's certificates, in the public lands, and
in the various evidences of the public debt, was the business of many who had money, and of many who had not.
Perhaps the fortunes some thereby acquired, may have excited envy, and thus increased the opposition to the system
which had its origin with some in political, and with others,
in moral reasons. Be this as it may, the Bank of the United
States was regarded as the cap-stone of a policy which
was viewed as very objectionable : and the democratic
journals of the day abounded in what one of our most respectable authors calls " abuse of the Banking and funding system."

Mr. Jefferson's opposition to Banks was of the most decided character. In his preface to Destutt Tracy's Political Economy, he denounces them as parisitical institutions :
and he seldom let slip an opportunity of expressing his ab-
horrence of their whole scheme of operations. His objections to the Bank of the United States on constitutional
grounds were equally strong. " I consider," he says, " the
foundation of the Constitution as laid on this ground, that
" all powers not delegated to the United States by the Con-

stitution, nor prohibited by it to the States, are reserved
to the States or the people." To take a single step beyond
the boundaries thus specially drawn around the power of
Congress, is to take possession of a boundless field of
power, no longer susceptible of definition. The incorporation of a Bank, and other powers assumed by this bill,
have not, in my opinion, been delegated to the United States
by the Constitution." After showing that the powers were
not among those specially enumerated, nor in any of the
general phrases, he says " It is known that the very power
now proposed as *a means* was rejected as *an end* by the
Convention which formed the Constitution : a proposition
was made to them to authorize Congress to open canals,
and an emendatory one to empower them to incorporate ;
but the whole was rejected, and one of the reasons urged
in the debate was, that then they would have power to
create a Bank, which would render the great cities, where
there were prejudicies or jealousies on this subject, adverse
to the reception of the Constitution."

The Bank was not established by a strict party vote,
for eleven out of thirty-nine who voted for it were democrats, and six out of twenty, who opposed it, were fede-
ralists; but it afterwards became, as Mr. Niles says, one of
the landmarks of party, and, in the second Congress, a
resolution declaring the Bank charter unconstitutional, was
within one vote of passing the House.

The hostility of the democratic party to the Bank, was
but little abated for many years ; but, as the time approach-
ed for the expiration of the charter, enmity to the institution gave way, in a great degree, to fear of the distress
which the winding up of its affairs would produce. The
pens of numerous scribes were employed in portraying the
manifold evils which must come upon the country, and
deputations of merchants and mechanics were sent from
Philadelphia to Washington, to beg Congress to avert the
impending danger.*

* See the public papers of the day.
Of the feeling with which a portion of the community regarded the
prospect of a non-renewal of the Bank charter, an opinion may be
formed from the following extract from a pamphlet, by Mr. Carey, entitled " Desultory Reflections upon the Ruinous Consequences of a
Non-Renewal of the Charter of the Bank of the United States," published in May, 1810.

The predictions that were so confidently made of the ruin that would overspread the land, if the charter were not renewed, had their intended effect on some of the democratic members. But, after a full discussion, the bill was indefinitely postponed on the 24th of January, 1811, in the House of Representatives, by a vote of 65 to 64. The National Intelligencer said, on recording the vote, that if the question had not been on the indefinite postponement, but

"In the history of nations, as well as of individuals, there are to be found occasional moments of *frenzy*, in which every movement baffles the calculations of the politician, the moralist and the philosopher. To the distractions and derangements of our affairs with the European world we are, with almost incredible folly, preparing, by allowing the charter of the Bank of the United States to expire, to add an *awful* scene of internal disorder and confusion, of private and public bankruptcy. I have gone over my calculations anew ; sifted the facts on which my opinions are founded: turned them in every possible point of view, to discover errors if any there were. But the result of every examination has been an invariable conviction of the reality of the danger, the momentary frenzy of too many of my fellow-citizens, and the awful consequences of the prevailing apathy, if it should continue."

By the next session of Congress, Mr. Carey's fears were in no degree abated, as will be seen by the following extract from another pamphlet, published December 15th, 1810, and entitled "Nine Letters to Dr. Adam Seybert, Representative in Congress for the City of Philadelphia."

"Never have I addressed my fellow-citizens with more solicitude than I feel at present. The question at issue, respecting the renewal of the charter of the Bank of the United States, in its consequences upon the character of the country, and upon the prosperity and happiness of a large portion of its most valuable citizens, I conceive to be of more importance than any one that has been agitated for twenty years." He then intimates to members of Congress from parts of the country remote from the operations of Banking, "that they are liable to be bewildered and led astray ; to be instrumental in dashing the Bank of public credit upon rocks and quicksands, and producing *an awful scene of destruction, the consequences or terminations of which elude the power of calculation.* At such a crisis, it behoves every man whose experience in any degree qualifies him to shed light upon the subject, to step boldly forward, and use his endeavors to preserve so many vital interests as are at stake from the destruction which menaces them. In such a cause, indifference and guilt would perhaps be synonymous. Influenced by these motives, and unalterably convinced of the reality of the impending ruin, I resolved, at the risk of the abuse, the calumny, the malignity, and the persecution, to which every man is liable, who, on such occasions, takes an active part, to raise my feeble voice in defence of a good cause. I fully resolved that, come the calamity when it might, I should be able to wash my hands from any participation in the guilt, even by neutrality."

on the passage of the bill, the majority would have been much greater.

Another bill was brought before the Senate ; but, on the 20th of February, the first section was struck out by the casting vote of the Vice President, George Clinton.

The Senate gave this vote, which was equivalent to a rejection of the bill, only *eleven* days before the charter expired. The Bank made application in this interval for such an extension of its charter as would enable it to wind up its concerns. But the Committee of the House to whom the memorial was referred, reported, through their Chairman, Mr. Henry Clay, " that, holding the opinion, (as a majority of the Committee do,) that the Constitution did not authorize Congress originally to grant the charter, it follows as a necessary consequence of that opinion, than an extension of it, even under the restrictions contemplated by the stockholders, is equally repugnant to the Constitution."*

Trustees were then appointed, and they proceeded so rapidly in winding up the concerns of the Bank, that on the 1st of June, 1812, they paid over to the stockholders 70 per cent. of the capital stock, and 18 per cent. more on the 1st of October.†

This was a rapid collection of the debts due to the institution, inasmuch as it enabled the trustees to pay 88 per cent. of the capital stock, in about a year and a half ; but it did not produce the universal ruin with which the country had been threatened. " Many persons" said Dr. Seybert, writing in 1816, " viewed a dissolution of the late Bank of the United States as a national calamity ; it was asserted that a general bankruptcy must follow that event. The fact was otherwise : every branch of industry continued uninterrupted—no failures in the mercantile community were attributable to that occurrence."‡

* Legislative History of the Bank of the United States.

† Another instalment, amounting to 7 per cent., was paid on the 1st of April, 1813. An additional payment of 5 per cent. was made in April, 1815, and another of 5 per cent. in December, 1817. Two or three small payments, of the exact amount of which we are not informed, were subsequently made. Some years before the expiration of the charter, the stock sold at 156.

‡ Statistics, pp. 522.

CHAPTER VI.

Of Banking from 1790 to 1810–11.

In Vol. III of the American edition of the Edinburgh Cyclopedia, published in 1813, the following table is given, " to exhibit in one view the names of the Banks most deserving of notice, the time of their institution, and the amount of their capital." The table is not complete, but it shows the time in which the Banking system was introduced into the different States.

Names.	Instituted.	Capital.
Bank of North America, Pa.	1781–2	$ 2,000,000
Massachusetts Bank at Boston, Mass.	1784	1,600,000
Bank of New York, N. Y.	1784	950,000
Bank of Maryland, Md.	1790	300,000
Providence Bank, R. I.	1791	400,000
Bank of Albany, N. Y.	1792	260,000
Bank of South Carolina, S. C.	1792	640,000
Union Bank of Boston, Mass.	1792	1,200,000
New Hampshire Bank, N. H.	1792	100,000
Bank of Alexandria, Va.	1792	500,000
Hartford Bank, Conn.	1792	930,000
Union Bank, New London, Conn.	1792	500,000
New Haven Bank, Conn.	1792	400,000
Bank of Columbia, N. Y.	1793	160,000
Bank of Columbia, D. C.	1793	500,000
Bank of Pennsylvania, Pa.	1793	3,000,000
Bank of Nantucket, Mass.	1795	100,000
Bank of Delaware, Del.	1795	110,000
Bank of Baltimore, Md.	1795	1,200,000
Middletown Bank, Conn.	1795	400,000
Bank of Rhode Island, R. I.	1795	100,000
Norwich Bank, Conn.	1796	200,000
Manhattan Bank, N. Y.	1799	2,000,000
Portland Bank, Me.	1799	300,000
Essex Bank, Salem, Mass.	1799	300,000
Washington Bank, Westerly, R. I.	1800	50,000
Bank of Bristol, R. I.	1800	120,000
Exchange Bank, Providence, R. I.	1801	400,000
Farmers' Bank, Lansinburgh, N. Y.	1801	75,000
State Bank of South Carolina, S. C.	1801	800,000
Maine Bank, Portland, Me.	1802	300,000
New Hampshire Union Bank, N. H.	1802	200,000

Names.	Instituted.	Capital.
Lin and Ken Bank, Wiscasset, Me.	1802	$ 200,000
Kentucky Insurance Company, Ky.	1802	150,000
Merchants Bank, N. Y.	1803	1,250,000
Bedford Bank, at N. B., Mass.	1803	150,000
New York State Bank, N. Y.	1803	460,000
Newburyport Bank, Mass.	1803	550,000
Saco Bank, Mass.	1803	100,000
Albany Mercantile Comp., N. Y.	1803	25,000
Plymouth Bank, Mass.	1803	100,000
Boston Bank, Mass.	1803	1,800,000
Stafford Bank, at Dover, Mass.	1803	150,000
Philadelphia Bank, Pa.	1803	2,000,000
Miami Exporting Comp., Cinn. O.	1803	200,000
Salem Bank, Mass.	1803	200,000
Roger Williams' Bank, R. I.	1803	150,000
Newport Bank, R. I.	1803	120,000
Warren Bank, R. I.	1803	68,000
Exeter Bank, N. H.	——	200,000
Union Bank of Maryland, Md.	1804	3,000,000
Bank of Cape Fear, N. C.	1804	350,000
Bank of Newbern, N. C.	1804	300,000
Newark Banking and Ins., Co. N.J.	1804	225,000
Trenton Bank, N. J.	1804	300,000
Hallowell and Augusta Bank, Me.	1804	200,000
Worcester Bank, Mass.	1804	150,000
Nantucket Pacific Bank, Mass.	1804	100,000
Marblehead Bank, Mass.	1804	100,000
Rhode Island Union Bank, R. I	1804	150,000
Smithfield Union Bank, R. I.	1805	50,000
Narragansett Bank, R. I.	1805	60,000
Rhode Island Central Bank, R. I.	1805	60,000
Bank of Virginia, Va.	1805	1,500,000
Mechanics' Bank, Baltimore, Md.	1806	1,000,000
Bank of Chilicothe, Ohio	1806	100,000
Bridgeport Bank, Conn.	1806	200,000
Derby Bank, Conn.	1806	200,000
Bank of Kentucky, Ky.	1807	1,000,000
Bank of Nashville, Ten.	1807	500,000
Bank of Marietta, Ohio	1807	100,000
Farmers Bk. of the State of Del., D.	1807	500,000
New Bunswick Bank, N. J.	1807	150,000
Farmers and Mechanics Bank, Pa.	1807	1,250,000
Hagerstown Bank, Md.	1807	250,000
Mohawk Bank, N. Y.	1807	200,000
New London Bank, Conn.	1807	200,000
Hudson Bank, N. Y.	1808	300,000

Names.	Instituted.	Capital.
Bank of Steubenville, Ohio	1809	$ 100,000
Chambersburgh Bank, Pa.	1809	250,000
Commercial Bank, R. I.	1809	50,000
State Bank of North Carolina, N.C.	1810	1,600,000
Commer. & Farm. Bk. of Balt, Md.	1810	1,000,000
Farm. & Merch. Bk. of Balt., Md.	1810	500,000
Franklin Bank, Do.	1810	600,000
Marine Bank, Do.	1810	600,000
Elkton Bank, Md.	1810	300,000
Farmers' Bank of Lancaster, Pa.	1810	300,000
Mechanics' Bank, N. Y.	1810	2,000,000
Bank of Troy, N. Y.	1811	500,000
Mechanics' & Farmers' Bank, N.Y.	1811	600,000
State Bank at Boston, Mass.	1811	3,000,000
Merchants' Bank at Salem, Mass.	1811	200,000
Cumberland Bank of Alleghany, Md.	1811	200,000
Bank of Newburgh, N. Y.	1811	400,000
Farmers' Bank of Wor. & Som. Md.	1811	200,000
Middle District Bank, N. Y.	1811	500,000
Bank of New Orleans, L.	1811	500,000
Union Bank, N. Y.	1811	1,800,000
Eagle Bank, Conn.	1811	750,000
Bank of America, N. Y.	1812	6,000,000
City Bank, N. Y.	1812	2,000,000
Farm. and Mechan. Bk. of Cinn., O.	1812	500,000
Bank of Muskingum, Zanesville, O.	1812	100,000
Monongahela Bank, O.	1812	250,000
New York Manufacturing Co., N.Y.	1812	1,200,000
Camden State Bank, N. J.	1812	800,000
Trenton Do. Do.	1812	300,000
New Brunswick State Bank, N. J.	1812	400,000
Newark Do. Do.	1812	400,000
Elizabeth Do. Do.	1812	200,000
Morris Do. Do.	1812	200,000
Utica Bank, N. Y.	1812	1,000,000
Pittsburg Manufacturing Co., Pa.	1812	1,000,000
City Bank of Baltimore, Md.	1812	1,500,000
B. of Wil'gton and Brandywine,Del.	1812	120,000
Farm. & Mechan. Bank of Del., D.	1812	75,000
Commercial Bank of Del., D.	1812	200,000
Farm. & Mechan. Bk. of Va.,V.	1812	1,500,000
Savannah Bank, Geo.	——	1,000,000
Union Bank, S. C.	——	1,000,000
Planters' and Mechanics' Bank, S.C.	——	1,000,000

Total, $77,258,000

The operations of Banks in those times, were much like their operations in our own days. Thus, Mr. Burwell, of Virginia,in a speech delivered in 1811, said, " In Baltimore, where the Bank capital has always exceeded the demand by solvent customers, and where, to give full employment to their funds, the Banks have been accustomed to accommodate mere speculators, failures have happened to the amount of a million, without property to pay the creditors twenty cents in the dollar. (A gentleman from Maryland corrected Mr. Burwell, by stating that the failures had in the aggregate exceeded the sum he had mentioned, but in no single instance had the loss to creditors exceeded 600,000 dollars.) I stand corrected only 600,000 dollars."*

It was in New England, however, that Banking operations were carried furthest. The author of a pamphlet, entitled " Remarks on Money," published at Philadelphia in 1814, says, some of the institutions in that quarter issued bills for so small a sum as twenty-five cents, whereby " it was rendered so difficult in some of the Eastern States, to get a dollar changed, that it became necessary to purchase change of the money dealers in towns for current travelling expenses in the country."

Of the principles of operation of some of these institutions, we have a curious memorial in a report made on the 20th of March, 1809, by a committee of the Legislature of Rhode Island, appointed to inquire into the situation ot the Farmers' Exchange Bank of Gloucester. The Committee state, "that the said Bank was incorporated, February, A. D. 1804. That by the charter, its capital stock was to consist of two thousand shares of fifty dollars each, payable in seven instalments, in gold or silver. It appears to the Committee that the capital stock was not paid in according to the provisions of the charter. Some of the stockholders paid the whole amount of the shares by them subscribed ; others paid a part and gave their notes for the residue. The directors did not pay any money whatever, for although, in common with the other stockholders, the directors lodged the amount of their first instalment in specie, yet, in a very few days afterwards, all the directors received out of the Bank the amount of said instalments in bills of said

* Legislative History of United States Bank.

Bank, for which no security whatever was given, and they gave five notes, without indorsers, for the five first instalments, payable on demand with interest : for the two last instalments, no payment was made or security given. The said notes remained in the Bank until the directors transferred their stock, when they were delivered up in the manner hereinafter mentioned. The directors were the holders of one hundred and three shares each, and in this manner did the Farmers' Exchange Bank, which by the charter was to consist of two thousand shares, commence its operations with only six hundred and sixty-one shares, on which any payments had been made in gold and silver, agreeably to the express provisions of the charter : and the whole money paid into the Bank at any one period whatever, on the said six hundred and sixty-one shares, amounted to nineteen thousand one hundred and forty-one dollars and eighty-six cents.

" Prior to the twenty-ninth of March 1808, sundry stockholders, holding four hundred and fifty shares, transferred them to the directors of said Bank. No money or other consideration whatever was paid by the directors with their own property to any of the stockholders who so transferred their shares, but they were uniformily paid for with the property of the corporation. Most of the said stockholders were indebted to the Bank in notes, and to them their notes were given up, and if their shares exceeded the sum due from them to the Bank, the balance was paid out of the Bank with the property of the corporation : and none of the said directors, or any person whatever, was debited for the said sums so paid, or for the notes surrendered.

" On the third day of June, 1805, the Board of Directors passed a vote permitting each director to take out of the Bank 200 dollars for the purpose of exchanging the the same. The said directors have never paid or accounted for said money to the Bank.

" When the Bank first commenced its operations, the capital paid in, including the money paid by the directors, and which was soon after repaid to them, as is herein before stated, amounted to the sum of eleven thousand eight hundred and six dollars and sixty one cents : when the directors had, as before stated, taken back in bills the amount they had paid in specie for their first instalment, the capital stock really paid in, amounted to only the sum of three thousand and eighty-one dollars and eleven cents.

" The directors never declared any certain dividend of the profits of the Bank, but once a year paid to the stockholders interest generally at the rate of eight per cent. per annum on the sums they had respectively paid in, and the residue, amounting in some years to one hundred and thirty dollars each, the directors divided among themselves.

" According to the books containing the weekly state of the Bank, there were several periods when the amount of bills in circulation far exceeded the amount of notes due the Bank ; for instance, on the twenty-fifth day of March, 1805, the amount of bills in circulation was seventy-two thousand two hundred and eleven dollars, and the amount of debts due the Bank was fifty-three thousand two hundred and seventy-five dollars : at some periods, anterior to the 29th day of March, 1808, the Bank had in circulation from sixty to seventy thousand dollars. On the 28th day of March 1808, there was in said Bank, in specie and bills of other Banks, three hundred and eighty dollars and fifty cents, and the Bank had twenty-two thousand five hundred and twenty-four dollars of their own bills in circulation."

Under this system, the Bank continued in operation about four years : and then eleven of the directors transferred their interest in the institution to the agent of Andrew Dexter, jun., of Boston. Each of the directors received thirteen hundred dollars in consideration of his transferring his shares ; and each of them received back the notes he had given for instalments, the whole principal and interest whereof were then due to the Bank. " The thirteen hundred dollars were paid to some of the directors by notes signed by Simon Smith and John Harris, as principals, and Andrew Dexter, jun., as surety : to others by surrendering them notes given by the Bank for money borrowed, and to others by giving them the notes of individuals which were the property of the Bank. It appears that *all* the money paid to the said directors, *was paid out of the Bank with the property of said corporation*, except that there is charged to said Dexter, three thousand seven hundred and eighty-five dollars and ninety-five cents paid on that account."

Dexter thus got control of the institution, and having a Board of Directors disposed to favor his views, he got from

the Bank, at divers times in the course of the year, its bills
to the amount of *seven hundred and sixty thousand two
hundred and sixty-five dollars,* and there was paid to sundry
persons for his use three thousand seven hundred and eighty-five dollars and ninety-five cents."

" From the first connexion of Dexter with the Bank, he
appears, by himself and his agents, to have had the entire
control and management thereof: all his schemes and
plans, however wild and extravagant, were adopted and
carried into execution without reserve : those of the directors who still pretended to superintend the concerns of the
Bank took no care whatever to guard the interest of the
stockholders or the public.

" Dexter was furnished with as much money as he thought
proper to demand, and prescribed his own terms as to the
security he gave, the rate of interest, and the time and manner of payment. The greatest secrecy was used respecting his negotiations at the Bank to prevent the public from
being alarmed at the immense sum of money which was
so suddenly put in circulation ; and at the request of Dexter, the Cashier signed the bills secretly and chiefly in the
night. Dexter never gave any security whatever, except
his own name, for any money received by him from the
Bank. For the first sums delivered Dexter gave his receipts : for other sums he gave receipts to the following
purpose, that he would employ the money as their agent for
their benefit, paying them six per cent. interest therefor, and
redeeming the bills by paying specie for them as often as
they returned to the Bank, the cost of redemption to be paid
by the Bank. After these receipts had been standing for
some time they were taken up by Dexter, and a note given
by him for the whole amount, of the tenor and effect following . " I, Andrew Dexter, jun., do promise the President, Directors and Company of the Farmers' Exchange
Bank, to pay them, on order, —— dollars, in two years from
the date, with interest, at two per cent. per annum : it being however understood, that said Dexter shall not be called upon to make payment until he thinks proper, he being
the principal stockholder, and best knowing when it will
be proper to pay the same." The said note was afterwards given to Dexter, and a note given by him for *five
hundred and seven thousand seven hundred and seventy-one
dollars,* bearing date on the 30th of November, 1808 : all

the money received by Dexter after that time was delivered to him by order of Harris and Fairbanks, the last of
which was delivered on the 9th of February, 1809, for which
Dexter gave his notes, which are now remaining in the
Bank : one bearing date on the 4th of November, 1808,
for *three hundred thousand dollars* : one bearing date on
the 30th of the same month for thirty-two thousand dollars,
and one bearing date on the 12th day of December, 1808,
for six thousand dollars : all which notes amount to the
sum of *eight hundred and fifty-five thousand seven hundred
and seventy-one dollars*, payable in eight years from their
respective dates, bearing interest at and after the rate of
two per cent. per annum.

" Out of the amount above stated, as due from the said
Andrew Dexter, jun. to the Bank, ought to be deducted certain drafts or orders drawn on said Dexter by the Cashier,
to take up the bills at different times returned to the Bank,
so far as the said drafts or orders have been paid by said
Dexter. The amount of said drafts or orders, according
to the books of the Bank, still outstanding and unsettled, is
two hundred and four thousand and five dollars, but of
this sum the Committee have no means of ascertaining what
part has been paid by the said Dexter.

" In December, 1808, the credit of the Bank had become very low, and the bills were selling at a large discount : but the said Andrew Dexter, jun., and the other persons who managed the affairs of the Bank, instead of putting
a stop to the emission of their bills, and making some provision for the payment of those in circulation, redoubled
their efforts to circulate sums to a large amount, when at
the same time they refused the payment of the smallest
sums at the Bank.

" The President and Cashier were incessantly employed
in signing bills :" and " Dexter was continually urging them
to sign bills as fast as possible," telling them that every thing
depended on his having them very speedily : that if they
were not soon finished, he should not be able to dispose of
them, and that at that time he should be able to sell some
of them very well. The bills were made with so much
precipitation, and the officers of the Bank were so much
pressed for time, that said bills were in some instances sent
to Boston without being dated or numbered.

" There is now in said Bank, eighty-six dollars and forty-six cents of specie. On the 9th of February, 1809, there had been emitted by said Bank, six hundred and forty-eight thousand and forty-three dollars of their bills, according to their books. Owing to the extreme confusion in which their mode of keeping their accounts has involved all their transactions, it is impossible to ascertain with precision the amount of their bills now in circulation: but from the inquiries and examinations made by the Committee, they are of opinion that the bills of said Bank now in circulation, amount to the enormous sum of five hundred and eighty thousand dollars."

From the testimony of the Cashier, which is appended to the report, it appears that the emission of six hundred and forty-eight thousand eight hundred and forty-three dollars in Bank bills, spoken of by the Committee, took place between the 29th of March, 1808, and the 9th of Febuary, 1809, and that previous to the first mentioned date, the Bank had bills in circulation to the amount of forty-five thousand eight hundred and twenty-one dollars.

This history of the Farmers' Bank of Gloucester shows what cunning men can do, when they have a legislative charter to work with.

When the explosion took place, other New England Banks exhibited proof that they had been trading on the same principles, though none, we believe, to the same extent. In a speech in Congress, in February, 1811, Mr. Desha, of Kentucky, said, " The Berkshire and Northampton Banks, both 'of Massachusetts, when their vaults were examined, one had perhaps thirty or forty dollars in it, the other, I believe, was entirely empty: the Coos Bank, (I believe it was called,) of New Hampshire, was nearly in the same situation, and thousands of their bills in circulation at the same time."

Mr. Burwell, of Virginia, said, " The State of Massachusetts found, upon examining the vaults of the Banks, the whole of them did not contain specie equal to the paper issued by a single one."

We have no list of the New England Banks that stopped payment previous to the war: but it is evident from all testimony, that the Banking institutions in that quarter had extended their operations so far, that the necessary reaction produced very disastrous consequences.

South of New England, the Banking system was, in some respects, less pernicious than it has been at any period since the war. The notes of the Banks were then " convertible" into either gold or silver. The old Bank of the United States issued no notes of a less denomination than ten dollars : whereby it was enabled to exercise a more salutary control over the local Banks, than the present Bank has ever found possible.

As long as a state of war existed between Spain and Great Britain, the citizens of this country were the carriers and commercial agents of Spain, and nearly all the metallic treasure of Mexico passed through our hands. From the Peace of Amiens, in 1801, this influx of silver abated : but it was still considerable. It could hardly be regarded as part of the currency of the country, being received by us in payment for European goods, and afterwards transmitted to those from whom we had obtained those goods; yet, temporary deposits of it were made in the Banks, whereby these institutions were sometimes prevented from feeling the effects their expansions must otherwise have produced. The specie constantly *in transitu* from South America through the United States to other parts of the world, was so great in amount, that a retention of the quarterly or semi-quarterly supply for only a month or two was sufficient to relieve the Banks from the difficulties into which they were occasionally brought by extending their operations too far.

The Bank of England having suspended specie payments in 1797, and paper money being in extensive use on the continent of Europe, the demand for the precious metals as a material for money was, in a degree, abated. This rendered the pressure on the American Banks less severe than it is at present.*

---

* The competition among the Banks being less than it is now, these institutions made very high dividends. In 1792, the Bank of North America divided 15 per cent.; in 1793, 13½ per cent.; from 1794 to 1799, inclusive, 12 per cent. per annum; from 1800 to 1802, 10 per cent.; in 1803, 9½ per cent.; from 1804 to 1810, 9 per cent. The dividends of the old Bank of the United States were from 7 5-8 per cent. to 10 per cent. From 1792 to 1808, the Bank of Pennsylvania never divided less than 8 per cent., and sometimes its annual dividends were as high as 10 per cent. Dr. Bollman, writing in 1810, says, " none of the Banks divided less than 8 per cent., and some of them much more."

High dividends were not the only profit those who had the control of the Banks derived from their situation. Banking was a closer monopoly than it now is, and circumstances were such as to render that monopoly very lucrative. Money being at this period worth more than Bank interest to mercantile men, facility of borrowing gave' to such as possessed it great advantages. Our commerce was exposed to frequent interruptions by the belligerents. These sometimes made the necessity of borrowing very urgent, which necessities the agents of the Bank directors used to meet by lending money at two or three per cent. a month.

The Banks expanded and contracted their issues then, as the Banks do now, and as credit Banks from the necessity of their nature always will do, and the occasional plenty of money produced by Banking operations, and the subsequent scarcity, had the same effects that they have in our own times. As a close veil was then thrown over Banking proceedings, it was not always easy to trace these effects to their causes: but even in those days it was not possible completely to conceal the connection of causes and consequences from the eyes of observers. The periodical demand for specie for the China and East India trade always caused a pressure in the money market. The specie at the Branch Bank at New York was, it is said, reduced on one occasion to 10,000 dollars.* Notwithstanding all the advantages the Banks then enjoyed, they were probably many times brought near the necessity of suspending specie payments, for they had the same inducements then that they have now for extending their operations as far as possible.

The effects of these operations were less severely felt, the further a county or a town was removed from the sphere of Bank influence. In many of the agricultural districts, the state of credit was sound, or nearly so. The " vulgar prejudices of the country people in favor of gold and silver money, were not then entirely subdued." The spirit of wild speculation did not often infect them. Industry and economy were considered as the true roads to wealth : and men of reputation found little difficulty in borrowing as

* Vide " A Peep into the Bank," New York, 1828.

much money as was wanted. The country capitalists did not then purchase Bank stock with their surplus funds, but lent them to their industrious neighbors for long periods. Little risk attended this mode of lending, and it was mutually beneficial to the parties concerned.

" Before the establishment of Banks in the interior," say a committee of the Senate of Pennsylvania,* " the farmer who possessed credit and character, experienced little difficulty in borrowing on his simple bond, for one or more years, any sum which it was thought could be prudently loaned to him. Embarrassments and failures, in those days, were scarcely known among our husbandmen, and society moved on by a regular, sure, and happy march. In our cities, on the contrary, where loans have been chiefly made by incorporated Banks, we have seen a continued succession of bankruptcies, and had it not been for the practice so universally prevalent amongst merchants *of securing the Banks for the sake of indorsers*, Banking long since would have been abandoned as an unprofitable trade."

" From the adoption of the Federal Constitution in 1788, down to 1804," says a writer in the Richmond Enquirer, " Banks were unknown in Virginia, with the exception of a branch of the old U. S. Bank in Norfolk, about 1799 or 1800. The paper of this Bank scarcely found its way into the interior of the country : and it may be truly said, the currency of the country was metallic. Until the year 1798, no people enjoyed more happiness or prosperity than the people of the United States—nor did any country ever flourish more within the space of time. The desk of every agriculturist in Virginia had some gold or silver to spare, if he was a prudent, industrious man ; or he had something like money to spare in the hands of his merchant, who, in the days of which I am speaking, acted as a banker to his prospering customers. Nor was any interest paid upon such moneys as might be deposited in the hands of the merchant : because both planter and merchant considered themselves accommodated by the arrangement : the planter in having his money safely kept for him, until he wanted to use it, and the merchant in having the use of the money

* Report on the renewal of Bank charters, Jan. 15th, 1821. Condy Raguet, Chairman.

until it was called for. Under such circumstances, none
will doubt the happy condition of both planter and merchant, and if the view be somewhat extended, it will be
found that this state of prosperity was not confined to one
or two classes of society, but extended to all. The man
embarrassed might readily sell something, and to advantage, to pay his debts. The currency of the country being
specie, was widely scattered through the land, and in diversified hands, so that its concentration at any particular
point was impossible, and consequently its removal from
the country could not happen to any great extent.

"I know there are many, who, in order to effect present
objects, insist that commerce could not be carried on without the aid of Banks. To this I answer, how was commerce carried on before we had Banks? Will any body
deny there was any commerce in this country at that time?
None will be found hardy enough to take this ground, for
every intelligent man of forty years, knows that, before
there were any Banks in Virginia, the foreign commerce
of the country was greater than it has ever been since, and
the country far more prosperous. Nor was there the least
inconvenience in transmitting money from one point to another through the merchants, whose credit *then*, was as good
as the credit of the Banks now, if not better. Banks have
destroyed the credit and confidence which men had in one
another.

" No people had more cause to rejoice than the people of
Virginia ; but alas, the Banks came, and all things became
changed. Like the Upas tree, they have withered and destroyed the healthful condition of the country, and inflicted on the people political and pecuniary diseases of the
most deadly character."

CHAPTER VII.

Of Banking from 1810-11 *to* 1814-15.

After the unsuccessful attempt to obtain from Congress a renewal of the charter of the United States Bank, overtures were made to the Legislature of Pennsylvania. The petitioners offered a bonus of five hundred thousand dollars, and a loan of five hundred thousand dollars more, for an act of incorporation under the title of the " American Bank," with a capital of five million dollars.* The offer was, in a fiscal point of view, very advantageous, but it was not accepted, less perhaps from any remains of the old democratic enmity to the system, than from a desire of individuals to get charters for the particular benefit of themselves and their friends.

" The anxiety displayed by the stockholders of the United States Bank to continue their business," say a committee of the Senate of Pennsylvania,† " and the successful appearance of their dividends, added to the locating of branches of the Pennsylvania Banks in the country, very naturally excited the attention of the public, and particularly of the inhabitants of some of the interior counties of the State, who fancied that much of the prosperity of cities was to be traced to the establishment of Banks, and that if that were the case, there was no reason why the country should not participate in their advantages.‡ Such considerations as these, urged on by the desire of accumulating wealth without the dull exercise of labor, engendered a spi-

* " Concise Observations on the Propriety of Incorporating New Banks," Philadelphia, 1812.

† Report on the Causes and Extent of the Present General Distress Read January 29th, 1820. Condy Raguet, Chairman.

‡ If they had supposed that the prosperity of *some* of the inhabitants of cities was owing to the establishment of Banks, they would not have been far wrong. Nor were they in error in supposing that Bank notes are money to those who issue them, if others are so simple as to receive them; nor that a universal rise in the price of land and commodities brings an increase of wealth to those who are fortunate enough to make sales while prices are high. Their error was in supposing that a system which is profitable to any, only because but few participate in it, might be extended so far as to be profitable to all who might wish to share in its advantages.

rit of speculation. It was supposed that the mere establishment of Banks would of itself create capital, that *a bare
promise to pay money*, was money itself, and that a nominal rise of the price of land and commodities, ever attendant upon a plenty of money, was a real increase of substantial wealth. The theory was plausible, and too well
succeeded. The Farmers' Bank, with a capital of three
hundred thousand dollars, was established in the county
of Lancaster, in the beginning of the year 1810, and was
accompanied by several others in the city, as well as in
other parts of the State.

" These early symptoms of a mania for Banking, induced
the Legislature, on the 19th of March, 1810, to enact a
law prohibiting unincorporated institutions from issuing
notes, or pursuing any of the operations of Banks; but in
defiance of its provisions, the system was persevered in,
and even companies incorporated for the purpose of con-
structing bridges, departed from the spirit of their charters,
converted themselves into Banks, and emitted notes for circulation.

" The war, as might naturally be expected, put a tempo·
rary stop to the exportation of specie, and thereby removed
the only check against inordinate issues of paper, which
can possibly exist. This cessation of the returning of notes
for payment, had the effect of inviting the Banks to enlarge
their issues. Loans were made to Government to an immense amount, and to individuals vastly beyond what the
absence of foreign commerce justified, and a gradual depreciation of the currency was the result. The increase
of dividends and the facility with which they appeared to
be made, extended throughout the whole Commonwealth
the spirit of speculation, already introduced into some counties. The apparent success of the Farmers' Bank of Lancaster, which from the enormous extent of its issues was
enabled to divide upwards of *twelve* per cent. per annum,
and to accommodate its stockholders *with loans to double
the amount of their stock*, had a powerful influence on the
public mind. A Bank by many was no longer regarded as
an instrument by which the surplus wealth of capitalists
could be conveniently loaned to their industrious fellow-citizens, but as a mint in which money could be coined at pleasure, for those who did not possess it before. Under these

delusive impressions, associations of individuals sprang up in every quarter, holding out inducements to the farmer, the merchant, the manufacturer, and mechanic, to abandon the dull pursuits of a laborious life, for the golden dreams of an artificial fortune.

" The liability, however, to individual ruin, attendant upon unchartered copartnerships, restrained in a degree the Banking mania, and impelled the projectors to apply for a legislative sanction.   During the session of 1812–13, a bill to incorporate twenty-five institutions, the capitals of which amounted to nine million five hundred and twenty-five thousand dollars, was passed by both houses of the Legislature, by a bare majority of one vote in each.   The bill was returned by the Governor with his objections, which were sensible and cogent, and on a reconsideration the votes were 38 to 40.   At the following session the subject was renewed with increased ardor, and a bill authorizing the incorporation of forty-one Banking institutions with capitals amounting to seventeen million dollars, was passed by a large majority.   This bill was also returned by the Governor with additional objections, but two-thirds of each House, (many members of which were pledged to their constituents to that effect,) agreeing on its passage, it became a law on the 21st of March, 1814, and thus was inflicted upon the Commonwealth an evil of a more disastrous nature than has ever been experienced by its citizens.   Under this law thirty-seven Banks, four of which were established in Philadelphia, actually went into operation.

" The immediate commencement of a number of these Banks, with scarcely a *bona fide* capital equal to the first instalment, *for the convenient mode of discounting stock notes to meet the subsequent payments, was soon discovered,* increased the mass of paper credits already too redundant, and depreciated the whole circulating medium so far below specie value, as to excite a want of confidence in its convertibility.   In the absence of a foreign demand for specie a domestic one arose.   The laws of the New England States had been so rigorous upon the subject of Banks, which were liable to a penalty of 12 per cent. per annum for the non-payment of their notes, that no depreciation of *their* currency took place.   The consequence thereof was, that the difference between the New England prices of commodities, stocks and foreign bills of exchange, and those of Pennsylvania, was equal to the extent of the depreciation of the currency of the latter, and as our Bank notes were redeemable on demand, the most profitable remittance which could be made to New England, in exchange for her commodities, was specie, and this demand created a run upon the Banks which they were not able to withstand. The situation of the southern and western Banks was precisely similar to that of our own. All had over issued, and a general depreciation had ensued. The same causes produced the same effects, and a general stoppage of all the Banks in the United States except those of New England, took place in August and September 1814.* The New England demand, it is true, was increased by two causes, viz : *first*, by facilities in foreign trade through neutral vessels, which were afforded them by an exemption from the blockade of the enemy, and *secondly*, by a well-grounded apprehension that the southern Banks, from their extensive emissions, would necessarily become embarrassed. Certain it is, however, that all these causes combined could not have produced a general suspension of payment, had our Banks observed the same caution in their issues as that which characterized the Banks of the Eastern States."

From this account it appears, that, one year before the expiration of the charter of the United States Bank, and two years before the commencement of the war with Great Britain, the Bank mania raged in Pennsylvania with so much violence as to require legislative interposition. In a year or two after, the mania infected the Legislature. It had received a check in New England, and was now, according to the natural course of things, spreading south and west.

The infatuation of the high authorities of the United States Government, was as strong as that of the people and of the local Legislatures. War was declared against

* It appears from other documents, that, when the British made an inroad into the State of Maine, some of the Banks in that quarter of the country suspended payment; that the Banks of Ohio and Kentucky maintained specie payments till the latter part of December, or the beginning of January ; and that the Bank of Nashville, (one of the two Banks then in operation in Tennessee,) did not stop payment till August, 1815. The Banks of Louisiana suspended payment in April, 1814, four months sooner than the Banks of Pennsylvania.

Great Britain in June 1812, and Bank notes and Bank credits were seized on to defray the expenses of fleets and armies. "The Bank capital has been stated at seventy-five millions," said the Committee of Ways and Means of 1813-14, of which Mr. Eppes was chairman. "On this capital we may calculate with safety on a circulation in notes and discounts of one hundred millions. From this sum deduct 47,569,120, the maximum of what is deemed necessary for circulation, and the sum remaining, viz. 52,430,880, constitutes the ability of the monied capitalists to loan. Of this sum we propose to borrow thirty millions."

In conformity with these principles, about six millions were borrowed in 1812, from the Banks, and about four millions more from individuals, who had obtained from the Banks the means of lending. These loans were obtained at par. In the next year the Government borrowed about twenty millions, for every hundred dollars of which it issued a certificate of stock for 113 dollars. In the following year it borrowed about fifteen millions, for twelve millions of which stock was issued at the rate of 125 dollars for 100 dollars paid in. Then, as Mr. Ingham said in Congress, "it seemed impossible to borrow on *any* terms."

The policy of carrying on the war by means of loans, cannot be said to have been an unwise one ; but what ought to have been an essential point in this policy, namely, drawing on the real resources of the country to an extent sufficient to support the credit of Government, was neglected. It was known before-hand, that the operations of the enemy would, by cutting up our commerce, diminish the revenue from the customs : yet, the first steps towards raising a revenue by internal taxation, were not taken till July and August, 1813 : and the acts which were then passed, did not take effect until the 1st of January 1814.

The consequence was, that the revenue for the three years, 1812, 1813, and 1814, amounted to only thirty-six millions, or about twelve millions a year. The charges on Government in time of peace, amounted to eight millions a year, and with the remaining four millions we were endeavoring to carry on a war with the most powerful nation on the globe !

As an auxiliary means of supplying financial wants, emissions were made of treasury notes, bearing an interest of five and two-fifths per cent. per annum, reimbursable one year after they were issued, and receivable in payment for duties, taxes, and public lands. Of these notes, nearly three millions were issued in 1812, about six millions in 1813, and upwards of eight millions in 1814. As great part of the revenue of twelve millions a year was received in treasury notes, the reader can judge of the condition of Government.

The mania which raged among the people, and which infected the Legislatures of the different States, would have produced great evils if we had remained at peace. But this fiananciering of the United States Government hastened the crisis and exacerbated all the symptons of the disease. The country was flooded with paper, which might, without impropriety, be regarded as a new emission of continental money, differing from the old only in having the Banks for indorsers. Gladly did these institutions avail themselves of the excuse for stopping payments, which was afforded by the inroad of the enemy into Maryland.

For some time after the suspension of specie payments by the Bank of England, its notes remained on a par with specie, and after they depreciated the paper of all the other Banks, inasmuch as they were convertible into Bank of England notes, experienced an equal degree of depreciation. The currency was at times depreciated as much as twenty per cent., but the scale of depreciation was the same throughout England and Wales.

The suspension of specie payments in the United States, differed from that of England in two important particulars. It did not take place throughout the country, and, as each Bank was independent, there was a different scale of depreciation for each county and each town.

The paper, however, still served as a medium of commerce. The merchant of Pittsburg put an additional price on his goods, equivalent to the depreciation of the currency in that quarter: and as he had obtained ten or twenty per cent. more on his sales, he was enabled to pay ten or twenty per cent. more on his purchases. A loss was sustained by individuals when the paper underwent an additional depreciation while remaining in their hands, but their indignation, instead of falling on the Banks, was vented on the innocent and useful exchange merchants.

On the 19th of November, or eighty days after the suspension of specie payments, the paper of the best Banks of
Philadelphia was at fourteen per cent. discount : yet but
little murmuring was heard, except at the refusal of the
Banks to receive southern and western paper on deposit.
Prices were rising, business was brisk, and if any man
experienced difficulties, he attfibuted them to the war.

Such was the state of things, when, on the 14th of
October, 1814, or *forty-four* days after the suspension
of specie payments, Mr. A. J. Dallas, Secretary of the
Treasury, recommended the establishment of a National
Bank, with a capital of fifty millions, of which twenty
millions should be subscribed by Government, and paid
in six per cent. stock. The residue of the capital was to
be subscribed by individuals, and was to be paid, six millions in gold and silver coin, in three different instalments,
six millions in treasury notes, and eighteen millions in six
per cent. stock. The Bank was to be bound to lend thirty
millions to Government, and was to be authorized to suspend specie payments, if the President of the United States
should deem such a suspension advisable.

So desperate was the state of credit, that this desperate expedient was regarded with favor by many members of Congress. Mr. Ingham, who was one of its advocates, said,
" should any unexpected difficulties menace the Bank, there
will be a resort to the power of suspending specie payments.
* * * I do not apprehend any serious consequences will result from the temporary suspension of specie payments. The
experiment was tried many years ago in England, and has
been continued up to this time, without injury to the commercial interests, and with essential benefit to the nation
at large. It has also been tried here, and, though Bank
paper is somewhat depreciated thereby, it is solely because it will not answer the purpose of paying balances
between people of different States, for which specie had
usually been employed. For example, the Bank paper of
the District will not enable you to trade east of Baltimore :
yet every article to be purchased with it here, is as cheap
as it was twelve months ago. It may, therefore, be fairly
inferred, that a paper which was receivable all over the
United States in taxes, and might be exchanged for notes
of smaller or greater denomination, or treasury notes in
each of the States, would, from its general convenience

continue to circulate without depreciation, even though a temporary suspension of specie payments should take place."*

Mr. Gaston, of North Carolina, compared this proposition to relieve the evil arising from too much paper by throwing more into circulation, to the remedy which Burke had described the French Convention as prescribing for every evil, viz : issuing *more assignats.*

The clauses in the bill to authorize the Bank to suspend specie payments, and to compel it to lend thirty millions to Government were struck out : and the bill was further modified, by a provision that the whole of the stock should be subscribed by individuals, and paid, with the exception of the six millions in specie, in treasury notes to be hereafter issued. In this form it received the approbation of a large majority of the House : but a select committee to whom it was referred, in one of its stages, received a letter from the Secretary of the Treasury, stating that the bill as amended would not answer the purposes of Government. It would, he said, give to the holders of the public stock cause for complaint ; and it would be very difficult, if not impracticable, to get into circulation, either with or without depreciation, the forty-four millions of treasury notes, which were afterwards to be subscribed as the capital of the Bank. After being made acquainted with the views of the Cabinet, the House rejected the bill, by a vote of 49 to 101.

A bill drawn up in accordance with the views of the Treasury Department, was then brought before the Senate. It proposed the establishment of a Bank, with a capital of fifty millions, whereof five millions were to be paid in gold and silver, twenty-seven millions in six per cent. stock, eight millions in treasury notes, and ten millions to be subscribed by Government. The Bank was to be bound to lend thirty millions to Government, and was to be authorized to suspend specie payments. In this form, the bill passed the Senate on the 9th of December, by a vote of 17 to 14.

In the House it was opposed with great ability by Mr. Webster and others, and rejected on the 2d of January, 1815, by the casting vote of Mr. Cheves, the Speaker.

* Legislative History of the United States Bank.

The next day this vote was reconsidered, and the bill was recommitted to a select committee, who, on the 6th of January, reported it with sundry amendments, reducing the capital of the Bank to thirty millions, of which fifteen were to consist of treasury notes, and ten of public stocks; and striking out the clauses to compel the Bank to lend thirty millions to Government, and to authorize it to suspend specie payments. The bill thus amended, was passed by the House on the 7th of January, by a vote of 120 to 37.

When the bill was in this form returned to the Senate, that body increased the capital of the Bank to thirty-five millions, and restored the clause authorizing the Bank to suspend specie payments. In this, the House refused to concur, and the Senate finally receded from its amendments.

The bill having thus passed both Houses, was sent to President Madison, but he put his *veto* on it. His objections were: "The amount of stock to be subscribed will not, it is believed, be sufficient to produce in favor of the public credit, any considerable or lasting elevation of the market price. Nor will any adequate advantage arise to the public credit from the subscription of treasury notes. The actual issues of these notes nearly equal, and will soon exceed, the amount to be subscribed to the Bank. The Bank will be free from all obligations to co-operate with public measures." [The meaning of this is, the Bank will not be compelled to lend thirty millions to Government.] Lastly: "The proposed Bank will commence and conduct its operations under an obligation to pay its notes in specie, or be subject to the loss of its charter. Without such an obligation, the notes of the Bank, though not exchangeable for specie, yet resting on good pledges, and performing the uses of specie in the payment of taxes and other public transactions, would, as experience has ascertained, qualify the Bank to supply at once a circulating medium, and pecuniary aid to Government. Under the fetters imposed by the bill, it is manifest that during the actual state of things, and probably during the war, the period particularly requiring such a medium and such a source for loans and advances to Government, notes for which the Bank would be compellable to give specie in exchange, could not be kept in circulation."

Another bill was then got up in the Senate to establish a Bank with a capital of fifty millions, of which five were to be paid in gold and silver coin, fifteen in six per cent. stock, twenty in treasury notes, and ten to be subscribed by Government. In one paragraph, it was declared "the said corporation shall be bound to lend to the Government of the United States, reimburseable at their pleasure, thirty millions of dollars, in such sums and at such periods as may be convenient to the Government of the United States." And in another paragraph, it was expressly provided, that " until the first Monday in April, 1816, it shall not be obligatory on said corporation to pay its notes in specie." Authority was also given to Congress to authorize, in certain contingencies, " the suspension of specie payments, for such time or times as they may deem proper."

This bill, which was framed in accordance with the views of Mr. Madison and of his Cabinet, was passed by the Senate on the 13th of February, by a vote of 18 to 16.

It was then sent to the House, where, after some debate, it was, on the 17th of February, indefinitely postponed, by a vote of 74 to 73.[*]

The news of peace was received on the 13th of February, and to the timely arrival of this intelligence, we must attribute the delivery of the country from the curse of a national paper currency. If Mr. Madison and the gentlemen of his Cabinet had been allowed to take their own way, we should have had a National Bank with a *paper* capital of fifty millions, issuing notes redeemable *in paper*.

CHAPTER VIII.

Of Banking from 1814–15 *to* 1815–16.

" At the time of the suspension of our city Banks, a public meeting of merchants and others was held, who publicly sanctioned the measure, under a pledge given by the Banks, that as soon as the war was terminated, specie

---

[*] Legislative History of U. S. Bank.

payments would be resumed.   That this measure was intended, is evident, from the curtailment of loans immediately consequent upon the suspension.*

" But, unhappily, the redemption of the pledge was not
demanded by the public at the stipulated time, and the
Banks, urged on by cupidity, and losing sight of moral obligations in their lust for profit, launched out into an extent
of issues unexampled in the annals of folly.   The fulfilling
of a promise to pay money, by tendering another promise
equally false, sanctioned by the public acquiescence, led to
the organization of additional Banks, under the act of
March, 1814, which had not till then been attempted to be
formed, and a scene of indiscretion in the loaning of Bank
credits was every where exhibited, which realized the an-
ticipations of those who had foretold the ruinous effects of
the paper system.   Money lost its value.   The notes of the
city Banks depreciated twenty per cent., and those of the
country Banks from twenty to fifty, and specie so entirely
disappeared from circulation, that even the fractional parts
of a dollar were substituted by small notes and tickets,
issued by Banks, corporations and individuals.   The depreciation of money enhancing the prices of every species
of property and commodity, appeared like a *real* rise in
value, and led to all the consequences which are ever
attendant upon a gradual advance of prices.   The false
delusions of artificial wealth increased the demand of the
farmer for foreign productions, and led him to consume in
anticipation of his crops.   The country trader, seduced by
a demand for more than his ordinary supply of merchandise, was tempted to the extension of his credit, and filled
his stores, at the most extravagant prices, with goods vastly

* This meeting was composed principally, if not exclusively, of owners of Bank stock, and of debtors to the Banks ; and the great body of the
public, knowing little of the nature of Banking operations, acquiesced
in the measure.

Peace was restored in *less* than six months after the Banks of the Middle States had suspended payment.

So confident were some of the public that these institutions would
then redeem the solemn pledge they had given, that " the chests and
secure places were unlocked, and hard money was again in the market, at three or four per cent. above par."   Even in May the discount
on Philadelphia notes was only 5 per cent.; but the Banks, under one
pretext or another, refused to open their vaults, and the paper sunk, by
June, to 9, and by November, to 16 per cent. below par.

beyond what the actual resources of his customers could
pay for, whilst the importing merchant, having no guide
to ascertain the real wants of the community but the eager-
ness of retailers to purchase his commodities, sent orders
abroad for a supply of manufactures wholly disproportioned
to the effective demand of the country. Individuals of every
profession were tempted to embark in speculation, and the
whole community was literally plunged in debt. *The
plenty of money*, as it was called, was so profuse, that the
managers of the Banks were fearful they could not find a
demand for all they could fabricate, and it was no unfre-
quent occurrence to hear solicitations urged to individuals
to become borrowers, under promises as to indulgences
the most tempting. Such continued to be the state of
things until towards the close of the year 1815."

The Secretary of the Treasury negotiated with the
Banks as independent sovereignties. His first effort was
" to associate them with a view of furnishing a uniform
national currency."* It is almost needless to say that this
effort did not succeed.

His next attempt was, " by their agency in circulating
treasury notes, to overcome the inequalities of exchange."
This, he says, was but " partially successful."

He then proposed a plan, " with the design to curtail
the issues of Bank notes, to fix the public confidence, and
to give each Bank a legitimate share in the circulation."
What the particulars of this plan were, he has not stated,
but it is evident from the context that it was through the
free-will of the Banks he sought to carry it into execution.
He soon found that a plan which was not fitted to promote
their particular interests, was " not likely to receive their
general sanction. The truth is," he adds, " the charter
restrictions of some of the Banks, the mutual relation and
dependence of the Banks of the same State, and even of the
Banks of the different States, and the duty which the directors of each Bank conceive they owe to their immediate
constituents upon points of security or emolument, interpose an insuperable obstacle to any voluntary arrangement,
upon national considerations alone, for the establishment

---

* Proposition relating to the National Circulating Medium, December 6th, 1815.

of a national medium, through the agency of the State Banks." The plain English of this is, that the directors of the Banks esteemed it a " *duty*" to make as much profit as they could, and Government did not see fit to interfere with them in the discharge of this sacred " duty."

In the effort " to overcome the inequalities of exchange, by the circulating of treasury notes, through the agency of the Banks," Government did indeed make some exertion of its power. The Secretary issued an order, declaring that, after the first of August, nothing should be received in payment of duties but specie, treasury bills and the notes of such Banks as would receive treasury bills in deposit at par. " The effect of this plan," says a contemporary writer,* " was clearly foreseen by all who fairly understood the subject. What was the result ? In places where treasury bills were in the market, at or above par, the Banks agreed to receive them : whereas, where they were below par, the proposition was rejected."

But this measure had not simply a negative effect. It increased the mass of Bank paper in circulation, and thereby still further vitiated the currency. This is abundantly proved in a pamphlet entitled " An Appeal to the Public," published at New York, in December, 1815.

In this pamphlet, Mr. Isaac Bronson, the author, states the active capital of the Banks of the city of New York to be 13,515,000 dollars, and computes the amount on which they were drawing interest to be twenty-two or twenty-three millions. " Admitting it to be twenty-two millions, it follows that the Banks make dividends on a sum which exceeds their active capital about *eight* millions and a half, yielding the stockholders about half a million in dividends. This profit is derived from their mere credit, without any cost or consideration whatever. Of the eight and a half millions excess beyond their capitals, five millions have been issued in the purchase of, and in exchange for, Government securities of various sorts, bearing interest.

" We have been speaking hitherto of ' *the* Banks,' as if no distinctions were to be made between them. It is now time to make the proper discrimination. Among each other the

* Inquiry into the causes of the present state of the Circulating Medium. Philadelphia, August, 1815.

directors have already, in their conversation, fallen into the
familiar distinctions of the ' debtor Banks,' and the ' creditor' Banks.   By the former, are meant those whose paper
has accumulated in the latter, to an amount which cannot
be taken up.   The debtor Banks, the Banks who are indebted to the others, have become so indebted, because
they hold large amounts of public securities, bearing interest, for which they have issued their Bank notes to
Government, and which notes have found their way into
the other Banks.   To keep the creditor Banks quiet, however, and as much as possible in good humor, it has been
stipulated that they shall charge interest on these accumulations.   The practical effect therefore is, that the debtor
Banks make their profit by trusting *Government ;* and the
creditor Banks make theirs by trusting the debtor Banks.
The debtor Banks give out their notes in exchange for
treasury notes bearing interest; and the creditor Banks
charge interest on the notes they receive of the debtor
Banks.   But if these notes accumulate in the hands of individuals, no interest is allowed *them*, unless they compel
its payment by law.   And thus the Banks have established
a rule of justice towards each other, in itself very correct,
but which they refuse, however, to extend to the rest of
the community.

   " It is important to our subject that the reader should
clearly understand the course of the Banks in relation to
treasury notes.   We hope, therefore, to be pardoned for
what to some may appear unnecessarily minute.

   " Some months since, the Secretary of the Treasury proposed, to all the Banks in the United States, that they
should receive treasury notes when offered them, and give
their own notes in exchange for them : accompanying this
proposition at the same time by a threat, that the treasury
should not receive the paper of those Banks which did not
receive treasury notes!   At a meeting of a select committee
of our Banks, appointed to consider these propositions, it
was resolved not to agree to them.   *Three* of the Banks,
and of course they are the three who have been called, because they have become, the *debtor Banks*, did afterwards,
however, by a private and separate arrangement, made by
agents sent to Philadelphia on purpose, agree to these propositions, without the consent or knowledge of the five

other Banks; so that these Banks now receive treasury notes from any one who presents them, and issue their bills in exchange for them when required. And here, we submit to the reader, whether it does not necessarily and inevitably follow, that these Banks have parted with all power of control over their issues? That department of the Bank has been abandoned to the Secretary of the Treasury; for it is very clear, that he may to-morrow, if he pleases, cause these Banks to add twenty millions to that excess of paper, which is the true cause of depreciation. That this excess is continually increasing, is most notorious: to what *extent*, is one of those Bank secrets which all their caution has not prevented us from penetrating.

" Among others, this singular and ludicrous consequence has followed: The United States take only the bills of those Banks which cannot keep their accounts even with the other Banks; and refuse to receive the bills of those Banks which are immense *creditors* of the Banks whose bills *are* received.

" And the practical result will be, that so long as the notes of these Banks continue to be worth more than treasury notes, so long will treasury notes continue to be presented and Bank notes issued in exchange for them. When the Bank notes, from the quantity afloat, become degraded below treasury notes, this practice will cease. But the affairs of the Banks will be, by that time, utterly irretrievable, and they will follow the fate of all the Banks which have been mere machines of Government.

" It appears from the reply to the Connecticut Banks, that in July, the *commercial* loans had been reduced nearly three millions below what their amount was when payments were suspended. But it is at the same time acknowledged, that the whole amount of loans had been increased *three* per cent. on the capitals of the Banks: and this *before* the system of receiving treasury notes was adopted. The effect of that system, as we have been recently enabled to ascertain, has been to produce in the creditor Banks an accumulation of the notes of the debtor Banks of between two and *three millions:* although the balances, when payments were suspended, were less than three hundred thousand."

The plentifulness of " money," whether caused by the

Banks trafficking with the Government, or by discounts to private persons, was very acceptable to the great mass of the people. The Banks of Pennsylvania added ten millions to the amount of their loans in the course of the year, and the Banks of some of the other States were equally liberal, if not more so. Never before had the country exhibited such an *appearance* of prosperity. The unequal value of the Bank notes of different districts, was productive of some inconvenience, but this was not sufficient to counterbalance the advantage of a general rise of prices, and the briskness of nearly every kind of business.

" We cannot," says one writer, " see, with some honest calculators, how the continuance of the present state of things can affect the interests of the country. If specie has been withdrawn from circulation, it is because it has been occupied abroad ,in a more profitable employment than it was engaged in at home. Its exportation has added to the stock and wealth of the nation, by the purchase of merchandise abroad, worth more than the specie itself. *To be sure, we are subject to some inconveniences in our transactions at market, and in petty dealings ; but as we become accustomed to the use of paper money, the disadvantage will vanish.* All large mercantile negotiations are conducted as they have heretofore been, by Bank notes, or checks upon Banks. As to the agios of exchange, where balances are due, they must of necessity continue : but before long they will be so completely understood, as to occasion no embarrassment. The merchant who sells his goods for foreign notes, will add to the price of his goods the amount of the loss he sustains upon the notes, and the purchaser will eventually discover, that the difference which he must pay for his goods, at a place where his Bank notes are at *a discount*, and at a place where they are *at par*, is at least equal to the agio on his notes. As to the solidity of the Banks, the suspension of specie payments has produced no alteration. Although the Banks do not pay specie for *any* of their notes, yet the time never has been when they could pay specie for them *all* : for a Bank that keeps on hand a sufficiency of specie to meet all its debts, can never divide six per cent. interest. The very principle upon which it is founded, requires that it

* Inquiry, &c., Philadelphia, August, 1815.

should trade beyond its capital. But the Banks have the
same means of discharging all their notes as they ever had,
viz : claims upon individuals who have borrowed their
money, and who are now as able to pay as ever they were,
if not in specie, in merchandise and property of equal
value."

In March, 1816, Mr. Carey addressed a series of letters
to the directors of the Philadelphia Bank, some extracts
from which will elucidate the state of affairs, and the state
of feeling.

" Blessed peace at length arrived.   *   *   *   *
About the middle of May, 1815, the first vessel from
Great Britain entered the port of Philadelphia. She was
quickly followed by others. They were all full freighted
with the most costly productions and manufactures of that
country. The news was rapidly conveyed into the interior.
The country storekeepers thronged to the city in crowds.
Never, probably, were there so many here before at one
time. The number has been calculated, and I believe
correctly, at two thousand.

" They were all eager to purchase—apparently fearful
of not being able to procure adequate supplies—and each
providing himself as largely as if he were to have the monopoly of the trade of his neighborhood.

" Thus, although the importations were uncommonly
great, they were sold off rapidly. The advances on the
invoices were universally high. And some of the importers
made independent fortunes on single cargoes.

" This was the golden age of Philadelphia. The rapid
circulation of property—the immensity of business done—
and the profits made on that business, produced a degree
of prosperity which she had, perhaps, never before witnessed. Almost every man in every kind of business, was
employed advantageously for himself and for the community. And so high were the prices of imported articles
generally, that domestic manufactures appeared likely to
stand the shock of competition.

" Of the immense quantity of business done in this city
during the last year, some idea may be conceived from the
astonishing fact, that the real bona fide auction sales on
which duties were paid, amounted in about eight months

to near ten millions of dollars. As this kind of business
was principally carried on upon credit, it may readily be
conceived that it must have created an inordinate quantity
of promissory notes. During the first epoch, (the months
of May, June, July and August,) which I have styled, and
I think justly, the golden age of Philadelphia, there were
few of these notes offered at the Banks which were not discounted. The Banks were in a most liberal mood. Few
men of fair character experienced refusals. Instances occurred of notes being discounted at the different Banks
for thirty, forty, fifty, sixty and seventy thousand dollars.
Cases of this kind were not, I believe, very numerous.
But enough of them did occur, to establish the fact of the
extreme liberality that prevailed on the subject of discounts.

" The Banks have been censured, and very severely, for
the extension of their discounts at this period. They have
been charged with taking advantage of the suspension of
specie payments, with over-trading and over-issuing of
notes.

" Superficial reasoners have carried these allegations to
a great extent—and have not scrupled to brand this conduct as fraudulent. These charges are highly unjust, except, perhaps, so far as respects those immoderate notes
above mentioned. These I do not undertake to defend."

Mr. Carey then attempts to refute the opinion of those
" superficial reasoners" who maintained that the Banks
had over-traded. " Never" in his opinion, " was a country in a more enviable state." The only cause of complaint he had against the Banks, was, that in the month
of September they began to curtail mercantile accommodations, whereby, in the months of October and November,
there was a considerable fall in the price of British goods.
The necessity for this curtailment, Mr. Carey shows to
have arisen from the extensive dealings of the Banks in
Government securities, thereby confirming the statements
of Mr. Bronson. The published accounts show that seven
of the Banks of Philadelphia, having nominal capitals of
the amount of $7,700,000, had invested about $3,500,000
in Government stock.

CHAPTER IX.

Of Banking from 1815–16 *to* 1816–17.

The *bona fide* revenue of Government for the year ending December 31st, 1815, was only fifteen million seven hundred thousand dollars, and the charges on Government in the same period amounted to upwards of thirty-nine million dollars: but with so much skill did the high officers of State exert those powers of financial metamorphosis which the funding and treasury note system gave them, that there was, at the end of the year, a balance in the treasury of upwards of *thirteen millions of dollars.*

The grand secret by which this balance was produced, was that of exchanging treasury notes, many of which bore interest, for inconvertible Bank notes which bore no interest. The officers of the treasury seemed highly pleased with the result of their operations: yet they found a difficulty in applying the balance where it was most wanted. But little of the money with which the treasury overflowed would pass current thirty miles from the seat of the Banks that had issued it, and paying the discount was a clear loss to Government or the creditors of Government. As was observed in a former chapter, the disadvantages arising from the various values of Bank notes, were not, in the case of individuals, sufficient to counterbalance the advantages arising from the advancing price of real estate, and the universal briskness of business. The time for general suffering, through the necessary reaction of the system, had not yet arrived.

The want of uniformity appears to have been the only evil the officers of Government discovered in the state of the currency. If the depreciation had been uniform, as it was in England, there is no reason to believe they would have complained.

In his message to Congress, on the 5th of December, 1815, President Madison said, "It is true, that the improved condition of the public revenue will not only afford the means of maintaining the faith of the Government with its creditors inviolate, and of prosecuting successfully the measures of the most liberal policy, but will also justify an immediate alleviation of the burdens imposed by the necessities of the war. It is, however, essential to every modification of the finances, that the benefits of an *uniform* national currency should be restored to the community. The absence of the precious metals will, it is believed, be a temporary evil : but, until they can be rendered again the general medium of exchange, it devolves on the wisdom of Congress *to provide a substitute,* which shall equally engage the confidence, and accommodate the wants, of the citizens throughout the Union. If the operation of the State Banks cannot produce this result, the probable operation of a National Bank will merit consideration : and if neither of these expedients be deemed effectual, it may become necessary to ascertain the terms upon which the notes of the Government (no longer required as an instrument of credit,) shall be issued, upon motives of general policy, as a common medium of circulation."

The Secretary of the Treasury, in his report on the 7th of December, entered at large upon the subject. "It is not intended," he said, " upon this occasion, to condemn generally the suspension of specie payments : for appearances indicated an approaching crisis, which would probably have imposed it as a measure of necessity, if it had not been adopted as a measure of precaution. But the danger which originally induced, and perhaps justified, the conduct of the Banks, has passed away, and the continuance of the suspension of specie payments must be ascribed to a new cause." The Secretary admitted the practicability of supplanting the paper currency by specie, and did not regard it as a very difficult operation : " But is it," he asked " within the scope of a wise policy, to create additional demands for coin, and in that way to multiply the inducements to retain and import the precious metals of which it is composed ? * * * * Even, however, if it were practicable, it has sometimes been questioned whether it would be politic, again to employ gold and silver for the purposes of a national currency. It was long and universally supposed, that, to maintain a paper medium without depreciation, the certainty of being able to convert it into coin was indispensable : *nor can the experiment which has given rise to the contrary doctrine be deemed complete or conclusive.* But, whatever may be the issue of that experiment elsewhere, a difference in the structure of the Government, in the physical as well as the political situation of the country, and in the various departments of industry, seems to deprive it of any important influence as a precedent for the imitation of the United States."

Lord Stanhope had laid it down as a principle, " that a pound sterling being the abstract value, by which the computed value of any object of consumption is measured, that value ought to be independent of the variable quantities of gold and silver, the representative signs of which may be found in circulation." In conformity to this doctrine by which an *abstract idea* was made the standard of value, the British Government had imposed a penalty on all who should presume to pay more than twenty-one shillings in Bank paper for a guinea : and so very profound and ingenious a doctrine could not fail to make proselytes on this side of the Atlantic.

It was the delusion of the day. A host of British ministerial writers had taken much pains to prove that Bank of England paper was as good as gold, and even better : and they had numerous copyists in America. Mr. Dallas, in admitting that inconvertible paper was not, whatever might be its abstract excellence, adapted to the situation of our country, was in advance of many of his cotemporaries.

After the Secretary had made his report, Dr. Bollman issued a pamphlet,* in which he declared : " The paper of the Bank of England preserves a value, as steady perhaps as any attainable, whilst the precious metals, like other commodities, fluctuate around this standard : and the system now in force, after an experience of eighteen years, is found so perfectly satisfactory, that the greater number of the most zealous bullionists, convinced of their former error, begin to doubt whether the resumption of specie payments would be at all expedient, should even no difficulty whatever stand in the way of this measure." The Doctor proposed the establishment of a National Bank, the notes of which should be redeemable in United States six per cent. stock. His plan was to be completed by making the notes

* Plan of an Improved System of the Money Concerns of the Union. Philadelphia, Jan. 16, 1816.

of the State Banks payable, not in specie, but in the paper of the National Bank.

Mr. Carey pronounced the plan of Dr. Bollman a " *magnificent*" one, and said it " would be a *sovereign* remedy for all the financial difficulties of the country."*

Another of the literati of Philadelphia published some essays in the National Intelligencer, in which he endeavored to refute, what he conceived to be, "the very fallacious and mischievous doctrines which some of the federal orators in Congress had recently uttered on the subject of a paper currency in general. Such, for instance, as the following : ' That paper not convertible can never have the quality of money. That the ability of a Bank to redeem, i. e. to pay specie, is the true criterion of excessive issues. That a paper currency is depreciated when it ceases to be of equal value with gold and silver. That the suspension of specie payments by the Bank of England in 1797, led to a depreciation of its paper. That the rise of specie, and a general increase of prices, are the certain indications of depreciation,' &c.—" All which propositions," said our American anti-bullionist, " derived from the report of the English bullion committee, were most triumphantly refuted, in the discussions to which that report gave birth, in and out of Parliament, and are now in England considered as absolutely exploded."

Mr. Carey, and the author of the essays published under the signature of " Anti-Bullionist," appear to have afterwards changed their views of the nature of inconvertible paper : but Dr. Bollman was, if we may judge by his latest publications, inflexible in error.

A new light was now, however, breaking on the people. To borrow the language of the committee of the Senate of Pennsylvania, " Towards the close of the year 1815, the doctrine so generally taught, and so generally received by the great mass of the community, that the paper currency was not depreciated, but that specie had risen in value, began to be abandoned. The intelligent part of the people became convinced that, although the nominal prices of property and commodities had been advanced, the substantial wealth of society had absolutely diminished."

* Letters to the Directors of the Banks, March 27th, 1816.

In Congress there were few, if any, open advocates of inconvertible currency.

On the eighth of January 1816, a bill was reported to establish a Bank of the United States. The bill was, word for word, nearly the same as that which had been brought before the House in 1814, excepting that it made the capital thirty-five millions instead of fifty, contained no provision to compel the Bank to lend to Government, and did not directly sanction a suspension of specie payments.

On the 26th of February, the House proceeded to consider the bill in committee of the whole, and Mr. Calhoun addressed them at length in support of the measure.

" There had been," he said, " an extraordinary revolution in the currency of the country. By a sort of under current, the power of Congress to regulate the money of the country had caved in, and upon its ruin had sprung up those institutions which now exercised the right of making money in and for the United States: for gold and silver are not the only money, but whatever is the medium of purchase and sale, in which Bank paper alone was now employed, and had therefore become the money of the country. A change, great and wonderful, has taken place, which divests you of your rights, and turns you back to the condition of the Revolutionary War, in which every State issued bills of credit, which were made a legal tender, and were of various values. We have in lieu of gold and silver, a paper medium, unequally but generally depreciated, which affects the trade and industry of the nation : which paralyzes the national arm : which sullies the faith both public and private of the United States. According to estimation there were in circulation, within the United States, two hundred millions of dollars of Bank notes, credits and Bank paper, in one shape or other. Supposing thirty millions of these to be in possession of the Banks themselves, there were, perhaps, one hundred and seventy millions actually in circulation, or on which they draw interest, while there were not, according to estimation, in the vaults of all the Banks, more than fifteen million in specie. The Banks had undertook to make loans to Government, not as brokers, but as stockholders—a practice wholly inconsistent with the system of specie payments. Of public stock the Banks held on, the thirtieth day of September last, about

eighteen millions and a half, and a nearly equal amount of
treasury notes, besides stock for long loans made to the
State Governments, amounting altogether to within a small
amount of forty millions. If the Banks would regularly
and consentaneously begin to dispose of their stock, to call
in their notes for the treasury notes they have, and mode-
rately curtail their private discounts : if they would act in
concert in this manner, they might resume specie payments. A National Bank, paying specie itself, would have
a tendency to make specie payments general, as well by its
influence as its example."

Mr. Ward, of Massachusetts, " acknowledged the correctness of the representation of the existing evil, for which
he appeared to think the remedy was near at hand, and
more simple in its application than the establishment of a
National Bank, viz., by refusing to receive the notes of
those Banks which do not pay specie, in dues to Government. But for an alliance which he considered disgraceful to the country, and unjust to individuals, between the
Secretary of the Treasury and the Banks which refused to
pay specie, the evil never would have existed."

Mr. Smith, of Maryland, " thought that, as far as he had
information, the Banks had not issued more notes than,
from the amount of their capital, they had a right to do."
He was friendly to the proposal to establish a National
Bank, but " he did not think it would do any harm, if the
Bank were to commence its operations without specie, but
with an assurance in its charter, of payment of specie at a
particular day. Such an assurance would make the Bank
notes equally good, in his eyes at least, as gold and silver."
The National Intelligencer said that, " with these views
Mr. S. concluded his *practical* speech."

Mr. Sergeant proposed to reduce the amount of the capital of the Bank, from thirty-five to twenty millions. " With
regard to the present time, he said, he should be glad to
know why the Treasury of the United States had not now
the command of specie payments, and the rate of exchange
in its own hands."

Mr. Ward thought that, " in the progressive state of the
country, it was not very important whether the capital was
thirty-five or twenty millions : the latter amount could be
used with nearly as much effect for any mischievous pur-

poses as the former—that sum would be quite sufficient to influence the destinies of the nation."

Mr. Tucker, of Virginia, was of opinion, that a capital of thirty-five millions would not be too large. " In New York, as I have understood, it is contemplated to put into activity an additional Bank capital of fourteen millions. In the State which I have the honor to represent, efforts have lately been made to establish fifteen new Banks, with a capital, I presume, of about seven millions. Do not these things prove that there is a fair prospect of profit?"

Mr. Webster said, " It was a mistaken idea that we were about to reform the national currency. No nation had a better currency than the United States—there was no nation which had guarded its currency with more care ; for the framers of the Constitution, and those who enacted the early statutes on this subject, were *hard-money men;* they had felt, and therefore duly appreciated, the evils of a paper medium; they therefore sedulously guarded the currency of the United States from debasement. The legal currency of the United States was gold and silver coin ; this was a subject in regard to which Congress had run into no folly.

" As to the conduct of the Banks, he would not examine whether the great advances they had made to the Government, during the war, were right or wrong in them, or whether it was right or wrong in the Government to accept them ; but, since the peace, he contended, their conduct had been wholly unjustifiable, as also had that of the Treasury in relation to them. It had been supposed that the Banks would have immediately sold out the stocks, with which they had no business, and fulfilled their engagements ; but public opinion had, in this respect, been disappointed. When this happened, the Government ought, by the use of the means in its power, to have compelled the Banks to return to their specie payments.

" The establishment of a National Bank not being, in his opinion, the proper remedy, he proceeded to examine what was. The solvency of the Banks was not questioned ; there could be no doubt, he said, if the Banks would unite in the object, they might in three weeks resume the payment of specie, and render the adoption of any measure by this House wholly unnecessary. The Banks, he said, were making extravagant profits out of the present state of things, which ought to be curtailed. He referred, for illustration of this point, to the state of the Banks of Pennsylvania, as exhibited in the return to the Legislature of that State, which, with a capital of 2,500,000 dollars, had done a discount business of 4,133,000 at the same time that it held 1,811,000 dollars of the United States' stock—so that, without taking into account a mass of treasury notes, real estate, &c., that Bank was receiving interest on six and a half millions, nearly three times the amount of its capital. That Bank had been pronounced by the Legislature to be in "a flourishing state;" it was so to the stockholders in the Bank, he doubted not.

"The Banks not emanating from Congress, what engine were Congress to use for remedying the existing evil? Their only legitimate power, he said, was to interdict the paper of such Banks as do not pay specie, from being received at the Custom Houses. With a receipt of forty millions a. year, if the Government was faithful to itself and to the interests of the people, they could control the evil, and it was their duty to make the effort. They should have made it long ago, and they ought now to make it."

After some members who were friendly to the proposal to establish a National Bank had spoken—

Mr. Randolph expressed his fears "lest gentlemen had got some of their ideas on this subject from the wretched pamphlets, under which the British and American presses had groaned, on the subject of a circulating medium. The proposal to establish this great Bank, he described as a crutch, and, as far as he understood it, it was a broken one: it would tend, instead of remedying the evil, to aggravate it. The evil of the times was a spirit engendered in this Republic fatal to republican principles—fatal to republican virtue: a spirit to live by any means but those of honest industry: a spirit of profusion; in other words, the spirit of Cataline himself—*alieni avidus sui profusus*— a spirit of expediency, not only in public, but in private life: the system of Diddler in the farce—living any way and well; wearing an expensive coat, and drinking the finest wines at any body's expense. If we wish to transmit our institutions, unimpaired, to posterity, we must put bounds to the spirit which seeks wealth by every path but the plain and regular path of honest industry and honest fame.

"It was unpleasant, he said, to put one's self in array against a great leading interest in the community, be they a knot of land-speculators, paper-jobbers, or what not : but, every man you meet, in this House or out of it, with some rare exceptions, which served only to prove the general rule, was either a stockholder, president, cashier, clerk, or door-keeper, runner, engraver, paper-maker, or mechanic, in some way or other to a Bank. The gentleman from Pennsylvania, might dismiss his fears for the State Banks, with their one hundred and seventy millions of paper on eighty-two millions of capital. However great the evil of their conduct might be, who was to bell the cat? who was to take the bull by the horns? You might as well attack Gibraltar with a pocket-pistol, as to attempt to punish them. There were very few who dared to speak truth of this mammoth: the Banks were so linked together with the business of the world, that there were very few men exempt from their influence. The true secret is, the Banks are creditors as well as debtors ; and if we were merely creditors to them for the paper in our pockets, they would soon, like Morris and Nicholson, go to jail (figuratively speaking) for having issued more paper than they were able to pay when presented to them. A man has their note for fifty dollars, perhaps, in his pocket, for which he wants fifty Spanish milled dollars: and they have his note for five thousand in their possession and laugh at his demand. We are tied hand and foot, and bound to conciliate this grand mammoth, which is set up to worship in this Christian land: we are bound to propitiate it. Thus, whilst our Government denounces hierarchy ; will permit no privileged order for conducting the service of the true God ; whilst it denounces nobility, &c., has a privileged order of new men grown up, the pressure of whose foot he, at this moment, felt on his neck. But, he said, a man might as well go to Constantinople to preach Christianity, as to get up here and preach against Banks."

The bill was read a third time on the 14th of March, and passed the House by a vote of 80 to 71.

When it came before the Senate, Mr. Mann, of N. H., moved so to amend it that the whole amount of specie to be paid in at the time of subscription should be two million eight hundred thousand dollars, instead of one million four hundred thousand. " The United States' stock subscribable and payable at the same time, to the amount of seven mil lions, would be no more aid to the Bank in discounting, with a view to redeeming its notes in specie, than so many Bank bills. The amount of one million four hundred thousand dollars in specie, divided among the different branches, which he presumed would be immediately established, would, he argued, be insufficient for any operation whatever. Let the Bank issue paper to produce any effect, and the specie in its vaults would be instantly withdrawn from them; twenty-five days would be sufficient for that purpose. It might be said the Banks would commence operations slowly and with caution ; but any man acquainted with the institution of Banks knows *that the sum first paid in is nearly all that the stockholders ever pay.* The Bank would continue in operation forever, without taking from the stockholders any considerable sum more than the first instalment : for, as far as the Bank discounted, the second instalment would be paid into the Bank with the specie of the first instalment, &c. This was a position so fully supported by all experience, that he presumed it would not be denied."

Mr. King, of New York, supported this motion. " The gentleman from New Hampshire had conclusively shown, that one and a half millions was the greatest extent to which, as it now stood, the Bank could safely issue on a specie system. Illustrating his view of the subject by a detailed statement of the process, he said, that the first discounts of the Bank being necessarily to those most pressed by the State Banks, the proceeds of the discounts would immediately find their way to the State Banks. Under this view, a million and a half would be a sum entirely too small to enter into a competition with the existing Banks."

Mr. Bibb, of Georgia, and Mr. Barbour of Virginia, opposed the motion. In reply to some remarks by these gentlemen, Mr. Mann said, " he knew of no *law* of the United States which authorized any officer of the Government to receive any part of the spurious money, which the gentleman said was in circulation. The laws were already perfect on this subject. If the executive officers had received other moneys in payment than those authorized by law, they had acted without law, without right. The remedy now proposed, was, Mr. M. thought, something like Sangrado's practice : more Bank paper of the same sort—more hot water for the same evil."

Mr. Mann's motion to amend was rejected.

Mr. Wells opposed the bill on constitutional grounds, and because he did not believe it would have the effect intended. " This bill," he said; " came out of the hands of the Administration ostensibly for the purpose of curtailing the over issue of Bank paper : and yet it came prepared to inflict upon us the same evil, being itself nothing more than simply a paper making machine; and constituting, in this respect, a scheme of policy about as wise, in point of precaution, as the contrivance of one of Rabelais' heroes, who hid himself in the water for fear of the rain. The disease, it is said, under which the people labor, is the Banking fever of the States; and this is to be cured by giving them the Banking fever of the United States."

So little effect have the strongest arguments on men whose minds are made up, that the bill was passed by the Senate on the 3d of April, by a vote of 22 to 12: and returned to the House for concurrence in certain amendments, not important enough to deserve special notice.

When the question on concurrence with the amendments of the Senate was stated, Mr. Randolph declared himself the holder of no stock whatever, except live stock, and had determined never to own any: but, if this bill passed, he would not only be a stockholder to the utmost of his power, but would advise every man, over whom he had any influence to do the same, because it was the creation of a great privileged order of the most hateful kind to his feelings, and because he would rather be the master than the slave. If he must have a master, let him be one with epaulettes—something that he could fear and respect, something that he could look up to—but not a master with a quill behind his ear."

Mr. Webster " animadverted on what he called a compromise of principle, on a great moneyed institution, and the desertion, not only of principles, but of friends, which had characterized the proceedings of this bill."

A motion to postpone the bill indefinitely, was decided in the negative on the 4th of April, by a vote of 67 to 91. The amendments made by the Senate were concurred in by the House; and on the 10th of April the bill was approved by James Madison, the President.

At the same session of Congress, a resolution was passed declaring that, after the 20th of February, 1817, nothing but gold and silver, treasury notes, and the notes of specie paying Banks, *ought* to be received in payment of dues to the United States.

An incident which occurred in the beginning of this year, deserves mention, as an example of the power the Banks had over the community. A Mr. Fisher, a gentleman of Richmond, wished to enforce the payment of ten notes for 100 dollars each, which had been issued by a Bank ฿in Virginia. It had been his wish to bring a suit against the Bank in 1815, but he could not find any gentleman of the bar at Richmond, who was willing to undertake the business. He at length succeeded in engaging a lawyer, and, in January, 1816, regular proceedings were instituted : but the President of the Bank refused to obey the summons. The sheriff called to his aid *a posse comitatus*, and the President was forcibly taken before the court. The Bank still refusing to pay the amount of its notes, its doors were closed by the sheriff. It then brought suit against Mr. Fisher, laying its damages at 10,000 dollars, and also took measures for instituting legal proceedings against the sheriff! The doors of the Bank were surreptiously opened, and the Bank continued its operations, thus gaining a new triumph over the laws.*

The Banks of other parts of the country, evinced an equal indisposition to obey the laws of the land. Notwithstanding that the resolution of Congress designated the 20th of February, 1817, as the day after which the notes of non-specie paying Banks ought not to be received in payment of dues to Government, " the principal Banks in the Middle States explicitly stated" to the Treasury Department, in the month of August, " their determination not to resume specie payments before the 1st of July, 1817."†

Mr. Dallas had, however, become weary of treating with

* Niles.   † Letter of Mr. Dallas, Nov. 29th, 1816.

the Banks as with independent sovereignties. He gave public notice, on the 12th of September, that the resolution of
Congress would be enforced. But the delegates of the
Banks of New York, Philadelphia, Baltimore, and the District of Columbia, assembled at New York on the 16th of
September, bid him defiance, by resolutions which they
published, fixing on the 1st of July for the resumption of
specie payments.

The resolution of Congress was, however, of such a nature that it could not easily be evaded; and it was not a little strengthened, by an act of the Legislature of New York,
imposing a penalty of twelve per cent. on any Bank within
that commonwealth, which should not pay its notes on demand. An act of this kind had been brought before the
Legislature in April, 1815, but the fair promises of the
Banks, and the exertions of their agents, prevented its
being adopted in that year. Tired out by the subterfuges
of the moneyed corporations, the Legislature at last adopted this salutary measure.

CHAPTER X.

Of Banking from 1816–17 *to* 1817–18.

During the year ending December 31st, 1816, the re
venue of the United States' Government amounted to the
enormous sum of *forty-seven millions of dollars*, or to
two millions more than the total of the national debt on
the first of January, 1812. The appearance of increasing
riches, and the general rise of prices produced by the free
use of paper money, had caused a consumption of foreign
commodities, the effect of which was felt by Government
in the great increase of its revenue.

But, with all this income, our fiscal affairs were not
free from embarrassment. " The public treasury exhibited a phenomenon in finance. Many millions of surplus
revenue, with as many different values as there were offices of collection, constantly accumulating at those ports of
entry where it was least valuable, and applicable only where
it was collected, while the great mass of public debt and

expenditures was at those places where the public moneys were least available: even the quarterly interest on the public debt, due where the currency was most valuable, could not be discharged but by the evidence of a new debt, in the form of seven per cent. treasury notes. Thus creating an invidious distinction as well between the debtors as the creditors of the public, in many cases exceeding twenty per cent. on the amount of their respective claims. The market value of the currency paid to the Government, was made to fluctuate according to the arbitrary decisions of Banks, and intrigues of brokers.

" In this situation, the State Banks which had been employed as depositories of the public money, withheld the indispensable facilities of exchange, for the payment of the public creditors, and finally refused to pay the balances due by them, but in the ordinary course of public expenditure; at their respective places of location claiming, under various groundless pretexts, the indulgence of Government, while the immense sums received by them on account of the United States in the paper of the Banks which did not participate in the public deposits, enabled them to control those Banks and protract their efforts to resume specie payments."*

Such was the state of affairs, that, though there was a balance of *twenty-two* millions in the treasury, the Government was compelled to borrow five hundred thousand dollars from the United States Bank, in anticipation of its regular operations, to pay the interest due on the public debt at Boston on the first of January, 1817.

The Bank of the United States opened its doors at Philadelphia on the 1st of January, 1817. Its capital then consisted of one million four hundred thousand dollars in specie, and fourteen millions in public stocks. About this time a second instalment in specie, of the amount of two millions eight hundred thousand dollars, was due : " but it is clear," says a Friendly Monitor, " that the Bank having commenced operations, and put its paper in circulation, could not enforce the payment of the specie part of the second and third instalments of the capital in *new acquisi-*

" A Friendly Monitor." Philadelphia, December, 1819. Rep., September, 1822. Mr. Gallatin says "it is well known that this pamphlet came from an authentic source." We have been told it was written by W. Jones, the first President of the United States Bank.

tions of specie. They would be paid either in the notes of the Bank, or in the specie which they would draw out of the Bank, or with checks drawn on the credit of the discounts, or not at all : for if the Bank had ceased to furnish facilities in the vain expectation of coercing payment, *no dividend* could have accrued * * * * The directors therefore acted *wisely* in discounting the notes of the stockholders payable in specie sixty days after date."

From the documents laid before Congress in 1819, it appears that the directors did not wait till the second instalment was due : but passed a resolution in December, before any notes of the Bank were in circulation, authorizing discounts on a pledge of stock. Such "facilities" enabled the stockholders either to comply with, or to evade, the requisitions of the law, as the reader is disposed to interpret its terms. A large part of the second instalment was not paid till months after it was due, and instead of two millions eight hundred thousand dollars, only three hundred and twenty-four thousand can, according to the report of a committee of Congress, be fairly presumed to have been paid in coin.

A third instalment, of two millions eight hundred thousand in coin, and of seven millions in Government stock, was due after the 1st of July. But the committee of Congress say that, " of the two million eight hundred thousand dollars which was to have been paid at the third instalment, it is believed that a very trifling amount was paid in coin, and as little of the funded debt, but that nearly the whole were paid by the proceeds of notes discounted on stock."*

To be brief, the capital of the United States Bank, when all paid in, consisted of about *two* millions in specie, instead of seven millions, and of about twenty-one millions in funded debt, instead of twenty-eight millions, and of about twelve millions in the stock notes of the original stockholders. Mr. Mann had predicted that the stock would be completed in this way, and it being the way in which Bank stock is usually completed, the result ought to occasion no surprise.

The manner in which the discounts on pledges of stock of the Bank were conducted, was very beneficial to some of the original shareholders. " The directors did not confine themselves to the amount prescribed in the resolution of De-

* Report to Congress, January, 1819.

cember 27th, that is, to the proportion of the coined part of
the second instalment, but discounted to the full par value
of the stock which was paid for by the proceeds of the
same discounts; and the discounts, the payment of the
second instalment, the payment of the price to the owner,
the transfer, and the pledge of the stock, were, as it is
termed, simultaneous operations.   All the discounts on
stock after the 20th of February, 1817, were made at the
par value of the shares, which enabled the discounter not
only to pay the whole of the instalments, including the
specie part, and the funded debt part, but also to draw out
of the Bank the amount which might have been paid in on
his shares.   * * * The effect of these discounts was, very
obviously, to enable those who had made large purchases,
to retain their stock without paying for it, and to derive a
benefit from its probable advancement in price.   Had the
Bank rigidly required the payment of the instalments, the
large stockholders must have sold that portion of their
shares which their real means did not enable them to hold.
Or, if the Bank had not exacted the instalments, and had
not afforded the means of substituting credit for payment,
the stock would not have advanced materially in price, and
the large holders of it would have had no inducement to retain
it.   In either event, a more equal diffusion of shares would
have been the consequence, and it would have reached the
hands of solid capitalists, who would have held only what
they could pay for."*

In August a resolution was adopted to grant discounts
on Bank stock, at the rate of 125 for 100 paid, with an
indorser for the excess.   "And in order to insure the
greatest amount of such loans, and at the same time afford
facilities to the prompt purchase and sale of stock," the
President and Cashier were authorized, " to discount all
stock notes that should be offered between discount days,
to a certain amount.   Stock-jobbing to an immense extent,
and wagers on the price of shares, were the inevitable consequences of this system.   It gave equal facilities to the
bankrupt, who had not credit enough to obtain an indorser,
and to the capitalist.   Stock could be, and was, purchased
without the advance of a cent by the purchaser, who had
only to apply to the directors, or to the President and

* Report to Congress, Jan. 1819.

Cashier between discount days, for a loan on the shares about to be bought, and, by what is termed a simultaneous operation, he obtained the discount, and with it paid for his stock. A rise in the market would enable him to sell his shares, pocket the difference, and commence operations anew. The loans actually made were most of them unreasonable, and excessive in their amount : they were not made to the merchant and trader, but to a few persons consisting of directors, brokers, and speculators : and have been renewed and continued almost invariably at the option of the borrower.

" One of the arts obviously intended to give the Bank stock a high price in the European market, was the establishment of an agency there to pay the dividends. On the 28th of November, 1816, a resolution was passed by the casting vote of the President, and against the report of a committee who had been appointed to consider the subject, authorizing John Sergeant, Esq., to make arrangements in Europe, for the payment of the Bank dividends at the par of exchange, and at the risk and expense of the Bank. When the committee find among the eleven who voted in the affirmative, the names of some directors who have been constantly and largely engaged in the purchase and sale of stock ; and that of the ten who voted in the negative, not one has been ascertained to have dealt in those transactions, they are almost irresistibly impelled to the conclusion, that the measure was adopted more with a view to enhance the price of shares, than for the permanent benefit of the institution.

" The root and source of all these instances of misconduct, was the illegal and reprehensible division of the stock. By the first fundamental article of the charter, no person, co-partnership, or body politic, shall be entitled to more than thirty votes : and yet, in violation of this provision, it was a common and general practice, well known to the judges of the election and to the directors, to divide shares into small parcels, varying from one to twenty shares to a name, held in the names of persons who had no interest in them, and to vote upon the shares thus held as the attorneys of the pretended proprietors. By some of the witnesses it is avowed that their object was to influence the election. Mr. Leiper, one of the judges of the first elec-

tion, states that he did so himself. The effect was, that
Baltimore, which had about one-seventh of the shares
owned by individuals, gave more than one-fourth of all the
votes that could be given. In that place there were 1172
shares taken in 1172 names, by George Williams, as attorney, the whole of which, it appears from his examination,
he owned. At Philadelphia nearly one-third of the shares
was owned, and the votes given at that place were about
two-ninths of the whole authorized. The same persons
who thus held the power of appointing directors, are found
to have the greatest loans on stock."*

It is time now to turn our attention to other operations of
the Bank.

In January, a convention of delegates from the Banks
of New York, Philadelphia, Baltimore, Richmond, and
Norfolk, met in Philadelphia, and resolved to resume specie
payments on the 20th of February, on certain conditions,
one of which was, that the payment of the balances which
might accumulate against these Banks, should not be demanded by the Bank of the United States, until the said
Bank and branches should have discounted for individuals
(other than those having duties to pay) 2,000,000 in New
York, 2,000,000 in Philadelphia, 1,500,000 in Baltimore,
and 500,000 in Virginia.

The Bank of the United States acceded to this arrangement, and thus engaged to extend its credit dealings as
the other Banks contracted theirs.

A favorite object was "the equalization of exchange
between different parts of the Union." This was unfortunately sought to be effected, not by compelling the
local Banks to redeem their extra issues, and thus bring
the currency in every part of the country to a level with
specie ; but by issuing notes payable at all the offices, and
by a system of drawing and re-drawing carried on by the
mother Bank and its branches. The directors of the
branches at the South and West, especially those at Baltimore, had their own speculations to promote, and issued

---

* The effect of these different proceedings was, that on the last of
December, 1816, Bank of the United States stock was at 41 7-8, for 30
paid, in April at 81 for 65 paid, in May at 98, on the 20th of August at
144 for 100 paid, on the 30th of August at 156¼, at which price it remained for some days, and then began to decline.

Report to Congress, Jan. 16th, 1819.

their notes and drafts in so great quantity, as to cause no little embarrassment to the Bank at Philadelphia, and the branches to the North.

The Secretary of the Treasury increased the inducements of the Bank to multiply its discounts, by redeeming with a portion of the public deposits, eleven millions of the funded debt which formed part of the capital stock of the Bank.

The effect of these various operations was, that the discounts of the Bank, which were less than 3 millions on the 27th of February, were increased to 20 millions by the 30th of April, to 25 millions by the 29th of July, and to 33 millions by the 31st of October. At the close of the year, the amount of unsound credit dealings was, taking the country throughout, greater than it was at the begining : for the " contraction " made by all the local Banks, did not equal the "expansion" made by the United States' Bank.

The Committee of the Senate of Pennsylvania,* describe it as only a *nominal* resumption of specie payments that was effected in this year. " Had the United States Bank," they say, " been conducted with the discretion and wisdom which were essential to so powerful a machine, its influence might have been productive of the most happy consequences. The public was aware that the currency of the State Banks was still depreciated from excess, and that nothing but a further reduction of their issues could remove its unsoundness ; and yet, with this fact evident to the most limited capacity, the directors of the new Bank fancied, that if they could only persuade the city Banks to *call* that a sound currency which was in reality an unsound one, the evil of depreciation would be cured ; and they accordingly proposed to them to enter into an arrangement to resume specie payment on the 21st of February following. The city Banks, sensible that their power over the community was so great that few individuals would have the boldness to make large demands on them for coin, and relying upon the forbearance that had hitherto been extended to them by an injured public, who had been for two years and a half paying them six per cent. per annum for their dishonored bills, consented to the arrangement, and specie payments were *nominally* resumed on

* Report on the Public Distress, January 29th, 1820.

the appointed day.   We say *nominally*, because, in point of
fact, a *bona fide* resumption did not take place, as is evident from the well-known circumstance, that, for a long time
after that period, *American* as well as foreign *coins* would
command on the spot a price in city Bank notes above
their nominal value.   Depreciation can as well result from
the forbearance of the public to demand their rights, as
from the refusal of the Banks to pay their engagements ;
and the arrangement alluded to, was not any real resumption of cash payments, but a mere change of one species of
inconvertibility for another.   No sooner, however, had the
directors of the National Bank succeeded in the desirable
object of rendering depreciated paper an equivalent for their
own convertible notes, than, instead of reflecting, from an
acquaintance with general principles and from the experience of the past, that the channels of circulation could
contain only, without depreciation, but a limited amount
of paper credits, and that that amount was already in these
channels, they began to add to the mass already redundant, by emissions of their own notes : and in the course of
a few months, added to the mass of Bank loans an amount
greatly beyond the reductions which had been made.   By
these means the currency, although *nominally* convertible,
was depreciated below its former low state, and was thrown
back instead of being advanced on the road to restoration :
and thus was rendered nugatory, all the pain and embarrassment which the public had suffered from the former
curtailments of the State Banks."

In the Southern and Western States, the operations of
the United States' Bank caused the local Banks to extend
their issues.   The Bank, say the committee of Congress,
" improvidently afforded a temptation to the western Banks
particularly, to extend their circulation of notes, by insist-
ing on its branches paying out their own notes in preference to those of the State Banks, and on their delivering
drafts on the eastern cities, whenever it could be done,
to prevent the remittance of their own notes.   The branch
notes and the drafts issued in consequence of these instructions, were swept away by the facility of remittance
thus unwarily given, as well as by the ordinary balance of
trade.   A vacuum in the circulation was thus produced,
which could be supplied only by the local notes, which were

readily received by the offices of the Bank of the United States, and were retained by them as a fund upon which interest was paid by the State Banks.   The committee are of opinion, that instead of conducting with the alleged rigor towards the State Banks, the Bank of the United States is liable to the more serious charge of having *increased* the amount of notes in circulation, by its acceptance of them in those places where it was known they would not be redeemed in specie, and by making them, in the manner before mentioned, the only circulating medium in that part of the country.   So long as the notes of each office were payable at all the others, and the office issuing was not exclusively liable for their redemption, the discounts at those places against which there was a balance of trade, became larger in proportion to their indemnity against demands.   As the notes of the offices were rapidly carried off, the payment of those discounts was necessarily made in the notes of the local institutions.   And thus it was one of the inevitable effects of the old system, to increase the debts of the State Banks to the offices of the United States Bank at those places."

CHAPTER XI.

Of Banking from 1817–18 *to* 1818–19.

In the first part of the next year, the Bank of the United States conducted operations on the same principles that had governed it in 1817.   In January and February, 1818, the amount of its discounts and exchange dealings was swelled to forty-two millions, and in March and April to upwards of forty-three millions.

During all this time the Bank had not succeeded in getting notes to the amount of ten million dollars in circulation, but this appears to have been owing not to any disinclination of the directors to issue paper in abundance, but to a physical inability on the part of the President and Cashier to sign as many notes as were wanted.   To get over this difficulty, application was made to Congress to grant authority to the President and Cashiers of the Branches to sign notes.   One of the objects in establishing the United

States' Bank, was to substitute a uniform paper currency for that variety of notes which made it difficult for many persons to distinguish between the genuine and the counterfeit. An objection was therefore made to granting the officers of the branches power to sign notes, as the variety of signatures would increase one of the evils the Bank was intended to remedy : but a bill was passed by the Senate to authorize the appointment of a Vice President and Assistant Cashier, whose special duty it should be to sign notes for the mother Bank and all its branches. When the bill came before the House on the 18th of April, much praise was bestowed on the Bank for the excellent manner in which it had been conducted, and the propriety of taking measures to enable it to circulate more paper was warmly urged. Mr. Smith, of Maryland, said, " one great object of the Bank was to afford an adequate circulating medium, that would be uniform throughout the Union. To effect this, it is necessary to have a sufficient number of notes signed to enable the Bank to put twenty millions of dollars in circulation. The President and Cashier cannot, (having their other business to attend to,) sign more than 1500 notes each day. At that rate it would require more than four years to sign the number and kind necessary for circulation.'' The bill was negatived by the House, chiefly from a fear, as would appear from the debates, that it would give the United States' Bank too much power over the local Banks.

In its charter, in the preference given to its notes by the Government, and in its being made the depository of the public revenue, the United States' Bank had great power. It was thus it was enabled to make discounts in little more than a year to an amount exceeding forty-three millions, including eleven or twelve millions on pledges of stock, though the specie part of its capital was hardly two millions.

To sustain its operations, the Bank exchanged part of its funded debt for specie in Europe, and purchased a large amount of coin in the West Indies and other places. Between July, 1817, and July, 1818, upwards of seven millions of specie were imported by the Bank, at a cost of five hundred thousand dollars. But the original cause of the specie's leaving the country, viz : the excess of paper issues, still continuing to operate, the money was exported by individuals faster than it was imported by the Bank. "I myself have seen," says a Friendly Monitor," a detailed statement of five millions dollars, exported in twelve months from the ports of Boston and Salem alone, and from this data the aggregate amount exported in twelve months from the United States, could not have been, during the same period, short of twelve million of dollars." This estimate is probably below the real amount, and the result would have been the same, if the Bank had imported seventy millions instead of seven millions. If we had mines as rich as those of Potosi, and paper should be issued in excess, we should not be able to retain in the country even that small amount of silver which is necessary to keep Bank notes convertible.

Notwithstanding the importation of specie made by the Bank, the amount at any one time in its vaults did not rise to three millions—an amount which, divided among the mother Bank and eighteen branches, was quite insufficient to sustain its operations.

In July the Board of Directors found it absolutely necessary to change their policy. A sudden reduction of discounts to the amount of two millions at the Bank in Philadelphia, two millions at Baltimore, seven hundred thousand at Richmond, and five hundred thousand in Norfolk, was then ordered to be made before the 1st of November, and it was resolved to require the payment of the balances due by the Banks of Cincinnati and of the District of Columbia.

By the 30th of October, the reduction of discounts at Philadelphia had exceeded the prescribed amount in the sum of five hundred thousand dollars. In Baltimore, Richmond, and Norfolk, the deficiency was one million seventy-seven thousand five hundred. The total reduction in the four cities was nearly four million five hundred thousand : yet an additional reduction to the amount of one million, was deemed necessary in Philadelphia ; and a committee of investigation was constrained to urge a steady perseverence in the curtailments of the discounts of the Bank and its offices, wherever it might be practical and useful. One of the reasons for this course of procedure, was " the premium paid at this time for specie, which is said to be ten per cent. on Spanish dollars, and a considerable though less premium for other coins."

" When, in July last," says the Committee of Congress,
" the Board directed a curtailment of discounts, it fell in
almost all cases on the business paper, while the immense
amounts loaned on stock pledges were but little affected, excepting at the offices at Richmond and Washington, where
the curtailment appears to have fallen equally on all the
notes. But the discounts at these places on stock were
very small, particularly when compared with Baltimore,
where the loans were such, and so long continued, as to receive the animadversions of the parent Board."

A reduction of discounts to the amount of four million
five hundred thousand dollars in four cities, in the short
space of three months and ten days, had a very disastrous
effect on the merchants, and through them, on the rest of
the community. Their sufferings were increased by the order not to receive on deposit at Philadelphia any notes except
those of the mother Bank, or at any one of the branches,
any notes except those of that one branch. Heretofore the
mother Bank and its branches had paid and received in-
discriminately, all their notes, without regard to the place
of issue. By the new arrangement, paper which was received from the Bank on one day was on the next no longer
available in paying debts to the Bank. In other words, the
merchants were called on to pay four or five millions, and
were not allowed the privilege of paying debts due to the
Bank itself in the paper of the Bank.

The local Banks, when a sudden demand was made on
them for balances due to the United States' Bank, had no
way of meeting those demands but by pressing on their own
customers. The pressure thus became general throughout
the country.

The Committee of Congress say, that the demands of
the United States' Bank against the local Banks, " were
suffered to accumulate improperly, instead of being gradually reduced as specie was required at other offices, and
in small quantities that would not have been felt. Their
reduction was not insisted upon sufficiently early ; and
when the Bank began to call for specie, its demands were
so considerable as not only to expose the local Banks, but
the citizens in their vicinity, generally, to very severe
pressure."

The situation of the community was very alarming. Mr.

Niles, in his Register of October 3d, intimates that " a grand scheme was maturing ' for keeping the paper-mill a going.' The first part of the scheme is to *prepare* the members of Congress to vote as directed at the ensuing session of Congress. Of what is designed to be done, when a sufficient number of members are secured, we are almost wholly in the dark at present : but we believe one of the things proposed is, the substitution of a *paper currency* as a LEGAL TENDER, instead of coin, which is frequently hinted at in certain newspapers, as if to feel the public pulse." In his Register, of November 7th, he says, " We have several times darkly hinted at a great intrigue which was going on to relieve the Banking system, generally, and especially to subserve the grand views of the Bank of the United States. I am just now informed of what this intrigue is : but private honor will not permit me to mention it, at present. The object is, *by bits of paper to prevent the Banks from being compelled to pay their debts*. This is the long and the short of the whole affair. Aye, and the pretence is most specious, the appearance most seducing : but the instantaneous effect will be to banish money, and bring about those happy times when lordly Banks issued notes for six and a quarter cents, and a copper coin was a rarity. To effect this arrangement, many of the local Banks will co-operate—to seal their own ruin ; for the bits of paper above alluded to, will immediately centre in the Bank of the United States. Perhaps, as the people are alarmed on this subject, the project may not be pressed ; though we have reason to believe that much exertion has been made to convince certain members of Congress of the propriety of it : and we were astonished to learn that a distinguished gentlemen, of whom, indeed, we expected a different conduct, had boldly predicted the triumph of the United States' Bank over the local institutions. Upon my conscience, I would rather agree to have a hereditary President and a Senate for life, than that this thing should happen. In the latter case, our President and Senators might be influenced to good actions by a sense of *individual* shame, or a love of true glory, and the choice of representatives would be left free to us : but in the other, an unknown and irresistible aristocracy would be raised up, secret as the " council of ten" and remorseless as the " holy inquisition." Give me to live under any despotism but that which springs from the command of money : for it is the most base and unprincipled of all.

" But Congress will not, cannot, *dare* not, pass the law, proposed to pamper speculation. They may prohibit the exportation of coin, if they please ;. still they cannot substitute a paper medium for it, and compel me to take it in payment of debts justly due me. And this it is which is fondly designed to be attempted—for the benefit of the rag-barons."

It is certain that letters were received at Washington from Philadelphia, in the early part of December, urging an emission of treasury notes ; and that, on the 7th of December, a meeting was held in Philadelphia, Mr. Matthew Carey in the chair, by which a committee was appointed to draft a memorial to Congress to prohibit the exportation of specie. Some of the members appointed on the committee declined acting, and no memorial appears to have been prepared; but a member of the Senate actually brought before that body a resolution to prohibit the exportion of the precious metals! What despotic Spain could never accomplish, was attempted in free America.

Towards the close of this year, public opinion became so adverse to the Banks as to call forth strong denunciations of them from some of the high officers of State. De Witt Clinton, the Governor of New York, in his Message to the Legislature, reprobated the system in strong terms. "The embarrassments," he said, " arising from the disordered state of our currency, have increased instead of diminishing, since I had the honor to address the Legislature on the subject. And unless efficient preventives are adopted, and suitable remedies applied, the evil will be in a state of progressive augmentation. A proposition to invest Banks with a power of coining money, would have no advocates, and yet it might not be so pernicious as the authority already granted of emitting Bank notes. Having uniformly opposed the multiplication of Banks, I now only express opinions formed for many years, after mature deliberation, and which are every day sanctioned by the progress of time and the voice of experience."

Governor Worthington, of Ohio, said, " The disordered state of the currency will claim your attention. The good

people of the State look to you, gentlemen, for such remedy as may be within your power. The obstacles you have
to encounter in effecting an object of so much importance
cannot be disguised : indeed, I fear it may be found impracticable, under existing circumstances, to answer public
expectation."

Gabriel Slaughter, the Governor of Kentucky, was very
emphatic in his denunciation of the system.   " I am indeed," he said, " ready to confess before my countrymen,
that my sentiments, or perhaps prejudices, ever have been,
and still are, strongly against the Banking system.   Time
and experience, instead of conquering these prejudices,
have tended to confirm them.   I have ever viewed these
moneyed corporations with jealousy. I consider the corporate powers and privileges conferred on them, as so much
taken from the power of the people, and a contrivance to
rear up in the country a moneyed aristocracy.   Money is
power, in whatever hands it is placed : but it is less dangerous when divided among individuals, than when combined and organized in the form of Banks.   In vain did
the American people, during their struggles for liberty and
independence, destroy the landed aristocracy, then existing
under the law authorizing estates to be entailed, if a moneyed aristocracy is to be substituted.   Instead of having
our National and State Legislatures filled with men representing the feelings and interests of the great agricultural
class of the community, I fear we shall see these Banking
aristocracies greatly preponderate on the legislative floor.
I must ever be opposed to any system of policy, which, independent of its pernicious and corrupting influence in
other respects, tends to diminish, if not destroy, the weight
and influence of the farming interest, upon whose virtue
and independence the duration of our free institutions so
essentially depends.

" While this system exists in other States, Kentucky can
do little to rescue the country from the evil and anti-republican tendencies of these moneyed corporations.   Let us
therefore invite a co-operation in some plan, co-exten-
sive with the Union, to redeem this young and rising Republic from the mischief and dangers of this paper system,
before it is too late.   If permitted to progress and inter-
weave itself with all the interests and concerns of society,

it may, in a more advanced and dense state of our population, explode in a convulsion of the Government.   The
disease, it is true, has taken deep root, but the American
Republic is young, and by a vigorous and determined
effort, may, in a few years, exterminate it.   Some time
may be necessary to enable these institutions to wind up.
To effect so desirable an object, I would recommend to
the Legislature, to propose an amendment to the Federal
Constitution, providing, that, after a certain period, no incorporated Bank should exist in the United States, or, if
this should be thought going too far, and Banks in any
shape, or to any extent, are useful and necessary, let the
Banking powers be limited, and the system so regulated
and restricted, as to secure the community against the
wide spread ruin and mischief with which we are threatened."

These views appear to have been adopted by some members of the Legislature, for on the 4th of January, 1819,
Mr. Bledsoe submitted the following resolutions :—

1. *Resolved, by the General Assembly of the Commonwealth of Kentucky*, that the establishment of a moneyed
monopoly is hostile to republican liberty.

2. *Resolved*, That Banks are such a monopoly, and do
not depend for their profits upon the correct employment
of the products of industry.

3. *Resolved*, That as the products of the labor of a nation are the only genuine sources of national wealth, any
corporation or institution which tends to substitute speculation instead of the proper and valuable fruits of this
labor, must be pernicious, and ought to be abolished.

4. *Resolved*, That any corporation not promotive of, or
essential to, public good, ought not to exist.

5. *Resolved*, That all Banks wherein individuals are interested, are moneyed monopolies, tending to make profit to
those who do not labor, out of the means of those who do :
not tending to increase the means of industry, but to profit
of those means unjustly : tending to tax the many for the
benefit of the few : tending to create a privileged order,
unuseful and pernicious to society : tending to destroy
liberty, and create a power unfriendly to human happiness :
tending inevitably to an unfeeling moneyed aristocracy, more
to be deprecated than monarchy itself : tending to the destruction of the best hopes of man here and hereafter.

6. *Resolved*, That it becomes the duty of the General Government, and of every individual State composing it, (gradually if necessary, but ultimately and certainly,) to abolish all Banks and moneyed monopolies, and if a paper medium is necessary, to substitute the impartial and disinterested medium of the credit of the nation or of the States."

We know not if these resolutions were adopted.

CHAPTER XII.

Of Banking from 1818-19 *to* 1819-20.

A committee of Congress, which had been appointed on the 30th of November, 1818, to investigate the affairs of the United States' Bank, arrived in Philadelphia on the 6th of December, and left it on the 26th. Some investigations were subsequently made of the state of the branches at Richmond and Washington; and on the 16th of January, 1819, the committee made a report, giving an account of the operations of the Bank, and concluding with a declaration that it had violated its charter, in four particulars, viz: in purchasing two millions of public debt; in not requiring the stockholders to pay the second and third instalments of the stock in coin and funded debt; in paying dividends to stockholders who had not completed their instalments; and in suffering certain individuals, under pretext of their being attorneys for others, to give more votes for directors than the charter allowed.

Mr. Spencer, the chairman of the committee, offered a resolution to cause a *scire facias* to be sued out, to call on the corporation of the United States' Bank, to show cause why its charter should not be forfeited, unless the Bank would consent to certain alterations in the act of incorporation. Mr. Trimble offered a resolution to cause a *scire facias* to be issued immediately. Mr. Johnson offered a resolution to repeal the charter of the Bank.

After debate, Mr. Trimble's resolution was rejected on the 24th of February, 39 members voting in its favor, and

116 against it.   Mr. Johnson's resolution was supported by
30 members, and opposed by 121 ; and Mr. Spencer, discovering by these votes the disposition of the House, withdrew his resolution.

"We learn," says Mr. Niles, " that about *forty* members are stockholders—some of them heavily so : *we hope
that none of them voted in their own case.*   The great danger of incorporations is, that the chief members of them are
our governors, judges, and legislators ; and thus their individual interests may be placed between the people and
the justice that they claim."*

The Bank was in more danger from its own operations,
than from any proceedings of Congress.   On the receipt
in Philadelphia of the report of the committee, the stock
fell to 93, and Mr. William Jones, the President, soon after
fled in affright from the institution.   Mr. Cheves, of South
Carolina, was invited to take his place, and Mr. James C.
Fisher, of Philadelphia, served as President *pro tempore.*

Three years afterwards Mr. Cheves gave the stockholders an exposition of the state of the Bank, from which
exposition we shall make a copious extract.

" The institution commenced active Banking operations
about 1st of January, 1817, and in the course of the year established eighteen branches.   The report of the committee of
Congress made in December, 1818, has made you so fully
acquainted with many of the details of the previous management, that I mean to do little more in relation to the
period which preceeded 1819, than present the results, as
they will be exhibited in the state of the Bank when I
came into it.

" The Bank immediately on its commencement did a
very extensive business, imported vast sums of specie,
paid its notes and those of the offices, without reference
to the places where they were payable, at the Bank, and
all the principal offices north of the Potomac, while they
were, under the charter, necessarily received every where
in payments of debts to the Government of the United
State : and drafts were given without limit, on the parent
Bank and northern offices, by the western offices, at par
or at a premium merely nominal.   As soon as the notes of

* Weekly Register, Feb. 27, 1819.

the southern and western offices were paid or received by the Bank and northern offices, they were returned to them and re-issued in perpetual succession. An accompanying exhibit will show the enormous amount of the notes of the southern and western offices, which became chargeable on the Bank, directly and indirectly, through the northern offices.* The result was, that the Bank and the great northern offices were drained of their capital, and on the 20th of July, 1818, only eighteen months after the the institution began its operations, it was obliged to commence a rapid and heavy curtailment of the business of the Bank and its offices. During all this time, it had the advantage of immense Government deposits. At the moment that curtailments were ordered, the Government deposits in the Bank and its branches, including the deposits of public officers, amounted to eight millions of dollars, and they had been larger at preceeding periods. Curtailments were ordered from time to time, at the southern and western offices, to the amount of seven millions of dollars, and at the parent Bank to the amount of two millions, though at the latter they were made to the amount of 3,600,000, and upwards, between the 30th of July, 1818, and the 1st of April, 1819. No curtailments were ordered at the offices of New York and Boston, because there was no room for them, yet necessity obliged them to reduce their business very much. The curtailments at all points within the above mentioned dates, being eight months, were 6,530,159 dollars 49 cents. Yet after these immense and rapid curtailments, the most sensible and vital points (Philadelphia, New York, and Boston) were infinitely in worse condition than when the remedy was devised.

" An accompanying exhibit will show the distribution of the capital at the close of this important period.† At that moment the discount line of the important office at Boston, was only 94,584 dollars 37 cents. And when in this

---

* The total was $14,893,661, or $20,422,642,95, if we include 5,528,981,96 of post notes which were issued by the parent Bank, and destroyed because they were used in the Southern and Western States, in lieu of Bank notes.

† The office at New York had a capital of 245,000 dollars : that at Richmond, 1,760,502, Baltimore, 5,646,000, Cincinnati, 2,400,000, Louisville, 1,129,000, Lexington, 1,500,000, &c.

wretched state, the southern and western circulation was pouring in upon these weak points, and the Government at liberty, according to the practice of the time, to draw on either office or the Bank for the gross amount of its deposits, throughout the whole establishment, whether North, South, East or West. The southern and western offices were not restrained from issuing their notes, which they did most profusely. The curtailments, in many instances, resulted merely in a change of debts bearing interest, for debts due by local Banks, or the notes of local Banks, on neither of which was interest received. The western offices curtailed their discounted paper, but they purchased what were called *race horse bills*, to a greater amount than their curtailments. The Bank itself continued, during the whole period, to purchase and collect drafts on the southern and even western offices, though almost the whole of the active capital already lay in those quarters of the Union, and though the great object of the curtailments was to draw funds from these points. The debt due in Kentucky and Ohio, instead of being reduced, was within this period actually increased upwards of half a million of dollars. An accompanying exhibit will show, that, instead of getting relief from the southern and western offices generally, where curtailments had been ordered, the Bank was still further exhausted by the intervening operations.

"At the commencement of this period, (a period commencing with the order for curtailments, and ending March, 1819,) the Bank was indebted to Baring, Brothers & Co., Reed, Irving & Co., Adams, Robertson & Co., and Thomas Wilson & Co., the sum of 1,586,345 dollars 47 cents, growing principally, if not entirely, out of its specie operations. Of this sum the greater part was paid during this period. It had, however, contracted new debts with Baring, Brothers & Co., and Thomas Wilson & Co., of which there remained due, including any balance which may have been due on the former accounts, the sum of 876,648 dollars : and within the same period it had disposed of 2,270,926 dollars 65 cents of its funded debt, furnishing, by these compound operations, ways and means, in addition to its curtailments, to the amount of 1,561,229 dollars 13 cents, and making, with these curtailments, a reduction in the productive capital of the Bank, within

the period of eight months, of eight millions of dollars
and upwards.

" At the close of this period, the discounts on personal
security at Philadelphia, had been so long the subject of
curtailment, that but a small portion of them admitted of
further reduction, and, after great efforts, a rule had been
established to reduce the discounts which had been granted on the stock of the Bank, at the rate of five per cent.
every 60 days. The latter constituted the bulk of the
discounted paper, and so small a reduction afforded no
relief against a great and immediate demand. Even this
small reduction was the subject of loud, angry, and constant remonstrances among the borrowers, who claimed
the privileges and the favors which they contended were due
to stockholders, and sometimes succeeded in communica-
ting their sympathies to the Board. All the funded debt
which was valuable had been disposed of, and the proceeds
exhausted. The specie in the vaults at the close of the
day, on the 1st of April, 1819, was only 126,745 dollars
28 cents, and the Bank owed to the city Banks, deducting
balances due to it, an aggregate balance of 79,125 dollars
99 cents.

"It is true there were in the Mint 267,978 dollars 9
cents, and *in transitu* from Kentucky and Ohio overland
250,000 dollars: but the Treasury dividends were payable
on that day to the amount of near 500,000 dollars, and
there remained at the close of the day more than one half
of the sum subject to draft, and the greater part of the sum
which had been drawn during the day remained a charge
upon the Bank, in the shape of temporary deposits which
were almost immediately withdrawn. Accordingly, on the
12th of the same month, the Bank had. in its vaults but
71,522 dollars 47 cents, and owed to the city Banks a
balance of 196,418 dollars 47 cents; exceeding the specie
in its vaults 124,895 dollars 19 cents. It must again be
remarked, that it had yet the sum before mentioned in the
Mint, as well as the sum *in transitu* from Ohio and Kentucky—this last sum (250,000 dollars) arrived very season-
ably on the next day, or a day or two thereafter. The
Bank in this situation, the office at New York was little
better, and the office at Boston a great deal worse. At the
same time the Bank owed to Baring, Brothers & Co. and

Thomas Wilson & Co., nearly 900,000 dollars, which it was bound to pay immediately, and which was equivalent to a charge upon its vaults to that amount. It had, including the notes of the offices, a circulation of six million dollars to meet, to which were to be added the demands of depositors, public and private, at a time, too, when the scarcity of money called forth every disposable dollar, and therefore created demands upon the Bank for an unusual portion of the ordinary deposits and circulation.

" The sums which were collected daily on account of the revenue, in branch paper, were demandable the next day in Philadelphia, and, at the same time, at every office of the establishment, at the discretion of the officers of Government. The revenue was principally paid in branch paper, as well at Boston and New York as at Philadelphia, and while the duties were thus paid at one counter, in branch paper, the debentures, which amounted to one million of dollars every three months, were demanded and paid at the other, in specie or its equivalent—money of the place. Many additional details, increasing the difficulties of the moment, might be added. The southern offices were remitting tardily, and the western not at all. All the resources of the Bank would not have sustained it in this course and mode of business another month !! Such was the prostrate state of the Bank of the nation, which had, only twenty-seven months before, commenced business with an untrammelled active capital of twenty-eight millions of dollars.

" But it would have been fortunate for the Institution if its danger had ceased here. There still remained in some of the trusts of the Bank, some of the men who had contributed most to involve it in this state of things. As I must be brief, and the subject is very extensive, I will advert only to the principal instance of the misfortune and profligacy to which I allude.

" In the office at Baltimore of which James A. Buchanan was President, and J. W. M'Culloh was Cashier, there were near three millions of dollars discounted or appropriated, without any authority, and without the knowledge of the Board of the office, or that of the parent Bank ! S. Smith and Buchanan, of which firm J. A. Buchanan was a member, James W. M'Culloh and George Williams (the latter a member of the parent Board by the appointment of Government,) had obtained of the parent Bank discounts, in the regular and accustomed manner, to the amount of 1,957,700 dollars, on a pledge of 18,290 shares of stock of the Bank. These men, without the knowledge of either Board, and contrary to the resolves and orders of the parent Bank, took out of the office at Baltimore, under the pretence of securing it by pledging the surplus value of the stock, already pledged at the parent Bank for its par value and more, and other like surpluses over which the Bank had no control, the sum of 1,540,000 dollars : this formed a part of the sum before stated to have been discounted by the President and Cashier of the office, without authority. When this stupendous fraud was discovered, attempts were immediately made to obtain security ; and it was obtained nominally to the amount of 900,000 dollars. It was probably really worth 500,000 dollars.

"The losses sustained at the office at ·Baltimore alone, the great mass of which grew out of this fraud and others closely connected with it, have been estimated at the immense sum of 1,671,221 dollars 87 cents. The aggregate of the losses of the Institution, growing out of the operations which preceded the 6th of March, 1819, exceeded considerably 3,500,000 dollars. The dividends during the same time amounted to 4,410,000. Of this sum, 1,348,553 dollars 98 cents were received as the interest on the public debt held by the Bank, which leaves, as the entire profits on all the operations of Banking, the sum of 3,061,441 dollars 2 cents, which is less by at least half a million of dollars, than the losses sustained on the same business ! !

"When I was invited, and consented to fill the station I now hold, I was alike ignorant and inapprehensive of the situation in which I have just described the Bank, (truly, I believe,) to have been. I was at the moment remotely situated from the scenes of its active business, and its important transactions. I had held, it is true, shortly before, to oblige my friends, a place in the board of the office at Charleston, at which I occasionally attended, and from what I saw there, as well as from the public facts concerning the transactions of the Bank, I was satisfied that there was a great want of financial talent in the management of it. But I had not the faintest idea that its power had been

so completely prostrated, or that it had been thus unfortunately managed or grossly defrauded. I never imagined
that when it had, at so much expense and loss, imported so
many millions of specie, they had been entirely exhausted,
and were not yet paid for : nor that the Bank was on the
point of stopping payment. It was not until the moment
I was about to commence my journey to Philadelphia, that
I was apprized by a letter from a friend, who had been a
member of the preceding Board, that he feared, in a few
months, the Bank would be obliged to stop payment.

   " This was, indeed, appalling news. When I reached
Washington, I received hourly proofs of the probability of
this event. In Philadelphia it was generally expected. My
memory deceives me if I found any one in or out of the
Bank, who entertained a sanguine belief of its being able
to sustain its payments much longer. On the contrary,
there was, (I think it cannot be forgotten,) a public and
general expectation that the nation was about to suffer the
calamity of a currency composed entirely of irredeemable
paper. The evil which thus threatened the country, is not
at all to be compared with a suspension of sound currency
in times of war and great national emergencies. The former can only be conceived by a people who have suffered
under a paper currency in profound peace. What a train
of evils does it produce ? The destruction of public and
private credit, the national torpor, the individual ruin, the
disgraceful legislation, and the prostration of the morals of
the people, of which you may discover within your own territories some examples, will give you some, but a faint idea
of the calamity which was about to fall on the country.

   " Thus stood the Bank at the organization of the present administration. I was elected and took my seat as
President of the Board on the 6th of March, 1819. But
some time, of course, was necessary to look into the state
of the Bank before measures of relief could be projected.
Its danger, however, was too manifest and too pressing to
allow much time for this purpose. The principal errors
which produced the danger were fortunately of easy discovery, and to them the proper remedy was immediately
applied. The southern and western offices were immediately directed not to issue their notes, and the Bank ceased
to purchase and collect exchanges on the South and West.

A special meeting of the Board was called, which the non-resident directors were summoned to attend, for the 9th of April, (the next month,) and a correspondence with the Secretary of the Treasury was commenced, entreating his forbearance and his aid. To this officer I should be ungrateful and unjust, if I were not publicly to acknowledge my obligations, and those of the Bank, for the countenance and support he afforded to both in this struggle.

" At a meeting of the directors on the 9th of April, which was very full, the state of the Bank was submitted to them, a select committee appointed, to whom the subject of its difficulties was referred, and after very mature deliberation that committee made a report, which was unanimously agreed to. The principal means of relief proposed and ageed to were :

" 1. To continue the curtailments previously ordered. 2. To forbid the offices, at the South and West, to issue their notes when the exchanges were against them. 3. To collect the balances due by local Banks to the offices. 4. To claim of the Government the time necessary to transfer funds from the offices where money was collected to those where it was to be disbursed, as well as like time (until the difficulties of the Bank were removed,) to transfer funds to meet the notes of offices paid in the Bank or other offices than those where they were payable according to their tenor. 5. To pay debentures in the same money in which the duties on which the debentures were secured, had been paid. 6. To obtain a loan in Europe for a sum not exceeding 2,500,000 dollars, for a period not exceeding three years.

" These measures, simple and obvious as they are, and some of them so strangely overlooked so long, lifted the Bank in the short space of seventy days, (from the 6th of March to 17th of May,) from the extreme prostration which has been described, to a state of safety, and even in some degree of power, enabled it to cease its curtailments, except at points where it had an excess of capital, to defy all attacks upon it, and to sustain other institutions which wanted aid, and were ascertained to be solvent: above all, to establish the soundness of the currency, which had just before been deemed hopeless; and in a single season of business (the first) to give to every office as much capital as it could advantageously employ."

The Bank was saved, and the people were ruined. For a time, the question in Market street, Philadelphia, was, every morning, not who had broken the previous day, but who yet stood. In many parts of the country, the distress was as great as it was in Philadelphia, and in others it was still more deplorable.

"From all parts of our country" says Mr. Niles,* "we hear of a severe pressure on men in business, a general stagnation of trade, a large reduction in the price of staple articles. Real property is rapidly depreciating in its nominal value, and its rents or profits are exceedingly diminishing. Many highly respectable traders have become bankrupts, and it is agreed that many others must "go": the Banks are refusing their customary accomodations: confidence among merchants is shaken, and three per cent. per month is offered for the discount of promissory notes, which a little while ago were considered as good as "old gold," and whose makers have not since suffered any losses to render their notes less valuable than heretofore."

Four months afterwards, he says,† "It is estimated that there are 20,000 persons *daily seeking* work in Philadelphia; in New York, 10,000 able-bodied *men* are said to be wandering about the streets looking for it, and if we add to them the women who desire something to do, the amount cannot be less than 20,000: in Baltimore there may be about 10,000 persons in unsteady employment, or actually suffering because they cannot get into business. We know several decent men, lately "good livers," who now subsist on such victuals as two years ago they would not have given to their servants in the kitchen."

A committee appointed by a meeting of the citizens of Philadelphia, on the 21st of August, to inquire into the situation of the manufacturers of the city and its vicinity, reported, on the 2d of October, that in thirty mechanical and manufacturing branches of trade, which they enumerated, which gave employment to 9188 persons in 1814, and to 9672, in 1816, there were but 2137 persons employed in 1819.

---

* Weekly Register, April 10, 1819.   † Ib. August 7th, 1819.

A committee of the citizens of Pittsburg, who made report on the 24th of December, stated that certain manufacturing and mechanical trades in their city and its vicinity, which employed 1960 persons in 1815, employed only 672, in 1819.*

" Never," said the Frankford (Ky.) Argus,† " within the recollection of our oldest citizens, has the aspect of the times, as it respects property and money, been so alarming. Already has property been sacrificed in considerable quantities, in this and the neighboring counties, for less than half its value. We have but little money in circulation, and that little is daily diminishing by the universal calls of the Banks. Neither lands, negroes, or any other article, can be sold for half their value in cash, while executions to the amount of many hundreds of thousands of dollars, are hanging over the heads of our citizens. What can be done ? In a few months no debt can be paid, no money will be in circulation to answer the ordinary purposes of human life. Warrants, suits, and executions, will be more abundant than Bank notes ; and the country will present a scene of scuffling for the poor remnants of individual fortunes, which the world has not witnessed."

A Kentuckian, writing in the Edwardsville (Ill.) Spectator, confirmed this gloomy account.‡ " It has always," he said, " been my opinion, that of all evils which can be inflicted on a free State, Banking establishments are the most alarming. They are the vultures that prey upon the vitals of the Constitution, and rob the body politic of its life-blood. Look now at Kentucky ! What a spectacle does she present ! Nothing is to be seen but a boundless expanse of desolation ! Wealth impoverished, enterprize checked, commerce at a stand, the currency depreciated, all that was promotive of individual wealth, and all that was indicative of State prosperity and advancement, plunged into the great vortex of irremediable involvement. What incentive, now, has the farmer to industry and exertion ? How fruitless would be the effort of the merchants, to raise from their torpidity the fallen energies of the State !"

* See the documents appended to the Report of the Senate of Pennsylvania.
† See Weekly Register, June 7th.
‡ See Niles, Sept. 11th, 1819.

A writer in the Kentucky Gazette, quoted by Niles on the 9th of October, observed : " Slaves which sold some time ago, and could command the most ready money, have fallen to an inadequate value. A slave which hires for 80 or 100 dollars per annum, may be purchased for 300 or 400. A house and lot on Limestone street, for which $15,000 had been offered some time past, sold under the officer's hammer for $1,800. A house and lot which, I am inform-ed, was bought for $10,000, after 6,000 had been paid by the purchaser, was sold under a mortgage for $1,500, leav-ing the original purchaser (besides his advances) $3,500 in debt. A number of sales, which excited at the same time astonishment and pity, have occurred in this town. Comparison of local sufferings should not be indulged in, but I am told that Lexington is less afflicted than almost any other part of the State."

Bankruptcies for large amounts were of frequent occur-rence. Mention is made, among others, of the bankruptcy of a merchant-tailor in the little town of York, Pennsylva-nia, who failed for the sum of eighty-four thousand dollars.*

This was, indeed, an important affair in a town contain-ing but 3,000 or 4,000 inhabitants ; but it sunk into insig-nificance when compared with some of the failures in the large cities. " So extensive were these among the mer-chants of the cities east of Baltimore, that it seemed to be disreputable to stop payment for less than 100,000 dollars : the *fashionable* amount was from 2 to 300,000 dollars ; and the tip-top quality, the support of whose families had cost them from 8 to 12,000 dollars a year, were honored with an amount of debt exceeding 500,000 dollars, and nearly as much as a million of dollars. The prodigality and waste of some of these were almost beyond belief: we have heard that the furniture of a single parlor possessed (we cannot say *belonging*) to one of them, cost 40,000 dollars. So it was in all the great cities—dash, dash, dash—venders of tape and bobbins transformed into persons of *high blood*, and the sons of respectable citizens converted into knaves of *rank*—through speculation, and the facilities of the abomi-nable paper system."†

" I am told that one merchant, who lately failed to the

* Weekly Register, November 9th.   † Ib. June 5th.

eastward, yet lives in a house for which, and its furniture, he was offered 200,000 dollars in real money and refused it."

" Scenes of speculation are revealed and revealing that sober people had no idea of.   Their effect penetrates through all classes of society. The day-laborer feels it, and suffers, because *Mr. Highflyer* could sign his name prettily, and thereby cause his paper to pass through *some* of the Banks.   The farmer who improved his plantation by building a costly dwelling on credit, is compelled to sell both farm and dwelling to pay the debts incurred in erecting the house !—a pipe of wine, or a Cashmere shawl, compels some merchants to stop payment! I have heard of one man who failed for more than $500,000, whose private wine vault, as it stood at the time of his bankruptcy, was estimated to have cost him $7,000.   This is said to have happened in the sober city of Philadelphia.*

" Twenty or thirty years ago, if a man failed for 100,000 dollars, the people talked as fearfully about it as about that time the old women did of the fulfilment of ' Love's prophecies,' who had determined that the world should come to an end before the close of the last century. But now, through the blessings of the ' paper system,' the facilities which it afforded, and the speculations it nourished, it is not *decent* for a man to break for less than 100,000 ; and if a person would be thought a *respectable bankrupt*, he ought to owe two or three hundred thousand or more. If with this extent of credit it should appear that he had not been worth one cent for twenty years, and was not entitled to be trusted for a pair of shoes, so much the better !—it is evidence of his qualities as a *financier*. And if, out of other peoples' money, he has given his wife 50,000 or 60,000 dollars, it shows his *prudence* in ' providing for his family.'†

" The Federal Gazette of the 18th instant, contains *six* solid, formidable columns of advertisements, by order of the commissioners for conferring the benefit of the ' insolvent laws' of Maryland—in all about sixty—which gives the names, perhaps, of nearly one-third of the persons who are ' going through our mill' just at this time ; several of whom are those that lately counted their affairs by hundreds of

* Weekly Register, June 12th.   † August 14th.

thousands, or by *millions* of dollars ; who erected palaces, and furnished them with a degree of magnificence superior to that which many German princes aspired to—*who still live in splendid affluence, and indulge themselves in the most luxurious viands*—their wives and children, or some kind relative, having been made rich through their swindlings of the people."*

On the 9th of December, a committee of the Senate of Pennsylvania was appointed to inquire into the causes and extent of the public distress, and on the 29th of January, 1820, the committee made a report, through Mr. Raguet, their chairman, in which they said—

" In the performance of a duty of such high importance as that which has been intrusted to your committee, they have felt it incumbent on them to enter at large into the investigation of the subject contemplated by their appointment, in order that the people of the present day may be correctly informed as to the extent and causes of the evil by which they are oppressed, and that the records of the House may be furnished with a document, which may afford evidence at a future day of the miseries which it is possible to inflict upon a people by errors in legislation, and by the bad administration of incorporated institutions.

" In ascertaining *the extent* of the public distress, your committee has had no difficulties to encounter.   Members of the Legislature from various quarters of the State, have been consulted in relation to this subject, and their written testimony in answer to interrogatories submitted to them by the committee, has agreed, with scarcely a single exception, on all material points.   With such a respectable weight of evidence, added to that which has been derived from the prothonotaries, recorders and sheriffs of the different counties, from an intercourse with numerous private citizens residing in different parts of the State, as well as from the various petitions presented to the Legislature, your committee can safely assert, that a distress unexampled in our country since the period of its independence, prevails throughout the commonwealth.   This distress exhibits itself under the varied forms of—

" 1. Ruinous sacrifices of landed property at sheriff's

* Weekly Register, October 23d.

sales, whereby, in many cases, lands and houses have been sold at less than a half, a third, or a fourth of their former value, thereby depriving of their homes, and of the fruits of laborious years, a vast number of our industrious farmers, some of whom have been driven to seek, in the uncultivated forests of the West, that shelter of which they have been deprived in their native State.

" 2. Forced sales of merchandise, household goods, farming stock, and utensils, at prices far below the cost of production, by which many families have been deprived of the common necessaries of life, and of the implements of their trade.

" 3. Numerous bankruptcies and pecuniary embarrassments of every description, as well among the agricultural and manufacturing, as the mercantile classes.

" 4. A general scarcity of money *throughout the country,* which renders it almost impossible for the husbandman or other owner of real estate to borrow at a usurious interest, and where landed security of the most indubitable character is offered as a pledge. A similar difficulty of procuring on loan had existed in the metropolis previous to October last, but has since then been partially removed.

" 5. A general suspension of labor, the only legitimate source of wealth, in our cities and towns, by which thousands of our most useful citizens are rendered destitute of the means of support, and are reduced to the extromity of poverty and despair.

" 6. An almost entire cessation of the usual circulation of commodities, and a consequent stagnation of business, which is limited to the mere purchase and sale of the necessaries of life, and of such articles of consumption as are absolutely required by the season.

" 7. A universal suspension of all large manufacturing operations, by which, in addition to the dismissal of the numerous productive laborers heretofore engaged therein, who can find no other employment, the public loses the revenue of the capital invested in machinery and buildings.

" 8. Usurious extortions, whereby corporations instituted for Banking, Insurance, and other purposes, in violation of law, possess themselves of the products of industry without granting an equivalent.

" 9. The overflowing of our prisons with insolvent debtors, most of whom are confined for trifling sums, whereby the community loses a portion of its effective labor, and is compelled to support families by charity, who have thus been deprived of their protectors.

" 10. Numerous law suits upon the dockets of our courts and of our justices of the peace, which lead to extravagant costs and the loss of a great portion of valuable time.

" 11. Vexatious losses arising from the depreciation and fluctuation in the value of Bank notes, the impositions of brokers, and the frauds of counterfeiters.

" 12. A general inability in the community to meet with punctuality the payment of debts even for family expenses, which is experienced as well by those who are wealthy in property, as by those who have hitherto relied upon their current receipts to discharge their current engagements.

" With such a mass of evils to oppress them, it cannot be wondered at that the people should be dispirited, and that they should look to their representatives for relief. Their patient endurance of suffering, which can only be imagined by those who have habitually intermingled with them at their homes and by their firesides, merits the commendation of the Legislature, and prefers a powerful claim to their interference.

" Having thus enumerated the most prominent features of the general distress, your committee will proceed to point out the cause which in their opinion has occasioned it. That cause is to be found chiefly in the abuses of the Banking system, which abuses consist, *first*, in the excessive number of Banks, and, *secondly*, in their universal bad administration. For the first of these abuses the people have to reproach themselves, for having urged the Legislature to depart from that truly republican doctrine which influenced the deliberations of our early assemblies, and which taught that *the incorporation of the moneyed interest, already sufficiently powerful of itself, was but the creation of an odious aristocracy, hostile to the spirit of free government, and subversive of the rights and liberties of the people.* The second abuse, the mismanagement of Banks, is to be ascribed to a general ignorance of the true theory of currency and Banking, and to the avarice of speculators, desirous of acquiring the property of others by an artificial rise in the mominal value of stock, and by the sharing of usurious dividends.

" In order that this subject may be clearly understood, your committee have thought that the following concise history of Banking in Pennsylvania would be acceptable."

The committee then give a short history of Banking in Pennsylvania, and of the operations of the United States' Bank, up to July, 1818, after which they remark—

" This unwise procedure of replunging the people into the debts from which they had been partially extricated, and of involving others who had hitherto escaped, was continued for a time, but the dreadful day of retribution at length arrived. The Bank, (i. e. the U. S. Bank,) discovered almost too late, that its issues had been extended beyond the limits of safety, and that it was completely in the power of its creditors. It also foresaw that the payment of that portion of the Louisiana debt, redeemable on the 21st of October, 1818, which was held by foreigners, might occasion a demand for a considerable amount of coin, that the enhanced prices of China, India, and other goods, *occasioned by the depreciation of the currency from the over issues of itself and the State Banks,* would lead to a demand for specie, and that as it was professedly a specie Bank, and liable, under a penalty of twelve per cent. per annum, to pay its notes on demand, the same delicacy and forbearance would not be exercised towards it as to the State Banks. These considerations compelled it to seek its own safety, and from that moment a system of reduction commenced. This reduction operating upon the State Banks, which had not profited by the opportunity afforded them of contracting their loans whilst the other was extending, obliged them also to diminish their transactions, and a general curtailment ensued which has not yet had its consummation. The severity of the second pressure commenced in the city in October, 1818, and was continued without intermission for a year; at the expiration of which time it is said that the reductions made there by the National Bank alone have exceeded seven millions of dollars, and those by the other Banks probably two or four more. The reductions of the country Banks during the three last years, may be inferred from the following statement, which exhibits the amount of their notes in circulation at four different periods.

November 1st,	1816	$4,756,460
Do.	1817	3,782,760
Do.	1818	3,011,153
Do.	1819	1,318,976

" From the foregoing history it will be seen, what influence has been produced upon the affairs of the community by the operation of the Banking system. Real property has been raised in nominal value, and thousands of individuals have been led into speculation, who without the facility of Bank loans would never have been thus seduced. The gradual nominal rise in the price of land, has produced an artificial appearance of increasing wealth, which has led to the indulging of extravagance and luxury, and to the neglect of productive industry. Foreign importations and domestic consumptions have thus been carried to an extent far beyond what the actual resources of the country and people would justify, and in pursuing a *shadow*, the community has lost sight of the substance."

A similar Committee of Investigation, appointed by the House of Representatives, on the 13th of December, 1819, made report through their chairman, Mr. Wm. J. Duane, on the 28th of January, 1820, that,

" As to the extent of the distress, it might be answered, in the language of the resolutions under which your Committee act, that it is general: it extends, indeed, to the pursuits and habitations of the former capitalist, as well as to those of the more humble farmer and mechanic : there is no part of the commonwealth into which calamity has not penetrated, or in which numerous victims have not been found. But with regard to the extent of the loss which the State has suffered from the destruction of capital, the emigration of our citizens to the wilderness, the stagnation of business, the deterioration of landed property, and the prostration of manufactories, and above all, in the change of the moral character of many of our citizens by the presence of distress, your committee are utterly unable to decide : the extent of the mischief, they believe, defies scrutiny and surpasses the power of calculation.

" From the numerous petitions which have been presented at the present session, your committee quote the following extracts, which describe scenes of distress such as have been seldom, if ever, before beheld on this side of the Atlantic :

Sundry citizens of Northumberland county declare—

" The currency is so diminished as scarcely to suffice for the transaction of the most ordinary business : the produce of the country has met with an unprecedented reduction : the greater part of the citizens of this once flourishing commonwealth, even with the utmost economy and industry, are scarcely able to obtain sufficient articles to sustain life: real and personal property are daily sacrificed, and become the prey of speculators : debts are unpaid, creditors are dissatisfied, and the prisons are crowded with honest but unfortunate persons, whose wives and children must be a burden on the township, or suffer for want of the mere necessaries of life."

Sundry citizens of Wayne county represent—

" From the fall of every kind of produce, the scarcity of the circulating medium, and other causes, the general distress in our part of the State hath become so great and alarming, as to call for the attention and wisdom of the Legislature.   Our most industrious citizens are no longer able to meet their engagements, but their hard-earned property is daily sacrificed at a nominal value, and falling into the hands of a few speculators."

Sundry inhabitants of Pike county assert—

" At no time, since the Revolution, has greater distress been felt than at the present moment.   We consider the Banking system to have been the principal cause : instead of becoming, as was predicted, blessings to the people, Banks have become like the scorpions among the children of Israel, perfect beasts of prey. The property of the great portion of our industrious people is brought to sale at one-fourth of its value, and struck off to speculators, leaving honest creditors unpaid, and families reduced to beggary "

Sundry inhabitants of Huntingdon county represent—

" That the mass of the people are utterly unable, at once, to pay their debts : that their property is selling at such rates, that even the fees of law-officers are not realized : that the industrious are impoverished, whilst the speculating part of the community are daily growing more wealthy : that the evil is only beginning, and demands legislative interposition."

A memorial from sundry citizens of the western parts of the State, asserts—

" That embarrassment is universal : that the sordid and avaricious are acquiring the sacrificed property of the liberal and industrious : that so much property is exposed to sale under execution, that buyers cannot be had to pay more for it than the fees of offices : that those mischiefs, instead of diminishing, are daily increasing, and that over-trading and the facility of getting credit have produced these effects."

The petition of the inhabitants of Fayette county represents—

" That the fictitious capital and boundless credit extended by Banking, the almost universal spirit of speculation, the prostration of manufactures by the mistaken policy of the National Government, the introduction of luxuries and extravagancies, and a reduction of exports, have produced a long train of calamities : that industry is paralized—that the precious metals have vanished—that the Banks are tottering—that litigation is unprecedented in extent, and ruinous in its effects—that many merciless creditors, not content with plunging unfortunate debtors into the most abject poverty, frequently take from them the whole of that property to themselves, which in better times would pay the sums due to all, leaving the unfortunate debtor in jail, and his family in misery.

" These are but a few of the extracts, which might be presented to the House and placed upon the journal : but these are deemed sufficient, accompanied by the remark, that these representations are not only supported by all the other petitions presented at this session, but by the testimony of the members of the Legislature, coming themselves from all quarters of the State."

The committee then give a short sketch of the commercial history of the country, after which, they say—

" In defiance of all experience, and in contempt of warnings almost prophetic, which were given to them at the time, the people of Pennsylvania, during an expensive war, and in the midst of great embarrassments, established *forty-one* new Banks, with a capital of seventeen and a half millions dollars, and authority to issue Bank notes to double that amount! In consequence of this most destructive

measure, the inclination of a large part of the people, created by past prosperity, to live by speculation and not by
labor, was greatly increased : a spirit in all respects akin
to gambling, prevailed ; a fictitious value was given to all
descriptions of property : specie was driven from circulation, as if by common consent, and all efforts to restore
society to its natural condition were treated with undis-
guised contempt."

These remarks are followed by a short view of operations
subsequent to the war, after which, the Committee declare—" A new measure, however, remained to be adopted,
that was really to close the last scene in the drama of error :
the currency had already nearly vanished, but was tempo-
rarily restored on the seaboard. The enormity of fictitious
credit began to be felt : the abusive extent of paper issues
was about to effect its own remedy in the State, when Congress created a *corporation*, with authority to circulate upwards of *one hundred millions* of a new paper medium—a
corporation spreading its branches over the Union with the
baneful influence of the fabled Upas.

" Awakened by the quick succession of events so disastrous, from the dream of perpetual prosperity under which
they had so long been entranced, the people now find
themselves involved in distresses, against which no provision had been made, and from which, they allege, they can
find no refuge but in legislative interference."

CHAPTER XIII.

Of Banking from 1819-20 *to* 1820-21.

Appended to the report of the committee of the Senate
of Pennsylvania, are a number of questions which were
propounded to members of the Legislature, together with
the answers which were given. From these answers we
have formed the following table of the price of the best improved land in Pennsylvania, at three different periods.
The second column gives the price the land bore in the
height of the speculation, which was in different coun-

ties in different years, as the Banks extended their operations into them.

	1809		1819
Bedford,	$30 to 40	80 to 100 (1815)	20 to 30
Lebanon,	40 to 60	130 to 150 (1816–17)	50 to 70
Bradford and Tioga,	6 to 14	10 to 20 (1814)	3 to 10
Somerset and Cambria,		15 to 50 (1814)	5 to 20
Cumberland,	40 to 60	150 to 200 (1813–14)	25 to 40
Dauphin,	16 to 24	35 to 45 (1815–16)	12 to 15
Adams,	30 to 50	60 to 100 (1814)	no price
Lancaster,	75 to 100	250 to 300 (1813–14)	50 to 70
Delaware,	75 to 120	100 to 150	40 to 75
Northumberland,	40 to 50	80 to 90 (1815)	30 to 40
Berks and Schuylkill,	80 to 100	150 to 200	80 to 100
Northampton Wayne & Pike,	80 to 100	100 to 140 (1815–16)	15 to 20
Bucks,	50 to 60	100 to 110 (1814–15)	55 to 65
Huntington,	20 to 30	40 to 60 (1815)	20 to 30

The official valuation of real and personal property in
the State of New York, exhibits an equally striking fall.
It was, in

1818,	$314,	913,	695,
1819,	281,	862,	793,
1820,	256,	603,	300.*

The depression of prices continued throughout the year
1820, and, though money was abundant with retired capitalists, the pressure on the great body of industrious people was very severe. " Our difficulties in commerce," said
a director of the United States' Bank, writing to a friend
in England, " continue without abatement. Men in business are like patients in the last stage of consumption,
hoping for a favorable change, but growing worse every
day till they expire. Dismal as are the prospects on your
side of the water, they are worse here. You have some
regular and profitable trade—*we have none*. It is all scam-
per and hap-hazard." The director then states that in
former times he would, without hesitation, have trusted
some men among his customers with goods to the amount
of **100,000** pounds sterling; but he adds, " now I do not

* Niles, December 24th, 1821.

know the persons doing business; and there is not one among them whose order I would take for 1,000 pounds. What a difference! A long continuance of distresses in the commercial world has had a bad effect on the morality of the country. The vast number of failures takes away the odium. Men fail in parties for convenience; and the barriers of honesty are broken down by a perpetual legislation suited to the condition of insolvent debtors. We have now no imprisonment for debt. Credit is become very rare, as you may well imagine, for we have nothing to depend upon but a man's honesty. Besides our commercial distresses, we are suffering great alarm in this city (Philadelphia) from incendiaries, who have succeeded in setting fire to a great number of buildings. On Sunday evening our theatre was entirely destroyed.

"Houses which rented for 1,200 dollars, now rent for 450 dollars. Fuel which cost 12 dollars, now costs $5\frac{1}{2}$ dollars: flour which was 10 and 11 dollars, is now $4\frac{1}{2}$; beef 25 cents, now 8 cents: other things in proportion. It is thus true we now pay less for these necessaries, but we can make no money. The farmer is become as poor as a rat: the labor of the farm costs him more than the produce is worth. He cannot pay the storekeeper, and the storekeeper cannot pay the merchant.

"Mail robberies and piracies are quite the order of the day. Two men were hung at Baltimore a few months ago for robbing the mail: two more will experience the same fate, in a few days, at the same place, for the same crime. Two men are to be hung there a week hence for piracy, and five others are under sentence of death."*

"Money is plenty," says Mr. Niles, on the 4th of March. "The six per cent. stocks are at 103 to 104; but there is little use for money in the hands of those who do not owe it. Hence it has a sluggish currency, and those who have it do not know what to do with it for themselves, and are afraid to trust it to others."

On the 15th of April, the same writer says—"It has become a serious affair to the laboring man to purchase himself a new garment—his wages, on an average, do not pur-

* See Niles, vol. 18, p. 387. The letter appeared in the **London Courier**, on the 11th of May, 1820.

chase him half as much as they did, and he is continually *uncertain* as to obtaining even that. Many of the mechanical professions have equally declined : as an instance, though our population is one-half greater than it was ten years ago, it is certainly a fact that the printing of books is not now half so extensive as it was then. The desire to read is not lessened, but the means of purchasing are denied—the most common school books are a drug. Hatters, shoemakers, and tailors, and even blacksmiths, whose work seemed to be indispensable, have lost, in general, much of their former businesses--from a fourth to one-half. This is the result of necessity, and those who might purchase, abstain, in looking to a fearful future."

On the 16th of September, he says—" Five years ago all the large stores in Market street, &c., Baltimore, were cut into two, and then there was not enough of them ; and a dwelling house could hardly be had—if a man talked of moving, fifty were applying for the property. The stores have resumed their old shapes, and dwelling houses are abundant. I believe we have 10,000 less inhabitants than we had in 1815; and, by calculation, I have concluded that the property on Market street at this time, if all on rent, would produce a sum less by $250,000 a year, than it would have produced as rent in that year.

" Desire no longer presses on enjoyment with the laboring classes, but necessity presses on necessity; and, one by one, they give up their enjoyments which they hitherto delighted to indulge themselves in. This is evident to every person who will look at society. The laboring people cannot get much money, and therefore cannot spend much. The average price of wheat is hardly more than fifty cents a bushel, and the farmer cannot buy many luxuries at that rate : a mechanic is hardly half his time employed, or at reduced wages, and must therefore limit his expenditure."

It was natural that, in this condition of things, the public mind should be employed on projects for alleviating distress, if not for preventing its recurrence.

One measure that was suggested, was the requiring of cash payment of duties. This would have been beneficial, insomuch as it would have lopped off one of the branches of the super-extended credit system, but it would have afforded no immediate relief. An effort was made in Congress to carry through a measure of this kind, but it was not successful.

Another effort, which was attended with no better success, was to restrict sales by auction. There is no cause to regret that this effort did not succeed. The only way in which the value of many kinds of property could be realized in this season of distress, was by sales by auctions, and restrictions on this business would have increased the sufferings of the public.

A large portion of society were very anxious that a bankrupt law should be passed, and it may be doubted if the mercantile part of any community ever stood more in need of relief. But the bill which was reported to Congress was modelled on the English system, and not adapted to the state of things in America. It might, if it had been adopted, have afforded relief to many worthy men; but in its general operation it would probably have been productive of great evils. It was rejected by a decided majority.

The measure from which most was hoped, and which was pushed with most vigor and most perseverance, was an increase of the duty on imports. The dullness of business, the lowness of prices, and the want of employment, which were produced by the re-action of the Banking system, were all urged as reasons why Congress should afford adequate " protection to domestic industry."

It is no part of our plan to discuss the tariff policy. But it belongs to the history of Banking, to state that the raising of the duties on imports, to a height which now threatens to convulse if not to rend our Union, was one of the consequences of the great re-action of 1819. As the effects of the re-action were felt for several years, the advocates of the restrictive system had full leisure for applying all the arguments in support of their favorite policy, which they could derive from the continued lowness of prices, dullness of business, and want of employment.

The evils produced by the system of paper money and moneyed corporations, are of such a nature that they cannot be remedied by acts of legislation. When they come they must be endured. If we *will* have the system, we *must* bear its consequences. But there was one measure which, as it might have alleviated the distress, we have sometimes wondered was not adopted : We have wonder-

ed it was not adopted, because it is a measure which has
been adopted in other countries, and in our own country
at other times. We mean an *equitable* adjustment of the
affairs of debtor and creditor. When the South Sea bubble bursted, the British Parliament saw that to require a
literal fulfilment of the obligations which were affected by
that stock-jobbing concern, would be to give the getters up
of that scheme all the property of their miserable dupes.
It therefore, in some cases, reduced the amount of money
to be paid, as much as nine-tenths. During the Revolutionary War, " scales of the depreciation" of continental money
were from time to time published by the Legislature, by
which the courts were governed in enforcing such contracts as were submitted to adjudication.

The great Banking bubble of America was the same in
principle as the South Sea bubble, but of longer continuance, and involved in it the fortunes of the whole community. But nothing like an *equitable* adjustment of the affairs of debtor and creditor was attempted. An obligation
to pay 10,000 dollars entered into in 1816 or 1818, when
the current dollar was in some parts of the country worth
perhaps but 50 cents in silver, was enforced according to the
strictness of the letter, in 1819 and 1820, when the current dollar was of equal value with the legal dollar, and
worth one hundred cents in silver.

It is an awful thing to change the money standard of a
country : but it is equally awful to refuse to recognize such
a change, after it has actually been made. Effecting an
equitable adjustment of the affairs of debtor and creditor,
by a legislative or a judicial recognition of the practical
changes which had been made in the standard of value,
would not have " impaired the obligation of contracts."
Both debtor and creditor, when they entered into the contract, had the " current" dollar in view. The disorder was,
however, so general, that an equitable adjustment of contracts would have been a work of great difficulty, if not of
impossibility. Perhaps the courts, looking forward to the
operations of future years, acted wisely in regarding the
dollar as a fixed quantity, though it was, in fact, during
these years, a quantity that was always changing.

CHAPTER XIV.

Of Banking in the Western States.

The first paper issuing institution west of the Alleghany mountains, was the Lexington Insurance Company, which was incorporated in 1802, with a capital of 150,000 dollars, and for which Humphrey Marshall, the historian of Kentucky, says, Banking privileges were surreptitiously obtained. The business being found to be lucrative to those who were engaged in it, the Kentucky Bank was instituted in 1807, with a nominal capital of one million of dollars.

The Miami Exporting Company was instituted at Cincinnati, Ohio, in 1803, with a capital of 200,000 dollars. As its title indicates that it was established ostensibly for commercial purposes of another nature, perhaps Banking privileges were obtained for it surreptitiously, as in the case, in the previous year, of the Lexington Insurance Company. Be this as it may, the Miami Exporting Company did Banking business; and in the nine years subsequent to its institution, five other Banks were established in different parts of the State, making in all six Banks in Ohio in 1812, with a nominal capital of 1,200,000 dollars.

These Banks maintained specie payments till within a month or two of the close of the war. This is a fact not generally known, but it is placed beyond doubt by a statement made by Mr. Hawkins in Congress, on the 17th of January, 1815, that " *even* the Banks of Kentucky and Ohio, where specie abounded, had *at length* been compelled in self-defence to stop payment of specie."

It must be evident from this, that if the United States' Government had immediately compelled the Banks of the great Atlantic cities to redeem the pledge they had given in the preceding August, the western country might have suffered but little from the suspension of specie payments. But, when the United States' Government connived at the suspension of specie payments, sanctioned the use of inconvertible paper, and by its fiscal manœuvering encouraged the issue of additional amounts of such paper, it was impossible that the mania which had reached Pennsylvania, from New England, through New York and New Jersey, should not extend into Ohio and Kentucky.

Kentucky was, however, at first comparatively moderate. All she did at the close of the war, was to authorize the Bank of Kentucky to increase its capital to three millions, and to establish thirteen branches. Seven of these branches were in operation in 1816. Ohio, apparently, went further into the system ; for, we have seen a list of twenty-one chartered institutions which were in operation in that State in 1816, and allusion is made to others which were carrying on the Banking business without charters.

Still, the issues of paper in the Western States were moderate when compared with those in the Middle States. Mr. William Jones, the first President of the United States' Bank, stated, in the documents laid before Congress in 1819, that, " at the time of the subscription to the stock of the Bank, specie was at six per cent. at the westward, and at fourteen per cent. in Philadelphia, New York, and Baltimore." In the table appended to Mr. McDuffie's report, the rate of exchange at Lexington on Boston, in July 1816, is stated to have been two per cent.—a sure proof that the currency of Kentucky was not at that time much, if it was any, depreciated.

The issues of the western Banks were probably increased considerably in the last six months of 1816: and in this or the following year, the system was extended into Indiana, Illinois and Missouri.

It was about this time, that branches of the United States' Bank were established in the West, and they sought to make a profit, less by circulating their own paper, than by giving drafts on the eastern cities, receiving in exchange notes of the local Banks, and requiring interest to be paid on the same. This was rather a round-about way of inducing the local Banks to extend their issues, but it was the most effective that could be adopted. Western Bank paper being exchangeable for United States' branch drafts, and United States' branch drafts being exchangeable for European products in the Atlantic cities, the effect was similar to that which would have been produced by making western Bank notes current in New York and Philadelphia.

The full effects of this system were felt in the year 1818,

or in the second year of active operations of the United States' Bank. Mr. Niles, then, speaking of " new Banks establishing or about to be established," says, " Behold forty-three new Banks authorized in Kentucky—half a score in Tennessee—eight in Ohio," &c. Of those authorized in Kentucky, at least *thirty-five*, since known as the Independent Banks of Kentucky, went into operation. Their nominal capital was between seven and eight millions of dollars, but their real capital must have been small : for, the American Quarterly Review says, the same specie was used for different Banks, and only remained long enough in each for the law to be complied with.

If the months of May, June, July, and August, 1815, were " the golden age of Philadelphia," the first months of the year 1818, were the golden age of the western country. Silver could hardly have been more plentiful at Jerusalem in the days of Solomon, than paper money was in Ohio, Kentucky, and the adjoining regions. But, when the United States' Bank found it necessary to curtail, money became as scarce in the West as silver is in Jerusalem under the Turkish despotism.

The Bank of the United States was very sudden in its demands, for its necessities were such as to admit of no delay. An Ohio paper says that the branch at Cincinnati called on the local Banks of that town for a balance of 700,000 dollars, in requisitions of twenty per cent. every thirty days. This compelled the Bank of Cincinnati to stop payment about the middle of November, 1818, and in two days afterwards the Bank of Kentucky unexpectedly followed its example. A strong expression of public opinion compelled the Bank of Kentucky to resume specie payments in less than a week, and it continued to pay specie till the early part of 1820.

It is stated that in the twelve months preceding June 26th, 1819, 800,000 dollars in specie were drawn from Ohio. If this be true, the wonder is not that only six or seven Banks in that State paid specie in August, 1819, but that they were not all bankrupt. This was the fate of the Independent Banks of Kentucky. Some of them maintained a show of specie payments till August, and afterwards paid out notes which were lent them by the Bank of

Kentucky, redeemable in 365 days after date : but, towards the close of the year few of them paid any thing.

The Bank of Vincennes (Indiana) had recourse to a very ingenious expedient. It issued notes payable at its branch at Vevay, nine months after date, printing the words "nine months after date" in very small letters. All this, however, availed nothing. It went with the others.*

The effect which the sudden withdrawal of specie and discrediting of Bank paper, had on prices in the western country was very distressing. "It is said" remarked Mr. Niles on the 2d of September, 1820, " but we know not how to believe it, that corn is selling at 10, and wheat at 20 cents per bushel, specie, in some parts of Kentucky. At this rate how are debts to be paid ?" Mr. Niles appears afterwards to have had other evidence sufficient to overcome his incredulity, for he remarked on the 15th of September, 1821 : " A gentleman in Western Virginia directs the Register to be stopped, because he used to pay for it annually with one barrel of flour, but that three will not do it now. Another, a miller in Ohio, on paying his advance to my agent, observed, that he had sold *four barrels of flour* to obtain the note of five dollars which was remitted."

In other publications we have evidence of the lowness of prices. For example : In the United States Gazette of May 23d, 1821, corn is said to have been sold at Cincinnati at 10 cents a bushel : and the same periodical of 1st of June, has a notice of a letter from a practical farmer in Harrison County, Ohio, stating that wheat had fallen to 25 cents a bushel, and in some instances to 12½ cents. A letter from Greenfield, Ohio, dated May 3d, 1821, and quoted in the Gazette of June 23d, states that wheat was sold at 12½ cents a bushel, and that whiskey was dull at 15 cents a gallon.† The Weekly Register of May 19th,

* The Banks in the *extreme* West did not all stop payment till a year or two after the failure of the Banks in Kentucky. The Shawneetown and Edwardsville Banks, in Illinois, paid specie in August, 1821. One, at least, of the Banks in Missouri, continued to pay specie until the latter part of 1821 ; and several of the Ohio Banks appear to have paid specie in the midst of all the confusion.

† Towards the close of the year 1821, flour rose at Cincinnati to $3 50 a barrel.

gives the following quotation from " a late Pittsburg Mercury." " Flour, a barrel, $1 : whiskey 15 cents a gallon : good merchantable pine boards, 20 cents a hundred feet : sheep and calves $1 a head. Foreign goods at the old prices. One bushel and a half of wheat will buy a pound of coffee : a barrel of flour will buy a pound of tea ; twelve and a half barrels will buy one yard of superfine broadcloth.''

While the staples of the western country were at this low price, the people were deeply in debt to the United States Government, to the merchants of the Atlantic cities, to the United States' Bank, to the local Banks, and to one another. The plentiful issues of paper had led to great speculations in the public lands. The wild lands of the West had been sold, in some instances, as high as forty or fifty dollars an acre. The sum due to Government on account of these purchases, exceeded twenty-two million dollars in the latter part of 1820. The sum due to one of the branches of the United States' Bank, that at Cincinnati, exceeded two million dollars. The sums which were due by the western people to one another, to the local Banks, and to the merchants of the Atlantic cities could not easily be calculated.

To relieve the public distress, the Legislature of Ohio passed a law to prevent property from being sold unless it would bring a certain amount, to be fixed by appraisers. This law operated very unequally. Another law of the same State, to prohibit buying and selling the notes of chartered Banks, would have increased the mischief, if it had not, happily, been such a law as, from the nature of things, could not be enforced.

Kentucky adopted what has been called the " relief system," in all its extent. Stop laws, stays of executions, and replevin acts, followed one another in quick succession. And Commonwealth's Banks, or State Loan Offices, were established in Kentucky, Indiana, Illinois, and Missouri, with power to issue millions of paper money. The creditor had no alternative but to receive this paper or wait for payment till better times should arrive.

Governor Adair, in his message to the Legislature, in October, 1821, said, that " the paramount law of necessity" had compelled Kentucky to resort to a policy against

which strong objections might be brought : but, he added,
" let it never be forgotten, that the measures adopted have
completely realized the proposed end : that an agitated and
endangered population of half a million of souls, has been
tranquillized and secured, without the infliction of legal justice, or the example of violated morality."

All the people of Kentucky did not think so highly of
the system, and the Judges of the Court of Appeals were
among the dissidents. They resolutely refused to acknowledge the constitutionality of the " relief laws :" and the
Legislature established a new Court of Appeals, the judges
composing which were friendly to the relief system.

The people divided into two parties, and the contest was
conducted with great violence. The party friendly to the
new Court of Appeals had the ascendancy for several years.
In 1824, they numbered sixty members of the Legislature,
while their opponents numbered but forty. In the session
of 1825–26, they appear to have been less powerful, for we
find that preparations were made to defend the records of
the new Court of Appeals with powder and ball.*   In the
fall of 1826, the friends of the Old Court elected a majority of members of the Legislature. A change of only
ninety-one votes at the polls, would have given their opponents the majority of members. The Old Court party has,
however, ever since retained its ascendancy ; and the relief system is at an end.

All parties now are willing to admit that this " relief system" did great evil. It did not effect an equitable adjustment of the affairs of debtor and creditor. That could
have been effected only by a legislative or judicial recognition of the changes which had been made in the standard
of value, and a separate adjudication in each case. It was
only by accident if a man received payment in paper of the
same value as that which was current when the debt was
contracted.

The Bank of Kentucky commenced discounting on the
27th of April, 1821. Its notes were sold almost immediately at 70 cents in the dollar ; and continued to depreciate
till April or May in the ensuing year, when the exchange
was 210 paper dollars for 100 silver dollars. On the 28th
of July, 1821, which was ten days after it commenced its

* See Philadelphia Gazette of January 1st, 1826.

issues, the notes of the State Bank of Illinois were 50 per cent. below par.   In addition to the loss which each creditor sustained by being paid in money of this description, he was liable to further loss from the paper depreciating while it remained in his hands.

The other branches of the relief system, the stop laws, the appraisement laws, the stays of execution, and the replevin acts, tended to destroy the confidence of men in one another and in the Government.

The relief system is at an end ; but its evil effects will be felt in the West for twenty years.   What, then, ought we to think of the Banking system, in which the relief system originated ?

CHAPTER XV.

Of Banking in the Southwestern States.

From Mr. Gallatin's and Mr. Crawford's tables, there appear to have been three Banks in operation in Louisiana, in 1814, with a capital of $1,432,300 ; two in Tennessee, with a capital of $212,962 ; and one in Mississippi, with a capital of $100,000.

The Banks of New Orleans suspended specie payments in the latter part of April, 1814,* about four months sooner than the Banks of Philadelphia.   The pretext was, that a contraband trade was drawing away all the specie.   The fact may have been as stated : but if the Banks of New Orleans had not issued to excess, no contraband trade, or any other kind of trade, could have deprived Louisiana of its metallic money.   The excuse was, however, quite as good as that made by the Banks of the Middle States, viz. " That dealings in British Government bills of exchange, and importations of foreign goods through the Eastern States, were drawing off all the silver."

The Bank of Nashville, Tennessee, did not stop specie payments till July or August, 1815, nearly a year after the Banks of Philadelphia.†

* See Niles' Weekly Register for May or June, 1814.
† Ib. August, 1815.

The Banks in Tennessee in 1817, were the Fayetteville Bank of Tennessee, with a capital of 200,000 dollars ; the Nashville Bank, with a capital of 400,000 dollars ; and the State Bank, with a capital of 400,000 dollars. In November 1817, the capital of the State Bank was increased to 800,000 dollars, and authority was given to it to accept a batch of Banks as branches, which thereby swelled its capital to 1,600,000 dollars. A similar union was effected between the Nashville Bank and a number of others, by which the capital of the Nashville Bank was augmented to 1,031,705 dollars.*

Between the years 1817 and 1820, the capital of the Bank of Mississippi was increased from 100,000 to 900,000 dollars : and the number of Banks in Louisiana was increased from three to four, and their capital from 1,432,300 to 2,597,420 dollars. About the same time, the system was introduced into Alabama, by the establishment of the Planters' Bank at Huntsville.

The same causes that led to the extension of Banking operations in Ohio and Kentucky, were what led to an extension of Banking operations in the Southwestern States ; and they all felt the reaction of the system about the same time.

In July, 1819, the Banks of Tennessee stopped payment : and, soon after, a law was passed forbidding the issuing of executions on judgments, for two years, unless the plaintiff would consent to receive " current notes" in payment.

As the " current notes," (i. e., the notes of the non-specie-paying Banks of the State,) were many per cent. below par, this was making a considerable abatement of the demands of creditors. It gave them cause for complaint, but did not effectually relieve debtors; and, as the public distress increased, a special meeting of the Legislature was held in June, 1820, to consider the state of affairs, The Governor told them, in his message, " He was fully persuaded much good would result to the country generally, by extending the time in which payments can by the present laws be forced, unless the creditor should, by his own voluntary act, make terms of accommodation, and, instead

* American Quarterly Review.

of cash payments, take from the debtor such valuable estate, either real or personal, as it may be in his power to give, and at such abatement under its estimated value as you may direct." The Legislature, in acting on this subject, not only adopted the proposition of the Governor, but established a relief Bank, with a capital of 1,000,000 dollars, to make loans to debtors only. As a fund for the redemption of the notes of this Bank of the State of Tennessee, as it was called, the proceeds of certain public lands were appropriated. At the same time, an act was passed authorizing defendants to redeem in two years all lands and negroes sold under execution, on paying to the purchaser ten per cent. on the money he might have advanced.

Gen. Jackson, Col. Edward Ward, and other citizens, remonstrated against these proceedings, pronouncing them inexpedient, injurious in their tendency, and in violation of the Constitution. Gen. Jackson, in particular, was very energetic in his opposition; and a number of the most respectable citizens of the State united with him in sentiment. Their combined efforts could not prevent the Legislature from adopting the system : but it would hardly be correct to say, that their opposition had no effect. The issues of the Bank of the State of Tennessee were moderate, when compared with those of the Bank of the Commonwealth of Kentucky : and Tennessee appears not to have suffered as much as her sister State, by the relief system.

In March, 1821, the notes of specie-paying Banks were at an advance, at Nashville, of 13 to 17 per cent., when estimated in notes of the Bank of the State of Tennessee, and the currency does not appear to have undergone any sensible improvement for several years ; for, we find Tennessee paper quoted in the Philadelphia papers, of August, 1824, at 25 per cent. discount.

In July, 1826, the Bank of Nashville gave notice of its intention again to resume specie payments. It commenced them accordingly, in September ; but 260,000 dollars in specie were drawn from it in seventy days, and it could bear no further drafts. The only Bank then remaining, (except the private Bank of Yeatman, Woods & Co.,) was the Bank of the State, the notes of which are quoted in the Philadelphia papers of 1829 and 1830 at ten per cent. discount.

The notes of the Banks of Mississippi and Louisiana appear, from the Philadelphia price currents, to have been subject to little, if any, more vacillation than those of the Banks of the Middle States : but the currency of Alabama has been very bad.

In 1821, the notes of the local Banks being discredited, no way was found of paying public expenses in Alabama, but by issuing comptroller's warrants. These would not circulate, as some thought, because they were on bad paper and not handsomely printed ; whereupon, it was proposed to send to Philadelphia for blank warrants, handsomely engraved, and printed on silk paper.

In 1824, Huntsville notes were at 30 per cent. discount at Philadelphia.

In the next year, the Bank of the State of Alabama was brought into operation. All the spare funds of the State were devoted to its establishment, and its capital has been augmented from year to year, as the means of the State Government have increased. ts loans are distributed among the different counties in proportion to their population. Its notes do not appear ever to have been at par in the Philadelphia market.

In 1828, there was no local Bank in operation in Kentucky, none in Indiana, none in Illinois, none in Missouri, but one in Tennessee, one in Mississippi, and one in Alabama.

Branches of the United States' Bank were, however, doing an extensive business in the West : and Judge Catron, of Nashville, in an address which he published in June 1829, pronounced the crisis a dangerous one. " Millions" he said, " have been loaned by a single Bank—the crush of 1819 must overtake us."

Directing his remarks " to the cultivators of the soil and the laboring people of Tennessee," he said—" The great pressure upon the people of this State for money, growing out of the excessive loans of the Branch Bank of the United States' at this place, and the yet more excessive usury (from 5 to 10 per cent. a month,) every where prevailing, has induced me to address you this note upon a subject maturely considered of, during the last ten years ; of the necessity of which, my convictions have been confirmed by experience and observation.

"I propose that the Legislature of Tennessee, at their next session, pass a law declaring—" That no one shall be bound for the debt or default of another, by writing or otherwise : Provided, that the act shall not extend to securityships entered into in the courts of justice. In other words, that no one shall be bound as security for another, in any case, by word, bond, note or indorsement, for an ordinary contract between man and man."

"Should such a law be passed, no man will be trusted, except upon the faith of his property, unless he has industry and honesty; debts will be small and few, cash payments generally required, and the necessaries of life cheaper to the consumer.

"Wives and daughters, I ask your powerful influence and aid, to procure the passage of a law, cutting off the powers of your husbands and fathers, to inflict ruin upon you, by standing the security of worthless adventurers. The writer begs your indulgence to his feelings, when he speaks of you in connection with ruined securities. He has seen you turned out from your happy homes upon the streets and highways in search of bread, the derision of those who had been the cause of your destruction.

"For the sake of your families, fellow-citizens, let me intreat you to refuse your names, should the Banks and usurers outvote us, and the law not be passed. If you go security, what right have you to hope that your house will be your own to cover the heads of your wife and children ; you whose labor furnishes us all with bread, I ask—is not the speculator, the idle and worthless coxcomb, who boldly solicits credit and obtains it, more encouraged in society than the most honest and industrious of you, who by hard and daily labor earns his bread ? I appeal to you who till the earth, whom I hail as especial friends ; I appeal to the mechanic, with the sweat and dust of labor upon him, are you not ridden down by unprincipled adventurers, in cloth and ruffles, who, but the other day, through sheer worthlessness, deserted the plough, the plane, or the trowel, now turned merchants, or mock gentlemen in some form, upon the credit of those from whose side they so lately deserted ? Bankrupts in purse, and knaves in principle, with nothing to recommend them save impudence, and the fine clothes bought with the money you have paid, or will be forced to pay, as their securities. Will you longer be imposed upon ? I hear you vociferate the energetic NO : you are mistaken, my worthy friends, I know your indulgent natures ; a hundred times have you determined, and been ready to take a solemn oath you would never again go security, and as often wanted firmness to resist the succeeding impudent request. Thousands have I known ruined, calling heaven to witness every time they lent their names, that they had gone security the last time. You cannot help it, citizens : it is a weakness of your nature. Step forward boldly and confess that you cannot conquer it, and instruct your representatives to pass a law to protect your frailty, and guard you against those mistaken friends, or designing knaves, threatening your destruction.''

Judge Catron may spare himself further labor. The present rage in the West and Southwest, is for State Banks of various forms. Political power and money power are to be henceforth in the same hands. Our present contests are less for the honors than for the emoluments of office. Their violence is to be increased by making the capital and the credit of the different State Governments the prizes of the successful party. In the regulations which may be made for the distribution of loans, there may be great apparent fairness ; but the practical operation of the system must be for the advantage of a small part of the community, and the disadvantage of all the rest. A new kind of aristocracy, a kind of half-political, half-moneyed aristocracy, will spring up in the land.

The State Governments have no constitutional power to establish State Banks, or any other kind of paper-money issuing institutions. They are expressly prohibited to " emit bills of credit." *Qui facit per alios, facit per se.* He who does a thing by others, does it himself. State Banks and incorporated paper-money Banks are palpable violations of the Constitution, and would be acknowledged to be so by every body, if interest did not blind men's eyes to the truth.

The business of lending money is no part of the duty of any Government, either State or Federal. If a Government has more funds than are required for public purposes, its duty is to remit part of the public taxes.   Banking and brokerage are the proper businesses of such private citizens as choose to engage in them, protected by the same laws that protect men engaged in other businesses.

CHAPTER XVI.

Of Banking in the Southern States.

The Banks of the South found it convenient to suspend specie payments, soon after this measure was resolved on by the Banks of Philadelphia; and an extension of Banking operations in that quarter was the necessary consequence.   Without resorting to other evidence, the following tabular view of the amount of Bank capital in the four Southern States, in two different periods, will be sufficient.*

	1814	1816
Georgia,	623,580	1,502,600
South Carolina,	3,730,900	3,832,758
North Carolina,	1,576,600	2,776,000
Virginia,	3,592,000	5,521,415
	9,523,080	13,632,773

According to Mr. Gallatin's tables, there were fourteen Banks in these States on the first of January, 1815, and twenty-three on the first of January, 1816.   Two of the Banks of Virginia had, in this interval, increased their circulation from 4,616,240, to 6,031,446 dollars.   Of the circulation of the other Banks in the South, we have no returns.   The aggregate increase was, no doubt, very considerable, but it was not sufficient to bring down the currency to a level with that of Maryland and Pennsylvania. In the tables appended to Mr. McDuffie's report, it is stated that, on the 1st of July, 1816, when subscriptions were made to the stock of the United States' Bank, specie was, at Philadelphia, at 17 per cent. advance, and at Washington, at 20 per cent., while it was only 9 a 10 at Norfolk, and 6 a 8 at Charleston.   The price of specie in North Carolina and Georgia is not mentioned, but North Caroli-

* See Mr. Crawford's Report in 1820.

na notes bore a premium of four per cent. at Philadelphia on that day, and New York notes were at a discount of 5 a 9 per cent. at Savannah.

The comparative moderation of the southern Banks is to be ascribed to the fact, that, as but a small portion of the revenue from the customs is collected in the South, they did not get many of the treasury notes which were issued in the year after the war.

When the United States' Bank began operations, it did not include the offices at Charleston and Savannah, in the plan for the "equalization of exchanges." It however gave these offices authority to do an extensive business. By the 29th of July, 1817, the branch at Charleston had made discounts to the amount of 850,000, and that at Savannah to the amount of about 300,000 dollars. On the 23d of June, 1818, the total of discounts at Charleston, including bills of exchange and stock notes, was about $2,700,000 at Savannah $1,000,000, at Fayettville $500,000, at Norfolk $1,400,000, and at Richmond $3,000,000.

This increase of credit dealings in the South did not improve the state of the currency : and the attempts that were made to support excessive issues of paper, by importing specie, proved utterly unavailing. The directors of the Bank of the State of South Carolina say, that "in the first six months of 1818, it is probable that upwards of $800,000 in specie were thrown into general circulation in the city of Charleston. It is probable that by the the first of November in that year, not 50,000 dollars of the whole sum remained in the State; we are confident that $10,000 could have been found in Charleston."

The Bank of the United States was, to promote its own views, very indulgent to the Banks of the South, at the commencement of its operations. Without being so, it could not, as its specie capital was inconsiderable, and as the deposits of public money were small in that quarter, have done much business at Savannah and Charleston. It freely received the notes of the local Banks, and as it did not press for immediate payment, it encouraged them to make additional issues. The Bank of the United States could not, however, defer its demands forever, and when it called for payment, a conflict commenced between it and the local Banks, which was not fairly terminated for several years.

As some movements in the Legislatures of Georgia and South Carolina had, at an early period, indicated a disposition to embarrass its operations, the United States' Bank did not deem it prudent to use the most rigorous measures with the Banks of Charleston and Savannah. Fully aware of this fact, the Banks south of Virginia began, in the crisis of 1819, boldly to *evade* specie payments, if they did not make a full and formal suspension.

The Bank of Darien, Georgia, for example, adopted the following course of procedure, as is described by an eye witness: "Persons making demands on the Bank of Darien must swear before a justice of the peace, *in Bank*, to each and every bill presented that it is his own : that he is not agent for any other person ; and that oath must be made in the presence of at least five directors and the cashier : it also makes the person so demanding specie subject to a charge of $1 37½ on *each* bill, which must be paid on the spot, and unless you find five directors and the cashier together, you cannot make a demand."*

As the United States' Bank could not easily get payment from the local Banks, and as specie was almost immediately demanded for such of its own notes as it issued in the South, it found it politic, if not necessary, to receive what was due on account of the imposts in North and South Carolina, and Georgia, in notes of the Banks of those States.   So far as it traded, it traded on those notes, issuing none of its own. This arrangement gave the southern Banks a monopoly of the profits deriveable from the circulation of paper : but they were not satisfied, because they had not also the profits deriveable from the use of the public deposits. When the United States' Bank, in the spring of 1820, made a demand on the Banks of Savannah, for payment of a considerable amount of notes, which had been received principally in payment of duties, those Banks refused either to make payment in specie, or to allow interest on the sum which was unliquidated.   The United States' Bank then protested a large amount of their notes : and soon afterwards, five hundred dollars in notes of the State Bank of Georgia were advertised to be sold by auction, for specie, in lots to suit purchasers, in front of the Exchange at Savannah.

* Nile's Weekly Register, August 14th, 1819.

In August the Banks of Savannah had again the reputation of specie paying Banks : but they refused to give
money to individuals for their paper, unless those applying
for it would agree to take half the amount in bills of the
Darien Bank. It cannot, however, be said that they refused all kinds of accomodation to the public, for while
they would not pay cash for their notes, they would oblige
a holder of them by giving him a draft on New York at
three per cent. advance.*

In this contest the local Banks enlisted the feelings of
the Legislature of Georgia in their favor : and an act was
passed in the beginning of 1821, to repeal the law allowing twenty-five per cent. damages on non-payment of notes,
so far as it might operate in favor of the United States'
Bank. Such a disposition in the Legislature, was an
encouragement to the Banks to evade payment to individuals : and we read, without feelings of surprise, that on a
demand being made in April on the Planters' Bank of
Georgia for 30,000 dollars in specie, the cashier replied
that he would pay in cents only : and that, when a gentleman of Augusta made a demand for specie in June, cents
were tendered to him and counted out at the rate of sixty
dollars a day.†

From that time to this, the people of Georgia have suffered the evils of irregular Banking, sometimes in one
form and sometimes in another. The paper of their Banks
is usually at a discount in the Philadelphia market, exceeding the natural rate of exchange, that is, the cost of
transporting specie. In 1824, complaints were made that
" change " bills, issued by individuals and corporations,
were in circulation. In the same year we find the Governor
declaring " that all the Banks should resume specie payments without delay." If they all resumed them, they
could not all maintain them, for Mr. White, of Baltimore,
in a letter to the Secretary of the Treasury in 1830, speaks
of " intelligence having just been received of the failure
of some of the principal Banks of Georgia to redeem
their notes with specie." Complaints of sufferings by the
people of the State have been frequent. In 1824 and
1828 these complaints were very loud. When the Legis-

* Niles, August, 26th, 1820.
† United States Gazette of April 30th, and June 22d, 1821.

lature attempted to relieve the planters, by establishing a Bank on the funds of the State, called the "Central Bank," and opened that Bank for business at Milledgville in 1829, "the rush for money was tremendous."

In South Carolina a disposition was evinced by a part of the population, to make the suspension of specie payments perpetual. Full proof of this is to be found in a long and elaborate report by the directors of the Bank of the State, dated October 1st, 1819, in which all the arguments of the English Anti-Bullionists are placed in prominent relief. The prosperity of the country from 1815 to 1817, is depicted in glowing colors. The effects produced by the resumption of specie payments are deplored as unnecessary evils. "It becomes necessary to inquire," say the directors, "whether, in the present state of the world, a metallic currency, sufficient for the wants of our country, is attainable, and whether, if it be obtained, it will be worth the necessary cost: whether, in fact, a currency equally good, perhaps better, may not be established, without any of those sacrifices which our country has already been obliged to make, and which it must for a long time make, to secure this fugitive and evanescent object. * * * In Great Britain, where alone, in modern days, gold and silver have for a short time been left freely to find their value in an unshackled market; they have been known to fluctuate in value nearly 50 per cent. in the course of a few months : a fluctuation which no paper currency has ever undergone, excepting such as has been issued by the mandates of arbitrary and necessitous governments, where no value is received for it on its emission, no pledge given or secured for its redemption."

The Bank of the State of South Carolina did not pay specie regularly till the year 1823, and the United States' Bank at Charleston, as it is stated in Degrand's Weekly Report, "fostered the irregularity by aiding the circulation of State Bank paper which was not convertible." Since that time, Banking does not appear to have been less "regular" in South Carolina than in Pennsylvania : but as "regular" Banking by corporations and with paper money may produce great evils, it might be worthy of inquiry if *part* of the sufferings of the people of that State have not their origin in this cause. The excitement, however, at this moment, appears too great to permit such an inquiry to be made.

Virginia has the honor of being the first State that took effectual measures towards reforming the currency. This she did in 1820, when she passed an act to prohibit the circulation of notes of a less denomination than five dollars. Her Banking operations have never been less regular than those of the Middle States: and she will probably be one of the first to establish a perfectly sound system of credit and currency.

Of the condition of affairs in North Carolina, the reader may judge, by the following extract from a report made to the Legislature, at the session of 1828–29.

" The Legislature having laid down, in the charters of the several Banks, certain fundamental articles for the government thereof, the committee assumed these articles as the basis of their investigations, and proceeded accordingly to inquire, in the first place, whether the stock of the several Banks had been raised in the manner required by their charters?—The evidence received by the committee on this point, shows that the charters of the Banks were disregarded and violated in the very creation of their capital.

" The charter of the Bank of Cape Fear, enacted in 1804, authorized that corporation to raise a capital stock of $250,000; and the charter of the Newbern Bank, enacted in the same year, authorized that Bank to raise a capital stock of $200,000; both charters directing the capital to be paid by the stockholders in gold or silver. The undersigned have received no evidence as to the mode in which these Banks got into operation. It would seem, however, that they contemplated, at the outset, an evasion of the provisions of their charters. It is in evidence to the undersigned, that soon after they went into operation, they contrived to get possession of nearly all the paper money which had been issued on the faith of the State, which, being at the time a legal tender, enabled them to evade demands for specie, which they did, by thrusting this ragged paper at those who presented their notes for specie. In 1807, $25,000 was added to the capital stock of each of these Banks; in 1814, their charters were extended, and they were authorized to increase their respective capitals to $800,000 each, viz. the Newbern Bank was authorized to raise an addition to its stock of $575,000, and the Bank of Cape Fear, an addition of $525,000. It is in evidence to the undersigned, that the whole of this additional stock was manufactured by the Banks themselves, and that, in many instances, favored individuals were permitted to acquire stock by subscribing their names, and putting their notes into Bank, without advancing a single dollar of actual capital. It follows, that the whole amount of the interest drawn from the people, on the loans made on this fictitious capital, was a foul and illegal extortion. The effect of the transaction was the same as if the pretended stockholders had individually executed their notes of hand, without interest, to the amount of the notes which they issued from the Bank, and exchanged them with the people for their notes, bearing interest, and renewable every ninety days. Taking the issues made on this fabricated capital to be in proportion with those made on the former capital, they must have put into circulation, on the faith of the assumed stock, between 3 and 4,000,000 of notes; and thus, a parcel of individuals, under the name of stockholders, but who, in fact, held no stock, contrived to exchange their notes, without interest, to the amount of 3 or 4,000,000, for the notes of the people, bearing an interest of more than 6 per cent.; and while the property of the people was pledged for the payment of the notes they had given to the stockholders, there was not a dollar or an atom of property pleged to them for the payment of the notes they had received *from* the stockholders; so that for the use of their notes, which, intrinsically, were of no value at all, the stockholders of these two Banks have drawn from the people, by way of interest, something like $200,000 annually.

"The charter of the State Bank, enacted in 1810, authorized that corporation to raise a capital stock of $1,600,000, and directed books to be opened to receive subscriptions for that sum, requiring, at the same time, that individuals subscribing for stock, should pay three-fourths of the amount subscribed in gold or silver, and the other fourth in the paper currency issued on the faith of the State. Books were accordingly opened, and the sum subscribed, including the subscription of $250,000 for the State, amounted to $1,175,600. Of this sum, only $500,000, or thereabouts, was paid into Bank, as required by the charter, in gold or silver. The balance was paid in Bank notes. Upon the capital thus constituted, the Bank went on to operate till November, 1818; at which time, the proportion between the notes in circulation and the specie on hand, was nearly 12 to 1. In other words, the Bank had largely upwards of 11 and nearly 12 dollars of their notes in circulation, for every dollar of specie in their vaults. The directors then ordered books to be opened to receive subscriptions for the $424,000 which remained unsubscribed when the books were first opened; and it forms a part of the order by which this additional subscription was authorized, that the subscribers *might* pay it in the notes of the Bank. The reason assigned for this operation of the directors, is, that they were desirous of applying the sponge to a part of their outstanding debt, and by way of calling in $224,000 of their notes, they authorized individuals who held them to subscribe for stock in the Bank to that amount, and pay for it in their notes. Thus, at a time when they had in circulation nearly 12 dollars in notes for every dollar of specie in their vaults, and when most obviously they were unable to redeem their notes with specie, they purchased them from the holders by the sale of stock which they themselves created by the mere act of subscription. This the undersigned conceive to have been a most flagrant and fradulent violation of their charter. The charter only authorized the Bank to operate on a real and intrinsic capital, and directed that the capital should be paid into the Bank by the stockholders. In the transaction alluded to, the Bank itself, by a scribbling process of its own, created the capital, and paid off a portion of its debt, by the very act by which it also increased its capital. A circumstance, too, which greatly adds to the enormity of the transaction, is, that before all the instalments became payable, the State Bank, the Bank of Newbern and Bank of Cape Fear entered into a formal resolution, through their delegates assembled at Fayetteville, in June, 1819, not to pay specie : and their notes immediately fell to to 15 per cent. below par. Then commenced the system of usury and extortion, which has since been carried on with such unparalleled audacity, under the *name* of *exchange*. Up to this time, viz., 1819, the high tide of commercial prosperity enjoyed by the country, enabled the Banks to keep afloat, notwithstanding the artificial character of their capital, without resorting to this daring and dishonest expedient. They had kept pace in their operations with the increasing resources of the country, so as to absorb, by way of interest on discounts, nearly all the profits on the immense business then doing ; and having raised against the people a debt equal to the vast resources which, from 1815 to that time, they had derived from their foreign commerce, as soon as the alteration occurred in our foreign relations and those resources were cut off, the business of the country, unable any longer to employ the immense circulating medium which had been created by the Banks, and their notes returning upon them for redemption, they determined to extort from the people additional premiums on loans in order to enable them to meet the demands of their creditors.   A scene of extortion and usury ensued, which has no parallel in the annals of avarice—the strange spectacle of moneyed institutions exacting specie in exchange for their notes, which they themselves refused to redeem with specie.   To show the gross character of the usury thus carried on, the undersigned will suppose a case : An individual applies to the Bank for a loan of 1000 dollars, and offers his note to be discounted for the amount.   He is told by the Bank that his note cannot be discounted, unless he will exchange with them 1000 dollars of specie funds, for 1000 dollars of their notes.   Taking their notes to be 5 per cent. below par, 1000 dollars of their notes would *in fact be* no more than 950 dollars.   So that the substance of such a proposition would be, that the borrower should give the Bank *fifty dollars* as a premium for the loan of 1000 dollars : which, added to the legal interest received in advance, would amount to something more than 11 per cent.   In some instances, the usury has been still more rank.   Quantities of their notes have been loaned to individuals on condition that the whole amount should be returned in ninety days in specie funds.   At the rate of depreciation before stated, such a transaction would be equivalent to the exaction of 26 per cent.   The evidence received by the committee, shows that the State Bank and Bank of Newbern have been guilty of such practices since the summer of 1819. There is no evidence that the Bank of Cape Fear has.   It appears in aggravation of the guilt of these practices, that, in the case of the State Bank, the specie funds thus extorted from the people in exchange for their depreciated notes, have been employed by the Bank in purchasing back those notes at a discount : That they have, at times, employed agents in New York and Petersburg, to buy up their notes : and that about twelve months since, a parcel of their notes was bought up by their agent at Petersburg at 8 per cent. discount. It is stated by the President of the Bank of Cape Fear, for whose testimony too much respect cannot be expressed, that the notes of that Bank have, at different times, been bought up at a discount by the Bank.   That a quantity of its notes were so purchased in anticipation of the late call of the stockholders ; and that during the panic occasioned by that call, something like 500 dollars of their notes were bought up by the Bank at a discount of 5 per cent.   The depreciation of the notes of all the Banks, occasioned by the refusal of the Banks to make good their notes with specie, has been productive of incalculable mischief to the community ; and it is no inconsiderable aggravation of the mischief to know that, in the case of the State Bank, large quantities of their notes have occasionally been thrown into circulation by themselves in the purchase of cotton.   It is in evidence to the undersigned, that they laid out at one time 30,000 dollars of their notes in the purchase of cotton, on which they made a profit of more than 8,000 dollars.   Another remarkable fact in the history of the State Bank, which the undersigned will notice in passing, is, that to protect themselves from demands for specie, they determined at one time to administer an oath to an individual, presenting their notes for specie, in which he was compelled to state that he was not a broker.   It further appears to the undersigned, that all the Banks have bought up United States' Bank notes, for which they exchanged their own notes at a discount ; and the State Bank and Bank of Cape Fear, in direct violation of their charters, have purchased stock to a considerable amount in the United States' Bank.   The State Bank appears to have made a most convenient use of this arrangement.   It appears from the evidence of the late President of that Bank, that they have been in the habit of rendering false statements to the Legislature ; and that in

May last, when they stated in their exhibit that they had on hand 214,000 dollars in specie, 140,000 dollars of it consisted of stock in the United States' Bank. So that, instead of keeping the specie in their vaults to take up their paper, they have vested it in the stock of another Bank, and were deriving interest from it. It further appears, from the evidence of the same person, that the amount of actual specie now in the State Bank at Raleigh, is not more than 300 to 400 dollars: at any rate, not exceeding 1000 dollars.

"The undersigned have now gone through the details of the evidence, and stated all the *essential* facts collected in the course of their examination. Having thus embodied a simple statement of the facts, they would here close their report, and leave the conclusions and arguments to the Legislature; but they feel themselves impelled, by a solemn sense of the duty which they owe to the Legislature and the country, to take a brief view of the present relation between the Banks and the people, and the consequence which *must* ensue if the Banks are permitted to continue their operations; and, in doing so, to advert to the report of the committee of the stockholders of the State Bank at their late general meeting. It appears that the people of North Carolina, having already paid to the Banks, since they went into operation, a profit of about 4,000,000 dollars on their stock—stock, too, three-fourths of which was manufactured by the Banks themselves in a fictitious and fraudulent manner—that having paid this immense sum, exceeding four times the amount of the actual capital stock ever paid into Bank according to law, they still hold the notes of the people for more than 5,000,000 dollars, about four times the amount of the whole circulating medium of the State. Thus it is in the power of the Banks *absolutely to extinguish* the currency of the country, and when they have taken every dollar out of circulation, still to have a debt against the people to the amount of about 4,000,000 dollars. We say it is in their power to do it; and they intimate pretty plainly that they *will* do it. The communication from the stockholders of the State Bank, now before the committee, expresses the opinion that it is for the interest of the stockholders to withdraw their money from the Bank, and take it under their own management; and contains a resolution by which they have proclaimed their resolution to assemble in June next, in order to determine whether they will proceed to *wind up* their affairs ; and, consequently, *the affairs of the people of North Carolina.* Thus having for years contrived, by illegal and fraudulent practices, to draw from the people all the *profits* of their labor, and having by these practices placed the people in an impoverished condition, where they can no longer pay them large profits, they are now preparing, by one fell swoop, to extort from them the *actual means of subsistence.* But the question occurs, will *you* permit it ? Will you permit a parcel of men, who have long set the laws of the country at defiance, to go on and complete the ruin they have already so nearly accomplished ? Will you not bring them to the observance of the law ? Will you not at length cause them to feel the rod of that law they have so long despised and violated ? These questions, your committee conceive, answer themselves. When the Legislature is called upon to determine whether their constituents shall live under a government of laws, or a government of corporations, it cannot be difficult to decide. The undersigned, therefore, recommend to the Legislature the adoption of the following resolution :—

" Whereas it appears to the Legislature that the State Bank of Newbern, and the Bank of Cape Fear, have violated their charters and committed great frauds on the people of North Carolina, whereby said Banks have forfeited the powers and privileges granted in their charters : Therefore,

" *Be it Resolved by the General Assembly of the State of North Carolina,* That the Attorney General be, and he is hereby, directed forthwith to institute a judicial inquiry into the conduct of the said Banks : and that he prosecute such inquiry by writ of *Quo Warranto,* or other legal process."

No such judicial inquiry appears to have been instituted. The practical sovereignty remains with the Banks of North Carolina : and they respect the laws and public opinion, just so far as they believe to be conducive to their own interest.

CHAPTER XVI.

Of Banking in New England.

We have searched the public libraries of Philadelphia for particulars respecting the New England Banks that broke previous to the war, but have been able to find no document of any importance, except the report of the committee of the Legislature of Rhode Island in relation to the affairs of the Farmers' Bank of Gloucester. Many writers allude to the great distress that the operations of the moneyed corporations produced in New England about the years 1808 and 1809, but they do not even give a list of the Banks that then stopped payment.

That the distress was great, we have incidental proof in the rigidity of the laws afterwards adopted to enforce specie payments. All experience shows that till the evils produced by moneyed corporations become absolutely unendurable, the proper remedy is not applied.

After the commencement of hostilities with Great Britain, the New England Banks were obliged, in order to maintain specie payments, to wind up nearly all their credit dealings. This operation necessarily produced much distress, and greatly increased the dissatisfaction with which the people of that section of the Union regarded the warlike policy of Government.

This distress does not appear to have terminated with the war. For, a Philadelphian, writing in August, 1815, says, after mentioning the curtailments made by the New England Banks, " Real estate would not command prices nigh its former value; merchandise fell greatly below its usual rate; whilst money in the market was worth two per cent. a month. This is the *existing* state of things in Boston. * * * * It is manifest that the operation of the rigid laws of Massachusetts is highly injurious to the commerce of their towns, and we do not see that the boasted capacity of their Banks to pay a *few* notes in specie, renders their situation more enviable than our own."*

The natural anxiety of the New Englandmen to get payment of what was due to them by the people of the Middle

* " Inquiry," &c.

States, was attributed to ill-feeling. "Circumstances," said
a New York writer, "have excited a spirit of envy at our
prosperity, which has superadded a restless malignity of
effort to increase artificially and aggravate the evils of an
unfavorable balance. Whoever has attended to the uniform
language of eastern men and eastern writers, cannot have
failed to discover this spirit—they will not believe that I
speak of its authors with undue severity."*

The *apparent* prosperity of the Middle States was such
as might well excite envy; but it was a wholesome adversity New England was experiencing. Her currency could
not, indeed, be called perfectly sound, for, as appears from
Mr. Crawford's Report, many of the inconvertible notes of
the other States found their way into her territory. But,
as the people had got them for less than their nominal value, they sustained no other loss except that which arose
from the notes undergoing an additional depreciation while
they remained in their hands. The standard of value by
which contracts were regulated in New England was not
affected ; and the Banks being prevented from suspending
specie payments, were prevented from exciting a wild spirit
of speculation in the people.

The natural consequence of the suspension of specie payments in the other States, was an influx of specie into New
England. That this was very great, may be inferred from
the fact that the Massachusetts Banks which had $1,560,004
in specie in 1811, had, in 1814, specie in their vaults of the
amount of $6,393,718. It was useless to keep such an
amount of specie lying dead. The abundant issues of treasury notes by the Government afforded easy means of paying duties. There was enough, either of specie or of notes
of different kinds in circulation, to supply all the wants of
domestic trade. The specie was, therefore, exported with
so much rapidity, that the amount in the Boston Banks,
which had been $5,466,759 in June, 1814, was, by June,
1815, or about five months after the return of peace, reduced
to $2,125,076; or, if the amount in the Worcester Bank be
included, to about $2,800,000. The exportation of specie
did not stop till there was no more left than was just suffi-

* "Statius," in the New York Columbian ; republished by Mr. Carey,
with commendations, as an appendix to his "Letter to Mr. Calhoun,"
1816.

cient to support the credit of the notes in circulation : so
that, when the United States' Bank commenced operations,
the other States could derive no important supplies of metallic money from New England.

From a combination of causes, the operations of the
United States' Bank were of limited extent in New England. The channels of circulation there were fully occupied by local Bank notes which had never been discredited. The new institution had so little metallic capital, that it could not enter into competition with the local
Banks; and all the funds it acquired as receiver of the
public moneys at Boston, were wanted to support its operations in the South and West.

Hence, the reaction of 1819 was less sensibly felt in
New England than in other parts of the Union.

The ordinary operations of Banking in New England,
are, however, such as to make men lament that the system
was ever invented. Expansions and contractions have, as
we have before had occasion to remark, a more striking
effect on the operations of manufacturers than on those of
agriculturists. So facile is production with modern machinery, that a small rise of prices causes a great increase
of manufactured articles. In a short time, the Banks are
forced to contract. Then there is a scarcity of money and
a glut of manufactures. Then the manufacturers petition
for new additions to the duties on imports. The tariff is
raised accordingly. Enterprize is again awakened. There
is a demand for capital : and the Banks supply —— credit.
There is, however, no more solid ground for an extension
of credit after the passage of a new tariff act than there
was before. Not more than a year or two elapses before
the necessary reaction commences. The manufacturers,
again startled with the prospect of ruin, apply for additional
" protection." It may be granted ; but it is doubtful if any
tariff that can be established, will, while this system of
money dealings continues, be able to protect multitudes
from ruin. We know some very zealous and very intelligent friends of the " American System," who are decidedly of opinion, that if there were no moneyed corporations
and no paper money in the country, the manufacturers
would require no protecting tariff. If the excitement in
relation to protecting duties were less violent than it is at

this moment, we might invite particular inquiry into the effect paper Banking has on manufactures. We might illustrate our argument, by showing the effects expansions and contractions of Bank medium have had on manufacturing operations in England.

The multitude of Banks in New England, makes it necessary for those concerned in them to resort to a variety of *expedients* to sustain them in their operations. Of these expedients none but the concerned could give a full account : but some idea of their nature may be formed from the disclosures which are occasionally made.

Mr. Niles, in his Weekly Register for September 8th, 1821, for example, gives the following quotations from the New York Journal:—

" We observe by a notice in the " Dutchess Observer," that the farmers of Dutchess County have been *shorn* of all their wool by a most singular operation—or, in other words, that nearly all the wool in that county had been sold to J. Butler, cashier of the Litchfield Bank, who had recently failed, and assigned his factory, wool, &c. to the Bank, as security for his debts, leaving the farmers to suffer.

" The story, as told by one of the shorn, is briefly this : —The Wolcotville Factory, formerly belonged to Mr. Wolcott, who failed, being largely indebted to the *Bank.* As the Bank is prohibited from buying and selling property, their Cashier, Butler, became nominally the proprietor. The belief that James Butler acted in behalf of the Bank, was so universal, that he obtained an unlimited credit. The agents for the factory have recently made large purchases of wool, in the usual manner, upon the notes of James Butler. A great proportion of the wool raised this year in Dutchess County has thus been purchased and carried over to Litchfield, and as soon as the same is well packed away, James Butler, the Cashier, is discovered to be a defaulter to the Bank for some **16,000** dollars, and he assigns his factory, and the stock thus fairly and recently acquired, to the Litchfield Bank. The Bank is paid—the farmer has a *Litchfield shearing*—and James Butler, the cashier, is an insolvent."

The art of forming Bank capitals by discounting the stock notes of subscribers, appears to be as well understood in New England as in Pennsylvania. The Kennebeck

Bank, in Maine, had a nominal capital of 100,000 dollars; but an official investigation, in the year 1826, showed that 89,370 dollars of the whole amount consisted of stock notes: that the directors held nine-tenths of the stock, and that they were in debt to the Bank not only for the amount of their stock notes, but in an additional sum of 34,400 dollars. For two years, this Bank divided 12 per cent. per annum.

The expose of the Bath Bank in the same State, was very similar to that of the Kennebeck Bank. Nearly three-fourths of the capital were represented by stock notes, and nine-tenths of the stock were owned by the directors. More than three-fourths of all the discounts, in addition to those on stock notes, were made to the same directors.

The capital of the Bank of Vassalborough consisted of 300 shares, of which 283 " belonged either personally or representatively to a partnership at Hallowell, A. & J. Leonard, the former of whom is President. The whole amount of *money* which the Bank had on hand on the 21st of June, 1826, was $40,000; $36,000 of which was in the hands of the firm above mentioned, and 4,000 in the hands of the Cashier. The Bank had no record or charge to exhibit against the Leonards, who had about the whole property of the institution, and the Cashier had taken up his bond. The Commissioners were requested to postpone their report, till the Bank concerns could be put into some form and comeliness, but the disorders of the body politic appeared too incurable to be thus tampered with."

On an investigation of the affairs of the Burrillville Bank of Rhode Island, it was found that only 6000 dollars of the capital had been paid even in stock notes.

Bank capitals being thus easily formed, and legislative charters conferring great privileges, we cannot wonder at the multiplication of Banks in New England. Rhode Island, which had thirty-four Banks in 1820, increased the number to fifty by the year 1830: and Massachusetts, in the same period, made an addition of forty to the number of her Banking institutions.

In some of their recent acts, the Legislature of Massachusetts have endeavored to guard against the formation of Bank capitals out of stock notes, but that it is possible for the getters up of Banks to evade, if so disposed, even the strongest legal enactments, may be learned from the following extract from a report made to the Senate of the State, on the 25th of January, 1830.

" The Sutton Bank was incorporated the 11th of March, 1828. The act of incorporation provides—" That the capital stock of said corporation shall consist of one hundred thousand dollars in gold and silver, to be divided into shares of one hundred dollars each, which shall be paid in the manner following, viz. one-half part thereof on or before the first day of October (then) next, and the remaining part thereof on or before the first day of March, in the year of our Lord one thousand eight hundred and twenty-nine." And it further provides, that no moneys shall be loaned or discounts made, nor shall any bills or promissory notes be made or issued from the said Bank, until the capital subscribed and actually paid in, and existing in gold and silver in said vaults, shall amount to fifty thousand dollars, nor until the said capital stock, actually in said vaults, shall have been inspected and examined by three Commissioners, to be appointed by the Governor for that purpose, whose duty it shall be, at the expense of the said corporation, to examine the money actually existing in said vaults, and to ascertain, by the oaths of the directors of said Bank, or a majority of them, that the said capital stock hath been bona fide paid in by the stockholders of said Bank, and towards the payment of their respective shares, and not intended for any other purpose, and that it is intended there to remain as part of said capital."

" On the 26th day of September, 1828, the Governor, in compliance with an application for that purpose, made by a committee of the subscribers for stock in said Sutton Bank, appointed Commissioners to examine the moneys actually existing in vaults of said Bank, as is provided in the second section of their act of incorporation. On the 27th day of September, 1828, the Sutton Bank borrowed, on a deposit of fifty-one thousand dollars in the bills of the City Bank, the sum of fifty thousand dollars in specie, for one day only ; this same specie was examined by the Commissioners, and the following certificates made out, viz.—

" We, the subscribers, Commissioners appointed for that purpose, have this day been shown, and have examined, fifty thousand dollars in specie in the vaults of the Sutton

Bank, which was paid in by the stockholders at their first instalment, agreeably to their Act of Incorporation, passed the eleventh day of March, 1828.

JONATHAN LELAND.
AMASA ROBERTS.
SAMUEL WOOD.

September, 27th, 1828.   *Commissioners."*

Boston, Sept. 27*th,* 1828.

" SUFFOLK, *ss.*

" Then personally appeared Hezekiah Howe, Jonas L. Sibley, Joshua W. Leland, and Thomas Harback, being a majority of directors of Sutton Bank, and made oath that fifty thousand dollars in specie by them shown in their vaults, was the first instalment paid by the stockholders of their Bank, towards the payment of their respective shares, and not for any other purpose, and that it is intended therein to remain, a part of said capital.

" Before me.

" ELIPHALET WILLIAMS, *Just. Peace.*

" *The bills and specie were then re-exchanged; this whole business, accomplished within an hour, and all of it done within the walls of the City Bank, in the city of Boston.*

" It appears from the books of the company, that the several payments for the first instalment were made on the first and sixth days of October, 1828, and on the same days, almost all the stockholders are charged with notes for the same amount as their respective instalments: in two instances, notes were taken from individuals equal to their own subscription and the sums due from their minor children, in whose names stock had been subscribed: in two instances only, and those for a small amount, it appears any payment was made in money.

" On a petition to the Legislature, praying that they might be allowed further time to pay in the remaining moiety of their capital, " An act in addition to an act to incorporate the President, Directors, and Company of the Sutton Bank,' was passed on the 20th of February, 1829, which provides, ' that the said fifty thousand dollars shall be paid in gold and silver, in the manner following:—twenty-five thousand dollars on or before the first day of June next, and the remaining twenty-five thousand dollars on or

before the first day of October next.' The payment in
June was made in the same manner as the first payment,
as was also the last, with the exception of some shares on
which the instalment was not settled, either by note or
otherwise. The object of the Corporation in requesting
an extension of the time of making payment for their stock
in the mode adopted by them, is not apparent, as it may be
supposed that it would be as convenient for them to make
their notes in March last, as in the months of June and
October following."

The case of the Eagle Bank at New Haven is deserving of notice. This Bank had a capital of 600,000 dollars,
and was accounted one of the safest Banks in New England. It failed in September, 1825 : and from a report by
a committee of the Legislature, we give the following extract.

" George Bradly, Esq., the President of the Institution,
was employed as Cashier of said Bank from its commencement, until the year 1817, when on the resignation of
the Hon. Simon Baldwin, he was elected President. From
that period, the President was permitted to be the sole
manager of the institution. Its funds were placed entirely under his control and disposal. No rules were prescribed by the Board of Directors regulating the mode of trasact-
ing the business of the institution, or requiring its officers
to bring their doings under the review of the Board during
the aforesaid time. The President had not only in his
hands the entire control of the concern of the Bank, but
had, by accumulation of proxies, the power of appointing
the directors. In the successive changes of the Board,
no examination was made into the state and condition of
the Bank. The funds of the institution were employed in
speculations, and adventures unknown to the directors and
stockholders, and entirely unconnected with, and remote
from, the business of Banking. Loans were made in various
forms, and to a great extent, which were not communicated
to the directors, and in some instances by arrangement
not to be communicated. In this course of management
individuals obtained, without the form of security, and for
various purposes, funds of the Bank, exceeding the capital, and to supply the exigencies created thereby, agents
were employed in whose hands the bills of the Bank were
placed to give them a forced and distant circulation, and

by that means to sustain the operations of the Bank. Those operations were not recorded in the regular books of the Bank, but vested in loose papers in the custody of the President, and in a book, in which the initial letters of the names of the agents were entered, and the figures containing the amount by them received. The statements annually rendered to the Legislature, have been calculated to mislead, rather than to afford any information on which the public could safely rely in relation to the true state and condition of the Bank. In one instance 220,000 dollars, issued upon the checks of the President, Normand Dexter, Henry C. Rossiter, the Messrs. Hinsdales, and other memorandums of indebtedness not entered upon the books of the Bank, were not included in the reported amount of circulation, making an error in the statement of the aforesaid sum of two hundred and twenty thousand dollars. In the course of the last spring, other and further expedients were adopted by the President to assist his operations. Without the order or consultation with the Board of Directors, a new post note was procured, and notes in that form payable on different times, were placed in the hands of an individual to an alarming amount, and without the precautions of security, to obtain by negotiations, the funds necessary to relieve the increasing pressures on the Bank. Those notes were not entered regularly into the books of the Bank, and not known otherwise than casually to the Board. The consequences of such expedients were in a few months developed. The inability of the institution to redeem its notes, brought to an end its operations as a Bank in September last, and the distress in which the creditors were involved, and the great body of the stockholders, who cannot be supposed to have any agency in the management, is too deep and too extensive to require to be stated by the committee."

In May, 1827, a report was made to the Legislature, that the amount of Bank notes and post notes of the Eagle Bank in circulation, was 815,478 dollars. In May, 1828, another report was made, in which it was stated that 1,451,507 dollars were owing to the Bank from four individuals, viz: from J. & D. Hinsdale, 530,466 50: from W. C. Holly, 236,779 47 : and from N. Dexter, and W. C. Holly, conjointly, 568,801 98. The amount of debts, good, bad, and doubtful, due from all other persons to the Bank, was then less than 200,000 dollars.

Governor Wolcott, in an address to the Legislature of Connecticut, in May 1826, said, " Except in limited districts of the United States, the condition of our circulating medium is not very dissimilar to that which has been established by arbitrary Kings in the North of Europe, and especially by the Autocrat of the Russian Empire. There, a Bank has been created, and its notes constitute a circulating currency throughout his vast dominions. The credit which these notes obtain, is derived from revenues which are established by his sole authority. These revenues are not indeed paid in Bank notes, but the demand for silver coin which the revenue establishes, imparts a forced, though precarious, value to the notes, which value is maintained and regulated by the reciprocating influences which are created between the supply and demand for paper and silver currencies. The effect is, that all property is subject to his will.

" With us the currency which is required by the daily exchange between all the people, and by which the transactions between farmers, mechanics, laborers, manufacturers, and traders is regulated, is almost exclusively in Bank notes, which are issued by a great number of independent corporations, which possess an exclusive privilege of creating notes for their own benefit.

" This monopoly is here so exercised, that neither the amount of currency which is issued, nor the amount of that which is suddenly suspended, withdrawn, or annihilated, is subject to any practical limitation, other than what must arise from the state of foreign and domestic exchanges, the speculations of individuals, political events, and the necessities or caprices of the numerous monopolizing incorporations, who entirely control the circulation of the country.

" These last observations require no other confirmation than a reference to the notorions facts, that no coins circulate among the people, except small sums of copper, and the fractional parts of a dollar in silver, which is our silver unit. Our unit of gold is a coin of ten dollars, which, with its fractional parts, in coins of five dollars, and two and one half dollars, have wholly vanished from circulation.

" The effects produced upon the people are, that no man can travel fifty miles, in any direction, without receiving paper notes of which he possesses no means of ascertaining the value, or even the authenticity, and this difficulty increases in proportion to the distance of an individual from some one of these Banks. From these causes, the whole country is subject to complex evils, arising from either a redundant or too restricted circulation of the only currency which can be obtained, and hence, sudden variations in the prices of all exchangeable commodities, far exceeding the customary profits of regular industry and commerce, thereby converting all transactions of business, especially at a distance from the seats of foreign commerce, into mere lotteries.

" It is amidst explosions of credit, principally occasioned by the conduct of Banks, that every class of industrious citizens, and all our enterprizing young men, are exposed to repeated losses, against which no vigilance can guard, and no prudence exempt them.

These distresses are inflicted upon the community, without any advantage being derived either to the State, to the stockholders, to the depositors of funds, or to the honest debtors to the Banks. They are so frequent, so extensive, and embrace so many personal interests and connexions, that it seems impossible to impute them, in many instances, to voluntary depravity. The inference must be, that our system of Bank administration is essentially defective, and that to correct it, all interests ought to contribute their best councils and united efforts.

" There are fewer inducements at this time, why we should submit to the evils of a paper currency, than exist among any other people on the globe. We are prosecuting an active commerce with states and nations where gold and silver are abundant, and are, indeed, staple articles of trade. With these countries, the intercourse of the people on both sides is founded on friendly and constant relations, both personal and political. Our fabrics of iron, wool, leather, wood, cotton, paper, and most other productions of our arts and industry, are as necessary to these countries, as a fair relative proportion of their metallic wealth has become essential to us.

" It is very consolatory to know, that the abuses of

credit which are so prevalent, did not commence in this State, and that although we have yielded to temptations which we ought to have averted, our neighbors ought to correct their own conduct before they censure us.

" In my opinion, we ought to manifest our sincerity by immediately retracing the folds of the web in which we, in common with our neighbors, have become entangled. We can perceive that the issues of notes from the Banks in this State have been annoying to the Banks in Boston and New York, while theirs, founded on no superior security, have been equally injurious to us. Both parties ought voluntarily to concur, in permitting specie to circulate throughont the country, thereby rendering the capitals and credit which exist conducive to mutual advantage.

" The objections to the measure which I deem it my duty to recommend, will most probably be, that paper is a cheaper instrument of circulation than metallic money : and that the proposed restriction would diminish the dividend of Banks, in which the State, the school fund, ecclesiastical societies, the colleges and academies, other incorporations, stockholders, and numerous individuals, are interested.

" But if all these objections were true in point of fact, they would form very inadequate reasons for inflicting *great, increasing*, and *remediless injuries upon all the people and the whole nation.* These evils have not proceeded from the *incorporations as such*, but merely because they have issued bills of credit, as substitutes for the general currency of gold and silver.

" If any principles are demonstrable by reason and experience, they are, that paper money is an interruption to productive industry : that industry is the main source of wealth, and that whatever diminishes production is injurious to the lenders of capital.

" The stockholders of Banks are only interested in having their capitals safely invested, in such a manner as to secure the payment of a regular interest equal to the use of the sums so advanced. It cannot promote their interests, that all the capitals of this country, whether invested in stocks or other transferable property, or in exchangeable commodities, should be constantly exposed to the hazards of rapid revolutions.

" In my opinion, Banks which deal in circulating notes,

and which are safely conducted, require a much more
elaborate and expensive organization and system of detail,
than such as deal wholly or principally in gold and silver.
Honest men assume frightful responsibilities under the
forms by which many of these institutions are now conducted, and their hazards increase in proportion to the
number and variety of the notes which are received. Many
counterfeited and altered notes are so skilfully prepared,
as to defy the scrutiny of adepts : and no safeguards are
provided to protect those who receive them from the most
offensive accusations.

" The case is far different, in respect to transactions in
gold and silver : for by hydrostatic and other balances
which are cheap instruments, which have been known and
used since the time of Archimides, the purity and value of
coins can at once be ascertained with unerring certainty."

The struggles of the New England Banks with one another, to decide which shall have the greatest share of "the
circulation," inflict great evils on the community, in addition to those which are inflicted by general contractions
and expansions of Bank currency. Sometimes a number
of country Banks form a coalition to extend their operations, and the city Banks form alliances to resist them.
Sometimes some of the city Banks enter into arrangements
to aid the designs of the country Banks, and sometimes
those latter find efficient auxiliaries in the city brokers
When a coalition succeeds in extending its issues of paper,
certain districts or certain classes of society experience all
the advantages, real or apparent, derivable from an increase of circulating medium. This continues till the
counter-coalition succeeds in reducing the circulation of
its rivals : and then follows a reaction, with " scarcity of
of money," and its usual concomitants of bankruptcies and
public distress. A detail of the different measures of these
combinations and counter-combinations, and an account of
their effects on the community at large, would be interest-
ing, but would exceed our limits.

A writer in the Massachusetts Journal endeavored, in
the fall of 1830, to show that the Banking system of that
commonwealth is the *worst* which could be devised ; and
recommended as a substitute for it, a State Bank and
branches. His prominent objections to the present system

are " that it renders necessary about seventy Banking institutions: that this number must every year be increased,
as the Legislature cannot properly withhold charters from
any who may apply for them: that the competition for
business between these numerous establishments, gives to
individuals a dangerous facility in obtaining loans, and
creates a system of fictitious credits, which, having no base
on real capital, must, at every pinch in the money market,
explode, and bring ruin upon the Banks and their debtors.
Other objections are, that the expenses of these various
Banks in salaries, rent, &c., amount to a very large sum,
(in Boston alone to 120,000 dollars,) which expenses are
a tax upon stock :" that the country Banks are put to a
great expense in redeeming their bills in Boston ; " and
that, after all, the notes of these Banks form a currency, of
different and fluctuating value, instead of that steady and
uniform currency which public convenience requires."

From accounts recently published, it appears that the
number of Banks in Massachusetts, in August, 1832, was
eighty-three, having nominal capitals of the amount of
$24,520,000, notes in circulation of the amount of $7,122,-
856, and specie on hand of the amount of $902,205 75.
Of these Banks, twenty-two were in the city of Boston.
The greatest amount of specie in any one of the city Banks
was $127,131 43 ; the smallest was $2,415 41. The greatest amount of specie in any one of the sixty-three country
Banks, was $22,966 90 ; the smallest was $1,022 97.

Massachusetts was first in adopting the paper money
system ; and she will probably be among the last to abandon it. Its ramifications there are so numerous, that nearly all the members of the community are compelled to give
it either a willing or an unwilling support.

CHAPTER XVIII.

General View of Banking Operations from 1814–15 to 1820–21.

In the tables appended to Mr. Secretary Ingham's Report on the Gold Coinage, the following is stated to have been the price of specie, at the dates and places below mentioned.

1814.					Baltimore.	Philad.	N. York.
September	-	-	-	-	20 pr.ct.adv.		
October	-	-	-	-	15		
November	-	-	-	-	10		
December	-	-	-	-	14		
1815.							
January	-	-	-	-	20		15
February	-	-	-	-	5		2
March	-	-	-	-	5		5
April	-	-	-	-	10		5½
May	-	-	-	-	14	5	5
June	-	-	-	-	16	9	11
July	-	-	-	-	20	11	14
August	-	-	-	-	19	11	12½
September	-	-	-	-	20	15	13
October	-	-	-	-	21½	15	16
November	-	-	-	-	15	16	12
December	-	-	-	-	18	14	12½
1816.							
January	-	-	-	-	15	14	12½
February	-	-	-	-	13	14	9
March	-	-	-	-	18	12½	12½
April	-	-	-	-	23	14½	10½
May	-	-	-	-	20	14	12½
June	-	-	-	-	20	16	12½
July	-	-	-	-	15	15	6
August	-	-	-	-	12	10	5
September	-	-	-	-	10	7½	3
October	-	-	-	-	8	9½	2
November	-	-	-	-	9	7	1¾
December	-	-	-	-	9	7	2¼
1817.							
January	-	-	-	-	3	4½	2¼
February	-	-	-	-	2½	4	2¾

From the rates of exchange on London, in New York and Philadelphia, in the months in which there are blanks in the table, the price of specie appears then to have been a few per cent. less in Philadelphia than in Baltimore ; and a few per cent. less in New York than in Philadelphia.

In the Appendix to the Report of the Committee of the Senate of Pennsylvania, the following table is given to show the *discount* on the notes of the country Banks—not as estimated in specie, but as estimated in Philadelphia paper.

BANKS.	1816		1817		1818		1819		1820
	May 6.	Nov. 4.	May 5.	Nov. 3.	May 4.	Nov. 3.	May 3.	Nov. 1.	Jan 31.
Bank of Gettysburgh,	10	9	6	3	4	3	3½	4	3
Harrisburg Bank,	pr	pr	6	5	4	pr	pr	½	1½
Carlisle Bank,	10	9	4	5	2½	3	3½	4	3
Bank of Chambersburg,	10	9	4	3	2½	3	3½	4	3
Westmoreland Bank,	10	9	6	5	2½	10	15	15	12¼
Lancaster Trading Company,	10	9	2	5	2½	3	3	2	2½
Marietta,	10	9	6	5	4	30	35	45	33
Centre Bank,	10	9	6	5	4	10	15	30	25
Farmers' Bank of Reading,	10	9	6	5	1½	2½	2½	15	8
Alleghany Bank,	10	9	6	5	4	10	15	50	50
Germantown,	10	9	6	5	4	pr	pr	pr	par
York,	9	10	6	3	2½	3	3½	4	3
Farmers' Bank of Lancaster,	10	9	6	5	4	pr	pr	pr	par
Swetara,	10	9	6	3½	2½	3	4	4	3
Easton Bank,	pr	pr	pr	5	4	pr	pr	pr	par
Pennsylvania Agri. and Man. Bank,	10	9	6	3½	2½	10	4		40
Bank of Washington,	10	9	6	5	4	10	15	50	45
Northampton Bank,	10	9	pr	5	4	10	pr	2½	2½
Juniata Bank,	10	9	6	5	4	10	15	50	40
Delaware Bank,	pr	pr	6	5	4	p	pr	pr	par
Chester County Bank,	pr	pr	6	5	4	p	pr	pr	par
Bank of Beaver,	10	9	6	5	4	10	15	60	50
Bank of Pittsburgh,	10	9	6	5	3	6	pr	5	4
Huntingdon Bank,	10	9	6	5	4	10	15	30	25
Monongahela,	10	9	6	5	4	10	15	15	12½
North Western Bank,	10	9	6	5	4	10	15	50	35
Union Bank,	10	9	6	5	4	50	60	50	50
Northumberland, Union &Columbia	10	9	6	5	4	2½	5	30	20
Bucks County Bank,	10	9	6	5	4		pr	pr	par
Farm's. & Mech's. Bank of Pittsburg	10	9	6	3½	4	10		50	40
Far. & Mec. Bank of Greencastle,	10	9	6	5	2½	15	30	50	35
Montgomery Bank,	pr	pr	pr	5	4		pr	pr	par
Silver Lake Bank,	10	9	6	2½	2½	2½	2½	50	40

In his speech of Jan. 2d, 1815, Mr. Webster said, " the depreciation of the notes of all the Banks in any place is, as far as I can learn, general, uniform and equal." In looking through Grotjan's Price Current, we have found the quotations of Pennsylvania and Ohio notes to be, for months together, from five to six, and afterwards ten, per cent. discount, and those of Virginia and North Carolina two to three per cent. So general seemed to be the rate of depreciation for each part of the country, that the names of particular Banks were not given in the Price Current, for more than a year after the suspension of specie payments. While Philadelphia paper, the standard in which they were estimated, was always varying in value, as compared with silver, the notes of most of the country Banks had, as compared with one another, a singular equality of depreciation.

This equality lasted for some time after it became the custom to give regular quotations of the price of Bank paper. It will be seen, by inspecting the table, that in May, 1816, the notes of twenty-seven out of thirty-five country Banks of Pennsylvania, were at a discount of ten per cent. It will also be seen that the discount was diminished with a regularity approximating to uniformity, up to May, 1818. In the succeeding July, the United States' Bank commenced its curtailment, and then the great confusion in exchanges begun.

In other States the confusion was as great as it was in Pennsylvania. This may be seen by the following table.

PRICES OF BANK NOTES.

	At New York, April 7th, 1819.	At Baltimore, August 7th, 1819.
New England notes,	par to 2 per ct. dis.	1 to 6 discount.
Philadelphia,	par	
Pennsylvania,		1 to 60
Delaware,	4 to 12½	1 to 8 and to 50
Baltimore,	1½	
Maryland,	2 to 20	1 to 40
District of Columbia,		1 to 60
Virginia,	2	1½ to 25
North Carolina,	2 to 3½	20 to 25
South Carolina,	1½	8 to 10
Georgia,	2 to 3	7 to 8
Tennessee,	7	
Kentucky,		15 to 25

	At New York, April 7th, 1819.	At Baltimore, August 7th, 1819.
Bank of Kentucky,	5	
Ohio Banks,	6 to 15	10 to 50
Unchartered Bank of Ohio,	25 to 75	
Louisiana,	6	
Indiana, Illinois, and Missouri,		15 to 60

Mr. Niles, from whom we have taken the items which form this table, says the prices of Bank notes varied several per cent. in the course of a week. The notes which were at par in one part of the country, were in other parts at a heavy discount. At the same time that exchange at New York or New Orleans on New York was at from seven to ten per cent. discount, exchange at New York or New Orleans was at six per cent. discount. A Bank's paying specie did not prevent its notes depreciating : for nobody knew how long any distant Bank would continue to pay specie. All the Banks whose notes were at a discount at New York of less than 5 per cent., and some of the others, were understood to pay specie on demand.

Of the increase and decrease of the local currency of Pennsylvania, the reader may form an idea from the following table.

NOTES IN CIRCULATION.*

		Cify Banks.	Country.	Total.
Nov.	1814,	3,363,802	1,942,479	5,306,281
	1815,	4,810,507	5,349,247	10,159,754
	1816,	3,416,248	4,787,722	8,203,970
	1817,	2,355,694	3,853,866	6,209,560
	1818,	1,987,945	3,093,966	5,081,911
	1819,	1,645,000	1,384,325	3,029,325

It will be seen that the great increase in circulation took place in the year after the war. Great as it was we ought not to wonder at it. The Government's receiving inconvertible paper in payment of duties, was quite as efficient a sanction of the continued suspension of specie payments as could have been afforded by an act of Congress passed with that express intent. What Government is

* The returns of the Farmers and Mechanics' Bank, in 1814, were for August 2d: those of the Pennsylvania Bank for August 30, and those of the Philadelphia Bank for September 1st. The returns of the other Banks were for November. No return was made in any of these years of the circulation of the Bank of North America.

willing to receive, individuals having payments to make to Government will not refuse. Institutions which are founded for private profit, must always be expected to take advantage of so many opportunities of acquiring gain as the policy of Government will allow, or its necessities compel it to afford.

In the year 1815, ten months and a half of which were months of peace, the Government issued twenty millions in treasury notes. As such of these as were of a less denomination than one hundred dollars bore no interest, they directly increased the amount of paper medium. The others, as has been shown in another chapter, indirectly increased the circulation of the Banks, as those institutions gave their own inconvertible notes in exchange for treasury notes

In 1816 there was a reduction of about twenty-five per cent. in the circulation of the Banks of Pennsylvania, and a very great reduction in the circulation of the Banks of the adjoining States. Of the manner in which this was effected, we will let the Secretary of the Treasury speak.

"At a moment when excessive importations of foreign merchandise had involved the mercantile and manufacturing interests in the greatest distress, and menaced them with impending bankruptcy, reason, humanity, and sound policy, all united against the curtailment of Bank discounts. Yet, so far as the knowledge of the Secretary of the Treasury extends, the reduction of the circulating paper has in no instance been attempted by the sale of the public debt held by the Banks. Curtailment of discounts has been the only process resorted to by them, where any efforts have been made to prepare for the resumption of specie payments. The disregard to individual suffering manifested by this procedure in the State Banks has been the result of a conviction, that when the national currency shall be restored by the efforts of the Government and the Bank of the United States, the public debt will be increased in value."*

This is true. But when we establish institutions to which it is impossible to impart moral responsibility, we ought not to expect them to pay much regard to " reason and humanity." The Banks acted with sound " policy "

* Letter of Mr. Dallas, November 1816.

in regard to their own interest, in pressing on the community and in holding on to the public stocks.

In 1817, there was a further reduction in the circulation of the Pennsylvania Banks, but the deficiency was supplied by the issues made by the United States' Bank. The returns of the Pennsylvania Banks, for 1818, were made some months after the Bank of the United States had begun its grand curtailment.

The local Bank mania may be said to have raged with more violence in Pennsylvania in the year 1815, than at any other period : but, if we take the Union throughout, the mania did not reach its height till the spring of 1818, or three years after the close of the war. It was in this year that Vermont, which had been without Banks since the grand New England explosion of 1808-9, began to revive the system : and the passion for multiplying paper issuing institutions became so great, that Mr. Niles was forced to exclaim—" We see every where new Banks establishing or attempting to be established. Behold forty-three new Banks authorized in Kentucky—half a score in Tennessee—eight in Ohio—a mob in little Rhode Island—some in Virginia, Massachusetts, &c.—sixteen petitioned for in New York—and some wanted in Pennsylvania—half a dozen new ones in Maryland—and from fifty to a hundred more proposed in various parts of the United States."*

Only three months after Mr. Niles had indited this paragraph, the United States' Bank was compelled to commence that course of measures, the effects of which have been narrated in our previous chapters.

The author of the pamphlet signed " A Friendly Monitor," says, " Every inquiry I have made has entirely convinced me, that every formidable difficulty with which the Bank has had to contend, has been produced by its agency for the Government, and particularly by the too rapid reduction of more than eighteen millions of the public debt, between the months of June 1817, and November 1818, and the utter impracticability of converting in due time any reasonable portion of the specific public deposits into such funds as the public creditors were entitled to demand, without hazarding the prostration of many respectable institutions."

* Weekly Register, April 11th, 1818.

As Banks are the creatures of Government, all the evils they produce must be ascribed to the Government.   It is to afford opportunities for speculation to themselves, their personal friends and their political partisans, that our law-givers establish Banks. It was through the attempt to carry on the war by means of Bank notes and Bank credits, that the suspension of specie payments was produced. It was through the connivance of the Government, that the suspension of specie payments was so long continued. It was through the issue of treasury notes, that the amount of Bank notes in cir-culation was immediately increased.   It was that a large amount of public stock might be absorbed, that a Bank was instituted with a capital of thirty-five millions, when there was not room for a credit Bank with a capital of thirty-five thousands. No doubt, also, the disinclination of the Govern-ment to suffer the Bank to retain the eighteen millions of public moneys, mentioned by " A Friendly Monitor," had its effect. If the Government had been content to con-tinue to pay the interest on a corresponding amount of public debt, and to let the Bank keep eighteen millions of the public money for its own uses, the crisis might have been—we will not say averted, but it might have been de-layed.   If it had been delayed, the evil would have been increased.   The notion of the early administrators of the Bank of the United States, appears to have been, that the Bank should do a business bearing the same proportion to its great capital, that the business of the local Banks bore to their small capitals.   If the payment of any portion of the national debt had been deferred to suit their conve-nience, they would have made a corresponding increase in their business. Even as it was, we have found them com-plaining, in the spring of 1818, that they could not sign notes fast enough : and the report of the committee of Congress shows, that all the energies of the directors were exerted to increase the circulation, extend the gene-ral dealings of the Bank, and raise the price of the stock in the market.

Other men in their situation would probably have acted as they did. It is of very little moment whether it is Mr. Wig-gins or Mr. Spriggins that is president of a Bank, or whe-ther the Jones' or the Giles' are directors. *The fault is in the system.* Give the management of it to the wisest and best men in the country, and still it will produce evil.   No new principles of action were introduced by the early administration of the United States' Bank. If the members of Congress who granted the charter did not know that the usual way of paying all instalments after the first is by discounting stock notes, they had not much acquaintance with either the theory or the history of Banking. As little credit must be given them for intelligence in respect to money corporations, if they did not know that the practice of those who wish to get the control of such institutions is, to divide their shares, as was done by certain gentlemen in Baltimore and others in Philadelphia. It was not, surely, to be expected, that men who associated with the professed design of making profit for themselves, and who admitted the Government as a partner, should trammel themselves with restrictions which the Legislature had, either through design or oversight, failed to impose. If the courts of law have not absolutely decided that whatever is not expressly forbidden is granted in a charter, the Banks find it very convenient to act on such an assumption.

The history of the country from 1814 to 1818, exhibits nothing more than the natural results of Banking by corporations, and with paper money, while the Government, embarrassed in its fiscal concerns, wanted the inclination or perhaps the ability to apply an adequate remedy. The reaction of 1818–19 was only the natural result of the different operations of the preceding years. The irregular Banking in the South and West in subsequent years, is only a link a little lower down in the same chain of consequences.

It would appear as if the suspension and resumption of specie payments might have been productive of little embarrassment, comparatively speaking, if the Government had, immediately on the close of the war, refused to receive inconvertible notes in payment of duties. The few Banks which then existed in Ohio and Kentucky had suspended payment only a month or two. The Bank of Nashville actually maintained specie payments. The dealings of the Banks in the Southern States were of moderate extent. The new Banks of Pennsylvania were not yet in full operation. The principal part of the over-issue was by the Banks of the great cities of the Middle States, and these Banks might, by a sale of the public stocks they held, have obtained the means of redeeming their excess of paper.

If this had been done we should have escaped the particular evils recorded in the foregoing chapters, but we should probably have experienced evils proceeding from the same source in another form. It was four or five years before the war, that Banking in New England produced consequences similar to those felt in the other States four or five years after the war. As the mania spread through New York, into Pennsylvania, and thence South and West, Banks were established without those restrictions which experience in New England had proved to be necessary.

To impose such restrictions would, in fact, have been hardly in accordance with the philosophy of the day. A ruling principle in this was, as may be seen by the quotations we have given from the writings of various eminent men, that inconvertible Bank notes, if they were not quite as good as gold and silver, were very little inferior to them as a circulating medium. Many of our readers may smile at such notions now; but perhaps if they had lived in those days, they would have thought as their neighbors thought. Perhaps the present popular notions on the subject of Banks, will, some twenty years hence, be regarded in the same light as those notions of the anti-bullionists are at the present period.

That " *love* of money which is the root of all evil," and which, operating through the medium of incorporations and paper bills, is productive of so much evil, would have brought on the nation great calamities, if we had remained at peace. The war, and the measures consequent thereon, gave that evil its particular form and feature. It is that same " love of money" which now gives plausibility to the sophistry by which the present Banking system is supported, as well in the minds of those who suffer as in the minds of those who are benefitted by the system. Hence it is that the former are so easily persuaded that what is gained by the use of paper money is so much gained by the nation, and not so much gained by *one part* of the nation from *another part*. It is so hard for any man, be he merchant, or be he drayman, to be content with his earnings—we are all so anxious to become rich in a hurry, that we readily become the dupes of one another, and sometimes in our haste we dupe ourselves.

CHAPTER XIX.

Of Banking from 1820–21 *to* 1825–26.

To tell of all the expansions and contractions that have occurred since the first grand curtailment was made by the United States' Bank, would require a large volume. Our country is so extensive, and the causes that affect Bank medium are so various, that, while one part of the Union is suffering all the evils of scarcity of money, another may be in the height of that apparent prosperity which is produced by an increasing paper currency. It is by no means unusual for a contraction to begin on the sea-board, before the full effects of the previous expansion have been felt in the interior ; or for expansions to recommence on the sea-board, soon after the inland Banks find the necessity of restricting their issues.

Each Bank has its own sphere of operation, within which there may be contractions and expansions not sensibly affecting any but those within that sphere. But, from desire to increase their profits, the different Banks not unfrequently encroach on each other's spheres, by which more extensive disorders are produced. The action of the Banks among themselves has been compared to that of so many drunken men passing along the street together, occasionally supporting one another, and occasionally knocking one another down. Their motion is vacillating, tottering. It is seldom in a straight line.

An attempt to enumerate all the vibrations of Bank medium, would therefore be idle. But, from a careful inspection of files of the United States Gazette for 1821 and 1822, and of the Philadelphia Gazette for subsequent years, we are able to give the following view of variations of the money market, embracing all the most important expansions and contractions.

1821. Business dull in the beginning of the year. The effects of an expansion apparently commenced in the Spring, begin to be felt in June or July, and by October the spirit of speculation is tolerably active.

1822. A reaction commences in May, the effects of which are felt through the rest of the year.

1823. The Bank of the United States receives the notes of all its branches, and begins to extend its operations.

1824. The Banks increase their issues, and the spirit of speculation becomes excited.

1825. The consequences of the great reaction of 1818–19 are not over in the interior : but on the seaboard the effects of the expansion, begun in 1823 and continued through 1824, are felt in the rise of property and general briskness of business. In July or August a violent reaction commences.

1826. The effects of the reaction are felt through the greater part of the year.

1827. Money plenty. The United States' Bank commences issuing Branch drafts for small amounts.

1828. Sudden and alarming scarcity of money in May, and again in September.

1829. Money is scarce till July. It afterwards becomes plenty.

1830. Money plenty.

1831. Money very plenty till October. Then a reactiou begins.

1832. Money scarce. Towards the close of the year, the pressure abates in Philadelphia : but it is not appa rently diminished in some other parts of the country.

In the Middle States are placed the United States' Bank, and some of its most important branches, and here are collected and disbursed the greater part of the public revenues. The heart of the Banking system is here, and while it is affected, in a greater or less degree, by whatever affects the extremities, it, in its turn, has a powerful operation on the remote parts of the Union.

In the years 1820 and 1821, the Banks of the Middle States settled down into what Mr. Niles calls a state of regularity. The notes of many of them became mere broker's merchandise, and the discount on those which remained current, did not exceed the cost of transporting specie from the place where they were issued to the place where they were circulated.

A fair field was then first opened for the credit operations of the Bank of the United States.   But by this time
confidence was destroyed, and the spirit of enterprize was
chilled.   " There is now," says Mr. Niles, on the 3d of
February, 1821, " little demand for money, except to answer the current purposes of life, and pay old debts, for
either of which it is difficult enough to get, though apparently abundant enough."   The capitalists of New York
made great complaints in March of the difficulty they
found in investing their funds : though at this very time,
the country papers were teeming with advertisements by
the sheriff; and three hundred and fifty persons in Baltimore made application, in the month of May, for the benefit of the insolvent laws of Maryland.   A tradesman in
Philadelphia advertised for a shop boy, and fifty applications were made for the place in three days.*   The building of a new ship excited quite a sensation, as something
out of the common order of things.   The fear of moneyed
men to embark in new enterprizes, left many laboring people without employment.   Solvent men had little disposition to borrow, for they could not tell if prices had yet
reached their lowest limit, or form a satisfactory conclusion
as to the state of affairs in coming years.
   In the interior of Pennsylvania, the people were clamorous for the establishment of a State Loan Office.   Nor is
this to be wondered at.   In the month of June, the Sheriff
of Bedford filled two newspaper columns and a half with
his advertisements : and the Sheriff of Berks offered for
sale 3000 acres of land, besides town lots.   In August,
fifty-seven farms were advertised for sale by the Sheriff of
Westmoreland, sixty-three pieces of property by the Sheriff
of Northampton, and thirty-seven by the Sheriff of Mifflin.
In October, the Sheriff of Cumberland advertised for sale
2,380 acres of land, besides twelve town lots with handsome improvements : and in December, the Sheriff of
Berks offered for sale the property of forty persons.   From
the state of things in six of the fifty-two counties of Pennsylvania, the reader may form some idea of the condition of
affairs generally.
   In April or May, 1821, as nearly as can be ascertained,

* See United States Gazette of June 20th.

the city Banks began to expand, and the effects of this expansion were sensibly felt in August, and still more sensibly in October. Tired of a protracted state of inactivity, many men began to employ their capitals and their credit, at a risk rather than on calculation. For some months things wore a pleasing aspect : but in April and May, 1822, the prospect was again clouded over. Some kinds of imported goods fell 15 per cent. in Philadelphia ; and United States' Bank stock, which had been held at 115 in in February, was sold in New York on the first of May at 102, and fell before night to 98½.

Other kinds of public securities experienced a depreciation, but the fall in United States' Bank stock being greatest, naturally attracted most attention. It was attributed by some to the machinations of brokers, and by others to a loan of five millions made by the Bank to the Government, and to the quantity of stock hypothecated to the different Banks and insurance offices in New York and other places.

It is certain that the evils produced by paper money Banks, are greatly increased by the dealings of these institutions with Government. The transactions are so large as usually to derange the regular train of mercantile operations. The heavy deposits of Government enable the Banks, at times, to extend their discounts further than is proper. Their payment of these deposits, and the making of heavy loans to Government, usually compel them to curtail their accommodations to men of business.

But it is of less moment for us to know what particular operations of the Banks caused the sufferings of 1822, than to know that these sufferings were the consequences of over-trading produced by over-banking. That there was an excess of paper issues in part of 1821 and 1822, is evident from the fact that, according to the official returns, the exports of specie in the year ending September 30th, 1822, amounted to 10,781,933 dollars, and those of bullion to 28,248, while the imports of specie for the same period amounted to only 2,958,402 dollars, and those of bullion to 411,444. A Boston paper says that from the 1st of January to the 1st of June, 1822, the imports of specie into that port amounted to only 70,000 dollars, while the exports, in the same period, to the East Indies, Brazil, England, and

Cuba, amounted to one million two hundred and five thousand five hundred and six dollars. At one time in 1821, there were 2,434,000 dollars in specie in the vaults of the Boston Banks, and by June, 1822, this amount was reduced to 430,000. In the same period, the specie in the vaults of the United States' Bank and its branches was reduced from 7,643,140 to 3,334,452 dollars.

On the 29th of June, Mr. Niles remarked that forty-two merchants of Boston had stopped payment within the period of a month; and on the 3d of August, he made a quotation to the following effect from a Salem paper : " We regret to learn that failures continue to take place almost daily at Boston, some of them of persons extensively engaged in commerce. We are informed that within the last two months, there have been more than eighty failures in that city. The embarrassment, distress, and alarm, which such a state of things must necessarily produce, are indeed a serious calamity." The amount of these failures, for the last two months, adds Mr. Niles, is said to be more than three millions of dollars.

There were also failures in New York, and many of the operative manufacturers of Philadelphia were deprived of employment.

Throughout the year business was very vacillating. In the latter part of it, there appears to have been another sudden shock given to trade ; for it is mentioned in the United States Gazette of December 13th, that some species of cotton and woollen goods had fallen fifty per cent. in the course of a few weeks.

Bills on London, which were at $111\frac{1}{2}$ a $112\frac{1}{2}$, in February, 1822, were quoted in the Philadelphia Gazette of May 14th, 1823, at $104\frac{1}{2}$. The true par being, according to Mr. Gallatin, seven per cent. above the nominal par, the foreign exchanges were decidedly in favor of the country. A combination of causes compelled the Banks to be cautious this year in their operations. The condition of things in the Southern and Western parts of the Union, prevented the United States' Bank from extending its dealings as far as it desired. The Pennsylvania Banks felt the uncertainty of their fate. The charters of many of them were about expiring, and applications for a renewal of them, made to the Legislature in the sessions of 1821–22, and 1822–23, had been defeated. The city of New York was flooded with the notes of a number of small institutions in the country parts of that State, and of other States. These notes, though they were not on a par with specie, constituted the principal medium of retail trade.

The Bank interest was very powerful in the Pennsylvania Legislature in the session of 1822--23 ; but the dominant party feared to pass a bill to extend the charters of the ⁓Banks of 1814, as it might have an unfavorable effect on the election for Governor in October. When the election was over, the chief obstacle to the operations of the Banking interest was removed, and a bill was passed in March, 1824, for re-incorporating *every one* of the Banks of 1814 which had applied for a renewal of its charter.* About the same time, the Bank mania broke out afresh in some of the other States, and it seemed, in the latter part of 1824, and the beginning of 1825, as if the days of 1815 and 1816 were about returning in America, and those of the South Sea bubble in England.

The infatuation, if we may be permitted to call it by so mild a name; was most violent in New York. The speculators of that city, not content with such privileges as their own Legislature could bestow, prevailed, by means of bonuses, on the Legislature of New Jersey to establish a string of small moneyed corporations along the shore of the North River ; and, in defiance of the statutes of Pennsylvania, took possession of coal lands within her limits, under the color of charters granted by another State. Their own Legislature they besieged in every possible form. During the session which commenced in January, 1825, application was made for charters for new Banking, Insurance, and other companies, with nominal capitals of the amount of *fifty-two million dollars.*

Money was never more abundant, if a judgment could be formed from subscriptions to the stock of such companies as succeeded in their applications for charters. Three million dollars were subscribed in one day, in January, to the stock of the New Jersey Lombard and Protection Company, though its capital, as fixed by law, was only three

---

* The Silver Lake Bank is perhaps an exception. Its charter was renewed, but we are not certain whether it was at this or at a succeeding session.

hundred thousand dollars. Nine million dollars were subscribed in April to the New York Water Works Company,
and by some contrivance its script was raised in the market
to thirty per cent. above par. Thirteen millions were subscribed in May to the stock of the Delaware and Raritan
Canal Company. Between the 5th and the 16th of February, the stock of the New York Gas Company advanced
28 per cent., and was sold at 178.

It was not alone in dealings in the stocks of chartered
companies that great activity prevailed. More commercial
business was said to have been done in Philadelphia, in the
month of February, than in any one month of the preceding ten years. The Banks were liberal in their discounts,
and the spirit of speculation showed itself in various forms.

While the public mind was in this state, seven expresses
arrived at Philadelphia from New York in one day (April
9th) with news of a great rise of prices in the markets of
Liverpool and London. The effect was electric. Twenty-
seven cents were offered for Upland cotton, and refused,
though the holders would, a week before, have been happy
to obtain twenty cents. Cotton yarn, No. 15, rose from 35
to 45 cents. Muscovado sugars advanced a dollar a hundred.
St. Domingo coffee rose from $17\frac{1}{2}$ to 21 cents a pound.
Quercitron bark rose from 27 dollars a ton to 35 dollars.
The rise in the prices of tobacco, drugs, and spices, was
very considerable.

Every body was in haste to grow rich : and the cotton
dealers were regarded with special envy. It was currently
rumored that such a man had made 20,000 dollars in one
day ; such another, 30,000 ; such another, 40,000, and such
another 50,000. Some firms, if reports were to be believed,
had realized 100,000 ; while the computed or prospective
gains of others were swelled to nearly half a million.

In New York, the speculations were carried to a much
greater extent than in Philadelphia ; and despatches sent
to the South spread the infection through all that region.
The Charleston Patriot, to show the state of feeling, mentioned that " the same parcel of cotton had changed owners six or seven times within a week, without leaving the
hands of the factor." It was in this year, that the growing crop of corn was rooted up in some parts of the Southern States, to make room for new plantations of cotton.

The cotton mania continued to rage, with more or less violence, through the months of May and June. But in July news was received of a decline of 3d. a pound in the price of cotton at Liverpool, and a pressure for money was soon felt in New York. In the next month, the pressure increased, and between August and December, there were fifty failures in New York, and thirty in the Southern cities. Towards the close of the year, the pressure for money in Boston was very alarming. Exchange on England, which was at five per cent. in the spring, rose to ten per cent. in September. New Orleans notes, which were at two or three per cent. discount at Philadelphia in the spring, fell on the 21st of September to fifteen per cent., and were quoted on the 28th of the same month, at fifty-six per cent. below par. On the 4th of December, the same notes were quoted at only four per cent. discount, exhibiting a remarkable example of rise and fall in the space of a few months.

Many of the Banks were in great difficulties. Several of them broke. And such were the straits of the United States' Bank, that one of the directors talked publicly on the Exchange at Philadelphia of the expediency of suspending specie payments.

Mr. Biddle, the President of the United States' Bank, says, " The fall of 1825 was probably the most disastrous period in the financial history of England. It was then that the wild speculations in the American mines, and the still wilder speculations in American cottons, recoiled upon England, and spread over it extensive ruin. In the midst of this suffering, it required little to produce a panic, and accordingly there ensued a state of dismay, which, for a time, threatened to involve all interests in confusion. There was, probably, at no period of English history, so intense and general a distress as there was in December 1825.

" Now, the very same storm which thus broke on England, passed over this country a few weeks before : it was on the eve of producing precisely the same results ; and certainly I have never felt any uneasiness about the Banks of this country except on that occasion. Just as the difficulties were commencing, the Government paid off, on the the 1st of October, a loan of seven millions, of which $3,366,761 64 were payable in Philadelphia. The payment of this sum by the Bank, of course diminished its means for active business, and brought it largely in debt to the State Banks both of Philadelphia and New York. It became, therefore, an object of extreme solicitude to prepare for the relief of the community, and provide for the danger which was obviously approaching.

" The first object of the Bank was to relieve itself from the debt which the payment of the seven millions threw upon it. Accordingly, it began by making sales of its funded debt and Bank stock at New York, and Boston, and Philadelphia, amounting, in the month of October, to $1,828,210 19 in funded debt alone, and by husbanding all its means till it could place itself in a state of perfect security.

" By the first of November, the Bank was extricated from debt, and continued daily to strengthen itself. In the midst of the difficulties of the community, two circumstances contributed to increase them : the one was a heavy demand for specie for the use of the British army in Canada ; the other was a similar demand for specie, to pay the instalments of a new Bank then recently established at New Orleans. This want was to be supplied before any ease could be extended to the community, and it was pressing with extreme urgency. The effect of it was to inspire a general distrust and alarm, and, by the middle of November, all the indications, which it was impossible to mistake, denoted an approaching panic, which would have been fatal to the country. If the strength and wealth of England could not withstand such an alarm, its effects on this country would have been incalculable. That moment seemed to me to be the very crisis of the country, to be met only by some decided and resolute step, to rally the confidence of the community. In such a situation I did not hesitate on the course which my duty prescribed. I went immediately to New York, where I sought the gentleman who was preparing to draw specie from the Banks of Philadelphia, in order to send it to New Orleans, and gave him drafts on that city. These drafts were not given to protect the Bank itself, which was then a creditor of the Philadelphia Banks for more than the amount of them, but they were employed to arrest from these city Banks a drain which could not fail to embarrass them. I then endeavored to ascertain the real state of things by separating the danger from the alarm, and having done so, on the 22d of November, the letter annexed was addressed to the Branch at New York, suggesting the propriety of increasing its loans.

" From this moment confidence revived, and the danger passed. I then thought, and still think, that this measure, the increase of the loans of the Banks, in the face of an approaching panic, could alone have averted the same consequences, which, in a few days afterwards, were operating with such fatal effect upon England. I have never doubted that the delay of a week would have been of infinite injury, and the prompt interposition of the Bank was the occasion of protecting the country from a general calamity."

It is very possible that the means taken by Mr. Biddle were the only ones by which a panic could be prevented ; but, what ought we think of a system by which the pecuniary salvation of the country is made to depend on one man's hurrying by night from Philadelphia to New York, to prevail on another man to accept drafts on New Orleans in place of specie ? The establishment of a new Bank is, in the United States, an event of every day occurrence : and the business is so well understood, that the amount of specie required for such a purpose is very trifling. What sum was wanted for the use of the British army in Canada, is not mentioned ; but as the British Government must have given an equivalent for it, it diminished, in the same amount, the demand for remittances to England. If there had not been the two particular demands mentioned by Mr. Biddle, there would have been demands for something else.

There is what Mr. John Quincy Adams calls, " a galvanic sympathy" between the paper money Banks of different countries : and it is certainly no small objection to our present system that it makes us liable to be affected injuriously by every derangement in the currency, commercial concerns, or financial affairs of Great Britain. So intimate and so manifold are the connections of the two countries, that an expansion or contraction never takes place in England, without being accompanied or followed by an expansion or contraction in the United States. We have, also, expansions and contractions independent of

those of Great Britain : but when the causes of the variations of Bank medium operate simultaneously in both
countries, the effects are very striking.

The state of confidence between man and man, and the
state of the currency in some parts of the Union, were not
such as to admit of as great an increase of Bank medium
in the United States as took place in England in 1824 and
1825. The effects of the great reaction of 1818–19 were
not yet over. In Kentucky, society was in a state border-
ing on anarchy. In Alabama and Tennessee, the paper
of the local Banks was much below par. Ohio, Indiana,
Illinois, and Missouri had not recovered from the effects of
the relief system. The currencies of Georgia and North
Carolina were very vacillating. The city Banks of New
York had for two years, beginning with the summer of
1823, been endeavoring to restrict the petty Banks of
their neighborhood, and in so doing had limited their own
circulation. In New England there was a war between
the allied Banks of Boston and the country Banks, which
caused a great pressure for money in the Eastern States,
in the month of May, or at the very time when there was
so much commercial activity in the southern cities. In
the interior of Pennsylvania, the sheriffs had not yet got
through the duty of selling the estates of those who had
been made bankrupt by the operations of the years 1818
and 1819.*

While the country was in this condition, it was impossible for Banks maintaining specie payments to make any
great addition to their issues. In point of fact, the actual
increase of Bank currency in 1824 and 1825, appears not
to have been very great : but the state of affairs was not
such as to admit of any increase of credit dealings, without

---

* The Sheriff of Adams County advertised thirty-three estates for
sale in the month of May. The Juniata Gazette, on one day of July,
contained thirty-two advertisements by the Sheriff. The Sheriff of
Fayette, in the month of June, offered for sale 118 tracts of land, containing 45,000 acres, or one-eleventh part of the county. Most of this
was the property of one person. In the same month the Sheriff of
Bedford offered for sale twenty-three estates, and the Sheriff of Westmoreland, twenty-six. In December, 48 estates, containing together
3342 acres of land, with farm houses, barns, grist mills, and other improvements, belonging to thirty-one different persons, were offered for
sale by the Sheriff of Berks.

jeoparding a great variety of interests. It was owing to this, that, though the expansion was such as might under other circumstances have been regarded as inconsiderable, the effects of the necessary reaction were felt through the greater part of the year 1826, in a general dullness of business. In the Southern States, the consequences were most trying, as the 'high price of cotton had led to an over-extension of the culture of that article, and as the planters, encouraged by the demand for their staple, had plunged themselves in debt to support their style of living. The manufacturers of cotton were, also, great sufferers. Cotton cloth which it cost 18 cents a yard to import in 1825, was imported in the spring of 1826, at 13 cents. It was said that of four thousand weavers employed in Philadelphia in 1825, not more than one thousand had employment in May 1826.

It must be admitted, however, that the reaction was attended with one good effect, and that was in checking the operations of the New York speculators. Unaffected by all the disasters which the community were suffering, they made application to the Legislature, at the session commencing in January 1826, for charters for *twenty-seven* new Banks in the city of New York, with nominal capitals of 22,500,000 dollars, for *thirty-seven* new Banks in the other parts of the State, with nominal capitals of 19,250,000 dollars, for *twenty-six* other joint stockcompanies in the city of New York, with capitals of 14,350,000 dollars, and for *thirty-three* in other parts of the State, with capitals of 5,437,000 dollars, making in all 123 Banking and other joint stock companies, with nominal capitals of the amount of 55,537,000 dollars. The Legislature having at its previous session incorporated *twenty-two* Banks and loan offices, and *twenty-six* insurance companies, prudently refused to extend the system any further for the present.

The wisdom of this course soon became manifest. In April 1826, the Marble Manufacturing Company, a newly instituted, bond-issuing concern, became bankrupt. This was followed in July by the bankruptcy of the Dundaff and New Hope Banks of Pennsylvania, the Jersey City Bank and Patterson Bank of New Jersey, the Green County Bank of New York, the United States' Lombard, the

Franklin Manufacturing Company, the Hudson Insurance Company, and the New York Life Insurance Company; these were again followed, in August and September, by the bankruptcies of the New York Mount Hope Loan, the Sun Fire Insurance, the Greenwich Insurance, and the Protection Fire Insurance Company.

When an injunction was issued in the case of the Tradesman's Bank, a run commenced on all the Banks of the city of New York. It is probable that if they had been exposed to such a run twelve months sooner, very disastrous consequences would have ensued. But by this time the foreign demand for specie had abated. The exports of gold and silver from the port of Philadelphia in the months of June and July were only 500,501 dollars, against 2,136,151 in the corresponding months of 1825. Credit dealings having been diminished, and the amount of specie in the country having been increased, the New York City Banks were enabled to save themselves, and thereby to save all the Banks from Maine to Louisiana; for a stoppage of payment by them, would have produced a run on all the Banks in the Union.

The bankruptcy of some of the New York moneyed corporations, revealed secrets to the public which led to a legal investigation, and as it is always the practice of the world to punish unsuccessful villainy, some of the concerned were severely dealt with. Previous to passing sentence on them, Judge Edwards made following observations: "During the trials which have taken place at the present term of this court, we have witnessed displays of depravity on the part of the agents of moneyed institutions of the most appalling nature. As common as crimes are in all great cities, yet this community was not prepared to expect from the *class of society* to which the perpetrators of the crimes belonged, a *burst* of such iniquity. Their offences have been characterized by breaches of official and personal confidence; by a course of misrepresentation and deception systematically pursued, and by injurious and crafty devices which no ordinary prudence could guard against. Nor was this all. Among the actors in those scenes were some of the principal agents in the management of moneyed institutions, and they have been found actually combining and conspiring together for the accomplishment of their nefarious purposes.

" From combinations of men of so much talent, availing themselves of their high standing, it is not surprising that they should have swept society with the besom of destruction. When crimes of such character, attended with such destructive consequences abound, it behooves the tribunals of justice to gather themselves up to meet the occasion, and to extend, as far as in them lies, the protecting arm of the law."

The court sentenced two of the persons who were convicted to imprisonment for two years, and two others for one year.

A writer in a New Hampshire paper, says, after briefly relating these facts—" In some of the other States, justice has too long slumbered. The guilty have escaped with impunity, but the innocent and unsuspecting have been plundered without redress."

CHAPTER XX.

Of Banking from 1826-27 to 1828-29.

Mr. John F. Watson, the Cashier of the Bank of Germantown, in his " Annals of Philadelphia," gives the following testimony of an ancient lady, respecting the manner in which commercial affairs were conducted previous to the Revolutionary War. " If a citizen failed in business, it was a cause of general and deep regret. Every man who met his neighbor, spoke of his chagrin. It was a rare occurrence, because honesty and temperance in trade were then universal."

In another part of his book, Mr. Watson speaks of the changes which have in this respect taken place, within his own short period of observation. " When I was a boy, as none got suddenly rich by monopolies, they went through whole lives gradually but surely augmenting their estates, without the least fear of misfortune or bankruptcy. When it did rarely occur, such was the surprise and general sympathy of the public, that citizens saluted each other with sad faces, and made their regrets and condolence a matter of common concern. An aged person has told me, that, when the proprietor of that large house, formerly the Post Office (now the National Hotel) at the corner of Chesnut street and Carpenter's Court, suddenly failed in business, the whole house was closely shut up. for one week, as an emblem of the deepest family mourning, and all who passed the house instinctively stopped, and mingled the expressions of their liveliest regret.   Now how are changed matters in those particulars."

They are so changed, that a certain number of bankruptcies and insolvencies in the course of a year, are regarded as being as much within the order of nature as a certain number of deaths.   Periodical redundancies and scarcities of money are looked for as naturally as cold in winter or heat in summer.   If a great storm occurs, or a pestilence sweeps over the land, the journalists record it : and so they record great pressures for money, but they think no more of noting the effects of ordinary "expansions" and "contractions" than of noting the ordinary variations of the weather.

A gentleman who resided for twenty-five years in the town of Barcelona, a town which does most of the import and export business of the fertile and industrious province of Catalonia, has told us that during the whole period of his residence there, but one bankruptcy occurred.   It may be difficult for many Americans of the present day to conceive such a state of things to be possible.   But it is possible; and a faithful relation of the pecuniary vicissitudes of one of our ordinary years, might be received as incredulously by many plain Swiss and Hollanders, as some Americans receive accounts of countries and cities where bankruptcies and insolvencies are events of rare occurrence.

But, to return to our narrative.   By September, 1826, the violence of the reaction which followed the expansion of 1824–25, had subsided : and through the year 1827, things went on smoothly.   The two first months of 1828 also passed over without any convulsion : but in the beginning of March, a sudden and unexpected scarcity of money was felt in Philadelphia.

If we were engaged in frequent wars, or if the state of the world at large was such as it was in the twenty years which followed the French Revolution, ingenuity might be able to give a plausible view of the causes of the frequent scarcities of money, independent of the operations of Banking institutions. But we have enjoyed peace for seventeen years in succession. Most other commercial countries have been in the enjoyment of peace. It has, therefore, become impossible to conceal from observers, the effects which paper money Banking institutions have on commercial affairs. That the scarcity of money in 1828 was owing to their operations, was so evident, that no body doubted, nobody disputed it. No other cause could be assigned for it. And Mr. Biddle, the President of the United States' Bank, published an essay in the National Gazette, on the 10th of April, in which he gave the following elegant and lucid exposition of one of the causes of the evils the community was then suffering.

" The question is, what is the cause and the nature of the present scarcity of money?

" The answer is easy.

" The currency of the United States consists of coin, and of Bank notes promising to pay coin. As long as the Banks can always pay the coin they promise they are useful, because, in a country where the moneyed capital is disproportioned to the means of employing capital, the substitution of credits for coins enables the nation to make its exchanges with less coin, and of course, saves the expense of that coin. But this advantage has by its side a great danger. Banks are often directed by needy persons, who borrow too much, or by sanguine persons, anxious only to increase the profits, without much pecuniary interest or personal responsibility in the administration. The constant tendency of Banks is, therefore, to lend too much, and to put too many notes in circulation. Now, the addition of many notes, even while they are as good as coin by being always exchangeable for coin, may be injurious, because the increase of the mixed mass of money generally.occasions a rise in the price of all commodities. The consequence is, that the high price of foreign productions tempts foreigners to send a large amount of their commodities, while the high price of domestic productions prevents these foreigners from taking in exchange a large amount of our commodities. When, therefore, you buy from foreigners more than they buy from you, as they cannot take the paper part of your currency, they must take the coin part. If

this is done to a considerable extent, the danger is that the
Banks will be obliged to pay so much of their coin for their
notes as not to leave them a sufficient quantity to answer the
demand for it, in which case the Banks fail, and the community is defrauded. To prevent this, a prudent Bank, the
moment it perceives an unusual demand for its notes, and
has reason to fear a drain on its vaults, should immediately diminish the amount of its notes, and call in part of its
debts. So, on a large scale, when the Banks of a country
perceive such a demand for coin for exportation as diminishes too much the stock of coin necessary for their Banking purposes, they should stop the exportation. This they
can always do if their affairs have been well managed : and
here lies the test of Bank management.

"The law of a mixed currency of coin and paper is,
that when, from superabundance of the mixed mass, too
much of the coin part leaves the country, the remainder
must be preserved by diminishing the paper part, so as
to make the mixed mass more valuable in proportion. It
is this capacity of diminishing the paper which protects it.
Its value consists in its elasticity—its power of alternate
expansion and contraction, to suit the state of the community; and when it loses its flexibility, it no longer contains
within itself the means of its own defence, and is full of
hazard. In truth, the merit of a Bank is nearly in proportion to the degree of this flexibility of its means. If a
Bank lends its money on mortgages, on stocks—for long
terms, and to persons careless of protests, it incurs this
great risk, that, on the one hand, its notes are payable on
demand, while, on the other, its debts cannot be called in
without great delay—a delay fatal to its credit and character. This is the general error of Banks, who do not always discriminate between two things essentially distinct in
Banking, a debt ultimately secure, and a debt certainly
payable. But a well-managed Bank has its funds mainly
in short loans to persons in business—the result of business
transactions—payable on a day named, which the parties
are able to pay and will pay at any sacrifice, in order to escape mercantile dishonor. Such a Bank has its funds,
therefore, constantly repaid into it, and is able to say whether it will or will not, lend them out again.

" A Bank so managed, if it finds too much demand for

its coin to go abroad, begins by not lending more than it receives every day, and then goes farther, by not lending as much as its income, declining to renew the notes of its debtors, and obliging them to pay a part or the whole : making it a rule to keep its discounts within its income. The operation proceeds thus : by issuing no new notes, but requiring something from your debtors, you oblige them to return to you the Bank notes you lent them, or their equivalents. This makes the Bank notes scarcer—this makes them more valuable—this makes the goods for which they are generally exchanged less valuable—the debtor, in his anxiety to get your notes, being willing to sell his goods at a sacrifice—this brings down the prices of goods, and makes every thing cheaper. Then the remedy begins. The foreigner, finding that his goods must be sold so low, sends no more. The American importer, finding that he cannot make money by importing them, imports no more. The remainder of the coin, of course, is not sent out after new importations, but stays at home, where it finds better employment in purchasing these cheap articles; and when the foreigner hears of this state of things, he sends back the coin he took away. He took it away merely because your own domestic productions were so high that he could not make any profit in his country by taking them. But when the news reaches him that his productions are very cheap in our country, he will also learn that our productions are cheap too, and he sends back the coin to buy these cheap productions of ours. We, therefore, get back our coin by diminishing our paper, and it will stay until drawn away by another superabundance of paper. Such is the circle which a mixed currency is always describing. Like the power of steam, it is eminently useful in prudent hands, but of tremendous hazard when not controlled ; and the practical wisdom in managing it lies in seizing the proper moment to expand and contract it—taking care, in working with such explosive materials, whenever there is doubt, to incline to the side of safety.

  " These simple elements explain the present situation of the country. Its disorder is over-trading, brought on by over-banking. The remedy is to bank less, and to trade less.

  " During the last year, money was very abundant—that

is, the demand for coin being small in proportion, the Banks distributed freely their discounts and notes. This plenty concurred with other causes, especially the expectation of a new tariff, to induce an increased importation of foreign goods, and, at the same time, furnish great facility for procuring them on credit. For instance, in the difficulty of procuring profitable investments, there were found capitalists who exported the coin of the country, and sold their bills for it on credit—thus obtaining a small profit on the shipment, and a greater on the discount of the notes taken for their bills. This fraction of a per centage on the shipment of coin, seems to be a trifling gain for the great inconvenience to which it often subjects the community ; but the profit, though small, is lawful, and no odium should attach to the agents, for the operation is often a wholesome corrective of excessive issues of paper. The effect was, that by the month of February, the exportations of specie to France and England had become unusually large, amounting, probably, in the preceding twelve months, to between four and five million dollars; and great importations were constantly arriving, and which, when sold, would require remittances to Europe. Hitherto, at this season, the demand for exchange had been supplied by the bills drawn on the produce of the South, when shipped to Europe ; but this year the crop, and with it the bills produced by it, has come tardily into the market, so that the demands of exchange for the proceeds of the arriving shipments were directed immediately to the exhausted vaults of the Banks. Such an effect was to be averted without loss of time. The directors of the Bank of the United States, as was their natural duty, were the first to perceive the danger, and the Bank was immediately placed in a situation of great strength and repose. The State Banks followed its example. They began by restraining their loans within their income, and gradually and quietly decreasing the amount of them, and more especially directing their retrenchments on those whose operations were particularly connected with the exportations they desired to prevent. The course of business has been this : A merchant borrows from the Banks and sends abroad $100,000 in coin, or he buys bills from one who has shipped the coin. With these he imports a cargo of goods—obtaining a long credit for the duties—sends

them to auction, where they are sold, and the auctioneer's
notes given for them. These notes are discounted by the
Banks, and the merchant is then put in possession of another $100,000, which he again ships, and thus he proceeds
in an endless circle, as long as the Banks, by discounting
his notes, enable him to send the coin, and tempt him to do
so, by keeping up prices here by their excessive issues.
The Banks, therefore, begin by diminishing or withdraw-
ing these artificial facilities, leaving the persons directly
concerned in this trade to act as they please with their
own funds, but not with the funds of the Banks. The immediate consequence is, that the auctioneers can no longer advance the money for entire cargoes—that they no
longer sell for credit, but for cash—that the price of goods
falls—that instead of being sold in large masses, they are
sold slowly and in small parcels, so that the importer is not
able to remit the proceeds in large amounts. This diminishes the demand for bills and for specie to send abroad.
In the meantime, the importer, finding the prices of his
goods fall, imports no more ; and the shipper of coin, finding less demand for exchange, and that he can make more
of his money by using it at home than by exporting it, ab-
stains from sending it abroad. Time is thus gained till the
arrival of the Southern exchange, which will supply the
demand without the aid of the coin, and then every thing
resumes its accustomed course.

"This is the point to which the present measures of the
Banks are tending. The purpose must be accomplished,
in a longer or shorter time, with a greater or less degree of
pressure, but the effect must and will be produced."

This account, *mutatis mutandis*, will serve for a history
of Banking in almost any year. "*Such is the circle a
mixed currency is always describing.*" The only difference is, that the circle is sometimes wider and sometimes
narrower.

"*The constant tendency of Banks is to lend too much,
and to put too many notes in circulation.*" Sometimes it
is a demand for specie to establish a new institution at
New Orleans, that compels them to diminish their issues ;
sometimes it is a demand for specie for the use of the British army in Canada, sometimes the crop of cotton comes
in tardily—sometimes it is something else : but a year

seldom passes without some cause of this kind occurring, and it is impossible in the nature of things that such causes should not occur.

It would seem from Mr. Biddle's statements in another part of this essay, that, though every thing appeared very smooth on the surface in 1827, great danger lurked beneath.   Speaking of the State Banks, he says, " what interest has the community in propping up many of these institutions ? Let any sedate man look at the returns made this winter of the state of the Banks in various parts of the United States, and then answer whether they need further exemptions from the necessity of accommodating their business to their means.   *   *   *   *   *   *
In the present and immediate example, no man can fail to perceive that, but for the warning restriction imposed by the Bank of the United States and the leading State Banks, the events of the last six weeks would have brought many of them to the verge of insolvency, whence they could only escape by some sudden shock to the community."

In 1825, the immediate danger was to the Banks, and through them to the community.   In 1826, the United States' Bank and the leading State Banks placed themselves " in a situation of great strength and repose," but the sufferings of the community were not the less severe on that account.   It was, in fact, by producing sufferings in the community, that the Banks placed themselves in that situation from which they regarded what was going on around them with so much complacency.   The people implored them for relief, but the President of the United States' Bank replied, " It is in the order of nature, that if men or nations live extravagantly, they must suffer till they repair their losses by prudence, and that neither men nor Banks should impose on the community by promises to pay what they cannot pay.   The laws of trade have their own remedy for such disorders, as infallible as the law of animal life, which enables the human system to relieve itself from its own excesses.   Both must have their course.   But the Bank of the United States is invoked to assume that which, whoever attempts, deserves the ruin he will suffer.   It is requested to erect itself into a special providence to modify the laws of nature, and to declare that the ordinary fate of the heedless and improvident shall not be applied to the United States. Our countrymen are to be indulged without restraint in the utmost extravagance of the luxuries of Europe, on credit from the Banks; and when the day of payment arrives, the debtor shall not be called upon for payment—the Banks shall not be incommoded to pay their own notes, for the moment any inconvenience is felt, the Bank of the United States will certainly interpose and pay the debt. But if the Bank of the United States blends any sense with its tenderness, it will· do nothing of all this."

This reply, though not very consoling, would have been unanswerable, if it had not been that "the disorder of the country was over-trading, *brought on* by over-banking."

The Banks continued to diminish mercantile facilities, in the month of May. In September there was another pressure on the community; and in December a great scarcity of money was felt in Boston.

The President of the United States' Bank, in a letter to the Secretary of the Treasury, dated July 18th, 1829, says the office at Portsmouth, "last year was nearly prostrated in the general ruin which spread over that country. Out of 460,000 dollars of loans, 148,000 dollars was thrown under protest: still further protests were expected, and the actual loss sustained there will not be less than 112,000."

In March 1829, there was a pressure in Philadelphia : and in the following months great apprehensions were entertained in New York for the safety of the country Banks in that and the neighboring States. A writer in the United States Telegraph endeavored to show that the Banks of that city were also in a perilous condition. The difficulties appear to have been greatest in that city about the beginning of June. In the middle of the month, it was announced that the money market was becoming easy. Many New York merchants were, however, compelled to make compromises with their creditors; and many mechanics were deprived of employment.

The greatest distress in this year, appears to have been in Rhode Island. The Providence Literary Subaltern, as quoted by the Philadelphia Gazette, on the 26th of June, says—" The embarrassments which have been realized in this immediate neighborhood for the last ten days, have had no parallel in the history of the Republic. Men of reputed capital, who have withstood the shock of former changes and times; men who for the last forty years have stood firm, erect and undismayed before the tempest of the times that have assailed them, are now tottering on the verge of bankruptcy and ruin. Their fall bears excessively heavy on the poor and laboring classes, who, by the way, are in reality the principal sufferers. Deprived of employment, destitute and friendless, they are thrown upon the world, and know not how to obtain a livelihood. Within the last ten days, within the circle of the ten adjacent miles, upwards of twenty-five hundred people have been suddenly and unexpectedly thrown out of employment, and the distress that such an event has produced, can be far better imagined than described."

CHAPTER XXI.

Additional Particulars of the History of Banking from
1824 to 1829.

The professors of natural science are able to give satisfactory accounts of the general causes of heat and cold in different latitudes, and of snow and rain in different seasons, but it is in most instances beyond their power to state in what degree each of the general causes known to be in operation, has contributed to the state of the weather at a particular time and particular place. Banking is like the weather. It is affected by a variety of causes, which present themselves in different combinations. Many of these causes are of such a nature that their operation, if separately considered, would be inappreciable, though when united they produce a very sensible effect. Others are so strongly marked in their consequences, that their operation can at times be calculated with all the accuracy which is necessary for illustrating general principles.

Among these latter causes must be ranked the conflicts of the Banks with one another, and their dealings with Government. These are sufficient to produce great commercial embarrassments, even when there is no very great demand for specie for exportation. We have seen that the war between the allied Banks of Boston and the country Banks, produced a great scarcity of money in New England, in May 1825, or at the very time when speculation was most active in the Middle and Southern States. The President of the United States' Bank speaks of the "reaction, as it is called," taking place in Philadelphia, "in October." But the newspapers make mention of the pressure in July, and it is well known that it is not till sometime after great pressures begin, that mention is made of them in the public journals. Taking into consideration the facts that the pressure was felt here some four or five months before the crisis in England, that exchanges were in favor of this country, and that during this time the English country Banks were, according to Lord Liverpool, increasing their issues, we are inclined to think that some *other* cause besides the foreign demand for specie must have contributed to the reaction of 1825—at least so far as it affected the United States' Bank, and through it the other Banks and the community. We have a cause adequate to the effect, in the loans of ten million dollars made by the Bank to the Government in 1824 and 1825. The amount may not be large, abstractedly considered, but a paper money Bank which has been doing business for several years, can seldom, unless it has a surplus stock of specie, make loans for a long period, without being afterwards forced to resort to such measures as operate with great hardship on its regular customers. " The constant tendency of Banks," as Mr. Biddle has correctly observed, " is to lend too much —to put too many notes in circulation." And the Bank of the United States, after having lent as much as it could to private traders, strained its credit and resources to lend to Government, and thereby put more notes in circulation than the state of trade required.

The peculiar force with which the pressure of 1825 operated on the United States' Bank, strengthens this reasoning. It receives additional corroboration in the fact that the reaction was over in the United States much sooner than in England : and also in the fact that the exports of gold and silver in the year 1825, exceeded the imports in only the small sum of 2,600,000 dollars, the imports for the year being $6,150,785, and the exports $8,787,055.

It must, indeed, be admitted that a very small export of specie sometimes produces very great confusion. Mr. Carey, in a work published in 1810, says—" The merchants engaged in the trade to the East Indies, made application last spring to the Bank of the United States for dollars to remit there, and offered a premium of one per cent. The directors took the matter under consideration, and with liberality resolved to furnish the necessary sums without premium What was the exact amount I cannot state, but I have reason to believe it exceeded half a million of dollars. They were applauded for their liberality. But, however extraordinary it may appear, the effect of the operation was absolutely to impel some of the other Banks to curtail their discounts considerably."

If our currency was metallic, the exportation of ten or twenty millions of gold and silver, would have no more effect on the general train of commercial operations than the exportation of so many dollars' worth of iron and copper, for the exportation of specie would never commence till the domestic demand was fully satisfied. But, now, the fitting out of a single East India ship, may derange the trade of a city : and diminishing the ordinary stock of specie in the amount of only two or three millions, may derange the trade of the country.

This may appear strange at first view, but Mr. Biddle, in his Address to the Stockholders of the United States' Bank, in September 1831, gives us very satisfactory reasons why a cause, apparently so very trifling, should produce so very great an effect. " It is the peculiarity of our moneyed system, that in many parts of the country the precious metals are excluded from the minor channels of circulation by a small paper currency, in consequence of which the greater portion of these metals is accumulated in great masses in the Atlantic cities, liable to be immediately demanded on notes previously issued in the confidence of the continuance of the same state of things which caused the abundant issue of them ; at the first turn in the tide of foreign exchange—when the supply of foreign exchange is unequal to the daily demand, the vaults of the Banks may be exhausted before any precaution can prevent it. These

very precautions too, consisting as they do almost exclusively of curtailment of their loans, made suddenly—most-
ly without concert, and always under the influence of anxiety if not of alarm, may fall with oppressive weight on the
community, by the pressure in which alone can be produced the necessary reaction.   This reaction, moreover, is
necessarily slow, since our distance from Europe makes it
less easy to restore the equilibrium than between adjoining
countries in the same hemisphere."

It certainly was not by any increase of its loans to merchants that the Bank of the United States was brought into
difficulty in 1825, for these loans, including in the calculation common discounts and bills of exchange, actually sustained a reduction of upwards of 300,000 dollars, between
the 1st of January, 1824, and the 31st of July, 1825. By its
loans of ten millions to Government, the Bank appears to
have added to its circulation, between the dates just mentioned, only 3,277,885. But this, it seems, was two millions six
hundred thousand more paper than the country could bear,
for in this amount the exports of specie exceeded the imports in 1825.

It is well worthy of observation, that the total import of
foreign merchandise in 1825, was, according to the custom-
house returns, $96,340,075, and the total export of domes-
tic and foreign produce, was $99,535,388.   If allowance
be made for freight of the exports, and profits on them in
foreign markets, it will be seen that the " balance of trade"
was decidedly in favor of the country. So that, altogether,
we have in the events of the year, an example that, in time
of profound peace, and when the balance of trade is in
favor of the country, and when the exports of specie exceed the imports in the sum of only two or three millions,
a whole community may, by the operations of paper money
Banking, be brought to the very verge of insolvency.

The evils produced by Banks' making loans to Government are occasional. These produced by Banks' trading on
Government deposits, are perpetual. These deposits vary in
the amount of millions in the course of a few months.   A
Bank may know that the Government will, in the course of
a short period, require its funds to pay off a portion of the
public debt, or for some other purpose, but as the constant
tendency of Banks is to lend too much and put too many

notes in circulation, a Bank having possession of such funds seldom fails to make discounts on them as freely as on its own capital, trusting that when the Government shall demand its own, means may be found of meeting the demand through a credit in Europe, or some other financial operation. The most common mode is that of reducing commercial discounts. In the voluminous documents appended to the report made by a Committee of Congress in April 1832, continual reference is made to changes in the operations of the United States' Bank, rendered necessary by Government's reclaiming its deposits for the purpose of paying off the public debt.

If the State Banks should be made the depositories of the public funds, the evil would be increased instead of being diminished. Paper money Banks cannot be employed in any way as fiscal machines, without embarrassing the operations either of Government or of the community, and sometimes of both. If we had a metallic currency, and if our fiscal concerns were managed without the agency of Banks, the paying off of ten or twenty millions of public debt in the course of a year, would have the same effect as the paying off of ten or twenty millions of private debt—would produce benefit instead of injury. But as matters have been managed through the agency of the Banks, the paying off of the public debt has indirectly contributed to the irregularities of the money market since the year 1825.

The pressure of 1828 operated with more force on the local Banks than on the Bank of the United States. It was, as we have reason to believe, with great difficulty that some of the principal Banks of Philadelphia placed themselves in a situation of repose. As the imports of specie had in the previous year *exceeded* the exports, the imports having been $8,151,130, and the exports $7,971,307, while the total value of exports was $82,324,827, and of imports only $79,484,068, we cannot resist the conclusion that the difficulties of 1828 were, as well as those of 1825, owing, in a great measure, to domestic causes. The pressure in that year appears to have been independent of any movements in Europe. Money was very plenty in England. The interest on commercial securities in London in August, was only two per cent. The Bank of France had it in contemplation in November, to reduce the rate of discount to three per cent. In December, there was, indeed, a pressure in both France and England, but our difficulties commenced in the early part of the year. The foreign demand for specie could not have been great, as the exports of gold and silver in the whole year amounted to $7,550,339, and were nearly balanced by the imports, which amounted to $7,489,741.

To account for the difficulties in the year 1828, it is necessary to take into consideration a fact which was mentioned by Mr. Biddle in the verbal expose he gave to the stockholders of the United States' Bank, at their meeting in August. He then stated that the circulation of the Bank had been increased between August 1822 and August 1828, from 5,400,000 dollars, to upwards of 13,000,000, and that this had been effected, without adding any thing to the aggregate amount of currency, but simply by displacing an equal amount of the notes of the local Banks. Admitting this to be the fact, we have a satisfactory reason for the pressure felt by the other Banks of Philadelphia, while the United States' Bank was in a situation of great strength and repose. It was in the previous year, or 1827, that the United States' Bank commenced the issue of branch drafts for the sums of five and ten dollars, by which it obtained a decided advantage over the State Banks. It was thereby able, in December 1827, to put a stop to the circulation of the notes of the Cape Fear Bank of North Carolina; and to this operation of displacing the notes of the local Banks by the small branch drafts of the United States' Bank, may be attributed great part of the difficulties of the year 1828. It must be evident to every person, that new and unexpected demands on the local Banks by the United States' Bank, must have the same effect on them as new and unexpected demands on them for specie to send abroad. The United States' Bank may expand in the same proportion as the local Banks contract; but it has a different class of customers, and thus while money is made plenty with one portion of the community, it may be made scarce with another. The pressure of 1828 did not seem to affect the dealers in public stocks. Its weight fell principally on the merchants, and other productive members of society.

The difficulties of the year 1829, appear to have been owing in part to the operation of displacing local Bank notes by the branch drafts of the United States' Bank, in part to local causes of different kinds in different parts of the country, and in part to the state of commercial affairs in Europe. The operations of the United States' Bank are so limited in New England, that the people of that quarter of the country must attribute the principal evils they suffer to the doings of their local Banks. The people of the other States must attribute their sufferings to the combined operations of the local Banks and the Bank of the United States, bearing in mind the fact, that the United States' Bank has a share in producing these evils, only in proportion to the amount of its capital, the number of its branches, the control it has of the funds of Government, and the changes it makes from time to time, in its mode of operation.

CHAPTER XXII.

Of Banking from 1829-30 to 1832-33.

Towards the close of the year 1829, money became plenty. For this various causes may be assigned. One of the chief was the extensive dealings of the United States' Bank.

This institution had, early in 1823, devised a plan for extending its operations, and in that year discontinued the practice of paying out the notes of the local Banks, and renewed the practice of receiving the notes of all its branches. But the condition of things was such, that, towards the close of the year, its circulation was diminished, instead of being increased. It stood, in November and December, at $4,081,842, which was less than it was at any previous period, except the three months which immediately followed the first opening of the doors of the Bank at Philadelphia.

In 1824 and 1825, the Bank increased its active capital, by the sale of three or four millions of forfeited Bank stock. It was by this operation, by adding upwards of three millions to its circulation, and by straining its credit, that it was enabled in these years to lend ten millions to Government. A part of the plan of the Bank was to ex-

tend its dealings in domestic exchanges. This it naturally preferred to increasing its business in other commercial
securities, as on theseit received only discount, whereas on
bills of exchange it received both discount and premium.
Being the depository of the public funds in various parts
of the Union, it possessed great advantages for dealings
in exchange, especially as the greater part of the public revenues was received in those cities which had naturally
the rate of exchange in their favor. The operations of the
Bank in its exchange dealings are thus described by its
President.

"The crop of Tennessee is purchased by merchants
who ship it to New Orleans, giving their bills founded on
it to the branch of Nashville, which furnishes them with
notes. These notes are in time brought to New York
for purchasing supplies for Tennessee. They are paid in
New York, and the Nashville Bank becomes the debtor of
the branch at New York. The Nashville branch repays
them by drafts given to the branch at New York on the
branch at New Orleans, where its bills have been sent, and
the branch in New York brings home the amount by selling its drafts on the branch at New Orleans : or the New
Orleans branch remits. This very plan of circulation, is
the basis of the whole interior trade of the United States."

The true basis of the interior trade of the United States,
is the fertility of the soil and the industry of the people.
The sun would shine, the streams would flow, and the earth
would yield her increase, if the Bank of the United States
was not in existence. What is now performed by it in
the way of exchange dealings, would, if there were no
corporations, be as well performed by private exchange
merchants. Perhaps they could not perform it at quite
as low a rate, for they would have to provide a capital
of their own, whereas the United States' Bank performs
it by the control it has of the public deposits, and by
means of the credit its charter gives it in different States.
Employing no capital of its own in the business—the
whole affair being a mere paper transaction between the
Bank and its branches, it may well afford to do it cheap.
It may, however, be questioned, if the reduction of the
price of exchange below its natural rate, is an equivalent
for the evils which must necessarily ensue from the substi-

tution of the discretion of the officers of the United
States' Bank and of its twenty-five branches, for the laws
of nature. Whenever and wherever the Bank of the
United States reduces exchange below its natural rate, it
removes the only effective check on over-trading. This in
a short time makes necessary a reduction of discounts, and
thus we have in the exchange dealings of the United
States' Bank a new element of commercial vicissitude. If
there were no paper money institutions, the rate of domestic exchange would be regulated.by the cost of transporting
specie from one part of the country to another. This, even
between the most remote parts of the Union, would not exceed two or three per cent., and it would be better to pay
this per centage than to be exposed to all the evils of an
interminable series of expansions and contractions.

There was, however, a serious obstacle to extending the
operations of the Bank as far as was desirable. It was
physically impossible for the President and Cashier of the
Parent Bank to sign all the notes wanted for the branches:
and Congress, though repeatedly solicited, had refused to
give authority to any other persons to sign notes for circulation. Counsel was then taken of some distinguished
legal characters, and they declared that the issue of small
drafts signed by the officers of the branches, either upon
one another, or upon the Parent Bank, was not prohibited
by the charter. The issue of these drafts was accordingly
commenced in 1827, and a great increase of paper medium has followed. The President of the institution has
said, " If branch drafts had not been issued, no notes at
all could have been issued, from the mere physical impossibility of preparing them. But branch drafts do not increase
the circulation more than branch notes would." This
is true, but the physical impossibility was made known to
Congress, when application was made for authority to be
given to other persons besides the President and Cashier
to sign notes for circulation.

In answer to a question propounded by Mr. Camber-
breleng, " In what manner can a National Bank diminish
the circulation of country Banks, with which it has no
transactions except by reducing its own circulation ?" the
President of the Bank replied, " Very easily and very naturally. The very increase of the circulation of a National

Bank, may be the most efficient cause of the reduction of
a State Bank, and in this way, a branch is near a local
Bank—the branch notes are more valuable than the local
notes—the local notes are exchanged for the branch notes
at the branch Bank, which thus becomes the creditor of
the local Bank, and makes it pay its debts, and thus
reduce its circulation.   Now almost all State Banks stand
in this relation to the Bank and its branches."

This is sufficient to show that the embarrasments of
1828 were produced in part by the conflicts between the
United States' Bank and the local Banks for the circulation.   Encouraged by the success of its experiment, the
United States' Bank took measures for extending the operations of its old branches and for establishing new ones.
It felt pretty secure in the emission of branch drafts, for
they were made payable at a distance of five hundred or a
thousand miles from the places in which they were issued,
and though receiveable every where in payment of debts to
Government, could at any time be refused to be received
in payment of debts due to the Bank.   The Bank did, indeed, and still does, receive these branch drafts on deposit, at all its offices.   This was necessary to give the
drafts a general circulation.   But if it should at any time
become the interest of the Bank not to receive them, it has
only to say so, and the merchants will, as they were in
1818–19, be denied the privilege of paying debts due to
the Bank in the paper of the Bank.   A portion of the paper
of each of the twenty-five offices, being distributed through
each of the twenty-four States, each office may, in case of
a "panic" be delivered from the effects of a "run," by a
refusal to receive or to discharge any but its own drafts.

Under these circumstances the Bank increased its
issues, and it is evident that after these issues were swelled
to a certain amount, they afforded a basis for new issues
by the the State Banks.   It is well known that the country
Banks of Pennsylvania discount as freely on deposits of Philadelphia notes as on deposits of specie ; for, Philadelphia
notes are, they say, "as good to them as specie," or even
better, inasmuch as exchange is usually in favor of Philadelphia.   The Banks throughout the Union regard United
States' Bank notes and drafts in much the same light as
the country Banks of Pennsylvania regard Philadelphia

paper; because balances are constantly accumulating against them, in the United States' Bank, through that institution's being made the depository of the public funds, and through its many extensive transactions. The operaration was briefly this :—local Bank notes which circulated freely only in the neighborhood of the Banks which issued them, were exchanged at the offices of the United States' Bank for branch drafts which were made to circulate every where. This diminished the circulation of the State Banks, and increased that of the United States' Bank. The circulation of the Bank of the United States being increased, a number of its notes were received by the State Banks, either on deposit or in payment of debts due to them by individuals. The local Banks finding they had on hand a considerable amount of United States' paper, which was " as good to them as specie, or even better," began to issue their own notes more freely. A portion of these were received by the United States' Bank, and the State Banks, on payment being required, satisfied the demand with branch drafts. Each extension of the business of the United States' Bank in exchanges, increased its circulation of branch drafts, and each increase of branch drafts, after the new mode of operation was fairly established, enabled the State Banks to increase their issues, by providing them with means to meet such demands against them as might be made by the United States' Bank.

From the reports made to the Legislature of Pennsylvania in November, 1828, by the various Banks of the State, and by the Bank of Pennsylvania in February 1829, it appears that their circulation then amounted to 7,238,991 dollars, and their deposits to 6,221,037 dollars—total 13,460,028 dollars. From similar reports made in November 1831, it appears that their circulation was 8,753,092, and their deposits 7,736,747—total 16,489,839 dollars. This shows an increase in the local Bank medium of Pennsylvania, of three millions of dollars, or about twenty-two per cent. between these dates.

Mr. Cambreleng states, that, between the 1st of January 1830 and the 1st of January 1832, the country Banks in the State of New York had increased their circulation from 3,974,345, to 8,622,277 dollars. The increase in 1831, in the circulation of the Banks of New York, Massachusetts,

Rhode Island and Pennsylvania, not including the Banks of Philadelphia, is estimated by him at eight millions.

The gross circulation of the Bank of the United States in January 1829, was 13,391,110 dollars, and in January 1832 it was 24,630,747 dollars. The net circulation was at the first of these periods, 11,901,656—at the second it was 21,250,545 dollars. The increase in the net circulation was about seventy-eight per cent.

Other causes besides the new mode of operation adopted by the United States' Bank have contributed to this increase of currency. Multitudes of those who were ruined by the events which followed the war, had found relief in death. Others had sought an asylum in the poor-house. The children of others had become old enough to till, as hirelings, the farms their fathers once owned. A new generation of business men had come on the stage of action, and the incidents of 1818–19 were fast fading from the minds of those who were then old enough to be observant of the course of affairs. In such a country as the United States, the silent operations of society work great changes in a period of ten or twenty years. Pernicious as the Banking system is, it cannot exhaust the natural sources of wealth, or destroy that desire in men to better their condition, which is the main spring of action. The country was more populous and more wealthy than it was at any previous period. It could bear more Banking, and more Banking it was made to bear.

The combined operations of these causes began to be very visible in their effects in the latter part of 1829, after the embarrassments caused by a pressure in Europe were over. The rise of property on Market street, Philadelphia, was a subject of newspaper boast in November.

An increase of the trade with Mexico, and a decline of the trade with China, contributed to swell the amount of specie in the country. In 1830, the exports of gold and silver were only 2,178,773 dollars, while the imports were 8,155,964. A method adopted by the Bank of the United States, and imitated by private capitalists, of drawing bills on England to be negotiated beyond the Cape of Good Hope, was one of the causes which, in this year, diminished the export of gold and silver. The committee of Congress say, " this new method of dealing in bills of exchange

does not economize the specie of the country at all. It is
a universal law of drawing, that funds must either go before or follow after the draft to honor it at maturity; and
whether it goes directly or circuitously, the funds to discharge it must sooner or later arrive at the place of payment. These bills are to be paid in England, but they go
round the Cape of Good Hope before they reach their place
of destination. Instead, therefore, of sending the specie
directly to India and China, as formerly, who does not perceive that it must now be sent to England, the country upon
which these bills are drawn, there to meet them upon the
arrival at the place where they are to be paid? The Bank
consequently becomes the shipper of the specie, to pay its
bills, in place of the merchant, to purchase his merchandise in the East Indies. It is simply and purely nothing
but a change of the destination of the specie, with only the
advantage of its going to London.

" The supplying of bills encourages an operation which
commences and ends without the employment of any capital whatever, and is similar in character to respondentia securities. The buyer is enabled, within the term of credit,
to make the voyage, dispose of his goods, and obtain from
the proceeds the funds to meet his obligation, and the Bank
to transmit the same to the place upon which the bills are
drawn,(which are at six months' sight,) long before they become due. It would seem to produce a greater export of
specie, eventually, than would otherwise take place, if the
operations were commenced with specie, and not with bills
purchased in the manner described: for the merchant, relying upon his immediate resources, would not engage to
such an extent in the business, and would combine in the
operation much of the produce of the country, whereas, relying upon an extensive credit, he hazards every thing on
the success of the enterprize. It is a species of speculation
in trade, leading to great risks, and certainly terminating
in over-trading—the evils of which the country is now sorely
experiencing. By loans of a similar character by insurance
companies, providing funds for traders to China, Government has sustained more loss than in any other branches
of trade."

All this is true enough, but this method of drawing bills
to be negotiated beyond the Cape of Good Hope, enables

the Banks to increase their issues, inasmuch as it *defers* the demand for specie for six months, a year, or longer. It contributed, with other causes, to swell the amount of silver in the vaults of the Banks, in the latter part of 1829, and in 1830, and 1831.

In March 1830, the Bank of the United States had in its vaults 8,038,246 dollars, which was more than it ever had before. In December, the Banks of the city of New York complained that they had so much specie that they did not know what to do with it. The amount in their vaults was said to be seven millions.

Throughout 1830 and the greater part of 1831, the Banks generally extended their operations. Money was unusually plenty, and little embarrassment was suffered, except what was produced by the action of the Banks on one another, in their struggle to determine which should circulate most paper. The effect in Philadelphia was to raise property, in many parts of the town, as high, or nearly as high, as it was during the suspension of specie payments. Great part of Market street was rebuilt with elegant stores. Rents rose enormously in business places. The trade with the Western country was increased greatly; and speculation showed its activity in a variety of forms. In almost every part of the country, the same effects were observable, in either a greater or a less degree.

This continued till October, 1831, when " an active demand for money" began, the consequences of which have since been felt in various parts of the country in various forms.

The President of the United States' Bank, in a letter dated April 16th, 1832, addressed to Mr. Clayton, the chairman of the committee of Congress, gives the following account of the state of affairs :

" In addition to the business of domestic exchange, the amount of local loans has increased, owing to the greater demand for the use of money during the last year, and the conversion into the more active form of business of the stocks repaid by Government to the Bank. The first grew naturally out of the state of trade. For eighteen months, the want of employment for capital, and the derangement of industry arising from political and other causes, rendered money very abundant in France and England, the two countries whose situation so much influences our own, and produced a corresponding ease and plenty in the United States, while at the same time, the disturbed state of Europe, and the Cholera which interposed new obstacles to trade, with certain parts of it, naturally directed the manufacturers of England and France to this country, which is by far the best and safest markets for their productions. These circumstances occasioned, during the past twelve months, an unusual importation of foreign merchandise. While the treatment of this temporary commercial disease was in progress, the sufferers naturally looked for the cause of it every where but in themselves, and the Bank was reproached with having contributed to occasion the importations. Without going into detail, one single fact is quite decisive on this subject. It will be seen from the following official statement, marked B, that the large importations last year began with the month of April, and of course they must have been founded, so far back as the Bank was concerned, on the state of things in this country a month or two previous, say the month of March last. Now, it will be seen from the state of the Bank before the committee, that, for nearly two years before the month of March last, (1831,) the local discounts of the Bank had undergone no perceptible increase—those for July 1829 being $34,196,000, and those for March 1831 being $34,220,000, an increase within that period of only 24,000 dollars."

This does not appear to be a correct mode of viewing the subject. The exchange dealings of the Bank ought to be taken into consideration as well as the local discounts. They contribute quite as much to credit traffic. It is through them the Bank is able to circulate its branch drafts. The arrival of these branch drafts in the great Atlantic cities, is, as the President of the Bank has stated elsewhere, " the signal of relief to the southern and western traders." The receipt of them at the office at New York, was nearly twelve millions in the year 1828, and upwards of eleven millions in 1829. The receipt of them at Philadelphia, and at the three offices of New York, Baltimore, and Boston, amounted to upwards of thirty-seven million dollars, in the two years of 1828 and 1829. It is with these branch drafts that the southern and western merchants pay for foreign merchandise. It is with these the importer pays the duties to the Government. Nothing, therefore, can contribute more efficiently to an increase of imports.

" The large importations must have been founded, so far as the Bank was concerned, on the state of things in this country a month or two previous." This is unquestionable, and the state of things in this country was then affected by the new system of operations begun by the Bank in 1827. Between the two dates mentioned in the extract, the net circulation of the United Sates' Bank was increased from 13,780,847 to 16,933,122, or about twenty-two per cent., and though the increase in the circulation of the local Banks may not have been in the same proportion, there is reason to believe it was considerable. It may be admitted that the state of trade in Europe, and, perhaps, the Cholera, tended to swell the importations, but any disposition to over-trading thereby induced, would, if we had been without moneyed corporations and without paper money, soon have been checked by the necessity of paying cash, or at least making engagements to pay in specie.—The President of the Bank proceeds as follows:

" Without having contributed to produce them, the Bank found, about nine months ago, large importations, requiring for their diffusion through the country, increased facilities connected with Banking : having the means of giving them, being in fact created for the purpose of giving them it gave them; it had the means of giving, because, in the early part of the year, it had been strengthened for business, purposely, by the addition of two millions of its funds in Europe transferred home, by the repayment of about ten millions of the funded debt paid back by Government since October, 1830, making an increase of active means amounting to twelve millions. When, in the progress of a few months, the continuance of these importations, and the revenue which had accrued on them, produced an effect on the actual state of the market, the Bank applied itself immediately to correct any disadvantages from it to the community. The actual position of things was simply this : There were large importations requiring means of remittance to Europe to pay for them : there were large amounts of revenue to Government, amounting in New York alone, from March 1831, to March 1832, to nearly seventeen million dollars, requiring great forbearance towards the

debtors.   In the mean time, the southern produce, which
furnishes the greater part of the means to pay for these importations, was, owing to a great variety of causes, the state
of the crops and the weather, unusually late in appearing.
This, therefore, was the condition of the country : an unusual importation, an unusual amount of debts payable to
Government, and an unusual delay in receiving the ordinary means of meeting these demands.   Undoubtedly, if
the Bank had chosen to adopt such a course, it would have
been easy, by an immediate diminution of its loans, to place
itself out of the reach of all inconvenience, but it would,
at the same time, have inflicted very deep wounds on the
community, and seriously endangered the revenue of Government.   These exertions of mere power have no attrac-
tion, and it was deemed a far wiser policy to deal with the
utmost gentleness to the commercial community, to avoid
all shocks, to abstain from countenancing all exaggerations
and alarms, but to stand quietly by, and assist, if necessary, the operations of nature and the laws of trade, which
can always correct their own transient excesses.   Accordingly, the whole policy of the Bank for the last six months.
[preceding April 16th, 1832,] has been exclusively pro-
tective and conservative, calculated to mitigate suffering,
and yet avert danger.   The point where these importations
occurred, and where the revenue was payable, was New
York.   The whole force of the institution was, therefore, directed to strengthen that place, and the distant branches
were directed to avoid incommoding it, and the Atlantic
branches near to it, by drafts upon them, but to pay their
balances to them with as little delay as the convenience of
their respective localities would permit.   This is the whole
policy of the Bank for the last six months.   It will be seen,
therefore, that, without a diminution, there has been an actual increase of business in New York, and a large increase
of the domestic bills of the branches : the increase in New
York being for the purpose of protecting the interest there,
and the increase of the bills being the remittances from the
West and South to sustain New York and the southern Atlantic branches.   In the mean time the Bank, out of its
own accumulations, and its own credits in Europe, supplied,
since the first of September last, the means of remittances
in its own bills to the amount of $5,295,746 52, and part-

ed with its surplus specie to the amount of 5,000,000, making an aggregate contribution to the commerce of the country of $10,295,746 52."

The letters from the Cashier of the Bank at Philadelphia to the cashiers of the branches, in the months of October, November, December, January, and February, 1831–32, exhibit a remarkable example of the manner in which the operations of the Bank "assist the operations of nature, and the laws of trade, which can always correct their own transient excesses." The general directions to the cashiers were to shape their business, not according to the natural demands of trade in their immediate vicinity, but according to the special demands of the Bank in New York, and other Atlantic cities. They were to withhold local accommodations, and to purchase bills of exchange on particular places, thus increasing facilities to one class of dealers, and denying them to others, when it was as likely as not that regard to the interests of the community in the neighborhood of the offices would have required an increase of local discounts and a diminution of exchange dealings, or exchange dealings of a different character from those which were ordered. It may be doubted if any Board of men sitting in Philadelphia, is able to direct money operations, in many and remote parts of the Union, without inflicting injury on the community, especially when that same Board has on its shoulders the additional burden of regulating the foreign exchanges of the country. It may be doubted if the discretion of any Board, however scientific and however experienced, is an andequate substitute for "those operations of nature and laws of trade," which, if left to themselves, "can always correct their own transient excesses."

The reduction of accommodations at the Bank in Philadelphia, between the 5th of January and the 29th of March, 1832, was $1,810,408 37, including both promissory notes and bills of exchange ; at the offices at Boston, between the 5th day of January and the 29th of March, it was $167,-860 85, on a discount line of less than two and a half million dollars; and at the office at Baltimore, between the 16th of January and the 2d of April, it was $123,741 63, on a discount line of little more than two million dollars. At the office at New York, the local discounts were, as

Mr. Biddle states, increased, but the dealings in exchange were diminished, so that the actual reduction of commercial accommodations at that office, was $259,305 43, between the 4th day of January and the 28th day of March. At the Bank in Philadelphia, the reduction between the 5th of January and the 5th of April, fell a little short of twenty per cent. of the whole amount of accommodations.

It appears, from a letter of the Cashier of the Bank in Philadelphia, dated November 24th, 1831, that the orders issued in October were, at some of the Western offices, " unfortunately misunderstood.   At some of them, our Cashiers ceased checking altogether upon Philadelphia and New York, and at Nashville the Board refused very large amounts of prime bills upon your city, (New Orleans,) and have thus dried up a few of the rills by which the stream of exchange would have been swelled in its course towards you and thence to us."   Thus, it seems, that, in addition to the evils to which the country is exposed from the attempts of the Board at Philadelphia to control the whole course of foreign and domestic exchanges, and through them the whole train of commercial operations—attempts which, from the imperfection of human nature, must necessarily be productive of evil—we are exposed to other evils from the officers of distant branches misunderstanding directions.

Explanations of the orders of the Bank were then given to such of the branches as had misapprehended them, and it must be stated, in justice to the Cashiers of the Southern and Western offices, that they obeyed orders so well, that, though there was a reduction of dealings to the extent of two millions and a half at Philadelphia, New York, Boston, and Baltimore, there was an increase between October 1831, and March 1832, of more than a million in the net circulation of the Bank, of more than six millions in the bills of exchange, and of more than eight millions in the total of discounts and bills.

The Bank perceived in February that it was necessary to change its policy, for branch drafts came from the South and West in such quantities into the great Atlantic cities, as to threaten difficulties of another nature.   Orders were then issued to the branches to keep down their business, as well in bills of exchange as in local discounts.   Notwithstanding this direction, the bills of exchange were, by May, increased to twenty-three millions, and the aggregate of discounts and bills to seventy millions.

The immediate causes assigned for the movement in October, were directions from Government to pay off six or seven millions of the public debt. Orders to pay off a small additional amount, only one million and three quarters, in April, are specially mentioned, in the instructions given to the southern and western branches, why they should shape their business so as to assist the principal offices in the Atlantic cities. If the Government had been willing to leave the national debt unpaid, and to suffer the Bank to have the public funds to trade upon, it would, perhaps, have kept on expanding. But the Government was, very properly, desirous of discharging the national debt while it had the means: and expressed a wish in March, to pay off in July one half of the three per cents. This rendered necessary a new movement on the part of the Bank, which is thus related by its chief officer.

" I received a letter from the acting Secretary of the Treasury, dated the 24th of March, 1832, informing me that the Government was about to issue a notice on the 1st of April, of their intention to pay on the 1st of July next, one-half of the three per cent. stock, and to do it by paying to each stockholder one-half the amount of his certificate. He added, 'If any objection occurs to you, either as to the amount, or as to the mode of payment, I will thank you to suggest it.'

" Thus invited by the Government, in a communication marked ' confidential,' to give my opinion on a measure contemplated by the Government, I felt it my duty to express my views of its probable operation. In my reply, therefore, dated the 29th of March, I stated, ' that so far as the Bank is concerned no objection occurs to me, it being sufficient that the Government has the necessary amount of funds in the Bank to make the contemplated payment.' I then proceeded to observe, that in the present situation of the mercantile community, and with a very large amount of revenue, [amounting to nine millions,] to be paid before the 1st of July, the debtors of the Government would require all the forbearance and all the aid which could be given to them; and that the payment proposed, by creating a demand for the remittance of several million dollars to the European stockholders, would tend to diminish the usual facilities to the debtors of the Government, and might endanger the punctual payment. For this reason, I thought it for the interest of the Government to postpone the payment till the next quarter.

" After weighing the circumstances, the Government was desirous of adopting the measure ; but the difficulty I understood to be this, that the sinking fund would lose the quarter's interest, from July to October, of the sum intended to be paid in July, and that the Government did not feel itself justified in making the postponement, unless that interest could be saved ; but that it would be made, provided the Bank would make the sinking fund whole on the 1st of October.   To this I said, that, as the Bank would have the use of the fund during the three months, it would consent to save the sinking fund harmless, by paying the three months' interest itself.   And so the matter stands."

It was not long, however, before the Bank discovered that it would be as inconvenient to pay the European stockholders in October, as to pay them in July.   One of the directors then made a voyage to Europe, and an arrangement was made through the medium of private Banker in London, by which the reimbursement of a portion of the three per cents. was deferred for a further period.

It is thus by means of its credit with Government, and its credit in Europe, that the Bank has sustained itself during the last six months. And it is well for the community that the Bank enjoys this credit.   From the accounts recently published, it appears that its circulation was reduced, from March to November, more than twenty per cent.   A further diminution would, by is operation on the local Banks, have added greatly to the sufferings which the commercial community endured during the last year.   If we except the real estate held by the Bank and the specie in its vaults, all its capital and all its credit may be regarded as invested in promissory notes and bills of exchange, and it cannot pay to the public creditors the funds entrusted to it for that purpose, without making a reduction of commercial accommodations in a corresponding amount.   The reduction during the past year was quite as great as the community could bear ; and though the Government has just cause of complaint, inasmuch as the sinking fund was not made whole on the 1st of October, according to agreement, it ought, perhaps, not to be very severe in its judgment, as an attempt to fulfil the contract literally, would have occasioned a great pressure on the people.

The President of the Bank said, in his letter to Mr. Clayton in April 1832, speaking of the plan of operation adopted in October 1831, " This has given time for the operations of the laws of trade : the country is recovering from the temporary inconvenience; the over-stocked market, by checking prices, has checked farther importations ; the southern crop so long delayed, is coming forward ; the exportation of specie has ceased ; the importations of specie, postponed by the troubles of Mexico, are resumed ; and in a short time, the whole operation will rectify itself."

The inconvenience has, however, continued to the present day, and if a man of Mr. Biddle's great powers of mind, still thinks the embarrassments of the people are such as spring only from " vibrations of trade," having their origin in natural causes, and that they are in no way increased by Banking operations, it must be that his situation at the head of the Banking system, has an influence on his judgment. He speaks of its being natural for men to look for the cause of their sufferings every where but in themselves. With equal truth it may be affirmed that statesmen, and men whose situation gives them the power of statesmen, are apt to attribute the sufferings of the community to any cause but their own measures.

If it should still be denied that the operations of the United States' Bank in particular, and of the local Banks in general, contributed to that state of things which led to the excessive importations in the spring of 1831, it must be admitted that the subsequent measures of the Banks have contributed to produce the heavier importations of 1832. It would be very illogical to argue that the " Cholera," when it visits the north of Europe, forces trade from it, and that when it visits the United States, it brings an increase of trade along with it. There must be some other cause than the " Cholera" for the excessive importations of the last year. Mr. Biddle, in the essay he published in 1828, pointed out very clearly the manner in which over-banking leads to over-trading.

In October 1829, the statements of the United States'
Bank showed a total of discounts and bills of exchange
of $39,960,052, and in May 1832, a total of $70,428,070.
In the short period of two years and seven months, there
was an increase of $30,668,018 in the accommodations the
Bank afforded to dealers. At the same time the local
Banks expanded ; and if such causes will not affect trade,
it is hard to say what will.

The present amount of currency would be redundant, if
over-banking had not induced over-trading. But in the
present condition of things, men cannot, notwithstanding
the abundance of paper money, meet their engagements
with ease; and their embarrassments are, at particular times
and particular places, increased by the action of the Banks
on one another, and by a system of exchange dealings in
which the interests of the community in one town or in
one State, are made subordinate to the interest of a Banking office, perhaps five hundred or a thousand miles distant.

Such consequences are inseparable from the present system, and must not be ascribed to faults in the men who manage it. Under another President and another Board of Directors, the Bank of the United States might not have committed precisely the same faults, but perhaps it would have
committed faults which would have inflicted still greater
evils on the community. A President and Board of Directors who would refuse to take the measures necessary to
raise the rate of dividends and the price of shares as high
as possible, would be very unpopular with the stockholders,
and would, probably, soon be dismissed from their official
stations.

If the State Banks were made the depositories of the
public funds, and if their notes were made receivable in
payment of duties, the evils of the system would be increased.

If the Government should, after the expiration of the present charter of the United States' Bank, resolutely refuse
to receive any thing but gold and silver in payment of debts,
and also refuse to employ any Bank as an agent in its fiscal
operations, the evils of the system would be greatly diminished.

CHAPTER XXIII.

Extent of Banking Operations at Different Periods.

For many years a veil of mystery was thrown over the operations of the Banks. Mr. Bland, a member of Congress from Maryland, in a speech made previous to the dissolution of the old Bank of the United States, said, "The nature of the loans, the deposits, and all the bargains, dealings, and contrivances, between the Government and the Bank, are wholly invisible to the public."

Dr. Bollman, who undertook the defence of the Bank, after mentioning that the nature of Banking operations was but little understood, spoke of " an idea prevailing with those whom curiosity and a turn for research has led to investigate the subject more deeply, that the interest of of these institutions, as well as their usefulness, required the preservation of what they deem salutary prejudices concerning them." The Doctor justified such revelations as he made by the necessity of the case.

" I have labored," says Mr. Carey, who was embarked in the same cause, " under a most discouraging destitution of materials. Those whose province it was to furnish them, have most cautiously forborne from the communication, in the most extraordinary manner."

In another sentence he says, " The obligation of secrecy in Banking transactions, precludes a writer who undertakes the defence of such an institution, from many of the most important data, on which his reasoning may depend. * * * Were I possessed of a statement of the specie in the different Banks of Philadelphia—and were it proper to disclose it."

For many years this veil of mystery was not removed; if, indeed, it can now be said to be removed. " I have found " said ' A Frienly Monitor,' writing in 1819, " considerable embarrassment in obtaining the most simple information in relation to the Bank (i. e. the present Bank of the United States.) If I ask a director, the seal of his finger is significantly impressed on his lips. There is a species of masonry in Banking which to a certain extent is highly proper and necessary. It implies a mutual pledge among the directors, that nothing shall be divulged which may be prejudicial to the interests of the Bank."

Before the suspension of specie payments, no regular returns were received by the Legislature of Pennsylvania from the Banks in this Commonwealth. Since that time, accounts have been published annually : but as the Bank of Pennsylvania and the Bank of North America have in many years made no returns, it is impossible to give a general table from which indisputable conclusions might be drawn.

In some of the other States, the difficulty of obtaining satisfactory accounts of the extent of Bank operations, is more difficult than in Pennsylvania. During the great excitement of 1818–19, Mr. Niles made an effort to collect information respecting all the Banks then in existence ; but, though his correspondence was very extensive, he does not appear to have succeeded in his object ; for the tables which he gave notice of his intention of publishing, do not appear in his Register.

In 1820, Mr. Crawford, who was then Secretary of the Treasury, made a report on the state of currency, in connexion with which he gave a table intended to show the amount of capital paid in, the notes in circulation, the public and private deposits, and the specie in the Banks in 1819. Mr. Niles, on publishing the table said, "it will be seen the preceding returns are very imperfect—as, for instance, the capital paid in, in Maryland is given at 86,290, whereas it is nearly eight millions of dollars. Several of the other items I know, from various documents in my possession, are pretty nearly correct ; yet some are also much deficient."

Mr. Gallatin, who was for many years Secretary of the Treasury, published in 1831, "Considerations on the Currency and Banking System of the United States." A comparison of his estimates with those of Mr. Crawford, will show the difficulty there is in arriving at a satisfactory conclusion.

Mr. Crawford's estimate of the amount of notes in circulation, is as follows :

1813,	-	-	-	-	$62,000,000
1815,	-	-	-	-	110,000,000
1819,	-	-	-	-	45,000,000

Mr. Gallatin's estimate is as follows :

1811,	-	-	-	-	$28,000,000
1815,	-	-	-	-	45,000,000
1816,	-	-	-	-	68,000,000
1820,	-	-	-	-	44,863,349
1830,	-	-	-	-	61,323,898

Mr. Gallatin appears to have had more data than Mr. Crawford, but still his tables are so imperfect that variations of from 5 to 25 per cent. may take place in the amount of currency, which they afford no means of ascertaining.

To collect and arrange the accounts of five or six hundred Banks which are, or which have been, scattered through twenty-four States and two or three Territories, would be no easy task.

If we had all these accounts collected and arranged to our hand, a question might arise as to the sense in which they should be understood. There is an ambiguity in many Bank statements which renders them useless. The word " cash" under the pens of some Bank officers, contracts and expands its meaning with as much facility as Bank medium contracts and expands its amount. Sometimes it includes " mint certificates," because cash can be got for them in the market. Sometimes, in the case of a country Bank, it includes city Bank notes, because they are to the country Bank " as good as cash." Sometimes cash and " bills of exchange" are given together.

If all ambiguity were removed from Bank statements, another question might arise, and that is, how far they are to be depended upon. We have seen a committee of the Legislature of North Carolina accusing one of the Banks of that State of rendering a false account of the amount of specie in its vaults : and a committee of the Legislature of Connecticut accusing one of the Banks of that State of rendering a false account of the amount of notes in circulation.

No doubt, the accounts of many Banks are fairly rendered, but it is impossible, in a general view of the subject, to say how many Bank returns are faithful and how many are not. There may be a literal exactness in the returns, and yet some fact may be suppressed, which, if generally known, might entirely change the impression the public receives from a Bank statement. " I could," says a writer in a Portsmouth, New Hampshire, paper, " name more than one Bank in this State, where a considerable portion of the debts mentioned in the return, were worth nothing ; and much of the specie was borrowed from individuals or Banks, laid in the vaults those two days, and then returned to the owners with the seals unbroken." The author of a pamphlet published at New York, in 1828, entitled a " Peep into the Banks," objected to a new law of that State, requiring the Banks to make semi-annual returns of the amount of specie in their vaults, for the following reasons. " It is well known, that institutions which, heretofore, have been required to make these exhibitions, have prepared, previous to the period of making them, to present as favorable statements as possible. If all the Banks in the State are to do so, it will produce a semi-annual pressure for money. Paper, payable a short time previous to these periods, will be discounted freely, when a general curtailment will be made. The notes and bills payable out of the State, will obtain a preference, that thereby funds of specie, in Philadelphia, Boston, &c., may be made for a few days the property of Banks in this State. In this and other contrivances, the officers will be employed to make a a display of that which has no permanent existence."

There is another question. Do even the directors know, in all cases, what is the exact state of a Bank ?—There are not in the city and county of Philadelphia, any men more astute in what regards their own interests, than some of the Directors of the Bank of the Northern Liberties ; yet a sum equivalent to the whole capital of the Bank, was taken from it by some of its clerks and their coadjutors out of doors, without any of the Directors, the President, or Cashier, being aware of the fact. The case of the City Bank of Baltimore, was still more remarkable. It had what was called a " solid" capital of 800,000 or 900,000 dollars, and its credit was good. But, about the time Mr. M'Culloh was removed from the cashiership of the United States' branch, the Cashier of the City Bank found it necessary to resign. An investigation was then made by a committee of the stockholders, and it was found that all the persons employed in the Bank, with the exception of one clerk and the porter, had made free with its funds. The over-drafts of the Cashier amounted to $166,548 85 : those of his particular friend to 185,382 dollars ; those of one clerk to about 30,000 dollars ; those of a second clerk to $15,082 70 ; and those of a third clerk to $6,324 99.*

It is to be hoped that most Bank officers are every way worthy of the trust reposed in them ; but even then we cannot be sure of the accuracy of their accounts. As is remarked by Governor Wolcott, " The stations of President, Cashier, Teller and Book-keeper, are incompatible, and yet some two or more of them are united in the same persons, contrary to established maxims of accountability, prudence, and even justice to the individuals who are so entrusted. If, at the close of the hours of business in every day, full accounts of all the funds issued and of securities obtained and discharged, are not immediately stated, their accuracy ascertained, and their results extended into records, which are regularly continued, by persons whose peculiar duty it is to note all these facts, according to established forms ; then the transactions of different days will be blended, and soon all individual responsibility will be irrecoverably lost."

While so much obscurity and so much uncertainty hangs over Bank accounts, the reader will be content with a mere abstract of the tables and statements of Mr. Gallatin. We have been for seven years collecting the accounts of the Banks, but so little success has crowned the labors of Mr. Crawford, Mr. Gallatin, and Mr. Niles, that we do not think it worth while to arrange our own materials.

Number of Banks in operation at different periods, and number of Banks that failed or discontinued business, from 1st January 1811, to 1st January 1830.

		1811.	1815.	1816.	1820.	1830.	Broken Banks.
Massachusetts,	-	15	21	26	28	66	6
Maine, - -	-	6	8	14	15	18	8
New Hampshire,	-	8	10	10	10	18	2
Vermont, -	-				1	10	
Rhode Island,	-	13	14	16	30	47	1
Connecticut, -	-	5	10	10	8	13	2
New York, -	-	8	26	27	33	37	10
New Jersey,	-	3	11	11	14	18	7
Pennsylvania,	-	4	42	43	36	33	16
Delaware, -	-		5	5	6	6	1

* Niles' Register, October 30th, 1819.

	1811.	1815.	1816.	1820.	1830.	Broken Banks.
Maryland, - -	6	17	20	14	13	9
District of Columbia,	4	10	10	13	9	4
Virginia, - -	1	4	12	4	4	10
North Carolina, -	3	3	3	3	3	2
South Carolina, -	4	5	5	5	5	2
Georgia, - -	1	2	3	4	9	1
Louisiana, - -	1	3	3	4	4	2
Alabama, - -				3	2	3
Mississippi, - -		1	1	1	1	
Tennessee, - -	1	2	4	8	1	9*
Kentucky, - -	1	2	2	42		43
Ohio, - - -	4	12	21	20	11	20
Indiana, - -				2		2
Illinois, - - -				2		2
Missouri, - -				1		2
Michigan, - -					1	1
Florida, - -					1	
	88	208	246	307	330	165

We have another list, which contains the names of twenty-eight broken Banks not mentioned in Mr. Gallatin's table, viz. one in Massachusetts, one in Maine, three in New York, three in Pennsylvania, one in Delaware, one in the District of Columbia, two in Virginia, one in Georgia, four in Kentucky, eight in Ohio, one in Indiana, one in Illinois, and one in Michigan. Even this, however, does not appear to be complete. No list has yet been published of the number of Banks in operation in the first six months of 1818, which was the time the mania reached its height; and Mr. Gallatin, with all his industry, has not been able to give a complete list of all the Banks which were in operation in the years mentioned in the above table. There were, for example, two if not three Banks in Missouri in the year 1820.

Mr. Gallatin's estimate of the capital of the Banks, the notes in circulation, and specie in their vaults, at different periods, is as follows:

		Capital.	Circulation.	Specie.
1st. Jan. 1811,	-	52.610,601	28,100,000	15,400,000
1815,	-	82,259,590	45,500,000	17,000,000
1816,	-	89,822,422	68,000,000	19,000,000
1820,	-	137,110,611	44,863,344	19,820,240
1830,	-	145,192,268	61,323,898	22,114,917

* Including five Branches.

In making these estimates, Mr. Gallatin was forced to *guess* at the amount of specie possessed by, and the amount of notes circulated by, thirty-eight Banks in 1811, eighty-eight Banks in 1815, one hundred and twelve Banks in 1816, ninety-five Banks in 1820, and forty-nine Banks in 1830. Where he had returns they were not all of the same dates, and in some years the returns were from but little more than half the whole number of Banks. After all, his *guesses* may be as near the truth as some Bank statements.

Nothing is more certain than political economy. Nothing is more uncertain than political arithmetic.

Bank statements, taken by themselves, are too vague to be made the basis of an argument. We have, however, throughout this book, received them without dispute, because we believed them to approximate sufficiently near the truth to serve the purposes of illustration. Abstract signs would, if generally understood, answer the same end. Bank statements may be used with this view, though, taking them in the aggregate, they may not be worthy of implicit confidence. That the Banks should make such reports as will place their operations in the most favorable light, is natural.

If any think differently, and are disposed to reason *a priori* with Bank statements for their basis, we hope they will avoid the error of some modern writers, who have represented an increase of some eight or ten millions in the circulation of a single Bank in a year or two as quite gradual and moderate. If Mr. Gallatin is correct in his conjecture, that the whole amount of medium, Bank notes, Bank credits, and specie in circulation, is but one hundred and ten or one hundred and twenty millions, an increase of ten or twelve, or fifteen per cent., in one of these components of the currency, must have a very considerable effect on prices. This able writer is confident that the amount of notes in circulation did not exceed thirty millions in 1811, forty-seven millions in 1815, and seventy millions in 1816 : yet this he thinks, and he probably thinks justly, is quite sufficient to account for the depreciation of the currency. He agrees with Mr. Crawford in the opinion that the notes in circulation were not reduced to a less amount than forty-five millions in 1820 : yet his judgment is, that the numerous failures which preceeded the year 1819, or which have since taken place, have been principally owing to the operations of the Banks.

Full and correct accounts of the amount of notes in circulation, and of the amount of deposits, would gratify curiosity : but, for practical purposes, they are not necessary. The effects of Banking are inscribed on every page of our country's history, from the year 1783 up to the present day. Those who have been in business can speak of these effects from their own experience. Those who have never been in business, have only to open their eyes, and they will behold the effects of the system in the condition of different classes of society.

Many of the operations of the system are such that they cannot be embraced in the annual reports made by the Banks to the Legislature. Fluctuation of prices is but one of the evils of paper money Banking, and that not the greatest. If it were possible for a metallic currency to vary in amount as Bank medium varries, such variations would be limited in their effects, for they would not operate on a false and super-extended system of credit, nor would the evil be aggravated by the machinations of irresponsible Boards of Directors. Paper money must be regarded as the foundation of the American Banking System, since the founders of Banks would not, if they were prevented from issuing paper money, accept of charters : but this paper money does less evil as an uncertain medium of commerce, than is produced by its being made the instrument by which the foundation is laid for a false and super-extended system of credit, and by its giving to corporations a power which enables them to exercise an influence on society nearly as great as that which was exercised by feudal lords in the middle ages.

CHAPTER XXIV.

General Reflections.

Our American Bankers have found that for which the ancient alchymists sought in vain ; they have found that which turns every thing into gold—in their own pockets ; and it is difficult to persuade them that a system which is so very beneficial to themselves, can be very injurious to the rest of the community. They exclaim, as perhaps some of the rest of us would exclaim, if we were in their situation, " every thing goes on very well :" thus verifying the remark of Say, that " some persons who, under a vicious order of things, have obtained a competent share of social enjoyments, are never in want of arguments to justify to the eye of reason such a state of society. If the same individuals were to-morrow required to cast anew the lots assigning them a place in society, they would find many things to object to."

Not a few who have no interest in Banks, are equally devoted to their support. They appear to think that if Bank notes were withdrawn, there would be no money in the country—no credit—no trade. They have a vague notion that the wealth of the country is chiefly, if not entirely, owing to the Banks.

This is not surprising. The institutions to which men have long been accustomed, they believe to be necessary to social order. Church establishments were once regarded in this light, and hereditary nobility also. The distinguished writer whom we have just quoted, says, " Certain individuals who have never caught a glimpse of a more improved state of society, boldly affirm that it cannot exist : they acquiesce in established evils, and console themselves for their existence by remarking that they could not possibly be otherwise—in this respect reminding us of the Emperor of Japan, who thought he should have been suffocated with laughter on hearing that the Dutch had no king. The Iroquois were at a loss to conceive how wars could be carried on with success, if prisoners were not to be burnt."

Some of our countrymen who are aware of the evils of the Banking system, seem to think all discussion of it superfluous, apparently regarding it as a system so deeply rooted that it must exist in perpetuity. What always has been, always will be : but we know of no reason why Banking should be exempt from the vicissitudes which usually attend human institutions. Banking with convertible paper has been known in England for about one hundred and forty years, and in the United States for about fifty. England, in prohibiting the issue of all notes of a less denomination than twenty-four dollars, has begun to retrace her steps. In the United States we are far behind England in this respect, yet Bank notes may, fifty years hence, be found only in the cabinets of the curious. The penny notes which were issued by the Bank of North America about the year 1790, are already regarded as rarities by the virtuosi.

Banking, it must be admitted, is deeply interwoven with all the business, the interests, operations, and even the rights of society, public and private. But so was the feudal system, which had an effect, in the middle ages, similar to that which the paper system has in modern times. Like the feudal system, the paper system divides the community into distinct classes, and impresses its stamp on morals and manners. In the progress of society it may be as necessary to pass through the one as it was to pass through the other ; but the feudal system is giving way in Europe to enlightened reason, and it may, at least, be hoped, that the paper system will not last forever in America.

The comparison some writers are fond of making between paper Banking and steam power, is—only a comparison. It is not an argument, and it is not, in all respects, just even as a simile. Steam power is *essentially good.* Paper money Banking is *essentially bad.* Against accidents in the use of steam, effectual guards may be provided. No checks which can be devised can make paper credit Banks innoxious.

We may amuse ourselves by contriving new modes of paper Banking. We may suppose that a kind of money which has been tried, in various forms, in China, Persia, Hindostan, Tartary, Japan, Russia, Sweden, Denmark, Austria, France, Portugal, England, Scotland, Ireland, Canada, the United States, Brazil, and Buenos Ayres, and which has every where produced mischief, would, if we had the control of it, be productive of great good. We may say, it is true that paper money has always produced evil, but it is because it has not been properly managed. But, if there is not something essentially bad in factitious money, there seems to be something in human nature which prevents its being properly managed. No new experiments are wanted to convince mankind of this truth.

Any new paper money that we may devise must be issued either by individuals, by corporations, or by the Government. If it should be issued by individuals, it would not be a new experiment, for that has been tried in Scotland. Of the result, an eye witness shall speak for us. Mr. McCulloh, in his Historical Sketch of the Bank of England, recently published, says, " the example of the Scotch Banks may here be referred to. They are most liberal of their advances so long as they conceive they run no risk in making them; but the moment alarm and discredit begin to make their appearance, they demand payment of every advance that is not made on the very best security; they cease, in a great measure, to discount; and provide for their own safety by ruining thousands of their customers."

Such must ever be the effect of " convertible " paper. Commercial credit is an excellent thing, but it requires metallic money as an accompaniment, to prevent its being carried to excess.

If we give to corporations the power to issue paper money, we produce other evils. The very act of establishing a money corporation destroys the natural equilibrium of society. As is remarked by Raymond, " sound policy requires that the natural equality of men should be preserved as far as practicable : and it is the duty of Government to preserve this natural equality, so far as equal laws and equal rights and privileges will preserve it; to keep all the members of the community as distinct and independent as possible ; to preserve the individuality of the citizens, and to discourage, as far as practicable, all associations for the purpose of giving to those combined an artificial power."

On the subject of paper issues by Government, the warning voice of Alexander Hamilton may be heard. His words are—" The emitting of paper money is wisely prohibited to the State Governments, and the spirit of the prohibition ought not to be disregarded by the United

States' Government.   Though paper emissions under a general authority, might have some advantages not applicable, and be free from some disadvantages which are applicable, to the like emissions by the States, separately, yet they are of a nature so liable to abuse—and it may even be affirmed, so certain of being abused—that the wisdom of Government will be shown in never trusting itself. with the use of so seducing and dangerous an expedient.   In times of tranquillity it might have no ill-consequence ; it might even perhaps be arranged in a way to be productive of good : but in great and trying emergencies, there is almost a moral certainty of its being mischievous."

Government issues of paper would be incentives to extravagance in public expenditures in even the best of times ; would prevent the placing of the fiscal concerns of the country on a proper basis, and would cause various evils. Nor is a system of Banking in which the Government should deal in exchanges, after the manner of the present Bank of the United States, at all desirable.   It would be as reasonable in a man to wish his flour transferred from Pittsburg to Charleston by the public officers, as to wish his money transferred through such a medium from St. Louis to Philadelphia. To manage its own fiscal concerns, and manage them well, is as much as is in the power of any Government.   The financial operations of the United States' Government should be strictly limited to the collecting, safe-keeping, and disbursing of the public moneys, and the transferring of them from the places where they are collected to the places where they are disbursed.   Further than this, Government should have no more concern with Banking and brokerage than it has with baking and tailoring.

Why should ingenuity exert itself in devising new modifications of paper Banking ? The economy which prefers fictitious money to real, is, at best, like that which prefers a leaky ship to a sound one. With private bankers trading on metallic money, and with public offices of transfer and deposit, we can secure all the good of the present system, and get rid of all the evils.

A reform will not, however, be accomplished, as some suppose it may, by granting charters to all who apply for them.   It would be as rational to attempt to abolish a political aristocracy by multiplying the number of nobles.

The one experiment has been tried in Germany; the other, in Rhode Island.

Competition in that which is essentially good—in farming, in manufactures, and in regular commerce, is productive of benefit : but competition in that which is essentially evil, may not be desirable. No one has yet proposed to put an end to gambling by giving to every man the privilege to open a gaming house.

"It has often been said" remarks the author of ' A Peep into the Banks,' " that the evils of Banking will work their own cure : and this doctrine has been advanced years ago. The evils have continued, and even increased, without the cure so long promised being produced. But even admitting the cure to the extent to which it is maintained, is it wise to create a disease, because a cure will be effected ? Is not prevention better than cure ? Is it desirable that confidence should be placed in the responsibility of persons and companies, and to suffer loss in order to shake the confidence of the community respecting all securities. The doctrine is so absurd, that it might be doubted whether it ever had any real advocates. The idea has been advocated upon the presumption, that whenever incorporated companies could not make interest for their capitals, no more would be applied for. This, however, is not the fact, inasmuch as the generality of applications have not been with a view of investing, but on the contrary, of creating capital. It is, therefore, futile to calculate upon a cure being effected by the small dividends such companies may make, as that is not the object of pursuit. So long, therefore, as there are any persons wanting capital, we may expect there will not be wanting applicants for the power to create capital. THE EVIL WILL BE CURED BY ITSELF, AS A NATURAL DISEASE IS ENDED BY TERMINATING IN DEATH. When a total annihilation of all credit takes place, and public confidence is destroyed, then the evil will terminate by self-destruction."

A bad system cannot be abolished, and a good one established in its place, without exertion : but the necessary labor will not, perhaps, be as great as many imagine. The common-sense notions of money, have never yet been obliterated from the minds of the great body of the people. The sophistry of the Bank men silences but does not satisfy

them. They may feel themselves unable to reply to the
ingenious arguments of the advocates of paper medium,
but they think within themselves, with an honest old German
farmer of Pennsylvania, " You may say what you will, but
paper is paper, and money is money." Thousands of them
know the evils of Banking by personal experience. Thousands of others have seen the effects of the system displayed in the ruin of their neighbors.

The power is at present in the hands of the Bank interest, but by exertion the seat of power may be changed.
If our leading politicians should be as zealous on this question, as they have been either for or against the tariff, that
want of inclination which is the only real obstacle to the
establishment of a sound system of credit and currency,
will be overcome. Great difficulties may be encountered
at the outset, but they will yield to zeal and perseverance.
Nine Americans in ten, if not ninety-nine in a hundred,
have an interest in the downfal of the paper money and
money corporation system, and it is impossible for them
not to see, sooner or later, where their true interest lies.

For the salvation of the country, we must look to the
farmers and mechanics. The mercantile classes are so
entangled in the meshes of the Banks that they cannot
yield much assistance. For similar reasons, little must be
expected from public journals in the towns where Banks
are in operation. If the editors are not in debt to these
institutions, they are dependent, in a great degree, on the
patronage of the Bank interest for support : and it would
be unreasonable to wish them to sacrifice the means of subsistence of themselves and families to promote a public
object, while the great body of the public is disposed to
make no sacrifice at all.

The good work should be begun in the country, where
there is the strongest motive to begin it; for, the present
Banking system enriches the towns at the expense of the
country, and the large towns at the expense of the small
ones. In some counties, there are, as yet, no Banks. There
the public papers may discuss the question freely. In due
time, the conductors of some city journals may find it possible to speak on the subject without reserve, and perhaps
find their interest thereby promoted.

If inducements are wanted for exertion, they are afford-

ed in the history of the country, from the time of the introduction of paper money into Massachusetts, up to the present day. Let any man think on the wrongs that were inflicted by the instrumentality of provincial paper money—
of the many thousand familes who were ruined by continental money, and who lie in ruins to this day—and of
the multitudes who have been reduced to poverty by various Banking processes. Let him then trace the system in
its remote consequences—in its effects on morals—on manners—on education—on happiness. Let him consider that
the same causes being now in operation must produce the
same effects, and he will, if he has one spark of real patriotism in his breast, be willing to make any exertion which
will not interfere with his duty to himself and to his family.

If the work were once fairly begun, assistance might,
perhaps, be obtained from some quarters, from which, on a
first view, the most violent opposition might be feared.
There are strong indications of dissatisfaction in the official reports of some of the Banks. From the language they
use in private conversation, no men appear to have
clearer views of the evils the public suffer, than some
of the officers of these institutions. They have comformed
to a system which they found established in the country,
but if a sincere desire should be evinced by the people to
introduce a better system, not a few Presidents, Cashiers
and Directors may be found willing to yield all the aid that
lies in their power.

There are reasons, besides those which spring from patriotic motives, which should make men of property very
desirous to see the foundation laid of a system of sound credit and sound currency. They now hold their wealth by a
very uncertain tenure. It may pass from them as rapidly
as it came to them. In one respect the comparison of paper Banking with steam power is an apt one. The danger
of an explosion is very great, and the effects of an explosion would be tremendous.

The attempts at corrective legislation which the sufferings occasioned by paper Banking are sure to induce, offer
other motives for reflection to men of property. The " relief system" of the West, and the " tariff system" of the
East, are but specimens of what is to be expected. As it
has become a kind of principle that when the evils pro-

duced by paper money rise to a certain height, they are to be cured by more paper money, we may see a return of the times spoken of by Dr. Witherspoon, " when creditors were seen running away from their debtors, and debtors pursuing them in triumph, and paying them without mercy."

If the virtue and intelligence of the nation should direct the movements of Government during the ten or twenty years which might elapse in the gradual withdrawal of Bank notes and Bank credits, the people would suffer less from the application of the remedy, than they must otherwise suffer from the operation of the disease. Clamors might, indeed, be excited; for some of the community are always mistaking want of money's worth for want of money—want of things to be circulated for want of circulating medium. But such clamors ought to be disregarded. The work of reform once begun, should be steadily persevered in. If a State Government, after having prohibited the issue of notes of a less denomination than five dollars, should afterwards be prevailed on by a complaint of " want of money" to repeal the law, it would act with the same wisdom as a surgeon, who, being engaged in the amputation of a diseased limb, should be frightened by the cries of the patient, and withdraw his knife after having cut through the first artery.

If we should go to work too hastily—if Congress should, for example, exerting its constitutional power over the currency, pass an act prohibiting on short notice, the issue of Bank notes of any and every denomination, its conduct would be like that of a surgeon who should endeavor by one random slash of his knife to remove a diseased member. This is an evil, however, of which no fears need be entertained. All that it will be necessary for Congress to do, will, probably, be to declare that, after a certain day, nothing but gold and silver shall be received in payment of dues to Government, and that no corporation shall be an agent in the management of its fiscal concerns. The people will then begin to distinguish between cash and credit: and public opinion will operate with so much force on the State Governments, that they will, one by one, take the necessary measures for supplanting paper money by metallic.

Proceeding gradually in winding up the affairs of the Banks, the stockholders will get the real worth of their stock, whatever that may be, and more than this they are not entitled to. Many of the officers of Banks will be subjected to little inconvenience, as it is to presumed that, under a better system, their talents and industry will insure them as ample a reward as they receive at present.

When the work is done, the condition of the country will be very different from what it would have been, if paper money and money corporations had never been known. A system which has been in operation in different forms, for more than one hundred and forty years, must, by this time, have affected the very structure of society, and, in a greater or less degree, the character of every member of the community. It may require one hundred and forty years more, fully to wear out its effects on manners and morals.

In getting rid of paper money and money corporations, we shall not get rid of that *principle* of evil, in which they have their origin : but we shall get rid of very efficient *instruments* of evil. Our political institutions will then have their proper influence. Conjoining equality of commercial privileges with equality of political rights, we shall no longer startle those philosophers of Europe who land on our shores, by exhibiting to them a state of society so different from that which their views of republicanism had led them to hope for. We have heretofore been too disregardful of the fact, that social order is quite as dependent on the laws which regulate the distribution of wealth, as on political organization. Let us remove these excrescences by which our excellent form of Government is prevented from answering its intended end, and our country will become, " THE PRAISE OF ALL THE EARTH."

APPENDIX.

Bank of North America.

Minutes of the Assembly, March 21, 1785.

Petitions from a considerable number of the inhabitants of Chester County were read, representing that the Bank established at Philadelphia has fatal effects upon the community ; that while men are enabled, by means of the Bank, to receive nearly three times the rate of common interest, and, at the same time, to receive their money at very short warning, whenever they have occasion for it, it will be impossible for the husbandman and the mechanic to borrow on the former terms of legal interest and distant payment of the principal; that the best security will not enable the person to borrow; that experience clearly demonstrates the mischievous consequences of this institution to the fair trader; that impostors have been enabled to support themselves in a fictitious credit, by means of a temporary punctuality at the Bank, until they have drawn in their honest neighbors to trust them with their property, or pledge their credit as securities, and have been finally involved in ruin and distress ; that they have repeatedly seen the stopping of discounts at the Bank operate on the trading part of the community, with a degree of violence scarcely inferior to that of the stagnation of the blood in the human body, hurrying the wretched merchant who hath debts to pay into the hands of griping usurers; that the Directors of the Bank may give such preferences in trade, by advances of money, to their particular favorites, as to destroy the equality which ought to prevail in a commercial country ; that paper money has often proved beneficial to the State, but the Bank forbids it, and the people must acquiesce : therefore, in order to restore public confidence and private security, they pray that a bill may be brought in and passed into a law for repealing the law for incorporating the Bank.

March 28.—The report of the committee, read March 25, on the petitions from the counties of Chester and Berks, and the city of Philadelphia and its viciuity, praying the Act of Assembly whereby the Bank was established at Philadelphia, may be repealed, was read a second time as follows, viz:

The committee to whom were referred the petitions concerning the Bank established at Philadelphia, and who were instructed to inquire whether the said Bank be compatible with the public safety, and that equality which ought always to prevail between the individuals of a republic, beg leave to report, that it is the opinion of this committee, that the said Bank, as at present established, is in every view incompatible with the public safety; that in the present state of our trade, the said Bank has a direct tendency to banish a great part of the specie from the country, so as to produce a scarcity of money, and to collect into the hands of the stockholders of the said Bank almost the whole of the money which remains amongst us. That the accumulation of enormous wealth in the hands of a society who claim perpetual duration, will necessarily produce a degree of influence and power, which cannot be entrusted in the hands of any set of men whatsoever, without endangering the public safety. That the said Bank in its corporate capacity, is empowered to hold estates to the amount of ten millions of dollars, and by the tenor of the present charter is to exist forever, without being obliged to yield any emolument to the Government, or to be at all dependent upon it. That the great profits of the Bank, which will daily increase as money grows scarcer, and which already far exceed the profits of European Banks, have tempted foreigners to vest their money in this Bank, and thus to draw from us large sums of interest.

That foreigners will doubtless be more and more induced to become stockholders, until the time may arrive when this enormous engine of power may become subject to foreign influence; this country may be agitated with the politics of European courts, and the good people of America reduced once more to a state of subordination, and dependence upon some one or other of the European Powers. That at best, if it were even confined to the hands of Americans, it would be totally destructive of that equality which ought to prevail in a republic. We have nothing in our free and equal Government capable of balancing the influence the Bank must create: and we see nothing which, in the course of a few years, can prevent the directors of the Bank from governing Pennsylvania. Already we have felt its influence directly interfering in the measures of the Legislature. Already the House of Assembly, the representatives of the people, have been threatened that the credit of our paper currency will be blasted by the Bank; and if this growing evil continues, we fear the time is not very distant when the Bank will be able to dictate to the Legislature, what laws to pass and what to forbear.

Your committee therefore beg leave further to report the following resolution to be adopted by the House, viz:

Resolved, That a committee be appointed to bring in a bill to repeal the Act of Assembly, passed the first day of April 1782, entitled, "An Act to incorporate the subscribers to the Bank of North America;" and also to repeal one other Act of Assembly, passed the 18th of March 1782, entitled, " An Act for preventing and punishing the counterfeiting of the common seal, Bank bills, and Bank notes of the President, Directors, and Company, of the Bank of North America, and for the other purposes therein mentioned."

The opinion the Legislature of 1786 had of grants to corporations, may be judged of by the following extract from a speech by Mr. Smilie.

" There are charters so sacred that they cannot be revoked. But there is a material distinction between charters, and the opinions of many have been very wrong on that head. When once an error is taken up, men go on a long time in delusion. There are many things which we now consider as absurd, which were formerly venerated, for want of being properly considered. The doctrine of hereditary right, which is now held odious, was once deemed sacred. There is a strong reason why persons from Europe are so highly prejudiced in favor of charters. In the twelfth and thirteenth centuries, Europe was in the lowest state of vassalage—the people were in some measure rooted to the soil, and sold with it. While affairs were in that situation, the kings and powerful barons granted charters of incorporation to towns and cities, thereby exempting them from the common vassalage of the state, and bestowing on them particular immunities; thus giving them political existence. These charters were sacred, because they secured to the persons on whom they were bestowed their natural rights and privileges. But, there are, sir, charters of a very different nature. And here it is necessary to fix the point of distinction. Charters are rendered sacred, not because they are given by the Assembly or by the Parliament, but by the objects for which they are given. If a charter is given in favor of a monopoly, whereby the natural and legal rights of mankind are invaded, to benefit certain individuals, it would be a dangerous doctrine to hold that it cannot be annulled. All the natural rights of the people, as far as is consistent with the welfare of mankind, are secured by the Constitution. All charters granting exclusive rights, are a monopoly on the great charter of mankind."

Mr. Lollar said, " the House which granted it (the charter) entertained no idea of its being for a perpetuity, or of its being out of the power of the Assembly to alter or new-model it, as they might see fit. In support of this, Mr. Lollar quoted the minutes of that House, where it appeared that a clause had been introduced as a rider to the bill, for the purpose of empowering the Assembly that should sit in 1789, to alter or amend the charter as might be necessary. This was rejected by twenty-seven to twenty-four, and the express reason assigned for the rejection was, that the charter of the Bank must necessarily be always in the power of the House."

" What is all this to us?" said Mr. Morris in reply. " Are we to regulate our conduct by the private opinions of former members of Assembly ?"

The friends of the Bank maintained, that the Legislature had no power over a charter once granted, and that the courts of law alone had power to declare a charter forfeited.

There are traces of a Bank in Virginia, previous to the establishment of the Bank of North America, but we have not been able to learn any thing satisfactory concerning its character.

NOTE.—This work has been printed in about half the time usually employed in printing works of this size, in consequence of which some typographical errors escaped correction. Of these it is proper to note the following :

PART I.

Page 18 line 21, for equivalent, read equivalents
  22   26, for creditors, read credits.
  24   1, for exchanged, read exchangeable.
  55   23, for first, read second.
  91   18, for reflux, read reflex.
 103   2, for Bank, read back.
 107   28, for currently, read concurrently.
 120   23, for this, read they.
       30, for discreditable, read indestructible

PART II.

Page 24 line 18, for appeared, read appear.
  55   17, for Banks, read Bank.
  80   3, for Banks, read Bank.